THE OHLONE

PAST AND PRESENT

Cover:

Danse des habitans de Californie à la mission de St. Francisco
Lithograph after L. Choris
Courtesy, The Bancroft Library, University of California, Berkeley

Ballena Press Anthropological Papers No. 42
Series Editor: Sylvia Brakke Vane

THE OHLONE

PAST AND PRESENT

Native Americans of the San Francisco Bay Region

Compiled and edited by

Lowell John Bean

A BALLENA PRESS PUBLICATION

General Editors: Sylvia Brakke Vane
                             Lowell John Bean

Volume Editors: Susan Cole
                             Karla Young

Ballena Press Anthropological Papers Editors:
                             Sylvia Brakke Vane
                             Thomas C. Blackburn
                             Lowell John Bean

Library of Congress Cataloging in Publication Data

The Ohlone past and present : native Americans of the
San Francisco Bay region / compiled and edited by
Lowell John Bean.
    p. cm. -- (Ballena Press anthropological papers : no. 42)
    Includes bibliographical references and index.
    ISBN 0-87919-130-9 (alk. paper) : $29.95 --
    ISBN 0-87919-129-5 (pbk. : alk. paper) : $22.95
    1. Costanoan Indians--Antiquities. 2. Costanoan Indians--History. 3. Costanoan
Indians--Social life and customs. 4. San Francisco Bay Area (Calif.)--Antiquities. I.
Bean, Lowell John. II. Series.
E99.C8744045 1994
979.4'6004974--dc20   94-38326
                                                                              CIP

Copyright 1994 by   Ballena Press
                           823 Valparaiso Avenue
                           Menlo Park, CA 94025
          Orders: Ballena Press Publishers' Services
                           P. O. Box 2510
                           Novato, CA 94948

Printed in the United States of America.

WHAT DOES IT MEAN TO BE OHLONE?

Linda Yamane

"What does it mean to you to be Ohlone?"
      a voice once questioned me.
That question stunned me—
      what would my answer be?
I wished I could say it was growing up
      hearing the stories of long ago—
or listening to old ones
      singing the old songs,
      explaining the ways of the world.
I wished I could say I knew secrets
      that many have longed to know.
But Spanish missions
      and circumstance
changed native lives irrevocably
      until—even collectively—
my living family no longer bore
      the ancient memories.
But snatches of song
      rhythms of dance
         split-stick clappers
            voices that chant—
these faint images of times long past
      were still a part of me.

So much was missing. . . I wanted to know.

So I searched and found the old words
      then sat speaking them alone.

It was something I just had to do. . .
and besides,
             no one else knew how to.
You might say that language is meant
             for speaking with people today,
             but this time it was a way
of communicating with my past.
Now that the words are familiar to me
and I can speak them readily
             I seem to be finding—
             one by one—
             my cultural family.
With the passage of these few short years
             we who are of the same blood
                   and heart
             are finding each other—
             we're no longer apart.
It's such a good feeling to be able to share
             with others who understand
                   and care.

We care about the old ones who came before,
                   and about our ancestral ways—
but we also care about who we are today.
As part of our recent history
             our families had to submerge
             their cultural identities—
             that's how they survived.
But now those faded traditions
             are ready to be revived.
There's lots of hard work involved in this endeavor
             but it must be done now—
             before it's too late
             forever.
And though the work is hard
             there's also great reward!
For knowledge we thought was lost to us
             is now being found and revealed—by us!
We're finding our songs
             as well as our lore—
such cultural wealth and
             there's much, much more!

A lot has changed since that day
when that probing question came my way.
Now I can say I know secrets
        that others have longed to know.
Yes, a few secrets we still hold
but for now, at least, they cannot be told—
        except within.
"What does it mean to be Ohlone?"
If someone should ask me that question again
        I wonder where I would begin?
I guess I'd say it's knowing who I've come from—
        imme amah—anumk selesium
        from the people—the ancient ones.
And knowing exactly where I belong—
        tsiaiaruka uti ruk
        the country around here was their home
        tsiaiaruka ka ruk
        this is my home.
This is where I belong.
Haxe lattui—
        I know that—
                and that's why I can never leave.

November 1991

CONTENTS

FIGURES

TABLES

FOREWORD

On November 14, 1992, at the fourth of a series of academic conferences sponsored by the C.E. Smith Museum of Anthropology at California State University, Hayward, fourteen scholars convened to present papers on Ohlone Indian culture and history. The content of their papers was drawn from several data bases—those on the prehistoric, ethnographic, historic, and the present—and merged broadly in their concern for issues as well as theory and method approaches.

This was, unfortunately, the last of a series of conferences, supported by California State University, Hayward (CSUH), and its School of Arts, Letters and Social Sciences, then under the leadership of Dean Alan Smith. His generous support was responsible for the success of these conferences. Additional funding for the scholars' conference and an associated exhibit was provided by the California Council for the Humanities.

This volume presents all but three of the papers presented at the conference, plus one, that by Ann Marie Sayers, that was submitted after the conference. The earlier conferences resulted in two volumes, also published by Ballena Press, *Seasons of the Kachina* and *California Indian Shamanism*. This volume completes the series.

This conference renewed and fulfilled a commitment on my part to contribute to the understanding of the Ohlone people and their descendants who had been neglected by the scholarly community so very long ago.

Many discussions with Ohlone elders and leaders were held, and several Ohlones worked on an almost daily basis for several months with CSUH students so that a balanced and intimate view of Ohlone culture, prehistory, and history could be presented.

It was our intent from the first to solicit papers that could be published, creating a volume that would provide a view of what scholars, Indian and non-Indian, know about the Ohlone people at the present time. We wanted to make known the vigorous development of research that has developed over the past decade, much of it the result of cultural resource management (CRM) studies and the renewal of interest in the Ohlone.

Fourteen papers were delivered at the Ohlone Conference, which began at 8:00 in the morning on November 14, 1992, with an opening prayer presented by Andrew Galvan, an active member of the Ohlone group.

The students and staff of the C.E. Smith Museum of Anthropology at California State University, Hayward were especially grateful for the opportunity the conference provided to work closely with Ohlone peoples who could suggest ideas from the point of view of contemporary Ohlones, a rare opportunity to learn about Native American values and concerns.

Special credit goes to Ann M. Cuccia, Assistant to the Director, and Debra Wohlmut, Museum Assistant, for their extraordinary efforts in the preparation of the conference, and to the following students who worked hard to make the conference a success: Jen Bright, Deborah Caine, Gina deLeo, Sandra Hauber, Steve Lane, Alan Morganti, Burr O'Brien, Geoffrey Prenter, and Chris Steiner.

The transformation of the conference papers into a book has been a long and time-consuming process. Ann Cuccia worked tirelessly to get hard copies and computer disc files, when possible, of each paper, and to have each author give us signed permission to publish. Pauline Sanchez, Susan Cole, Heather Singleton, and Karla Young, under the direction of Sylvia Vane, have been responsible for editing, proofing, and formatting each paper. They have checked each paper's "References Cited" for accuracy, and have learned by hard experience that computer indexing is not as easy as it seems in the software brochures. Finally, they have added the photographs, maps, and tables, bringing the manuscript to "camera-ready" stage. My sincere appreciation to all of them.

THE EXHIBITION

The museum exhibition accompanying the conference, which was designed and executed under my direction by students at CSUH, museum staff, and members of the Ohlone community ran from April 10 to November 13, 1994. After several months of planning, exhibits were mounted covering a wide variety of expressions of Ohlone culture and history. Traditional culture was represented by exhibits on basketry, ethnobotany, subsistence technology, tools and weapons, tool making techniques, rock art, a boat, prehistory, and plants and animals used by the Ohlone Indians. These were enhanced by reproductions of Choris drawings and sketches of Ohlone activities seen and prepared by Choris in 1816.

Historical and contemporary issues were dealt with as well, e.g., materials on federal recognition, legal issues, the establishment of a land base at Indian Canyon with materials provided by Ann Marie Sayers; an exhibition on Alisal *rancheria*, the role of the missions in Ohlone history; and a photo wall of Ohlones in the 20th century.

We received generous cooperation and support from the Ohlone peoples: The Amah-Mutsun-Ohlone Costanoan Tribe of Santa Clara County; Mr. and Mrs. Tony Corona; Andrew Galvan; Mr. and Mrs. Felipe Galvan and family; Jacquelin Kehl and family; Joseph Mondragon; Victor Mondragon; Rosemary Cambra and other members of the Ohlone/Costanoan Muwekma Tribe of Indians; Ruth Orta and family; Alex Ramirez; Ann Marie Sayers, Indian Canyon Costanoan Tribe; Irene Zweirlein; and Linda Yamane, many of whom provided photographs of Ohlone peoples and activities in the 20th century. These were among the most favored of the exhibits, drawing many Ohlone visitors, who had not seen them, to the exhibit. Ohlone elders spent considerable time with visitors describing and explaining historical matters to visitors.

The following museums, schools, and groups donated items for the exhibition: The California Academy of Sciences; Norm Kidder and Coyote Hills Regional Parks; the Bancroft Library; De Saisset Museum of San Jose; Ohlone College in Fremont; Old Mission San Jose and historian Kerey Quaid; the Orinda Unified School District; Point Reyes National Seashore; the Santa Barbara Museum of Natural History; the Santa Cruz City Museum of Natural History; and the United States Geological Survey.

Special consultants were Rosemary Cambra, Tony Corona, Andrew Galvan, Felipe Galvan, Mark Hylkema, Jacquelin Kehl, Alan Leventhal, Malcolm Margolin, Margaret Mathewson, Randall Milliken, Joseph Mondragon, Ruth Orta, Beverly Ortiz, Ann Marie Sayers, Alex Ramirez, Lauren Teixeira, Linda Yamane, and Irene Zweirlein.

The CSUH students who helped in the design of the exhibition were Leticia Banks, Deborah Caine, Elena Cotarta, Gina deLeo, Michael Filson, Andrew Galvan, Sandra Hauber, Mary Kiernan, Steve Lane, Barbara LaVey, Burr O'Brien, Robert Oldham, Geoffrey Prenter, Kenneth Riley, Sonja Rongstock, Maria Santiago, and Dawn Swanson. Michael Robert Amrine was Exhibits Coordinator.

Lowell John Bean

INTRODUCTION

Lowell John Bean

The Ohlone speaking peoples (also referred to as Costanoan peoples) lived in the area from San Francisco Bay south to the Big Sur region and eastward toward the Central Valley. There were approximately fifty politically autonomous groups, ranging in population from about 50 to 500 each (Levy 1978:486). Recent research by Randall Milliken (1995) provides more precise estimates of these various groups, derived from information acquired from an intensive examination of mission records.

The Ohlone lived in permanent communities which they would leave as occasion demanded to acquire foods and other necessary resources. There were several such communities in some of the groups. Some eight linguistically separate groups have been noted: Karkin, Chochenyo, Tamyen, Ramaytush, Awaswas, Mutsun, Rumsen, and Chalon (Levy 1978:486).

Richard Levy has suggested that Ohlone peoples came into the San Francisco Bay Area about 500 A.D. from the San Joaquin-Sacramento River areas—probably displacing Hokan speakers—coinciding with what the archaeologists have referred to as a Late Horizon assemblage. The prehistory of these people remains a challenging but aggressively pursued focus of study—a rapidly advancing field of knowledge, as several of the papers in this volume attest.

The ways of pre-contact Ohlone have been reviewed by several scholars. Lifeways remembered by Ohlone peoples are being consulted by anthropologists and historians, and data recorded in the Spanish-Mexican and American periods are being recorded. The full impact of these sources is only now being felt as they are analyzed and presented by scholars. A catalyst of this research has been the increased interest of

Ohlone peoples in learning about their past (see Field et al. 1992), and the enthusiastic work of archaeologists, linguists, and ethnohistorians.

The Ohlone first appear in the historical record in a colonial context. The Spanish, as they colonized the west coast, brought Ohlones into their system rapidly, either into the missions themselves, which were "total" institutions that enculturated their "wards" very rapidly, or in the secular pueblos and presidios where the labor of Indians was necessary. It wasn't long before traditional communities were abandoned by many of them, whose traditional life style was no longer able to sustain them because of demographic losses due to European diseases, loss of resources, and the threats and inducements of the Hispanic culture.

Several missions were established between 1770 and 1777. From these missions came new ideas—religious, social, and political; new economic pursuits—agriculture, cattle raising, and other new technologies; and devastating diseases that reduced the populations significantly and created social milieus that incorporated not only the Ohlones, but also Indian peoples from the north, east and south of the Ohlone boundaries—Yokuts, Miwoks, Esselens, and Patwin peoples.

When the missions were secularized in the 1830s, even more changes, equally cataclysmic, occurred. Indians at the missions were incorporated into the secular ranching life of the area, but became in effect landless.

Despite decades of Hispanic enculturation, the Ohlone maintained many of their traditional ways—linguistic, religious, economic and social—but nonetheless become the economic mainstay of the Mexican system, providing labor, ranching skills, agricultural knowledge, skilled craftsmanship, and the like. In several communities of Indian people, of which *Alisal* near Pleasanton was a notable example, much of the traditional system persisted well into the 20th century.

The American period has been characterized by considerable neglect of the Ohlone. Many of them assumed alternate identities in the workplace. As time went on, they increasingly wore the clothing, ate many of the foods, lived in the houses, and spoke the language of the people around them, even while maintaining many elements of their traditional culture. Their hardships not being conspicuous, no lands were set aside for them; they were not recipients of government assistance for housing, education, and the like; they were, for the most part, ignored as a significant Native American population. Only a few ethnographic *entradas*, from the late 1800s until the 1930s, were accomplished.

Early anthropologists, concerned with recording and under-standing traditional culture, failed to appreciate the importance of the processes of adaptation and persistence for the scientific understanding of peoples. A look backward at the research conducted by anthropologists in the past provides an opportunity to review some of the goals and constraints of the discipline at the time and the consequent lacunae in the data that have been so distressing to those wanting to know.

At the time that A.L. Kroeber and his colleagues at the University of California, Berkeley (UCB) were conducting research on California Indians, they were among the very few who cared about the California Indian peoples from the point of view of understanding their past culture and subsequent travails. Those few dedicated scholars, and especially Kroeber, saw before them the formidable task of observing and understanding what is now known as one of the most complex and varied culture areas in North America.

A major effort, but one significantly impoverished of personnel and funding, was launched by Kroeber—one that lasted a half century, its goal to find out as much as possible about the traditional life ways of California Indian peoples. Kroeber selected for study those peoples who were accessible and who had managed to maintain a significant degree of their traditional culture—usually those least impacted by the Europeans, and those whose ways were most readily apparent. Thus, Kroeber and his students focused upon Pomos, Hupas, Patwins, Miwoks, Yuroks, and others. Other groups received less attention.

A very specific circumstance affected the UCB ethnographic effort among the Ohlone. A scholar with a strong sense of territoriality, and relatively independent of the UCB establishment, was working with the Ohlone—John Peabody Harrington. Harrington, retained by the Smithsonian Institution in Washington, was doing extensive work among the Ohlone, but was not willing to share his findings with Kroeber. Since Harrington was a very skilled linguist/ethnographer and was already familiar and successful with the Ohlone, Kroeber sent his students elsewhere. An interesting account of their relationship has been provided by Robert Heizer, a protegé of Kroeber. He recounts:

> When the Culture Element Distribution Survey was being organized by Kroeber, the Costanoan and Chumash tribes were a problem. Kroeber . . . was reluctant to send ethnographers to search out and interview the few surviving Costanoan and Chumash informants to fill out the element lists because Harrington had long preempted them as "his." According to Kroeber, he simply informed Harrington that if he refused the invitation to provide the Central California Coast elements lists, people would be sent out to secure these. And Harrington agreed and did provide the filled-in questionnaire list. This must have been something of a pill for Harrington to swallow, not only because he felt such an antipathy toward

Kroeber, but also because he was forced to disgorge some of the treasured facts of Costanoan and Chumash ethnography which he had secured. I would guess that the whole affair was as galling to Harrington as it was satisfactory to Kroeber. One keeps hearing that when Harrington's Costanoan and Chumash notes are published that we will finally know a great deal about the languages and cultures of these tribes. Let us hope that this is true.

I have also heard it said, by people who neither knew Kroeber nor what they were talking about, that Kroeber really fell down on the job by failing to work with these Central California groups. It is true that Kroeber and his students neglected the Chumash and Costanoans, but this was done because Harrington made it quite clear the he would resent Kroeber's "muscling in," and since there was plenty else to be done, Kroeber did not press the issue. Harrington may have felt that he had Kroeber bluffed, but when the issue was finally raised it was Harrington who backed down (Heizer 1975).

A major change in the attitude of most anthropologists toward the Ohlone was precipitated by two legal suits brought against the U.S. government by Indians of California (1928-1964) for reparation due them for the loss of traditional lands. Anthropologists, historians and Indians were consulted regarding the nature of traditional land holding. A review of what was known about Indians for the entire state of California commenced. The political organizing necessary to mount this action on the part of Indians led to the formation of political advocacy groups throughout the state. The Ohlone participated. A roll of descendants was established, bringing a new focus upon the community and a reevaluation of rights due its members.

By the 1960s, further political action took place and the Ohlone increasingly asserted their Native American identities. In San Francisco the American Indian Historical Society, a vigorous activist group formed by Rupert Costo, researched, published about, and lobbied for contemporary Native American peoples. Among these were the Ohlone. The Galvan family of Mission San Jose worked closely with the American Indian Historical Society and "successfully prevented destruction of a mission cemetery that lay in the path of a proposed freeway. These descendants incorporated as the Ohlone Indian Tribe, and now hold title to the Ohlone Indian Cemetery in Fremont, California" (Yamane 1994).

In 1978, Malcolm Margolin wrote and published his now classic *The Ohlone Way*. This book markedly contributed to public and scholarly interest in the Ohlone. Margolin apparently did not make use of the papers of John Peabody Harrington, but apparently did make use of Harrington's *Culture Element Distributions: Central California*, whose publication Kroeber had forced.

Harrington had died in the 1960s, leaving behind the notes from over half a century of research among the Native Americans of California and other parts of North America. The Smithsonian then embarked on the decades-long task of putting them in order. The existence of the Harrington papers was called to public attention in the 1970s, in part by Ballena Press publication of Jane Walsh's book, *John Peabody Harrington* (1976). There was also in the 1970s a resurgence of interest in mission record research by such scholars as Milliken and Chester King, and continuing interest in the Ohlone language by linguist Levy and others. All of these factors somehow conjoined to encourage scholars and the Ohlone themselves to undertake the review of available literature, research in new directions, and the development of new data bases.

Various Ohlone groups also became active in local Indian matters, protesting the conduct of archaeologists working on Indian sites, the repatriation of Ohlone artifacts held by museums, and arguing for better educational materials concerning them, better historical research, better health care, social services and the like.

In 1975, an archaeological circumstance united various Ohlones with other Indians and some scholars. Linda Yamane reports:

> In 1975 . . . a situation occurred in Watsonville, California, when a burial ground was discovered during construction of a warehouse. Local Native people resorted to an armed barricade in order to prevent destruction of the site, but the incident was resolved peacefully and the Pajaro Valley Ohlone Indian Council was formed to oversee future protection (Yamane 1994).

From that time on the Ohlone presence became well-known to the Bay Area community. Their history and concerns for their history and their future became known to many because of media coverage. Their participation in scholarly and social matters became aggressive and progressive. The California law that requires that the "most likely descendants" be called in as monitors when Native American remains are discovered at construction sites, has brought them increasingly into contact with archaeologists conducting cultural resource management (CRM) studies in order to make recommendations as to the disposition of the remains (Yamane 1994).

Because of federal action providing that groups presently unrecognized by the federal government may be recognized under certain circumstances, and receive certain benefits, four groups of Ohlone are now seeking recognition—the Amah-Mutsun Band, the Carmel Mission Band, the Indian Canyon Band, and the Muwekma/Ohlone Tribe. With the development of CRM studies, these efforts of Ohlone groups to achieve federal recognition, and the success of negotiations to have Stanford University repatriate the human remains in its archaeological collections, the fact that there were in the San Francisco Bay Area not only individuals of Ohlone descent, but also organized Ohlone peoples, has come to the attention and the consciousness of scholars and the public (Yamane 1994).

The future of the Ohlone people promises to be an interesting example of what is happening with many contemporary Indian peoples who have not previously been recognized by our federal government, people largely ignored, forgotten and neglected, who have taken charge of their history and future in forceful and creative ways. They are no longer a forgotten people but a people moving toward the future with a firm appreciation of their past. The literary and visual arts were important aspects of Ohlone life—poetry and its public reading, folklore performances, painting and sketching. Today Ohlone language, crafts, religious activities, educational and scholarly pursuits, and self-help activities are a model for other groups who have been so neglected.

Religious activities both traditional and European are also important aspects of contemporary behavior, especially in family contexts but important, too, for the protection and recognition of traditional sacred sites and used in the protection of places of religious and traditional historical significance.

As in traditional Ohlone culture one's particular Ohlone identity remains significant to contemporary socio-political organization. Individuals belong and identify with one group or another, one usually formally organized. And, of course, the family, which has served as the primary social unit of activity and identity, continues to do so, each family maintaining its special activities, social and religious.

Yamane says, "We are a modern people, and although much of our aboriginal culture is gone, we are still a people with a sense of identity, a strong sense of heritage, and a spiritual connection to our cultural past" (1994).

Our state of knowledge regarding the Ohlone is now expanding exponentially, much of the research toward that end conducted by, commissioned by, or aided by Ohlone peoples. Consequently, an especially rich data base is being developed as the Ohlone people continue to act out their cultural ways in a 20th century context.

This volume reflects these recent new directions and places the Ohlone in a new perspective, a perspective from which further studies can be done as a firm base of data develops, and Ohlone Indian peoples and more scholars address Ohlone issues.

The papers in this volume represent the interests of anthropological scholars, Ohlone peoples, and government agencies in Ohlone culture and prehistory. They demonstrate the extraordinary contributions forthcoming for many California Indians from the efforts of a new generation of scholars using records of the Hispanic period—mission records, baptisms, deaths, birth, and marriage—and having a renewed interest in reexamining other Hispanic documents and using them in new ways—asking new questions of data, for example.

The archaeological component of scholarly disciplines is also represented in a new way. Since archaeology has been guided and supported with new legislative mandates, agency policies, and direct Native American participation in that process, very different ways of acquiring, using, and explaining data have emerged in the United States.

The Ohlone peoples have been increasingly public about their identity during the past decade. Their original identity was never lost—it was proudly recalled within each of the groups, talked about *en famille*, and recorded on occasion by working with anthropologists and others. This held true despite a history often characterized, as was that of many other Native American groups, by pejorative statements in the literature, even in educational materials and church history.

Ohlone identities often merged with other ethnic identities, whether Hispanic, German, or something other. It is remarkable that their Ohlone identities have persisted, but despite, or perhaps because of, ethnic boundaries so constantly signalled, their Indian ethnicity has provided a sense of personal worth.

Many have been closely involved with the Catholic church, but others have belonged to other Christian denominations. Their political alliances have been mixed, raising a broad spectrum of regional and national polity. Their social actions have been expressed in many ways—advocacy for education, church activities, social and economic welfare, medical aid to their members and others, and scholarly pursuits—history, archaeology and ethnography.

Milliken and C. King, who have worked long and diligently solving problems regarding the nature of groups among the traditional Ohlone, and in the process reviewing the work of earlier scholars, e.g., Kroeber, Levy, and Harrington, present two important papers. They have noted the fluidity of dialectical groups within the area and that linguistic boundaries were gradual rather than abrupt. Precise political boundaries at the period of contact, they note, are now impossible to define. They also note that even then local groups were autonomous. Especially interesting to readers will be their discussion of the nature of conflict, warfare, raiding, marriage patterns, residence, and sex roles, all somewhat different than those described for other California groups. Most importantly, their level of organization was less structured than that of their neighbors, probably a late development in Ohlone history, quite different from an earlier, more complex systematic nature (T. King and Hickman 1973).

C. King and Milliken have made extraordinary use of mission records, a relatively new data base for the understanding of California Indian groups exposed to the missions. These data are becoming less mysterious in terms of use, largely due to the work of these scholars and others, from Zephyrin Engelhardt and S. F. Cook to John Johnson, William Mason, David Earle, Joan Oxendine, and others.

Similarly, Gary Breschini and Trudy Haversat use the mission records in their article, where they provide data suggestive of seasonal rounds among the Rumsen people. Combining the data regarding baptism with those on food resources available in the Rumsen territory, they are able to construct a model of seasonal patterns and population dispersal at various times. They address the issue mentioned above of changes in cultural development over a long period of time, and the need for models that explain it. They cite the model developed by Thomas King and Patricia Hickman (1973) that suggests the development of hierarchical systems and their relationship to developing trade systems between neighboring groups, a model applicable to many other groups throughout California.

Alan Brown's translation and analysis of diaries of the earliest Spanish period expeditions, along with his comparisons of the different versions of the same diary, and the diaries of one diarist with those of another on the same expedition, reminds us clearly of how much more data is available for the ethnohistorian if such methods be used.

If Brown's research on the Fages expedition of 1772 provides an important case study for such research, so does his use of historic material of the late period when he discusses the history of the use of the term "Ohlone."

Another article of historical interest is that of Edward Castillo. Castillo draws our attention to the damaging and incorrect characterization of Ohlone Indians by some church historians. Castillo focuses especially on Francis F. McCarthy's book on the history of Mission San Jose, published in 1958 and republished in 1977, but now withdrawn from sale. He is especially concerned that McCarthy and others have seen California Indians as wretched, debased, ugly, dishonest and other such biased views which in effect blame the victim for their sad history after European contact.

In a like manner, Robert Jackson argues that Indians have been ignored by some historians, their contributions and essential roles in the economy of colonial Spanish California life being ignored as if they were but passive receivers of a colonial system, rather than as peoples who engaged in significant tasks and participated actively in the changes through time at a mission.

E. Breck Parkman discusses the ways in which bedrock mortars can be analyzed in order to provide an explanation of how they were used and their social context. He suggests that bowl-shaped bedrock mortars were used to process such oily seeds as acorns, pine nuts, and buckeye, whereas cone-shaped ones were used to process hard grass seeds and some berries. He further suggests that the density of mortars in an area may suggest the level of complexity in the social unit that used them.

He, too, refers to historical data to assist his explanation, and uses catchment concepts and the possibilities that certain odd rock stone constructions may have been associated with religious activities, along with his analysis of bedrock mortar sites to show how a subsistence model developed from that of T. King (1974).

Jeff Fentress writes on rock art in and near the Ohlone area (Alameda and Contra Costa counties). Despite the common impression that there is no rock art in the Ohlone area, there are 41 possible sites. He has visited 38 of them, and thinks that more are likely to be found. He reviews the styles found—abstract and representational—noting the types of locations in which they are found.

Alan Leventhal, Les Field, Henry Alvarez, and Rosemary Cambra (the latter two being Ohlones) review the role of anthropologists, especially that of Kroeber and his students at the University of California, Berkeley, in creating the impression that the Ohlone were extinct, and trace the course of the recent revitalization of Ohlone culture. They also point out the misconceptions created by linguists, who distorted pre-contact realities when they developed linguistic classifications. They describe the difficulties caused for them by the popular idea that they no longer existed as a people. Legislation initiating the claims cases, that requiring cultural resource management studies, and that creating the possibility of federal recognition to previously unrecognized groups have brought the Ohlone into contact with archaeologists and anthropologists, made working relationships with them possible, and encouraged their own study of their culture and their past. Now, the Ohlone are laying claim to their own culture and history, and are making the public aware of their presence.

Another area of anthropology represented in this volume is that of folklore and storytelling. Beverly Ortiz, as are others, e.g., Yamane, is working carefully with Ohlone oral literature, utilizing published works as well as the formidable records of J.P. Harrington. Ortiz, in collaboration with Alex Ramirez, provides a comparative analysis of various texts, noting regional characteristics, and culture changes. She evaluates and compares the contributions of various collectors of data, and reminds us how sensitive the data is—reflecting the many feelings of the Ohlone people, toward their heroes in literature and the human qualities of sadness, sympathy, and the like.

Mark Hylkema, in his account of his CRM work on the Tamien Station Project provides a fine example of Native American, archaeological, and public agency cooperation resulting in the resolution of conflict between the varying needs of disparate parties.

The problems forthcoming from the destruction of archaeological sites—sites of special historical and social significance to Native Americans—are omnipresent in today's world. The collaborative efforts of the Ohlone, the State of California Department of Transportation (Caltrans), and archaeologists provides a good lesson on how to do it, the problems in resolving planning, facilitations and different goals.

The Ohlone participated actively in many ways in the conference from which this book is derived, and participated in several of the papers already discussed: Cambra and Alvarez as co-authors of the paper, "Back from Extinction"; and Ramirez as translator and interpreter of Ohlone narratives for Ortiz in her paper on narrative literature.

This book opens and closes with the work of two other Ohlones. Linda Yamane's touching poem, "What Does It Mean To Be Ohlone?" serves as a fitting preface, expressing what follows in terms of the feeling and emotion of one Ohlone person. Ann Marie Sayers' account of how she acquired the land that her grandfather lived on brings the book full circle, expressing the universals of Ohlone experience, and indeed those of all Native California people, in terms of the struggles of one family, however unique those struggles have been.

REFERENCES CITED

Field, Les, Alan Leventhal, Dolores Sanchez, and Rosemary Cambra
1992   A Contemporary Ohlone Tribal Revitalization Movement:
            A Perspective from the Muwekma Costanoan/Ohlone
            Indians of the San Francisco Bay Area. California
            History. Vol. LXXI, No. 3 (Fall):412-431.

Harrington, John Peabody
1942   Culture Element Distributions: Central California. *In*
            Anthropological Records. Vol. VII. Berkeley:
            University of California Press.

Heizer, Robert F.
1975   A Note on Harrington and Kroeber. The Journal of
            California Anthropology. Vol 2, No.2 (Winter):233-234.

King, Thomas F.
1974   The Evolution of Status Ascription Around San
            Francisco Bay. *In* ?Antap: California Indian Political
            and Economic Organization, Lowell J. Bean and Thomas
            F. King, eds., pp. 35-54. Ballena Press Anthropological
            Papers No. 2, Lowell J. Bean, ed. Ramona, California:
            Ballena Press.

King, T.F. and P.P. Hickman
1973   The Southern Santa Clara Valley: A General Plan for
            Archaeology. San Felipe Archaeology I. Submitted to
            National Park Service, San Francisco. Ms. on file (E-4
            SBN), Northwest Regional Information Center of the
            California Archaeological Inventory, Rohnert Park.

Levy, Richard
1978   Costanoan. *In* Handbook of North American Indians,
            Vol. 8 (California). Pp. 485-495. Robert F. Heizer, ed.
            William C. Sturtevant, gen. ed. Washington:
            Smithsonian Institution.

Margolin, Malcolm
1978   The Ohlone Way: Indian Life in the San Francisco-
            Monterey Bay Area. Berkeley: Heyday Books.

Milliken, Randall
 1995   A Time of Little Choice: The Disintegration of Tribal
                Culture in the San Francisco Bay Area 1769-1810.
                Ballena Press Anthropological Papers No. 43, Thomas C.
                Blackburn, ed. Menlo Park: Ballena Press.

Walsh, Jane MacLaren
 1976   John Peabody Harrington. The Man and His California
                Indian Fieldnotes. Ballena Press Anthropological Papers
                No. 6, Lowell J. Bean, ed. Ramona, California: Ballena
                Press.

Yamane, Linda G.
 1994   Costanoan/Ohlone. *In* Native America in the Twentieth
                Century: An Encyclopedia. Mary B. Davis, ed. Pp.
                143-144. Garland Reference Library of Social Science,
                Vol. 452. New York: Garland Publishing Inc.

THE EUROPEAN CONTACT OF 1772 AND SOME LATER DOCUMENTATION

Alan K. Brown

If anything holds the topics of this paper together, it is a rough adherence to chronology and a conviction that old and even supposedly well-known documents can successfully be re-examined in order to learn a little more about a populace who have left so broken a track in written records. The oldest records in some ways are the best known ones—and yet, to a considerable extent, not widely known at all, a situation that needs a little introduction.

In the spring of the year 1772, a Spanish expedition of fourteen soldiers and some other personnel, all on horseback and led by Captain Pedro Fages, explored from Monterey up through the length of the Santa Clara Valley and along the east side of San Francisco Bay to the mouths of the rivers, with a return by way of present Walnut Creek and the Pleasanton vicinity (Figure 1.1).

In other words, the tour was entirely or almost entirely within the district inhabited by peoples known at present as "Ohlone," or, in other terminology, Costanoan-speaking groups. Particularly after the party had passed beyond present Hayward, the journals kept by the European officer and by the accompanying missionary record the first meetings between two branches of humanity with many thousand total years of separate cultural development lying behind and between them. For the natives of the land, as these accounts make clear, this contact was an immeasurably strange experience. For the Spanish-speaking visitors, it was a story that had familiar elements—well-established protocols such as bestowing glass trade beads and trading foodstuffs—but that also represented a present crisis with conseqences just as important and

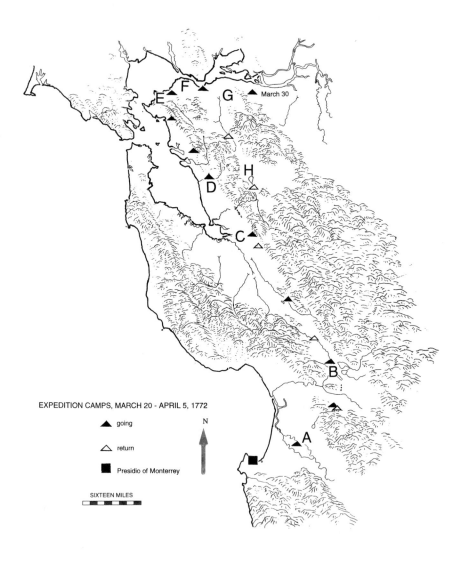

Figure 1.1. Expedition Camps, March 20-April 5, 1772

unpredictable as discovering whatever sea or river might lie beyond the next hill.

The chief recorder of this exploring tour was the missionary Juan Crespí, whose journals covering thousands of other miles of explorations are well known indeed. For the San Francisco Bay Area exploration of 1772, an original autograph manuscript is accessible. Although unpublished, it is the source of this journal's previously known version, the derivative text preserved in Francisco Palou's memoirs,[1] but the original manuscript, which is entirely in its author's own handwriting, is nearly twice the length of the previously published and translated "Palou" text. The original shows its closeness to the events by a considerable number of corrections and inserted afterthoughts; in fact, some breaks in the expression and changes of ink show that it stands now pretty much as it was written up in the field, at intervals during the march itself. For example, the writer puts in a large asterisk to mark a break in his text, with the remark "I had written thus far, when. . . ." Again, anticipating a geographical discovery, he writes "The scouts have gone out. . .; we shall see what report they bring back"; this is followed directly by "The scouts came back and gave their report" that no inland sea lay ahead, after all.[2] There would be no reason for leaving such passages unchanged in a revision, and at some of these same points, the handwriting shows slight changes that are consistent with the pauses in composition.[3]

---

[1]The "diaries" commonly attributed to Crespí were published in Spanish in the 1800s, and the well known English translations by Herbert Eugene Bolton appeared just about two thirds of a century ago. However, the original Crespí manuscripts (those in his own handwriting, plus a few early copies which, however, were all made from the same existing autograph texts) are considerably more extensive than the published texts ultimately based on them, and are richer in details. In fact, the accessible published versions have been cut down, altered, and often conflated with other people's writings. This severe editing, evidently inflicted on the missionary's works during his lifetime by his own colleagues, was demonstrated in my article, "The Various Journals of Juan Crespí," (1965:375-398). In justice, it should be mentioned that Crespí's companions Junípero Serra and Francisco Palou did apparently change their minds about the wisdom of this treatment. Their repentance came too late only because Palou died before circulating the original versions, and the altered documents, preserved among his papers, were taken up into an official historical source collection. For two centuries, therefore, Palou's sadly abbreviated and adulterated versions have been the standard texts. An example (in Bolton's translation) is given below, for comparison, among the excerpts labeled (E).

[2]For a translation of this last passage and several others—though few of them deal with native contacts or are included in this present paper—see Stanger and Brown (1969:125), etc.

[3]This manuscript, therefore, is at the stage of composition which I referred to as the "early draft," in my 1965 survey of Crespí texts, that is, exactly equivalent to the field-draft fragment of the July-November 1769 journal, which also lies in between the author's (lost) field notes and his

It has been known since 1965 that Crespí also composed a finalized manuscript, and twenty-two years ago, after a private collector published some sample translations from a document in his collection, it became clear that the autograph copy of the final version of the 1772 journal was actually still in existence.[4] Unfortunately, only the translated short sample passages have ever been made accessible. Fortunately, the sample published in 1971, when compared with this same manuscript's early copies and epitomes preserved in government and church archives, and with the earlier draft, shows that this final holograph text of Crespí's 1772 journal was much shortened from the draft and mainly represents material that is available elsewhere. Naturally, its publication would still be desirable in order to settle some textual questions. For instance, in the encounter with natives at Walnut Creek on March 30, 1772, where the Galvin sample translation describes how presents were left hanging on a bow-stave and how the expedition's commander reciprocated for them (compare extract G, below in this article), one wonders what lies behind the translation "tossing over in return a stick with glass beads"[5]—possibly, *hechando*? However, *parando* seems possible (translated more or less as if *pasando*), since in the more detailed draft version used in this paper, the corresponding entry says that Captain Fages drove into the ground (*incó*) a different pole, with glass beads. Fages's own journal, quite possibly following notes by Crespí, says he hung the beads on the *same* pole as the natives had used, but then his account goes on to describe

---

final, polished copies. (The published Palou abridgment of the documents never shows any special relationship to Crespí's final versions.)

[4]Galvin (1971:107-124 and plates). In a review of Galvin's book, I (Brown 1971:222-224) pointed out that the document is a holograph by Crespí, and not just another copied text with "unusual details" (Galvin 1971:107); and by matching an 18th-century library catalogue's entries (already used in my 1965 study) with some documents known to belong to the modern collection to which the manuscript belongs, I nailed down the identification with my earlier description of the (then missing) finished revision. I also pointed out that such details as could be ascertained agreed with those which, in my earlier publication (1965:388, note 29), I had assigned to the then missing final version. One of the predicted details was a "detour to the top of the hills" for a view *after* going up present Willow Pass. The epitomes which I had cited have: "*Para hacerlo mejor suvimos lo más alto de la sierra en que estábamos, y vimos una inmensidad de tierra llana de tal suerte que no alcanzó la vista su término,*" with which compare the sample translation: "To see it best [sic], we went to the highest point of the hill range that we were on, and we saw clearly that the region had an immensity of terrain as flat as the palm of the hand . . . all flat as far as the eye could see" (Galvin 1971:113). The draft version used in the present article speaks only of the pass itself: "*subimos un Portuzuelo [sic], y de lo alto vimos una gran inmensidad de llanura.*" The other predicted detail fulfilled by the published scrap of translation is a passage consisting of "further remarks on crossing the bay," which, so far as one can tell from the translation, agrees *verbatim* with my prediction.

[5]Galvin (1971:113).

another, very similar incident soon afterward, and this is not in either of Crespí's versions. Did Crespí's draft wrongly telescope two events into one, or did his confused notes lead to a duplication in Fages's version? The exact wording of the final version, if it were made accessible, might conceivably help settle this.[6]

However, in view of the continuing unavailability of the final text, it seems high time to make at least the material of the draft manuscript accessible to those who can use it, and that is what I am doing here.

A reliable full translation of the Fages journal by the late Theodore E. Treutlein was published in 1971.[7] Despite the availability of this, it seems desirable to give parts of the captain's journal here (in the original language as well as in new translations) in order to fill out the descriptions, if only where his own account is not verbally identical with Crespí's texts. This agreement with the other existing accounts is rather complex. Sometimes in detail Fages's descriptions resemble what is known about the final Crespí version rather than the draft, as in the March 28 entry when the width of present Carquinez Strait is given as a quarter league *and more*[8] and shell mounds are not mentioned until late in the entry. In the March 29 entry, among the gifts left by the natives, feathers are listed in first place rather than third; later there are mentions of *grassy friable soil planted with oaks*, of lines of trees off in the distance apparently indicating streams *running into the river courses*, of a camp at a stream of *poor* water, and of *deer* and tracks of *a mule-like animal*—the italicized phrases show the special agreement with the missionary's final text. On the other hand, there are other phrases which

---

[6]Another example: Crespí's draft text tells how while walking away from the April 1 camp "in order to make water," he accidentally discovered a running stream. It seems likely that it was the Captain's own idea to add, in his version of the journal, that the soldiers (of course) named it Father Juan's Creek. But just possibly the final version will show otherwise.

[7]Treutlein (1972:338-356). The translation includes typographical marks (contributed by myself at Treutlein's invitation) to indicate the material that is *not* found in Crespí's previously known texts. Some extracts mainly illustrating the expedition's geographical discoveries were also translated in Stanger and Brown (1969:120-128).

[8]Probably a misunderstanding of some typically awkward phraseology by Crespí, "a quarter league, or half a quarter and more."

do go more closely with Crespí's draft text in the same entries,[9] so that it is possible that many of the details given by Fages originally came from some unknown version of the missionary's journal, and if they did, this can hardly have been anything except lost daily notes, such as Crespí seems to have used in recording his other explorations.[10]

So, let us begin. The force that set out from Monterey on March 20, 1772, contained both colonial frontiersmen and European Spaniards, with a single "Christian Indian" from Lower California who accompanied the missionary. The journals mention seeing Monterey natives "camped on the shores of the lakes here at the harbor," but "no other heathens" during the first march as far as the river "known by the soldiers as the Monterey." Early the following morning, the armed and mounted party reached the banks of present Alisal Slough at the city of Salinas and scared some Americans out of two straw-roofed booths. The description of the fish traps, amplified by Crespí in his April 5 entry when he returned by the same route, seems to imply that these were emplaced for many miles along the watercourse.

(A)

Crespí. *Por donde lo[11] pasamos encontramos dos malas casuchas de gentiles, de ramas y algún sacate encima. Assí que nos sintieron, vimos correr de las dichas casitas diez gentiles que se corrieron como venados; y ahunque se llamaron y se les hicieron señas que no temieran, no atendieron a nada, sino en correr más recio. Nos paramos un rato cerca de sus malas casitas que estavan a la orilla del dicho arroyo corriente; nos divertimos un rato en mirar muchas trampas que en diferentes partes tenían formadas[12] de juncos a modo de nanzas,[13] con las que asseguraron los soldados cojían gran*

---

[9]Under March 28-30: A native gift of a smoking pipe (*pipa*); (twenty) natives follow the party; walnut trees; and two figures for distances agree with those originally present in the draft but later crossed out and altered.

[10]At the start of the March 31 entry, Fages's journal is much more correct about the course and topography than is either version of Crespí's entry, which clearly has distorted the description in order to square with that day's inaccurate latitude observation.

[11]*Es decir, un arroyo.*

[12]Sic; *formado.*

[13]*Estas cuatro palabras están añadidas en margen.*

multitud de pescaditos . . . El uno de estos arroyos corre al
pelo de la tierra, y por todo su curso que es bien largo tienen
los gentiles de este paraje puestos[14] lazos, que son a modo de
nanzas clavadas y tendidas por todo el curso del agua, de las
que vi en poco trecho como veinte, y con ellas asseguravan los
soldados que cojen grandes porciones de pescados, y que
explorando esto les[15] havían visto rimeros de ellos.

Where we crossed the stream, we came upon two poor
huts belonging to heathens, built of branches with a little grass
atop. As soon as they had heard us, we saw ten heathens
running away like deer from those little houses, and although
they were shouted and signed to, not to be afraid of us, they
paid no attention save to run faster. We stopped for a while
close to their poor little houses, which were at the edge of the
same running stream, and amused ourselves for a bit in
examining a great many traps that they had constructed in
several spots, a sort of fish-traps, made out of rushes, by which
they were catching a great amount of small fish, or so the
soldiers assured us. . . . One of these streams flows at ground
level, and along the whole length of its course, which is quite
far, the heathens belonging to this spot have set snares, a kind
of fish-traps staked down and stretched all along the water's
course, some twenty of which I saw within a short distance, and
the soldiers assure us they catch large amounts of fish in them,
piles of which they had seen while scouting through here.

The route the Europeans took across the range, approximately the
old road to San Juan, is described as a well-trodden native trail.[16] A day
later, they are between present Hollister and Gilroy, traversing the Santa
Clara Valley from south to north. Captain Fages has been through here
before, riding fast with a smaller troop, fifteen months ago; Crespí's
remark suggests that Fages' own mention of seeing fishermen should
really refer back to that earlier exploration. Just across what was then the

---

[14]Sic; *puesto.*

[15]*¿Es decir, vieron a los gentiles con? O ¿vieron en las nansas?*

[16]Crespí: *"Desde la loma redonda"* (= Sugarloaf Hill) *"seguimos un camino mui trillado de los*
gentiles, pero no vimos a gentil alguno . . . ."

head branch of the Pajaro River, about two miles east of the present
highway, the 1772 party meets a large village with a remarkable feature,
a bridge built of a sort of hurdles, to cross the large stream.

(B)

Crespí. *Tiene esta cañada un laberinto de lagunas de
agua dulce, mui grandes, mucha ciénega y tular, no sé quántos
arroyos grandes corrientes, y dos o tres rancherías mui grandes
de gentiles. Díxome señor capitán que el año pasado que
exploraron esto, cerca de las lagunas que algunas vimos de
lejos, havía una[17] ranchería y que tenían diferentes balsas de
tule con remos, con que pescavan en las lagunas. De lejos
vimos correr a quatro gentiles al trote, que desde luego irían
a avisar a otra ranchería, que decían estava más arriba por el
camino que seguíamos. . . . Como a los dos leguas de andar
por esta cañada llegamos a un mui caudaloso arroyo que
pasamos con algún trabajo por su mucha agua, y cerca de éste
estava una mui crecida ranchería de gentiles que assí que nos
vieron se empesaron algo a alborotar; y nos precisava pasar
por cerca de ella para proseguir el camino. Se adelantó para
ella el señor capitán con unos soldados, y todos luego se
metieron dentro de sus casas, que contamos como treinta y
tantas casas techadas de sacate. (Al arroyo que pasamos
tenían los gentiles hecha[18] una puente a modo de tapestle para
pasar de un lado a otro.) La ranchería estaría algo más de
tiro de fusil de este arroyo. Pasado este arroyo seguíamos el
camino mui trillado de los gentiles, y en dos distintas partes
havían incado quatro flechas, haciendo señas desde la
ranchería que tomáremos aquellas flechas. El señor capitán,
que como decía se havía adelantado, llevava dos de las dichas
y lo mismo los soldados que le acompañavan. Les dio el señor
capitán avalorios y no quisieron tomar ninguno, ni tampoco
pudo lograr que nos acompañara alguno para enseñarnos el
camino. Estuvimos un buen rato parados, y pasamos adelante
y a poco de andar huvimos de pasar otro más grande arroyo
corriente de mucha agua; los dos arroyos bien poblados de
álamos y alizos. (Luego de pasada la ranchería vimos un*

---

[17]*Corregido; era: dos.*

[18]Sic.

*hormiguero de gentiles que havían salido afuera de sus casas,
en donde se havían escondido al llegar nosotros.)*

There is a positive maze of very large freshwater lakes
with a great deal of swamp and bulrush patches in this hollow,
and I know not how many large running streams, and two or
three very large heathen villages. Our captain told me that
when they explored here last year, there was a village close to
the lakes, some of which we saw from afar off, and they had
several tule-rush floats with oars [sic], with which they fished
in the lakes. We saw four heathens running far off at a trot,
obviously going to give warning to the other village that was
said to be farther up along the route we were following. . . .
We came to a very full-flowing stream which it took us some
trouble to cross because it had so much water, and close to this
there was a very big heathen village where as soon as they saw
us they commenced a bit of a disturbance, while we were
forced to pass close to it in order to follow the route. Our
captain went out ahead toward it with some soldiers, and they
at once went inside their houses, of which we counted some
thirty-odd, roofed with grass. (In order to get from one side to
the other of the stream we had crossed, the heathens had made
a bridge, of hurdles, as it were.) The village must have lain a
bit over a musket shot away from this stream. We followed the
well beaten trail of the heathens beyond this stream, and they
had driven four arrows in the ground in two separate places
and, from the village, were signing to us to take those arrows.
Our captain, who, as I was saying, had gone out ahead took
two of them, as did the soldiers with him. The captain gave
them beads but they would not take any nor could he get any
one of them to go with us and show us the way. We spent a
good while stopping here, and then went on, and on going a
short way had to cross another, larger running stream with a
great deal of water; both streams being well lined with
cottonwoods and sycamores. (Immediately after crossing the
stream we saw a swarm of heathens who had issued from their
houses where they had hidden at our arrival.)

Fages. *Vimos tres ranxerías[19] muy grandes, y en una laguna vimos algunos indios que con unas balsitas estavan pescando, y otros casando patos. . . . Serca de éste [arroyo] estava una cresida ranxería, que luego que nos vieron enpesaron alborotarse. Y como nos presisava pasar por serca de ella me paresió ser nesesario adelantarme con algunos soldados por ver si los podía amansar, lo que no pude conseguir, ni que tomasen algunos abolorios;[20] pero ellos me dieron algunos plumajes y flechas, y otras que yo tomé que estavan clavadas de punta a tierra en señal de pas, a lo que se les correspondió dejándoles, al pie que estavan ellas, algunos abolorios.[21]*

We saw three very large villages, and some Indians who were fishing in some small *balza*-floats at a lake, with others hunting ducks . . . Close to this stream was a big village, where they commenced raising a tumult as soon as they saw us. And as we were faced with having to go close by it, I thought it necessary to go out ahead with a few soldiers to see whether I could calm them, which I was unable to do, or even to get them to take some beads, though they gave me some featherwork and arrows and other things that I took from where they had been driven point downward into the ground as a sign of peace; leaving for them, in return, some beads at the foot of where [sic] the arrows had been.

The next day's march is to pass without native contact, or rather with only a mutual spooking, after the party has camped at present Coyote. When the soldiers try some duck hunting, the noise of the shots is instantly echoed from a hill by loud shouts from six natives who cannot be enticed to visit the camp. At the end of the March 24 journey, the expeditionary party is halfway between Milpitas and Warm Springs, at the foot of the range. The journals of the missionary and the captain have different details. The latter's remark about the Europeans being able to ask for water in sign language is interesting, as of course are the first of the repeated comparisons with the Canaleño culture far to the south.

---

[19]Sic; *rancherías.*

[20]Sic; *abalorios.*

[21]Sic.

(C)

Crespí. *En toda la jornada no vimos a gentil alguno (Pasamos antes de llegar una grande ranchería desamparada que tenía cerca un corral quadrado bien hecho, y siete u ocho[22] palos altos con colgajes de tule);[23] sólo al llegar en donde paramos el real, nos salieron como unos catorze gentiles, los más de ellos bien armados de buenos carcajes de flechas, y mejores arcos cortos mui bien trabajados como los de la canal de Santa Bárbara si no son éstos mejores. Vinieron dos con todo el cuerpo embijado de blanco, y nos empesaron a dar vozes y a predicarnos. Se adelantó el señor capitán con unos soldados, les repartió avalorios y yo también, y se apaciguaron y se acentaron un rato con nosotros. Como a medio qüarto de legua de nosotros en una loma cerca de otro arroýto se ve una ranchería con siete casas, y como en la misma distancia en una oyanca por el curso del arroýto en donde estamos, otra ranchería, y por dos partes de esta dilatada llanura miramos dos grandes humederas.[24]*

On the whole day's march we saw not a single heathen. (Before reaching here we passed a large abandoned village close by which there was a well constructed square pen, with seven or eight tall poles in it with bulrushes hung on them.) It was only on our reaching the place where we camped that some fourteen heathens met us, most of them well armed with good quiversful of arrows and even better short bows, very well wrought, like those on the Santa Barbara Channel, unless indeed these are better than they. Two of them came up with their whole bodies painted white and commenced shouting and preaching at us. Our captain went out ahead with some soldiers and distributed beads to them, as did I, and they were mollified and sat down for a while with us. On a knoll close to another small stream a village having seven houses is visible about half a quarter-league away from us here, with another village at about the same distance in a hollow along the course of the

---

[22] *La palabra falta.*

[23] *Añadido en margen.*

[24] Sic.

small stream where we are; and we viewed two large smokes on two sides of this wide-reaching plain.

Fages. *Antes de pararnos, nos salieron al encuentro como ocho jentiles muy armados, con varios ademanes que nos hasían, y se les hiva ajuntando por instantes varios que venían de todos rumbos, los que procuramos agasajar y sosegar, explicándoles por señas a dónde havía agua, a lo que nos contextaron[25] acompañándonos en un arroyito muy bueno quasi en medio de dos rancherías que heran de los mismos jentiles, como un qüarto de hora una de otra. Heran las casas de forma esphérica; la una tenía 7 casas y la otra nueve.*

Before our halt, some eight heathens came out to meet us, heavily armed, using various gestures toward us, and moment by moment others joined them coming from all directions; we managed to please and pacify them, while conveying to them, by signs, Where was there any water? - to which they replied by going with us to a very good small stream almost in the midst of two villages belonging to those same heathens, one about a quarter-hour's distance from the other. The houses were spherical in shape; there were seven of them in one village and nine in the other.

The next day's march along this side of the bay ends at San Lorenzo Creek. It is not so clear here whether the corresponding entries in the two journals are independent, since the captain's may be summarizing detailed notes by Crespí, since lost.

(D)

Crespí. *Como en cosa de dos o tres leguas pasamos cinco rancherías de gentiles mui mansos y buenos, que todas sus rancherías estavan en la orilla de arroytos corrientes al pie de la sierra en esta llanura immensa. Todas las rancherías tenían sus casas mui bien hechas, aunque pocas, que sólo a una ranchería contamos ocho casas; las demás, tres, quatro o cinco, techadas al parecer de junco. Casi todos llevan el pelo largo los hombres: nada boruquientos, pues al pasar que no era mui lejos de ellos, davan alguna voz, y otros se estuvieron*

---

[25]Sic.

mui callados sin chistar. . . . Vimos diferentes humederas[26]
arrimadas al estero.   . . . Assí que huvimos llegado a este
paraje, pasaron por cerca de nosotros algunos gentiles y
mugeres que havíamos visto a lo lejos por esta dilatada
llanura.

At around about two or three leagues, we passed by
five villages belonging to very good well-behaved heathens, all
of whose villages lay in this enormous plain at the banks of
running streams at the foot of the range. All the villages had
the usual well made houses, although few of them, as we
counted eight houses only in a single village, the others having
three, four or five of them, roofed seemingly with rushes. The
men almost all wear their hair long; nowise are they unruly, for
as we passed not very far off from them they would give an
occasional shout, while others stood quite silent not making a
sound. . . . We saw several smokes over close to the inlet. .
. . A few heathen men and women passed by close to us as
soon as we had reached this spot; we had seen them afar off
across this wide-spreading plain.

Fages. *Divisamos por el llano varios jentiles que*
estavan dando voses como que se alegravan de vernos.
Dejamos a mano derecha sinco ranxerías que a poca diferensia
cada una tendría como seys casas de forma esférica y bastantes
jentiles que las abitavan. A mano esquierda[27] nos quedavan
algunas ranxerías; no podimos[28] divisar muy bien las[29] que eran
y las casas que tenían, por estar algo distantes; . . . Divisamos
desde el real muchos jentiles de ambos sexos que según señas
se mudavan de ranchería assia[30] nuestro rumbo.

---

[26]Sic.

[27]Sic; *izquierda.*

[28]Sic; *pudimos.*

[29]Sic; *lo.*

[30]*Assi a.* Sic; *hacia.*

Over the plain, we made out several heathens shouting
as though from joy at seeing us. To our right hand, we left
five villages each one holding more or less six houses spherical
in shape, with a good number of heathens dwelling in them. A
few villages lay to our left; we were unable to see what they
were very well or the number of houses they had, since they
lay some way off; . . . From our camp, we spied a great many
heathens of both sexes who, according to the signs, were
shifting their village in our direction.

Not until the third day's march further is another village found.
Captain Fages, under March 27, suggests the lack of natives in the entire
Oakland-Berkeley area is due to their fear of the large numbers of grizzly
bears.[31] The one that is successfully hunted near that day's camp is a
godsend for the hungry explorers, who will also be able to trade some of
the extra meat for edible seeds at the villages in the next few days'
march; within a few weeks, the captain will send a group of soldiers back
from Monterey to this area to shoot more bear.[32] On March 28, the first
new village met is at San Pablo Creek on the north side of Richmond,
and the other groups are encountered all the way to the day's camp at
modern Pinole. The foods that the European captain calls "wild onions
and potatoes" the missionary's next entry (under F) specifies in precise
Mexican terms as *cacomites* and *amoles* (terms mentioned even in the
miserably abbreviated entries of the Palou version, as given here for
comparison)—allowing us to identify them as *Brodiaea* bulbs and
soaproot.

(E)
Crespí. *Del otro lado del arroyo encontramos una
bonita ranchería de gentiles mui rubios y bien barbados que no
sabían qué hacerse con nosotros, demostrando mucho contento,
y[33] hiciéronnos grandes rasonamientos y nos dieron diferentes
bateas de unas como sebollitas tatemadas, que gusté, y tenían
un agridulce mui sabroso. El señor capitán y yo les dimos*

---

[31]"*Vimos pocos jentiles, que discurro será por los muchos ossos que abitan por aquellos
parajes.*"

[32]These details are from Corporal Mariano Carrillo's representation of December 1772, in
Archivo general de la Nación Mexicana, Californias, tomo 66, folios 34-40. No details about the
May 1772 visit of the hunters seem to be preserved.

[33]Sic.

avalorios, y le regalaron a él unos como mecates de plumas mui bien hechos y dos ánzeres[34] rellenos secos, y de éstos tendrían como tres dozenas, que tienen assí para la caza de otros, tan bien[35] compuestos que parecen vivos, y qualquiera se ha de engañar con ellos, pensando que son vivos. Pasamos adelante y a poco encontramos otra ranchería de la misma buena gente; y siete u ocho gentiles de la primera ranchería nos acompañaron motu proprio[36] *largo trecho. Todos ivan sin armas, salvo dos que cargavan dos buenos carcajes de mui buenas flechas, todas de pedernales prietos, y los arcos mui bien hechos y cortos. . . . Llegados a este paraje, de otra ranchería de este paraje lo mismo que los pasados, vinieron como unos ocho y llegaron con uno baylando con un pito en la boca y un gran plumero en la cabeza, y vinieron con una buena porción de sus raízes tatemadas a regalarnos. Regalaron al señor capitán una bandera compuesta de plumajes y una red que trahía el baylador; le regalaron también una pipa de piedra labrada negra con que ellos chupan, que era mui buena. Les regalamos avalorios y carne de osso del que mataron ayer. Estuvieron un buen rato ascentados con nosotros y después se bolvieron mui contentos. Nos quadraron mucho esta gentilidad; y parecen unos españoles.*

We met with a fine little village at the other side of the stream, belonging to very fair-haired, well-bearded heathens who showed so much happiness that they were at a loss how to handle us, but gave us long speeches; they gave us several bowls full of a sort of barbequed small onions, which I tasted and found to have a very agreeable sweet-sour flavor. The captain and myself gave them beads, and they made him a present of a sort of very well made cords of featherwork, and two dried stuffed geese. These they must have had some three dozen of, made for the purpose of hunting other [geese], and they are so well prepared they seem as though living and anyone would be fooled into thinking them alive. We went

---

[34]Sic.

[35]*También.* Sic.

[36]*Es decir, de su motivo propio, de su propia voluntad.*

onward and shortly came upon another village of the same good folk; and seven or eight heathens belonging to the first village went with us a long way at their own instigation. All of them were going unarmed except for two of them carrying two good-sized quivers full of very good arrows, all of which had black flints, and with very well made short bows. . . . On our reaching here,[37] just like the last ones they came over from another village, belonging to this place. Some eight of them came, and as they approached one of them was dancing, with a pipe in his mouth and wearing a large feather headdress. They presented our captain a flag made out of feathers and a net that the dancer had been carrying; they also presented him with a carved black stone pipe of the sort they use to smoke with, that was very fine. We made them a present of beads and meat from the bear that was killed yesterday; they sat with us a good while and then went off very well satisfied. We were greatly pleased with this heathen folk; they are like just so many Spaniards.

Palou's "Crespi" (for comparison; translation by Herbert Eugene Bolton).
. . . on its banks we found a good village of heathen, very fair and bearded, who did not know what to do, they were so happy to see us in their village. They gave us many cacomites, amoles and two dead geese, dried and stuffed with grass to use as decoys in hunting others, large numbers being attracted in this way. We returned the gift with beads, for which they were very grateful, and some of them went with us to another village near by.[38]

Fages. A la orilla de los dos [arroyos] encontramos dos rancherías con bastantes jentiles, mujeres y niños. Nos regalaron de unas sebollas silvestres, papas y varios plumajes, con dos ánzares rellenados de secate,[39] sin saber qué aser con nosotros, con varios ademanes de júbilo y contento. Les correspondimos en darles varias sartas de vidrio, de lo que

---

[37]Present Pinole.

[38]Bolton (1927:291).

[39]Sic; zacate.

quedaron muy agradecidos, y nos instaron mucho para que nos
quedáramos, y nos fueron siguiendo como ocho jentiles. . . .
Nos vinieron a visitar algunos jentiles con muchas muestras de
alegría. Uno de ellos venía tocando un pito de uesso, con un
plumaje a la cabesa disforme,[40] dando bueltas a proporsión que
hiva veniendo.[41] Nos regalaron de bastantes plumajes, una
bandera con una red, una pipa muy grasiosa de piedra. Les
correspondimos con abolorios[42] y otras cositas.

At the edges of both streams we came upon two
villages with a good many heathen men, women and children.
They presented us with some wild onions, potatoes, and pieces
of featherwork, together with two geese stuffed with straw—at
a loss what to do about us, with so many gestures expressing
joy and happiness. We responded by giving them several
strings of glass beads for which they were very grateful and
pressed us a great deal to remain; about eight heathen men
came following us away. . . . A few heathens came to seek us
with a great many signs expressing happiness. One of them
came up playing on a bone pipe, wearing an enormous feather
headdress and turning this way and that as he approached
apace. They presented us with a good many pieces of
featherwork, a flag with a net, and a very handsome pipe made
of stone. We responded with beads and other trifles.

Going on around the south side of Carquinez Straits, the explorers
do not mention any cultural differences, such as might correlate with a
linguistic one. Crespí's insistence on the especially light complexion of
the people he met here drew down on him the perhaps well-deserved
criticism of a slightly later missionary visitor to the area (Pedro Font).
On the other hand, the unusually noticeable beards of the San Francisco
Bay Area men are mentioned in a number of other sources, evidence used
by Professor Mary Barnes of Stanford, a hundred years ago, to decide on
the genuineness of the last San Mateo native's ancestry. Do we know,
even now, whether this feature was due more to biology, or to culture?

---

[40]*Diforme.* Sic; *es decir, "disforme de grande."*

[41]Sic; *viniendo.*

[42]Sic.

(F)

Crespí. *Hemos encontrado quatro o cinco rancherías
de gentiles mui bellos y manzos, mui rubios, barbados y
blancos, que todos se desacían para que fuéramos a sus
rancherías, y darnos*[43] *de comer. Hemos pasado por tres o
quatro de ellas, y nos han regalado en todas ellas muchas
porciones de cacomites y de amoles: que los cacomites, es una
raizita redonda poco más de una avellana grande, y los amoles
una raicita a modo de cebolla. De uno y otro nos regalaron
buenas porciones. Unos solos eran tatemados, y otros después
de tatemados estavan pasados al sol; uno y otro de un buen
agridulce mui agradable al paladar; que según vimos, éste*[44] *es
su comida y pan. Las rancherías tienen quatro o seis casas,
techadas de sacate. Llevan estos gentiles el pelo largo, y, los
más, amarrado con mecates que tuercen de pieles y plumas, y
remedan mucho a los de la canal de Santa Bárbara. Las
mugeres van más honestas que las de Monte Rey, porque éstas
todas las hemos obcervado bien tapadas de pieles por delante
y detrás. Los arcos y flechas sin diferencia como los de la
canal. En todas las rancherías hemos visto mucho conchaque
de almejas. Pero estos gentiles les ganan a los de la canal en
lo blanco, y hemos visto diferentes muchachos y mozetones que
no parecían otra cosa que unos españoles en lo blanco. Y
gente toda mancíssima: assí que salíamos de una ranchería nos
acompañavan* motu proprio *a la ranchería que se seguía, o a
largo trecho del camino, todos mui contentos sin arma alguna.
—Bolvamos al estero que seguíamos. Luego de la otra banda
del estero—que como llevo dicho es de un qüarto y medio
qüarto de legua su anchor—empesamos a oír vozes de la otra
banda como que nos llamavan, y luego vimos unos que venían
con balzas o canoas, remando. Nosotros pasamos adelante,
pero los de la reqüa que venían atrás dieron razón que havían
pasado con balzas de tule. Preguntamos a esta gentilidad por
señas si corría largo este estero, y entendimos que sí corría
largo pero que abría*[45] *mucho a lo retirado.*

---

[43] *Es decir, para que allí nos dieran.*

[44] *¿Es decir, los amoles?*

[45] *Habría.* (Sic.)

We have come across four or five villages of very fine well-behaved heathens, very fair-haired, bearded and white-skinned, all of whom were dying for us to come to their villages and have them feed us.[46] We have passed through three or four of the villages and in each one they have presented us with a great many servings of *cacomites* and *amoles*: *cacomites* are a small round root only a bit larger than a large hazelnut, while *amoles* are a small root like an onion, and they gave us good-sized servings of both sorts, some of them being only barbequed while others had been dried in the sun after barbequeing. Both kinds had a good sweet-sour flavor that was very agreeable to the palate, and this,[47] by what we saw, is their food and daily bread. In the villages are four to six houses, roofed with grass. The heathen men here wear their hair long, most of them having it tied with cords twisted out of skins and feathers,[48] and resembling a great deal the men on the Santa Barbara Channel.[49] The women go about more decently than the ones at Monterey, for the ones we have noted here are well covered by hides worn in front and behind. Their bows and arrows have no difference from the ones on the Channel. We have seem a great amount of mussel shells at each of the villages. But the heathens here beat those of the Channel in point of whiteness; we have seen several boys and youths seeming to be nothing else but so many Spaniards in whiteness—and the folk are all exceedingly well behaved. As soon as we would set out from a village they would accompany us at their own instigation as far as the next village or for a long stretch of the way, all of them very happy, without a single weapon. —Let us return to the inlet which we were following along. At once we commenced hearing shouts as though of people calling to us from the other side of the inlet which as I have said is a quarter-league or half a quarter in

---

[46]The fragmentary translation of Crespí's final version mentions "making big speeches" in this connection. (Galvin (1971:111).

[47]Or: the latter (i. e., the *amoles* [soaproot]).

[48]"Very well done and everything in place," the final version apparently adds (Galvin 1971:111).

[49]"Only they" (the present natives) "are not boisterous like them" (Galvin 1971:111).

width. And at once we saw some of them coming over rowing floats or canoes. We ourselves went onward but the men coming behind with the pack team reported that they had crossed over in tule-rush floats. Using signs, we asked the heathens here whether this inlet ran far along, and we understood from them that it did but that it spread out a great deal in the distance.

Fages. *Por unos lados y otros de los brasos del estero se ven muchas umaredas, y nos hasían señas los jentiles que heran rancherías. Es sierto que todos los jentiles que vimos en el curso del estero heran muy afables, dósiles y amigos de regalarnos quanto tenían. Heran quasi todos de un altor grande, los más blancos y[50] rubios de todos quantos se han visto por estas tierras, y se asemejan en la vivesa, traje y[51] idea de armas[52] a los jentiles de la canal de Santa Bárbara. Las mujeres las más onestas que se han visto; los hombres llevan el cabello largo, y los más atado a modo de rabo. No estilan robar nada. . . . Los jentiles de la otra parte del estero vinieron con varias balsas de juncos, que nos querían pasar al otro lado, y en una de ellas ivan sinco jentiles. Les agradesimos sus agasajos, y les dimos algunos avalorios y trapos, con lo que quedaron muy contentos y se fueron por sus tierras.*

A great many smokes are to be seen on both sides of the inlet; the heathens told us by signs that those were villages. No question that all of the heathens we have seen all along the inlet were very friendly and tractable and given to making us a present of whatever they had. Almost all of them are tall in stature, most of them are the whitest and fairest-haired of any that have been seen in these lands, and in quickness, clothing and the nature of their weapons they resemble the Santa Barbara Channel heathens. The women are the most modest we have seen; the men wear their hair long, most of them with it tied into a kind of queue. They are not in the custom of

---

[50]*La palabra falta.*

[51]Sic.

[52]"*De armas*" *añadido.*

stealing anything. . . . The heathens from the other side of the inlet came over in several rush floats, wanting to take us across; there were five heathens riding in one of them. We thanked them for their favors and gave them a few beads and items, with which they were well pleased and left for their own district.

Between Martinez and the low hills beyond Concord, two new instances of cautious contact at a distance might indicate that some linguistic or other cultural barrier had been crossed. As the party stops to prepare the crossing of a large creek bed, from behind its trees (including "ones that seemed similar to walnuts") they hear shouting from the plain beyond, to which they reply but get no response; however, the very cautious first exchange of gifts takes place as soon as they have crossed. The second meeting does lead to a successful face-to-face exchange when a fair-sized group (Fages's "50" may be a misreading of Crespí's "14") catches up with the European party.

Crespí. *Luego de entrados a este valle torcimos el rumbo derecho al nordeste y tuvimos los gentiles que nos gritavan (que eran 4)[53] como poco más de tiro de fusil; que havían incado en el suelo un arco con flechas y un cuero de animal con plumajes, y nos hacían señas lo fuéramos a tomar, sin quererse arrimar a nosotros. Señor capitán se adelantó con un soldado a tomar lo que nos havían puesto, y se retiraron los gentiles un trecho, y allí mismo les incó señor capitán un palo con avalorios y les hizo señas que lo fueran a tomar, y nosotros cruzamos adelante el valle[54] por el nordeste a ir a subir un portuzuelo que hacía la sierra. Assí que huvimos cruzado trecho fueron los gentiles a tomar lo que les havíamos puesto, y vimos que después se ivan corriendo a una de dos humederas[55] que mirávamos a lo retirado por dos partes del llano. Al estar ya para desamparar el valle ohímos otra vez gritar y obcervamos que venían algunos gentiles cargados y que nos llamavan y eran de la ranchería de donde se havían*

---

[53] *Añadido en margen.*

[54] *Es decir, nos adelantamos atravesando el valle.*

[55] Sic.

ido los quatro primeros. Nos paramos un rato, y llegaron como unos catorce gentiles, y algunos cargados de las sebollitas que llaman amoles tatemados, que hecharon en el suelo y de los nuestros tomaron las porciones que quisieron. Les dimos avalorios, y quedaron mui contentos. Eran gentiles como los antecedentes, mui rubios y blancos, y los más unos gigantones.

On coming into the valley here, we changed course to due northeastward and had the heathens who had been shouting to us (there were four of them) a little more than a musket-shot distant. They had driven a bow into the ground, with arrows and an animal skin, with featherwork, and were signing to us to go and take it, being unwilling to approach us themselves. Our captain went ahead with one soldier to take what they had set out for us and the heathens drew back a way; and our captain in the same spot drove in a pole with beads for them and signed to them to come take it, while we proceeded on northeastward across the valley to go up through a gap in the range. As soon as we had proceeded some way, the heathens went to get what we had left for them, and then, as we saw, they went running off to one of the two smokes that we had been viewing off in the distance on two sides of the flat. As we were just about to leave the valley we once again heard shouting and noticed a few heathens coming, laden, and calling to us, who were from the village that the four first ones had come from. We stopped for a while, and some fourteen heathens arrived, some among them laden with the small onions they call *amoles*, barbequed, which they cast upon the ground while some of our men took whatever share they wanted. We gave them beads and they were very well pleased. They were heathens like the previous ones, very fair-haired and white, most of them like just so many giants.

Fages. *Salimos a un llano, en donde encontramos quatro jentiles que por varias dilijensias que hisimos no los podimos[56] amansar. Nos dejaron plumas, un pellejo montés y unas flechas en un palo, apegado todo y ellos a distansia de nosotros como dosientas varas. Me arrimé con un soldado al palo y cojí lo que había a él, y en el mismo palo colgué unos*

---

[56]Sic.

*abolorios con algunas otras cositas para que las cojieran, todo
en señales de pas. Vimos a distansia de una legua de nosotros
en medio de un llano su ranxería, que hera muy grande y
pobladísima de jentiles. . . . Serca de éste,[57] nos salieron otros
quatro jentiles, que hisieron lo propio que los pasados, pero
logramos que uno de ellos tomase las sartas de vidrio: motivo
fue, que a corto tramo de andar nos salieron a resibir[58] como
sinquenta jentiles, trayéndonos varios regalos de plumajes,
pieles y amoles, con demostraciones de mucho contento y
alegría, pero algo asorados. Es sierto que todos los jentiles
heran muy altos y bien dispuestos.*

. . . we came out upon a level where we met four
heathens whom we were unable to mollify despite several
efforts for the purpose. They left feathers, a wild animal skin
and arrows for us upon a pole, all of it close by and themselves
about two hundred yards off from us. I went up with a soldier
and took what was on it, and hung beads and some other small
things on the same pole for them to come and take, all for a
sign of peace. At a league's distance from ourselves in the
middle of a level we saw their village, a very large one
exceedingly populous with heathens. . . . Close to [the gap[59]],
four more heathens came to meet us, doing the same as what
the previous ones had done, but we succeeded in getting one of
them to take glass beads. And this was the cause that on going
a short way further, we were met and greeted by about fifty
heathens bringing us a number of gifts of featherwork, hides
and *amoles* with gestures of great happiness and pleasure, but
still a bit flustered. Certainly, they were all very tall, healthy
heathens.

A long time—thirty-eight years—afterward, another missionary
visited the site of the first encounter, the lower end of Walnut Creek, and
wrote in his own journal that the end of the Arroyo de los Nogales, the
sloughs, the plain with its large trees including walnuts, and the hills

---

[57]*Es decir, de un portezuelo.*

[58]*Arresibir.*

[59]Willow Pass.

around it, were the lands of the *Jarquines*—most of them having gone as recent converts to San Francisco, but their ranchería was said (presumably by military personnel who had been familiar with the place since 1804) to have been at the willow swamp next to the bay.[60] These *Carquines*, or *Karkín*, people are well recorded as speakers of the Monterey-San Francisco language, the one variously named Costanoan, Taresan or "Ohlone," forms of which the Fages party in 1772 had certainly been hearing all along the way from Monterey. On the other hand, despite this specific reference of the year 1810, somewhat later records assign the exact site, along with the valley to the southeast of it, to a different tribe, the *Chupcáns*, and Randall Milliken now has shown that these people had a different sort of language, Bay Miwok (1991:418-420). All that seems certain is that this was the same village that was once surrounded or assaulted by Spanish soldiers who gave to its enormous willow swamp the name Monte del Diablo, after their attempt was frustrated by some eerie experience, possibly nothing more than the escape of the populace. Milliken's history, using a remarkable variety of sources, plausibly dates the occurrence to 1804 or 1805.[61]

The 1772 explorers' second meeting, since it presumably included some verbal interchange, has a bearing on how we interpret Crespí's one explicit comment about language affiliation—an interesting scrap of information to which I called attention in a note in the *International Journal of American Linguistics* twenty years ago (Brown 1973:186). The missionary's remark appears only considerably further on in the journal, in the April 1 entry, since, all during the time that the exploring party moves eastward toward Pittsburgh and then begins its return by first going southwestward via Kirker Pass and then turning south past our city

---

[60]José Viader, diario, Santa Barbara Mission Archive no. 536: "... *unos esteros al nordeste de un llano famoso, y bien poblado de arboleda (entre otros nogales grandes.) . . . cuyas tierras son de los Jarquines, que los más, o casi todos son christianos de San Francisco . . . ."* "*En todo este parage mui famoso por su cielo, buenas tierras, mucha leña, y nogales, no hemos encontrado más agua que una laguna de agua corrompida, otra de buena, aunque detenida de las aguas, un ojo que corre poco, y está junto a un zauzal immediato al estero [= la bahía principal], en donde dicen estaba la ranchería de lo[s] Jarquines.*"

[61]Milliken (1991:308-310). Perhaps it should be noted that the circumstantial-sounding story of the inhabitants' mysterious disappearance (recovered by Milliken from an early newspaper account) does seem to have been recorded later than Mariano G. Vallejo's tale involving a horrifyingly-dressed shaman; and Erwin G. Gudde's scornful remark on the latter version, "This is certainly quite fanciful," seems to be mainly directed toward General Vallejo's attempt to tie the name directly to the mountain and perhaps toward the exaggerated-sounding claim of a military defeat, since Gudde goes on to cite Dr. Marsh's corrective testimony, which seems right about the location but, if Milliken's supposition is correct, wrong about the date: it is still hard to know what version of the event to believe (Gudde 1949, *sub voce* Diablo, Mount).

of Walnut Creek toward the Livermore Valley, none of the inhabitants will let themselves be seen or heard except from a distance, on the hilltops, where they stand silently or else shout warnings to each other. The explorers then go straight past two villages, although the inhabitants of one come out and shout to them. Finally, a pause at two villages close together south of Dublin calls forth the missionary's statement that "all of the villages this far up"—i. e., "this far north," the meaning which *adentro*, literally "inward," always has in Mexican geographical usage[62] and in the Crespí journals—employ some common Monterey-Costanoan (*Rumsen*) words. Three of these are cited, naturally using the *Rumsen* dialect forms with which the writer is familiar: "bear, my brother, deer." In my view, Crespí is unlikely to be using the phrase "all of the villages" loosely or vaguely; he must mean that he had heard at least one of these words used among each group contacted while his exploring party circled through the area that is now known to have held tribes that spoke Bay Miwok languages. At the same time, in view of Randall Milliken's overall findings suggesting extensive bilingualism, the remark that all of the native villages "seemingly have a great deal of the Monterey language" can also be understood as meaning exactly what it says. In other words, the natives encountered near Pacheco on March 30, 1772 can well have been basically speakers of a Bay Miwok language, who still would have had no trouble in recognizing and using the commonest Costanoan vocabulary, once the Spanish missionary or some of the soldiery tried it out on them.

(H)

Crespí. *Encontramos otras dos grandes rancherías que estarían una de la otra apartadas un qüarto de legua. Pasamos por la una que estava al camino que seguíamos; no bajarían los hombres grandes de ser como unos sesenta o setenta, fuera de las mugeres, niños y niñas que eran muchos. Paramos un ratillo para darles unos avalorios, y nada se alborotaron. Eran unos hombres mui grandes, rubios y blancos; todos estavan fuera de sus casas, sin verles arma alguna en las manos. Todas las rancherías de acá dentro, parece tienen mucho de la lengua de Monte Rey, porque les*

---

[62]The directional and locational phrase *tierra adentro*, best translated as "upcountry," had been used since the earliest years of the New World conquest for the gradual widening of the continent northward from Mexico City—the Aztecs' land of the *Chichimecas*, or savages. In the late eighteenth century, the phrase was formalized into the title of *Provincias Internas*, "Interior Provinces."

ohímos el orres, *que es el osso, el* cattaus, *hermano, el* tot, *venado, y otros.*

. . . we met with two more large villages that must have been a quarter-league apart from each other. We passed through one of them, which was on the way that we were following. There must have been not under about sixty or seventy grown men, besides a great many women and boy and girl children. We stopped for a bit to give them beads, and they were not disturbed at all. They were very tall, fair-haired and white men; all of them were standing outside their houses, without a weapon in sight in their hands. All of the villages this far up seemingly have a great deal of the Monterey language, since we hear *orres,* which is "bear," *cattaus,* "brother," *tot,* "deer," and other terms, from them.

Fages.   *Divisamos a mano derecha muy serca de nosotros una ranxería bastante cresida de jentiles, y porque nos llovía no quisimos llegar a ella. Los jentiles nos davan muchas voses, ya de la ranxería ya de los montes vesinos, indisios según comprehendimos para avisar las ranxerías vesinas; de lo que a corto tramo de haver andado nuestro camino nos sersioramos de algún modo, porque encontramos al lado de un buen arroyo de agua una ranxería cresidísima de jentiles que quisás pasarían de dosientos de ambos sexos. A mano esquier-da[63] como tiro de fusil havía otra algo menos que la pasada. Les dimos sartas de vidrio; les preguntamos por señas a dónde estava el estero de San Francisco y si hera distante a lo,[64] que nos contextaron con seña assial[65] sur y el dedo bajo, que quiere desir serca.*

To the right, very close to ourselves, we espied quite a large heathen village but as it was raining we refused to go there. The heathens were shouting at us a great deal both from the village and the nearby woods, which we took for a sign they were notifying nearby villages. We received a certain

---

[63]Sic.

[64]Sic; *es decir, a ello.*

[65]Sic; *hacia el.*

proof of this after going a short distance further on our way, for beside a good-sized stream of water we came upon an extremely big heathen village, with perhaps over two hundred of both sexes. About a musket shot away to the left was another one, smaller than the last. We gave them strings of glass beads and asked them using signs where the San Francisco inlet lay and whether it was far off, and they answered by signing toward the south with the finger held low, which means close by.

Captain Fages' description of an actual gesture in the local dialect of American sign language—pointing with the finger held low means "nearby"—is exceptionally interesting among most other explorers' very general observations on the subject. An example or two: "They make very vivid signs and one very easily gathers the sense of what they want to say" (this from a missionary, speaking of the Chumash and others on the coast-to-desert trade route north of Los Angeles). Or, from a frontier officer, proud of his skill: "they are wont to make signs which a person of some moderate experience can understand"; although at another time, when this same frontiersman's interpretations had failed to produce useful results, a European fellow officer sneered at "laughable and meaningless faces and pointings. . . a dumb-show from which little indeed could be understood, and . . . the rest of us could make nothing of" (Stanger and Brown 1969:102, 133). The fault no doubt lay with the observers, not with the communication system.

Our 1772 party of Hispanics followed the sign-language indication southward to upper Alameda Creek, where they camped and on the next morning continued along its *alameda* of streamside trees (while it may be only a coincidence that Crespí actually uses the term *alameda* here, it is not common elsewhere in his writings). On their way up the east side of Mission Pass, they "went close to a good-sized village of heathens camped at the edge of another good-sized running stream well lined with trees and very large laurels";[66] the grove of exceptionally tall laurel trees here was destroyed by freeway construction in the year 1960. Fages's entry does not seem to mention this village, unless it has mistakenly transposed it to the west side of the pass: "There was quite a large village at the foot of the descent, with considerable heathens, who

---

[66]"*. . . al subir el puerto pasamos por cerca de una buena ranchería de gentiles que estavan arranchados a la orilla de otro buen arroyo corriente bien poblado de arboleda y de mui grandes laureles, que también pasamos y tuvieron que componer algo de su caja por acantilada.*"

were shouting."[67] Crespí, in turn, does not directly mention this place but says that as they turned south, now retracing their northward bayside route of eight days earlier, "we did not see the heathens belonging to this spot" (the campsite of March 24) "but did see some belonging to the villages before there," settlements which are more expressly described by Fages as lying to the left (east) and being "three not very large villages" out of those that the explorers had passed on March 25th when, it will be remembered, five settlements, in all, were counted east of the way as far as San Lorenzo Creek.[68]

From this point, we can let the explorers of 1772 find their own way back to Monterey, since their only remaining native encounter was with the inhabitants of two huts who, as others had done on the way up, ran inside and refused to come out despite offers of glass beads.[69] (This was in the plain south of present Gilroy, close to what within five years would become known as the Lomita de la Linares—"Ms. Linares's knoll," one of the stops along the way to which the first Mexican settlers, on their march to found pueblo San José, gave names in order to mark the stages of their journey. Another of these way stations was at the Lomas de las Lágrimas, just south of San José, so called "because the children cried" from lack of food near the end of their long march.)

Let us stay in the San José and Mission San José area, where as early as the 1790s, local natives independently experimented with agriculture, as we learn from Spanish records of a preliminary examination of the future Mission San José site: "the heathens irrigated the corn planting that they have had here"; "as for getting out the water [for irrigation], I've nothing to say [i. e., no worry], since the heathens

---

[67]"Y al pie de la bajada estava una ranxería bastante grande, con sufisientes jentiles que davan gritos."

[68]Crespí: "No vimos los gentiles de este paraje que a la venida estavan, pero vimos algunos de las rancherías antecedentes." Fages: "dejando a mano esquierda [sic] 3 ranxerías no muy grandes las que se pasaron el propio día mentado" (es decir, el 25 marzo).

[69]Crespí: ". . . encontramos en la dilatada llanura dos casitas de gentiles que luego que éstos nos vieron se entraron dentro de sus casitas. Pasávamos poco más de tiro de fusil de ellos; el señor capitán assí que vio que se entraron dentro se adelantó y fue a ellos a que no tuvieran miedo; y no pudo lograr que ninguno de ellos tomaran [sic; es decir, tomara] unos hilos de avalorios." Fages: ". . . encontramos dos casitas de jentiles que luego que nos vieron se asoraron y se metieron dentro de ellas. Les quise dar unos hilitos de abolorios [sic] pero no uvo remedio de quererlos recibir." (Es decir que el escritor no pudo conseguir que los naturales admitieran el obsequio.)

took it out at two separate spots."[70] Down nearer the Pueblo, there is also some possible evidence, connected with the place name Milpitas, for an early adoption of agriculture by natives who were not yet drawn into the Spanish mission system.[71] But even in the 1790s these were events of the past; the future, as we know, was to be represented by the 1797 foundation of Mission San José. Here has stood, read by uncounted numbers of visitors during most of our own century, the well known series of plaques commemorating the lives and deaths of several thousand Ohlone or Olhone people who passed through the mission system.[72]

Before and beyond the effect of the memorial plaque, I believe that most of the popularity of this native name has been due to Frederic Hall's *The History of San José* (1871), which flatly stated that "the tribe of Indians which roamed over this great [Santa Clara] valley, from San Francisco to near San Juan Bautista Mission . . . were the Olhones or

---

[70]Santa Barbara Mission Archive no. 282 (Hermenegildo Sal): "*la saca es sumamente fácil, [el arroyo] corre al pelo de la tierra fuera de la sierra, los gentiles regaron [dél] la siembra de maiz que aquí han tenido*"; no. 284 (Antonio Dantí): "*la saca de(l agua) no digo nada, porque los gentiles la sacaron en dos distintos parages.*" The examination was made on November 23, 1795.

[71]A Mexican family who moved into San José may have had a role in teaching this technology to the native people. Many decades afterward, the rancher Máximo Martínez testified in court that the name Milpitas came about when his father José María Martínez "sowed, cultivated and lived there, and after raising the crop, left for the pueblo [San José, where he was alcalde by 1797]. *Some Indians were living with us*" (quoted in Gudde 1949, sub voce Milpitas). The phrase I have italicized is not one that any *Californio* would have bothered to add if the natives had been ranch servants. For background on the circumstances and official policies that first allowed and then discouraged cooperation, outside the limits of the mission system, between Penitencia Creek area natives and Spanish-Mexican settlers, see Milliken 1991:453-454, 255, and 154 and following. The place originally named Milpitas certainly was on Berryessa (formerly Milpitas) Creek, since this is also referred to as *arroyo del finado Martínez*, "stream of the late Martínez," in land records; the exact location must have been up near the foot of the mountains, or within about half a mile from them, where its permanent stream of water used to cease. (The story that the name Milpitas—"little corn fields"—referred to Pueblo San José settlers' small vegetable plots down near the present town, where harvest festivals were held, seems to be more or less well-intentioned folklore growing out of a misunderstanding.) For a late use of the name Milpitas Creek, see Hoffman 1873. Santa Clara County Surveyor's map book A:63 is a manuscript survey plat that gives a good picture of the Milpitas land claim in 1851, including Nicolás Berelleza's small cultivation on the south bank of the stream later named for him, at the same spot that may have been where non-Christian natives once farmed.

[72]Older (1938:214) reported the spelling on the original plaque as "Olhone," which I think may be her own correction.

(Costanes)."[73] In 1973, I very briefly sketched out an argument to the effect that the name "Ohlone" is the result of a series of obvious misunderstandings, as follows (Brown 1973:188-189). The San Francisco Mission registers show that the name of a tribelet that once lived on the ocean shore midway between San Francisco and Santa Cruz was *Oljón* (Milliken 1991:445-46). The published account of Captain Beechey's round-the-world expedition, which spent considerable time at San Francisco in the 1820s, gives a short but reasonably impressive general account—anyway, one of the few which exist—of the world view of a local native society:

> The Olchone, who inhabit the seacoast between Sán [sic] Francisco and Monterey, worship the sun, and believe in the existence of a beneficent and an evil spirit, whom they occasionally attempt to propitiate. Their ideas of a future state are very confined [i. e., limited]: when a person dies they adorn the corpse with feathers, flowers and beads, and place with it a bow and arrows; they then extend it upon a pile of wood, and burn it amidst the shouts of the spectators, who wish the soul a pleasant journey to its new abode, which they suppose to be a country in the direction of the setting sun. Like most other nations, these people have a tradition of the deluge; they believe also that their tribes originally came from the north (Beechey 1831:78).

The published narrative of the Beechey expedition was very well known and widely read. To see the equivalence between its spelling of "Olchone" and the *Oljón* of the Spanish registers, one should compare the use of "ch" in "Machin," the spelling which the same account uses for the Christian name of the Santa Clara missionary *Magín Catalá*.[74] The phrase "inhabit the seacoast between Sán [sic] Francisco and Monterey" is clearly ambiguous and could easily be misunderstood as meaning the entire stretch of shoreline.

An 1850 report on natives formerly under the jurisdiction of Mission San Francisco by Sub-agent Adam Johnston specified that,

---

[73]Hall (1871:40). The parentheses around the last word are doubtless meant to stand for italics. Another example of the use of "Santa Clara Valley" in a wide sense is in Hall (1871:196): "One José de la Cruz Sanchez remarked at the time of the [Christmas 1848] snow, that he was then 64 years old, and born in this country, and never had seen snow in the valley before. He resided north of San José thirty-three miles, on the Buri-Buri ranch, but in the valley."

[74]Beechey (1831:46) "padres José and Machin" at Santa Clara.

among a number of other small groups once living on the San Francisco Peninsula, "the Olhones are called in Spanish Costanos" (he means *costeños*) "or Indians of the Coast."[75]   But quite inconsistently, the word "COSTANOS" was also introduced as the headline for this entire section of the report. The only obvious reason for such a shift of reference in the heading is that some person responsible for the publishing (no doubt the learnèd editor of the volumes in which Johnston's report was printed, Henry Rowe Schoolcraft) must have thought of the prior Beechey publication, with its ambiguous mention of a coastal tribe bearing what looked like—and certainly was—the same native name, Olchone, Olhone. Within a number of years after the report's publication, the headline itself caused the invention of the term "Costanoan" for native languages between San Francisco and Monterey.

The printed sources used by Hall obviously included the two I have mentioned above—in fact, he criticizes the Beechey expedition account for spelling Olhone improperly (1871:42)—as well as the later anthropological studies that had begun to use "Costano" in a very wide sense. More than the obvious learning, however, it is a sense of the author's expertise in local traditions that impresses a reader of Hall's *History*, and I think that has led to its being taken as gospel on this subject, so to speak. One or two passages such as the following are especially effective:

> The rivulet known as the Aguage, but erroneously called by some La Penetencia [sic], and named by the Indians Shistuk, . . . floods the land on which stands the patch of willows near the premises of James Murphy, and whence springs the little stream, the true appellation of which is La Penetencia (Penitence). Its Indian name was Yukisma (Hall 1871:12-13).

Hall goes on to explain that Penitencia Creek was so named because members of "the gowned fraternity," priests from Missions San José and Santa Clara, met there to confess each other—a topic amusing for an Anglo-American audience, and presented as such.

A point to be noticed, however, is that these local spots were known landmarks in San José's municipal land claims dating from

---

[75]The particular segment of coastline midway between San Francisco and Santa Cruz had already begun to appropriate this term as a local name—see Brown 1976, s. v. *the Coast*.

Spanish times,[76] a subject to which the author devotes a full chapter and
two appendixes of his book, and with which he was deeply familiar as a
lawyer involved in land-title practice (Starr 1973:392).   For example,
when in another passage he gives (though in distorted forms) the native
names *Chual* and *Umunhum* for summits in the Santa Cruz Mountains he
is repeating information that was quite well known due to the enormous
New Almaden title litigation (Hall 1871:9).

Hall's *History* was admired in its own time by such extremely
different historical critics as Hubert Howe Bancroft and Josiah Royce,
and in many ways it is worthy of its reputation. Published only twenty-
two years after the Gold Rush, at a time when grossly derogatory remarks
about non-Anglo populations were still in fashion and almost required,
the book at least covers any depreciatory comments with a certain amount
of wit, as when the author, on behalf of the California natives, thanks a
negligent British authority for failing to include them in a catalogue of
the "uncivilized nations" of the earth (Hall 1871:44-45).   Or, when
ridiculous anecdotes are told about natives or Mexicans, as in the cases
of the *Californios* who thought North Americans must be very pious to
have erected so many crosses between San Francisco and San Jose or
who "waited nearly all one day to see the mail pass on the wires," the
author will immediately add some equally stupid behavior on the part of
an Anglo, like the fellow who thought he had to provide an envelope to
be sent with his telegram along that same line of poles with their
crossbars (Hall 1871:258).[77]

This broadminded approach, however, changes abruptly when it
becomes a question of land titles, above all of the re-plattings through
which the descendants of San José's founders had lost their main
patrimony, the *suerte* lands, a subject on which Hall is extremely
defensive and partisan.[78]   One hears only indirectly of the existence of
any valid *suerte* claims.[79]   The town *alcalde* appointed during the

---

[76]See, for instance, the folding engraved "Map of Pueblo Lands of San Jose Finally Confirmed
to Mayor and Common Council of the City of San Jose . . . July 1866" that accompanies this book.

[77]The anecdote about the old California lady's view of telegraph poles and Protestant piety was
a very popular one, but not even Hall's retelling acknowledges that she must have meant the remark
as a joke in the first place.

[78]See Hall's long legal-historical disquisition aimed at this topic, pp. 50-56, and the third-person
argument on p. 180. For a description of the actual *suerte* properties in San José (which I originally
contributed), see Hoover et al. 1990:403; 1966:432).

[79]Hall's later annals barely mention the mass meetings (p. 275) and legal proceedings on the
issue.

Mexican War, who is first depicted as a bumbling, semi-literate Yankee clown (with many amusing or horrifying anecdotes about his handling of cases) (Hall 1871:171-175), becomes a shrewd commonsense detective, "honest John Burton," when faced with this issue:

> While Mr Campbell was surveying the land where Santa Clara and First streets cross each other, Mr. Charles M. [i. e., Carlos María] Weber presented himself and forbade the survey . . . Weber exhibited a title from Anistasio [sic] Chabolla . . . Burton looked at the title for a moment, then raised his head, and said "Captain Weber, this won't do, it smells of fraud;" . . . we have seen suits instituted by Chabolla's heirs and their grantees to obtain possession of the two suertes. . . . No proposition was clearer in the mind of honest John Burton, than that all claims within the survey of Campbell were without any valid foundation (Hall 1871:177-179).[80]

Land-title injustices lie at the beginning of the histories of a number of modern cities—for example the dispossessions and evictions of the native residents (by then called ex-Mission Indians) who were the original settlers of Mountain View and San Mateo.[81] The point being made here is that, following the Mexican War and the Gold Rush, the extraordinary amount of litigation about land property did allow someone with Frederic Hall's interests to become familiar with some local native place names, without his necessarily having any special access to wider information about the original native populace. In 1871, a hundred years had passed since the representatives of Spanish culture first arrived: three

---

[80]Since I am quoting this passage in order to show how the author establishes his general approach to the subject of *suerte* claims, it is not necessary to consider how valid Anastasio Chabolla's claims really were, or the exact nature of his right, at that time, to sell lands that had originally been entailed under Spanish law (a point which might have been part of Burton's objection, supposing this actually occurred). In any event, the North American town survey was very soon extended to cover even the most valid Spanish *suerte* claims, a point that Hall evades.

[81]On Mountain View, see just below. For the San Mateo case, see Brown (1973-4:[13-15]). For the record, I want to disassociate myself from the remark on p. [14], touching this crime, that "Their [the natives'] life could not have been very happy there [at San Mateo]." This was an insertion by the editor. A letter of 5/20/1974 containing this and other corrections is on file with the San Mateo County Historical Association. Pedro Evencio, almost the last survivor of the original San Mateo settlement, testified in 1869 that "when they [the San Francisco County sheriff's men] put us off [in 1853], they said it was Howard," i. e., the eviction was due to W. D. M. Howard's agents pursuing his land claim.

or four generations during which most of a people had died, whose
survivors may easily have forgotten whatever terms were once used that
corresponded to our "Costanoan" or "Ohlone"; even in the eighteenth
century, a Spanish missionary could only suggest using the word for
"man," *tares*.[82] The use of local names is obviously a different matter.

That minor native place names could survive as long as the
natives did, and longer in land records, can be illustrated in terms of
settlements on the lands of ex-Mission Santa Clara[83] (Figure 1.2). In
addition to the *Ulístac* tract, which bears a native name and was granted
to natives in 1845, there was a very large area in present-day Sunnyvale
and Mountain View that was claimed by natives in the 1830s and 1840s.
The original sketch map presented by the headman Lope Iñigo and others
with their petition for the claim showed two settlements, *Posolmi* and
Sojorpi, both names being followed by the Spanish phrase *en lengua
matriz*, "in the mother-tongue." The trail from *Sojorpi* to *Posolmi* and on
to the Santa Clara Mission embarcadero is the present Mountain View-
Alviso highway. At *Posolmi*, located close to the south corner of Moffett
Field (which represents roughly the tract of relatively low-grade soils to
which the land grant was later shrunk by surveyors and courts), a cloth-
making industry was pursued, all the way from sheep to woolen wares.
Sojorpi,[84] near where present El Camino crosses Stevens Creek, supported
large fields of melons and other crops, which were commercially vended,
at first by the raisers, eventually by Mexicans and finally by North
Americans.[85] This settlement gave rise to (Old) Mountain View, though
only after the Indian title had been extinguished by the enlargement of a
land grant to Mariano Castro and Francisco Estrada and the southwest
side of present El Camino Real had been declared United States public
land.

An early record of some of these affairs is a petition to the
government in which Gorgonio, an ex-Mission Santa Clara native, as

---

[82]More properly, *tares*. I do not know whether it meant "human being."

[83]In 1839, the headman of the main ex-Mission ranchería, in present Santa Clara itself, was
Tulareño (i. e., of the Yokuts) who was unable to speak enough Spanish to testify in court.
However, it is likely that most of the other settlements mentioned here were staffed, or at least led,
by ex-neophytes descended from the local population.

[84]In some of the documents connected with the land grant, e. g., Chester H. Lyman's survey
(1847), the place is labeled *Sitanjun* or *Gitanjun*. I think this is just the end result of careless
copying of the original spelling.

[85]I contributed some of the foregoing material to the third edition of Hoover, Rensch and
Rensch (1966:433), but it is not in the fourth (1990) edition.

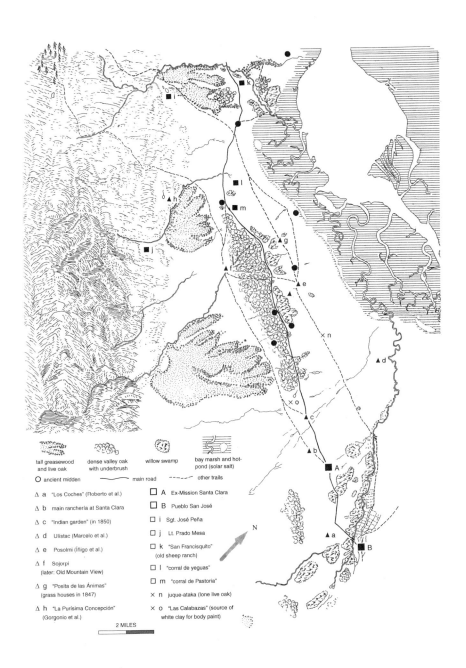

Figure 1.2. Settlements on the lands of ex-Mission Santa Clara

representative of his "relatives" occupying still another tract of former mission lands—roughly, the present northern part of Los Altos Hills—complains of his Mexican neighbors. The document is in his own handwriting and in acceptable Spanish for its time and place.

> *Ecselentísimo señor*
>
> *El ciudadano Gorgonio, vecino de la misión de Santa Clara: ante vuestra señoría con el más devido respeto comparece y dice: que hace el tiempo de cinco años que le fue concedido el parage de la Purísima Concepción, con anuencia del señor comandante general y de los reverendos Padres ministros de aquel tiempo; bajo este concepto, que tengo a mi favor; y de que el señor Peña se me quiere ahora introducir hasta mi sitio; digo que si vuestra señoría lo haya [es decir, halla] por comviniente que lo ejecute, y si no que se retire; además hay muchos parientes míos que reclaman por el dicho sitio: y aunque le fue ordenado al señor don Mariano para el fin de que, que inmediatamente prosediese a señalarme mi sitio; aun sin embargo, este señor no, [sic] lo ha verificado, hasta la fecha: para que [¿es decir, porque?] no se le ha concedido y aun sin embargo, él pide desde el camino hasta arriba de las lomas y desde a [sic] Sántaca, hasta el horno de los Toroquis, y dey [sic; de ahí] para dentro hasta la horía [orilla] del chamisal; concluyendo con el arroyo del que colindo con el alférez Prado. Esto es decir que entre ambos me ban a oprimir en este caso: Por tanto vuestra señoría rendidamente suplico se digne atender a mi suplicatoria*
>
> > *Santa Clara 21 de Julio de 1839*
> > *Gorgonio[86]*

Most Excellent Sir

The citizen Gorgonio, domiciled resident of Mission Santa Clara, with most due respect appears before Your Lordship and states: That it has been five years since the place of La Purísima Concepción was granted to him by approval of the Commandant General and of the Reverend Father Ministers of that time. In view of which fact, which I have in my favor, and [of the fact] that Señor [José] Peña now intends to come

---

[86]Monterey County Courthouse (Salinas), Recorder's Office, Old Spanish Archives (archive of the Monterey Court of First Instance) vol. 9, pp. 425-426. I have modernized the capitalization and accentuation and expanded the abbreviations, but otherwise have not changed the punctuation or spelling.

[i.e., to extend the lands occupied by him] onto my tract, I say: let him do so, if Your Lordship finds it fitting for him to; and if not, let him withdraw. In addition, there are a great many relatives of mine with claims upon that tract. And although Señor don Mariano [Castro] was ordered to the purpose of proceeding [sic] immediately to mark out my tract for me, still nonetheless, up to the present, this gentleman has NOT carried that out. Because, [although] it has not been granted to him, nonetheless he is petitioning for [a land grant running] from the road to above [i. e., up to?] the hills, and from to-*Sántaca* [sic] over to the *horno de los Toroqüis* [the oven of soapweed], and thence inward [or: north?] to the edge of the *chamizal* [grease-wood jungle], ending with the creek that forms my boundary with Sublieutenant Prado [Mesa].[87] Which is to say, in this case, between the two of them [i. e., Peña and Castro] they are going to squeeze me out [or: oppress me]. Wherefore I humbly pray Your Lordship to vouchsafe your attention to my petition.

Santa Clara, July 21st 1839
Gorgonio

In this document, the place name *Sántaca* has the well known suffix found in native location names (in the spelling often used at Santa Clara Mission, *-taca*), and, interestingly, a feeling for the suffix's locative sense seems to have affected the writer's Spanish syntax, giving "from to Sántaca" in literal English translation. Since *toroquis* (for *torogüis*) is the well documented native word for *amoles*, i. e. soapweed, soaproot, the place name containing it will have referred to a spot used for roasting the roots.[88]

---

[87]I. e., present Adobe Creek (formerly the *arroyo de las Yeguas*, so named from the Santa Clara Mission mare corral); Mesa's grant is the one labelled on maps as San Antonio. José Peña's original settlement (1824) was at present Lagunita on the Stanford campus. His son Narciso Antonio Peña much later started a ranch near present Middlefield and San Antonio Roads, on an "augmentation" of 500 varas south of Adobe Creek that may be part of the planned encroachment to which Gregonio refers.

[88]Gorgonio's calls for Castro's claim seem to describe it as lying between the main road (later called the lower San Francisco road) and the hills, i. e., as having those limits for its width northeast and southwest. The other places may be mentioned in order to define the length from southeast to northwestward, perhaps along or near the upper or *desecha* route (in part present El Camino Real), and if that is so, *Sántaca* would presumably have lain in Sunnyvale, and the *amole* oven would be somewhere in Mountain View. Of course, the boundaries as later determined for the Castro-Estrada "Pastoria de las Borregas" grant (so named after the Mission sheep range of the 1830s), for Peña's

Of course, eventually the forgetting process took over. One of the landmarks for the *Posolmi* claim was a lone tree labeled on the original sketch map as *juque ataka*, which recognizably means at or to a live-oak.[89] A witness in the land case in the late 1860s, one Félix Buelna, a local *Californio* who had pretensions to literary culture and also had been employed by the U. S. government as an Indian agent (at ex-Mission San Antonio, in "Salinan" territory), was able to interpret part of the term, probably because the native word had passed into local Spanish as the name for the Coast live-oak, *encino juque*. The same witness, however, rather ridiculously mistook the locative suffix for a distortion of Spanish *estaca*, stake.

Let us return (as one of the above-quoted passages by my explorer Juan Crespí puts it) to our subject, in this case the name Olhone/Ohlone.[90] A general conclusion ought to acknowledge that we live with many a misnomer, consciously or unconsciously, and when we become conscious of one, we handle it however we see fit—there is no general law, and "America" and "Indian" are two famous problems which we easily may wish to solve in opposite ways. A closer parallel might be the case of such well known peoples as the Greeks and the Germans, who get their English names from otherwise long-forgotten small tribes. "Greek" and "German," for that matter, also seem much less euphonious than "Ohlone" with its present trisyllabic pronunciation, which obviously provides a sound-echo evoking the well known native California name Ahwahnee with its pleasant associations. As Juan Crespí wrote on another occasion, people as a whole are free to give names according to what pleases them. But the record of choices needs to be kept clear.[91]

"Rincón de San Francisquito" (actually occupied by his son Narciso Antonio), and for the U. S. public lands, show how Gorgonio's fears came true.

[89]The form in recorded "Costanoan" vocabularies is, more or less, *yukis*; e. g., in Heizer 1955:168. Francisco Palou, in 1774, refers to it as *yuccs* (the Monterey form of the word), translating it as "acorns."

[90]In Bancroft 1875:453, the spelling Ohlone appears in an inaccurate quotation from the Adam Johnston report, as well as in an adjacent quotation, equally drawn from Johnston, that is attributed to an article by Alexander Taylor in *The California Farmer*, 1861. However, these citations are obviously interchanged, and in the same paragraph, a quotation from a third source, also originally dependent on Johnston, spells the term correctly! I have not tried to discover whether Taylor may have been the one originally responsible for switching the *l* and the *h* in the name; the new spelling, of course, became enshrined on the plaque at Mission San José.

[91]"*Y para toda claridad . . . expresaré unos y otros [nombres], dejando a la libertad de los que planten después las misiones (y ahun desde ahora a todos) a que los nombren como gustaren.*" (Mexico manuscript, folio 24v; Rome manuscript, folio 6r; cf. *The Americas*, 8 (1951:218.)

Acknowledgements
        I am extremely thankful to Ann Cuccia, Gina deLeo, and Burr O'Brien for an excellent last-minute job of reproducing the handouts of documents that were distributed at the conference.   In the documentary portions of the present publication, some corrections and other changes have been made.

REFERENCES CITED

Bancroft, H. H.
1875   The Native Races of the Pacific States. Vol. 1. New
               York.

Beechey, Frederick W.
1831   Narrative of a Voyage to the Pacific and Beering's Strait:
               . . . under the command of Captain F. W. Beechey, R. N.
               Vol. 2. London: H. Colburn and R. Bentley.

Bolton, Herbert Eugene
1927   Fray Juan Crespi, Missionary Explorer.   Berkeley:
               University of California Press.

Brown, Alan K.
1965   The Various Journals of Juan Crespi. The Americas
               21:375-398.

1971   Review of The First Spanish Entry into San Francisco
               Bay, 1775. The Americas 28:222-224.

1973   San Francisco Bay Costanoan. International Journal of
               American Linguistics 39:186.

1973-74   Indians of San Mateo County. La Peninsula 17 (4)
               Winter:[13-15]. San Mateo, California.

Carrillo, Mariano, Corporal
1772   Representation of December.   Archivo general de la
               Nación Mexicana, Californias, tomo 66, folios 34-40.

Crespí, Juan
1951   The Arrival of the Franciscans in the Californias—1768-
               1769, According to the Version of Fray Juan Crespí,
               O.F.M. Maynard Geiger, ed. The Americas 8:209-218.

Galvin, John, ed.
1971   The First Spanish Entry into San Francisco Bay, 1775.
               San Francisco: John Howell.

Gorgonio
1839   Petition to the government, July 21. Monterey County
                Courthouse (Salinas), Recorder's Office, Old Spanish
                Archives (archive of the Monterey Court of First In-
                stance), Vol. 9:425-426.

Gudde, Erwin G.
1949   California Place Names, A Geographical Dictionary.
                Berkeley: University of California Press.

Hall, Frederic
1871   The History of San José and Surroundings. San Fran-
                cisco: A. L. Bancroft.

Heizer, R. F.
1955   California Indian Linguistic Records--The Mission Indian
                Vocabularies of H. W. Henshaw.   Anthropological
                Records 15 (2):168. Berkeley and Los Angeles.

Hoffman, C. F.
1873   Map of the Region Adjacent to the Bay of San Francisco.
                State Geological Survey of California.   First Edition
                published in 1867.

Hoover, M. B. et al.
1966   Historic Spots in California. 3rd edition. Revised by W.
                M. Abeloe. Stanford University Press.

1990   Historic Spots in California. 4th edition. Revised by D.
                E. Kyle. Stanford University Press.

Lyman, Chester H.
1847   Survey of Rancho Posolmi. In U.S. District Court land-
                case papers, Northern District, Pastoria de los Borregas,
                Bancroft Library, University of California, Berkeley.

Milliken, Randall
1991   An Ethnohistory of the Indian People of the San Fran-
                cisco Bay Area from 1770 to 1810. Ph.D. dissertation,
                Department of Anthropology, University of California,
                Berkeley.

Older, Fremont, Mrs.
1938   California Missions and Their Romances. New York:
               Coward-McCann.

Stanger, F. M. and A. K. Brown
1969   Who Discovered the Golden Gate? The Explorers' Own
               Accounts. San Mateo, CA: San Mateo County Histori-
               cal Association.

Starr, Kevin
1973   Americans and the California Dream, 1850-1915. New
               York: Oxford University Press.

Treutlein, Theodore E.
1972   Fages as Explorer, 1769-1772.   California Historical
               Quarterly 51:338-356.

Viader, José
n.d.   Diario. Santa Barbara Mission Archive no. 536.

THE BEDROCK MILLING STATION

E. Breck Parkman

The Ohlone people, like all native Californians, have long demonstrated their ability to adapt to the world around them (see Galvan 1968; Parkman 1992). Indeed, the very fact that Ohlone communities still survive today, after so many dark years of Euro-American conquest, brutality, and forced assimilation, is a testament to their passion for life. The protection of The Ohlone Cemetery by members of the Galvan family and the American Indian Historical Society in the 1960s (Anonymous 1971), and contemporary Ohlone organizations, such as *Muwekma* (Field *et al.* 1992), continue the tradition of self-determination inherited from the ancestors. Like their modern-day descendants, the ancestral Ohlone had a passion for life, and the ability to adapt to their surroundings. This paper discusses an aspect of that adaptability as it pertains to subsistence strategies.

As hunters and gatherers, the ancestral Ohlone of the southeastern San Francisco Bay Area employed a subsistence strategy that focused on seasonal exploitation of their environment. Although a great variety of foodstuffs was utilized, major importance was given to the use of vegetable foods, primarily acorns (*Quercus* spp.), hard grass seeds (including *Bromus* spp., *Hordeum* spp., *Elymus* spp.), and bulbs (especially *Brodiaea*), all of which were readily available at different times of the year. The methods used by the Ohlone in processing these food plants rank among the most advanced of all native technologies. Indeed, they served as a focal point in the exploitive pattern, and may have represented an important aspect of the integration of Ohlone social and economic life.

Like other native Californians, the Ohlone are known to have utilized bedrock milling stations (Harrington 1942:11). These stations are defined as locations at which vegetable foods (and, less often, other foodstuffs and non-food resources, such as hematite) were ground by the use of mortars and/or metates located in bedrock outcroppings. Much of the labor associated with the processing of the vegetable crops took place at these sites.

The history of archaeological inquiry in the southeastern San Francisco Bay Area reveals an understandable bias in favor of the investigation of large and materially-rich shellmound villages (cf. Bickel 1981; Davis and Treganza 1959; Phebus 1973; Rackerby 1967). This materialist tradition resulted in the neglect of the smaller and materially-simplistic sites, such as bedrock milling stations. Fortunately, the advent of the legally-mandated cultural resource management programs of the 1970s helped to alter this historical bias. In 1978, an archaeological survey was conducted on Walpert Ridge (Parkman 1981; Parkman *et al.* 1978), marking the first major study of the local hinterland, while the 1979 excavation of Ala-60 (Miller 1982; see also Bard *et al.* 1989), marked the first major investigation of a bedrock milling station in the area.

As a part of the Ala-60 investigation, a bedrock milling feature typology was developed, and used to identify and segregate structural variations (Parkman 1982). Additionally, a model was developed by this author that sought to explain the prehistoric subsistence patterns of the southern Alameda County bay shore (Parkman 1980). The model was based in part on the morphology and distribution of bedrock milling features, and was an elaboration of a subsistence model first proposed by Thomas King in 1974. In developing his model, King presented the following hypothesis concerning sedentism:

> . . . it is predicted that sedentary settlements of hunter-gatherers would be most likely to develop where catchments contained a wide variety of biotic resources exploitable according to an annual schedule with few "gaps" (King 1974:40).

King continued his argument with the observation that, ". . . bayshore Marin is a better place for sedentism than is bayshore southern Alameda County or any other major part of the Bay Area" (1974:45). This paper is, in part, a test of King's hypothesis concerning Bay Area sedentism. A model is presented to demonstrate the semi-sedentary and seasonal nature of the settlement of the southern Alameda County bay shore, an area that is characterized by a broad plain separating the bay shore and bay hills. The model is based on the bedrock milling feature typology, and on certain observations generated by it. It is my hypothesis that the socioeconomic organization of the people who utilized the bedrock milling station affected their use of it, as reflected by the types and distribution of milling features within the site. This hypothesis results from the observation that bedrock milling features are fossilized reflections of socioeconomic organization.

THE BEDROCK MILLING STATION

There has been little research conducted to date that addresses the socioeconomic implications of the bedrock milling station. The existing archaeological literature concerns itself with the technical aspects of the sites, while ignoring the social and economic aspects; therefore, it is possible only to speculate on the forms of socioeconomic control exercised on this type of site, and on the site's role within the Ohlone subsistence pattern. Considering the variation in size and form of bedrock milling stations, it is likely that various types of social groups used the sites to the exclusion of others. This is better illustrated by Table 1.1, which presents a possible range of social agents attributable to the bedrock milling station, and serves as an explanation for the diversity found among sites of their types in the southeastern San Francisco Bay Area. The model results from certain archaeological observations from southeastern San Francisco Bay, and is considered valid for only that area. The cultural and environmental variations found elsewhere may have necessitated a different subsistence strategy.

For the purposes of this discussion, I have designated four categories of bedrock milling stations. The differentiating factors are the number of milling features attributable to each, and the type of social group thought to have utilized the site. The latter factor is an internal reflection of the former, and coalesces archaeological inferences with ethnographic realities. The model inherent to this approach attempts to interpret the form of the bedrock milling station by the number of milling features occurring at it. It is similar to the approach taken by James Bennyhoff (1956) for the Yosemite region. Bennyhoff proposed a classification scheme that equated 1-7 bedrock mortars with a single family or house site, 8-19 mortars with a small village, and 20 or more mortars with a large village (1956:13). For southeastern San Francisco Bay, I hypothesize that 1-5 bedrock mortars might be associated with a

TABLE 2.1. TYPES OF BEDROCK MILLING STATIONS

Type	Milling Features	Social Agent Using Site
A	1-5	single family (nuclear or extended)
B	6-10	single family (extended) or corporate unit (clan)
C	11-19	corporate unit (clan or moiety)
D	20+	corporate unit (moiety) or village

single family or house, 6-10 mortars with an extended family or clan, 11-19 mortars with a clan or moiety, and 20 or more mortars with a moiety or village.

A functional approach might also be taken by analyzing the types of milling features found to occur at the site. The typological analysis of food-processing bedrock mortars in central California indicates that most of them fit into one of two broad categories (cf., Johnson 1942:323; McCarthy *et al.* 1985:312, 314-317; Moratto 1968:28-33, 1972:325-330; Parkman 1982:151-152). The categories are characterized by mortars with profiles of either bowl or cone shape. These profiles resemble the letters "U" and "V," respectively. Bowl-shaped mortars are rounded and relatively shallow, while cone-shaped mortars are conical with deeper and more pointed bottoms. Bowl-shaped mortars tend to have more irregular and less parabolic walls than do the cone-shaped variety. This variation in mortar types suggests a functional division.

In 1980, this author suggested that bowl-shaped bedrock mortars were used to process acorns, and cone-shaped mortars to process berries and hard grass seeds (Parkman 1980). In the central Sierra Nevada, the Miwok are known to have utilized shallow bedrock mortars for grinding acorns, and deeper ones for processing manzanita berries and seeds (Barrett and Gifford 1933:208). Only an inch or two of acorn material and other soft seeds and pulpy materials were ground in the mortar at any one time, and the mortar was no longer used for grinding acorns after it reached a depth of about five inches (Barrett and Gifford 1933:143; Johnson 1942:324). To grind these materials required that they be pulverized using a pounding motion, in which a pestle was repeatedly raised then lowered into the mortar. Only a small amount of material could be effectively ground at any one time. Franklin Fenenga (1952:342) noted that, "Oily seeds (acorns, pinenuts, and buckeyes) could be ground only in the shallow pits because otherwise they congeal into a pasty mess." Apparently the acorns of the Black Oak (*Quercus kelloggi*) are the most oily of all the acorns (Helen McCarthy, personal communication 1992).

More recently, ethnographic data for the Mono has substantiated the same pattern in the southern Sierra Nevada (McCarthy *et al.* 1985).

On the other hand, the cone-shaped bedrock mortar acquired its shape through the grinding of hard grass seeds and certain berries. The parabolic nature of the conical mortar's profile indicates that the feature was utilized as if it were a "vertical" metate. In other words, the mortar was filled with grass seeds or berries, and a pestle was then rotated around the inside of the mortar, remaining in constant contact with the mortar's rim and/or walls. Some of the portable stone mortars from Ala-328, one of the large shellmounds at Coyote Hills, appear to have been used in a similar fashion (Bickel 1981:198). The conical mortar would appear to have been more energy-efficient than the bowl mortar, since a larger amount of material could have been ground at any one time. The pestles that were used with them were probably elongated, with pointed distal ends, somewhat similar to Lillard *et al.*'s Type A.1 (1939:10-11), and Beardsley's Type IIB3 (1954:10).

A SEASONAL SUBSISTENCE MODEL FOR
SOUTHEASTERN SAN FRANCISCO BAY

In her analysis of the Coyote Hills shellmounds, Polly Bickel noted a scarcity of portable stone mortars and pestles at Ala-328 that suggested that "either seasonal residence changes or short forays away from a base settlement may be indicated" (1981:199), and that, "Several patterns of movement may have been involved, varying with the food exploited" (1981:202). Bickel's conclusions fit a subsistence model first proposed by Thomas King (1974) and further developed by this author (Parkman 1980). The model, which follows, pertains to the Ohlone inhabitants of the southeastern San Francisco Bay Area during the late prehistoric period (ca. AD 300-1800).

Winter

Winter was spent in a large permanent village, such as Ala-328, located near the shore of San Francisco Bay. Great quantities of shellfish were collected and consumed, and represent one of the major food items utilized during this season. Migratory waterfowl were hunted, and, along with fish, and stores of acorns and grass seeds served to supplement the shellfish diet. Portable stone mortars and milling stones were used to grind stores of acorns and hard grass seeds. With the entire population in residence, the winter village was the scene of intense ceremonial activity.

Spring/Summer

With the arrival of spring, the winter village fragmented, as many of the villagers moved inland to collect the ripening plant foods, first bulbs and greens, and then hard grass seeds. Communal base camps, occupied by the members of an extended family, or, more likely, a ceremonial unit such as a clan or moiety, were made near the interface of the bay plains and the bay hills. Portable grinding stones were located at some of the camps. Individual family units, either nuclear or extended, formed separate collecting units, and their collecting areas were dispersed across the plains. Bedrock milling stations were established by the collecting units. A constant flow of traffic united the milling stations with the base camps, and the camps with the winter village, as stores of food materials were transported home. At this same time, deer hunters ventured into the hills in search of their prey. Some of the villagers remained in the winter village to hunt waterfowl and collect shellfish along the bay shore. Certain craft specialists, and the young and infirm also remained in the winter village. The other villagers returned home periodically during their spring and summer collecting forays.

Fall

With the arrival of fall, some of the base camps were moved into the bay hills in order to collect the ripening acorns. The camps were re-established near oak groves, and traffic flowed back and forth between the camps and the winter village. Conveniently located spring and summer camps were also used in the fall. With the abundance of food available from one oak tree, multiple collecting units could harvest a single grove. Thus, the associated bedrock milling stations were sometimes communal rather than single family work-sites. Some camps were also equipped with portable stone mortars. The members of the collecting units were members of either nuclear or extended families, while the consolidated collecting units represented a ceremonial unit, such as a clan or moiety. In addition to collecting acorns and other vegetable foods, and hunting deer, the members of the fall camps prepared for the ceremonial events that would highlight the end of the fall harvest and the advent of winter. Prior to the arrival of winter, the fall camps broke up, and the members reassembled in the winter village. Thus, the Ohlone year began once again.

The model presented above is supported by the preliminary data generated by the typological analysis of bedrock milling features. This preliminary analysis indicates that, with few exceptions, the bedrock milling stations located in the southeastern San Francisco Bay Area consist of sites with no more than 10 bedrock mortars. Most of the sites are characterized exclusively by either bowl-shaped or cone-shaped mortars. This distribution does not appear to be coincidental, but rather suggests small spring and summer encampments focused on bulb and hard grass seed exploitation, and small fall camps focused on acorn exploitation.

Using the faunal data derived from several Contra Costa County bay shore sites (the Stege Mounds and the Ellis Landing Shellmound), Dwight Simons tested the King (1974) and Parkman (1980) model, and found that it was valid for the northeastern San Francisco Bay Area (Simons 1981:18, 32-33). At the same time, William Hildebrandt analyzed the faunal remains from Ala-12 and Ala-13, at Coyote Hills, and noted a late period hunting shift from locally-available elk to more distant-ranging deer, which he thought to be a probable result of over-exploitation (Hildebrandt et al. 1984:56, 62). Diane Watts (1984) noted a similar pattern at Ala-328 and Ala-329. These findings suggest some validation of the King/Parkman model.

Support for the King/Parkman model might also be found in the ethnohistoric record. In an 1806 visit, Langsdorff noted that the Ohlones whom he found near the site of the present-day city of Fremont were nomadic (Langsdorff 1814:164). Fages found Ohlones at Stiver's Lagoon in Fremont on November 27, 1770 (Fages 1911:151-153). They were apparently hunting geese, as they presented Fages with several decoys stuffed with straw. On March 31, 1776, Anza noted six villages between the Coyote River and San Lorenzo Creek (Bolton 1930, 3:135). In a

1795 expedition, Hermengildo Sal and Father Antonio Danti noted three villages on the bay plains between Milpitas and San Lorenzo Creek, and two villages near Coyote Hills, as well as an empty village of seven houses near San Lorenzo Creek (Cook 1957:140; Mayfield 1978:146-147). Earlier, on March 25, 1772, Fages had noted five villages located at the foot of the bay hills between Milpitas and Castro Valley, each of which contained about six houses (Fages 1972:10). Although he also noted some bay shore villages, Fages observed that the Ohlone were shifting their residences from the bay shore eastward toward the bay hills (Fages 1972:10). A village shift from the bay shore to the foot of the bay hills corresponds with the King/Parkman model.

DISCUSSION

Southeastern San Francisco Bay was home to a small nation or tribe probably known as *Tuibun* (Margolin 1978:2), members of which spoke the *Chochenyo* Ohlone language. For the purposes of this discussion, the *Tuibun* tribal area is delineated as running from Coyote Hills west through the marshlands to the bay shore, a distance of 5 kilometers (km); east to the bay hills, a distance of about 10 km; and along the bay shore for a distance of about 10 km north and 15 km south. This reflects the minimum area that was necessary for obtaining all of the major foodstuffs (i.e., fish and shellfish, bulbs and grass seeds, acorns and deer) utilized by the Ohlone of southeastern San Francisco Bay, regardless of distance from the bay shore villages.

King (1974:44-45) suggested that the degree to which a winter village was permanently occupied was a reflection of the ecological diversity found within the local catchment area. A "catchment" is normally considered the resource area about a habitation site that is within convenient walking distance, and can be exploited in one day's work (e.g., King 1974:Map 3; Thomas 1989:650). For example, !Kung women are known to exploit an area of about 9 km around a waterhole of vegetable and animal foods (Lee 1968:31). However, studies have shown that foraging beyond a distance of about 5 km is uneconomical (Vita-Finzi and Higgs 1970:7). Thus, the area that I have delineated as the *Tuibun* tribal area may be too large to have been effectively exploited from sedentary bay shore villages. Given the distance (10-15 km) separating the bay shore and bay hills environments (see Mayfield 1980:18-19), it is clear that the area required a subsistence strategy that included some kind of seasonal shifting of residence. Thus, a seasonal shift from a large bay shore winter village to smaller bay plains and bay hills non-winter camps is likely. Such a seasonal shifting of residence is not unique to this area. For example, Kent Flannery (1976:111) has illustrated a similar subsistence strategy in the Valley of Tehuacan, Mexico, where middle Formative Period (ca. 2,800-2,500 BP) villages utilized mountain camps 20 km away for hunting deer and gathering vegetable foods. By establishing seasonal camps in the hinterland, a community increased the size of its catchment area, and increased its effectiveness in exploiting it.

In this discussion, it is assumed that the large shellmounds at Coyote Hills (Ala-12, -13, -328, and -329), and some of the shellmounds to the north and south represent the remnants of *Tuibun*'s winter villages, of which three or more were occupied at any one time.[1] This occupation probably began about 4,000-3,000 BP (Moratto 1984:255). It is also assumed that these villages established seasonal base camps inland near the base of the hills. Such base camps were probably established in the vicinity of Mission San Jose (at or near a site called *Oroysom*) (Kroeber 1925:465, Figure 42; Levy 1978:485, Figure 1), in and around Stiver's Lagoon in Fremont (e.g., Ala-343), in Hayward (near the Holy Sepulchre Cemetery at the foot of the hills below the university), and near Warm Springs (e.g., Ala-342). While the base camps were usually located near the interface of the bay plains and bay hills, at least one camp (Ala-468) was established in the ridgelands at an elevation of 1,720 feet.

Fifty-eight archaeological sites have been recorded within the *Tuibun* Tribal Area. Fifteen of the sites are located along the bay shore, 14 on the bay plains, and 29 at the base of or within the bay hills. Eighteen of the sites are bedrock milling stations (see Table 2). The other sites consist primarily of bay shore shellmounds, seasonal encampments, and special task sites scattered across the bay plains. Additionally, several unrecorded sites are known to occur on top of Mission Peak. These sites appear to be associated with religious activities, and include stone constructions similar to the *tsektsels*, or "prayer seats," of northwestern California (cf. Buckley 1986, 1992:134-

---

[1] An alternative interpretation has been offered for at least one of the sites at Coyote Hills. Alan Leventhal (Leventhal *et al.* 1992) believes that Ala-329 was not a village, but rather a special mortuary and "cry" site. Leventhal's argument is based, in part, on the paucity of shellfish refuse in the Ala-329 mound. He believes that the mound was intentionally constructed for the purpose of interring the dead, much like the earthen burial mounds of eastern North America. Furthermore, he explains the site's non-burial associated artifactual and ecofactual remains (see Coberly 1973) as having been deposited there as a result of the area's use as a "cry" or feast site. Although it is conceivable that Ala-329 was used for such a purpose (I have proposed a similar feast-site function for CA-CCO-320, near Mount Diablo), the evidence offered to date is not convincing.

**TABLE 2.2. BEDROCK MILLING STATIONS LOCATED IN
OR NEAR THE *TUIBUN* TRIBAL AREA**

Site   Milling Features

Ala-60 25 conical BRMs, 6 bowl BRMs, 13 untyped BRMs, 182 cupules

Ala-344   1 bowl BRM

Ala-396   10 bowl BRMs

Ala-400   3 conical BRMs, 2 incipient BRMs

Ala-410   2 bowl BRMs

Ala-418   2 conical BRMs

Ala-419   3 bowl BRMs

Ala-431   7 BRMs

Ala-469   2 BRMs

Ala-470   3 BRMs

Ala-471   1 BRM

Ala-472   2 BRMs

Ala-505   20+ BRMs and cupules*

Ala-512   4 conical BRMs

Ala-513   3 conical BRMs, 2 cupules*

Ala-530   1 BRM

Ala-533/H   9 BRMs, 1 cupule*

Ala-535/H   1 BRM, 2 cupules*

*These cupules may represent incipient mortars.

135; Chartkoff 1983). Other kinds of ceremonial activities may have been conducted elsewhere on Mission Peak (see Anonymous 1965:53; Banks 1985:30). It is very probable that other unrecorded sites are to be found in the bay hills, and beneath housing tracts and other developments on the bay plains.

One of the most important of the special task sites is Ala-342, located at the base of the bay hills. Excavations conducted by Chester King in 1968 revealed that Ala-342 was a bulb-roasting site utilized circa AD 1400-1780 (King 1968:3-4). Numerous ovens and storage pits were encountered in the excavations, as were 29 burials (see Jurmain 1983). King noted that,

> Ala-342 was evidently used as a campsite by groups of people living at a village fronting on San Francisco Bay. Such campsites were probably quite common along the southern edge of San Francisco Bay, as the Bayshore and the foothills are some distance apart in this area. The camp site was evidently used in the spring as a center for the processing of various corms which were fresh in this season. Probably small groups of people lived on the site at this time without shelter. The site was probably also used in the fall as a base from which to gather acorns (King 1968:7-8).[2]

Leventhal and Jurmain (1983:1-2) noted that the Ala-342 artifactual assemblage indicated, "strong affinities, culturally and temporally, to the large bayshore village site CA-ALA-329, at Coyote Hills" (cf. endnote 1).

Ala-343, near Stiver's Lagoon in Fremont, represents another seasonal camp (Wildesen 1969:28). Both it and Ala-342 fit the King/Parkman model well. Just as Ala-328 is the ideal winter village type of site, so are Ala-342 and Ala-343 the ideal seasonal camps.

The various bedrock milling stations also fit the model well. Fourteen of the eighteen stations consist of five or less bedrock mortars. Four of these sites consist of conical mortars, and another three consist of bowl mortars. The mortar types were not recorded at the other six sites.

Three of the bedrock milling stations consist of 6-10 mortars. At one of the sites, the mortars are all bowl-shaped. The mortar types were not recorded at the other sites.

---

[2]Dr. King (personal communication 1992) now believes that Ala-342 may have been occupied year-round.

A single bedrock milling station, Ala-505, has 11-19 mortars. Although the types of mortars were not recorded, their measurements suggest that they are probably of the bowl variety.

A single bedrock milling station, Ala-60, has 44 bedrock mortars. This site consists of 25 conical mortars, 6 bowl mortars, and 13 untyped mortars. (The latter are features that were too badly broken to type, or else not available for study).

The large number of conical mortars at Ala-60 appears to be an anomaly, and might possibly be explained by the site's antiquity. The site is thought to have been occupied as early as 8,000 BP, with occupation continuing intermittently into the late prehistoric period (Bard *et al.* 1989, 12:18, 13:2). The conical mortars were probably utilized to process hard grass seeds, perhaps at a time prior to the introduction of the acorn industry. A single oval bedrock metate was also recorded at Ala-60. In addition to the metate and conical mortars, there are 6 bowl-shaped bedrock mortars, including 4 "incipient" mortars, which might reflect a later use of the site by *Tuibun* groups harvesting the local acorn crop. Bard *et al.* (1989, 13:8) noted that the distribution of the ground stone implements at Ala-60 suggested that a well-developed acorn economy was in place between circa 4,500-4,000 BP. If this observation is valid, then the conical mortars at Ala-60 represent an earlier use of the site, or else a seasonal function (i.e., the processing of hard grass seeds) separate from the acorn industry.

CONCLUSIONS

Within the *Tuibun* Tribal Area, bedrock milling stations consist of either bowl-shaped or cone-shaped mortars, and most of the sites consist of five or less mortars. With the exception of Ala-60, sites with more than five mortars tend to be characterized by bowl-shaped features. Four inferences might be drawn from these data:

(1) The bedrock milling stations reflect seasonality.

(2) Most of the stations were utilized by small collecting units.

(3) The stations were more likely to have seen communal use during the fall acorn harvest.

(4) Hard grass seeds were as important as acorns to the local diet.

Additionally, I would propose that certain bulbs of the lily family, especially *Brodiaea*, were also of major importance.

In conclusion, the data suggest that the subsistence model discussed herein is applicable for southeastern San Francisco Bay. Whereas a sedentary lifestyle was enjoyed by many of the Ohlone nations, the people of the Coyote Hills area found it necessary to employ a seasonal round that precluded a completely sedentary lifestyle. However, the seasonal round was very effective, and these Ohlone enjoyed an abundant life. Thus, the subsistence strategy that they employed represented a successful adaptation to a rich but expansive environment.

Acknowledgements

I thank Leigh Jordan and Lisa Hagel for the assistance they provided me at the Northwest Information Center, California Archaeological Inventory, Sonoma State University. I also thank Diane Watts and Helen McCarthy for taking the time to discuss their research findings with me, and George Rodgers who assisted me in various ways. Finally, I am very grateful to Diane Askew for her editorial suggestions. Any errors, of course, are the sole responsibility of the author.

REFERENCES CITED

Anonymous

1965   History of Washington Township. Fremont, California:
            the Country Club of Washington Township.

1971   The Ohlone Story. The Indian Historian 4(2):42. San
            Francisco.

Banks, Peter

1985   A Cultural Resources Investigation of the Mission Peak
            Regional Preserve, Fremont, Alameda County, California.
            A report prepared by California Archaeological
            Consultants, Inc., for the East Bay Regional Park
            District.   On file at Northwest Information Center,
            California Archaeological Inventory, Sonoma State
            University, Rohnert Park (S-7820).

Bard, James C., Colin I. Busby, and Larry S. Kobori

1989   Archaeological Data Recovery of CA-ALA-60 Located
            on Route 580, Castro Valley, Alameda County,
            California.   A report prepared by Basin Research
            Associates, Inc., for the California Department of
            Transportation. On file at Northwest Information Center,
            California Archaeological Inventory, Sonoma State
            University, Rohnert Park (S-10732).

Barrett, S. A., and E. W. Gifford

1933   Miwok Material Culture. Bulletin of Milwaukee Public
            Museum 2(4):117-377. Milwaukee.

Beardsley, Richard K.

1954   Temporal and Areal Relationships in Central California
            Archaeology, Part One.   University of California
            Archaeological Survey Reports 24:1-62. Berkeley.

Bennyhoff, James A.

1956   An Appraisal of the Archaeological Resources of
            Yosemite National Park.   University of California
            Archaeological Survey Reports 34:1-71. Berkeley.

Bickel, Polly McW.
1981   San Francisco Bay Area: Sites Ala-328, Ala-13 and Ala-
              12. Contributions of the University of California
              Archaeological Research Facility Number 43.

Bolton, Herbert Eugene
1927   Fray Juan Crespi: Missionary Explorer on the Pacific
              Coast 1769-1774. Berkeley: University of California.

1930   Anza's California Expeditions. 5 volumes. Berkeley:
              University of California Press.

Buckley, Thomas
1986   Lexical Transcription and Archaeological Interpretation:
              A Rock Feature Complex from Northwestern California.
              American Antiquity 51(3):617-618.

1992   Yurok Doctors and the Concept of "Shamanism." *In*
              California Indian Shamanism, Lowell John Bean, ed., pp.
              117-161. Ballena Press Anthropological Papers No. 39,
              Sylvia Brakke Vane, ed. Menlo Park, California: Ballena
              Press.

Chartkoff, Joseph L.
1983   A Rock Feature Complex from Northwestern California.
              American Antiquity 48(4):745-760.

Coberly, Mary B.
1973   The Archaeology of the Ryan Mound, Site ALA-329, a
              Central California Coastal Village Site. Museum of
              Anthropology Occasional Publications in Anthropology,
              Archaeology Series 4. Greeley: University of Northern
              Colorado.

Cook, Sherburne F.
1957   The Aboriginal Population of Alameda and Contra Costa
              Counties, California. University of California Anthropo-
              logical Records 16(4):131-156. Berkeley.

Davis, J. T., and A. E. Treganza
    1959   The Patterson Mound: A Comparative Analysis of the
                  Archaeology of Site Ala-328. University of California
                  Archaeological Survey Reports 47:1-92. Berkeley.

Fages, Pedro
    1911   Expedition to San Francisco Bay in 1770: Diary of Pedro
                  Fages. Herbert Bolton, ed. Publications of the Academy
                  of Pacific Coast History 2(3):141-159. Berkeley.

    1972   Expedition of 1772. *In* The Fages-Crespi Expedition of
                  1772. Translation of Folios 211-216r, Archivo General
                  de la Nacion, California 66, Bancroft Library, Berkeley.
                  Livermore: Amador-Livermore Valley Historical Society.

Fenenga, Franklin F.
    1952   The Archaeology of the Slick Rock Village, Tulare
                  County, California. American Antiquity 17(4):339-347.

Field, Les, Alan Leventhal, Dolores Sanchez, and Rosemary Cambra
    1992   A Contemporary Ohlone Tribal Revitalization Movement:
                  A Perspective from the Muwekma Costanoan/Ohlone
                  Indians of the San Francisco Bay Area. California
                  History 71(3):412-432. San Francisco.

Flannery, Kent V.
    1976   Empirical Determination of Site Catchments in Oaxaca
                  and Tehuacan. *In* The Early Mesoamerican Village,
                  Kent V. Flannery, ed., pp. 103-117. New York:
                  Academic Press.

Galvan, P. Michael
    1968   "People of the West": The Ohlone Story. The Indian
                  Historian 1(2):9-13. San Francisco.

Harrington, John P.
    1942   Culture Element Distributions, XIX: Central California
                  Coast. University of California Anthropological Records
                  7(1):1-46. Berkeley.

Hildebrandt, William, et al.
1984   Prehistoric Hunting Patterns in Central California. *In*
               Papers on Central California Prehistory: I:43-67. Coyote
               Press Archives of California Prehistory Number 3.
               Salinas.

Johnson, E. N.
1942   Stone Mortars of Contra Costa County, California.
               American Antiquity 7(3):322-326.

Jurmain, Robert, ed.
1983   The Skeletal Biology of CA-ALA-342.   Salinas,
               California: Coyote Press.

King, Chester D.
1968   Excavations at Ala-342: A Summary Report. Manuscript
               on file at California Department of Parks and Recreation,
               Sacramento.

King, Thomas F.
1974   The Evolution of Status Ascription Around San
               Francisco Bay. *In* ?Antap: California Indian Political
               and Economic Organization, Lowell J. Bean and Thomas
               F. King, eds., pp. 35-54. Ballena Press Anthropological
               Papers No. 2, Lowell J. Bean, ed. Ramona, California:
               Ballena Press.

Kroeber, A. L.
1925   Handbook of the Indians of California.   Bureau of
               American Ethnology Bulletin 78. Washington: Smithso-
               nian Institution.

Langsdorff, Georg Heinrich von
1814   Voyages and Travels in Various Parts of the World
               During the Years 1803-07.   Volume 2.   London:
               Colburn.

Lee, Richard B.
1968   What Hunters Do for a Living, or, How to Make Out on
               Scarce Resources. *In* Man the Hunter, Richard B. Lee
               and Irven DeVore, eds., pp. 30-48. Chicago: Aldine-
               Atherton.

Leventhal, Alan, Hank Alvarez, Dolores Galvan Lameira, Rosemary
Cambra, Joe Mondragon, and Irene Zweirlein
1992   Back from Extinction: The Cultural Heritage, Biological
              Continuity and Contemporary Revitalization of the
              Muwekma Ohlone, Amah-Mutsen and Carmel Mission
              Band of Costanoan Indians. Paper presented at the
              Ohlone Scholar's Conference, November 14, Hayward.

Leventhal, Alan, and Robert Jurmain
1983   Introduction. In The Skeletal Biology of CA-ALA-342,
              Robert Jurmain, ed., pp. 1-4. Salinas, California: Coyote
              Press.

Levy, Richard
1978   Costanoan. In Handbook of North American Indians,
              Volume 8 (California), Robert F. Heizer, ed., pp. 485-
              495.   William Sturtevant, gen. ed.   Washington:
              Smithsonian Institution.

Lillard, Jeremiah B., R.F. Heizer, and Franklin Fenenga
1939   An Introduction to the Archaeology of Central California.
              Sacramento Junior College, Department of Anthropology,
              Bulletin 2.

Margolin, Malcolm
1978   The Ohlone Way. Berkeley: Heyday Books.

Mayfield, David W.
1978   Ecology of the Pre-Spanish San Francisco Bay Area.
              M.A. thesis, San Francisco State University.

1980   Ecology of a Discovered Land.   Pacific Discovery
              33(5):12-20.

McCarthy, Helen, Robert A. Hicks, and Clinton M. Blount
1985   A Functional Analysis of Bedrock Mortars: Western
              Mono Food Processing in the Southern Sierra Nevada.
              Appendix F of: Cultural Resources of the Crane Valley
              Hydroelectrical Project Area: Volume I, Ethnographic,
              Historic, and Archaeological Overviews and Archaeo-
              logical Survey. Prepared by Theodoratus Cultural

Research, Inc., for the Pacific Gas and Electric Company.

Miller, George R., ed.
1982   Final report of Archaeological Test Excavations of CA-
              ALA-60 Located on Route 580, Castro Valley, Alameda
              County, California, P.M. 26.0/29.0. A report prepared
              by the Institute of Cultural Resources, California State
              University, Hayward, for the California Department of
              Transportation.

Moratto, Michael J.
1968   A Survey of the Archaeological Resources of the
              Buchanan Reservoir Area, Madera County, California.
              San Francisco State College, Occasional Papers in
              Anthropology 4(1):1-121. San Francisco.

1972   A Study of Prehistory in the Southern Sierra Nevada
              Foothills, California. Ph.D. dissertation, University of
              Oregon, Eugene.

1984   California Archaeology. Orlando: Academic Press, Inc.

Parkman, E. Breck
1980   Toward a Paradigmatic Interpretation of the Seasonal
              Exploitative Pattern of Native California: Archaeological
              Inferences from the San Francisco Bay Area. Manuscript
              on file at California Department of Parks and Recreation,
              Sacramento.

1981   An Incised Tablet from Northern California. Journal of
              California and Great Basin Anthropology 3(2):286-290.

1982   Bedrock Mortars and Cupule Petroglyphs. In Final
              Report of Archaeological Test Excavations of CA-ALA-
              60 Located on Route 580, Castro Valley, Alameda
              County, California, P.M. 26.0/29.0, George R. Miller,
              ed., pp. 133-174. A report prepared by the Institute of
              Cultural Resources, California State University, Hayward,
              for the California Department of Transportation.

1992   Dancing on the Brink of the World: Deprivation and the
              Ghost Dance Religion. In California Indian Shamanism,

Lowell J. Bean, ed., pp. 163-183.   Ballena Press
Anthropological Papers No. 39, Sylvia Brakke Vane, ed.
Menlo Park, California: Ballena Press.

Parkman, E. Breck, Diane C. Watts, and Joseph S. Eisenlauer
1978   An Archaeological Reconnaissance of a 2500 Acre Parcel
            on Walpert Ridge, Alameda County, California. A report
            prepared by the Institute of Cultural Resources,
            California State University, Hayward, for Ecumene
            Associates.

Phebus, G., Jr.
1973   Contributions to Costanoan Archaeology: Archaeological
            Investigations at 4-Ala-330 and 4-SMa-22.   Treganza
            Anthropology Museum Papers 12. San Francisco.

Rackerby, F.
1967   The Archaeological Salvage of Two San Francisco Bay
            Shellmounds. Treganza Anthropology Museum Papers
            3(1):1-86. San Francisco.

Simons, Dwight D.
1981   Avian and Mammalian Remains from Prehistoric Sites in
            the Richmond Harbor Area. Appendix I of: Investigation
            of Cultural Resources within the Richmond Harbor
            Development Project 11-A, Richmond, Contra Costa
            County, California, by Peter M. Banks and Robert I.
            Orlins. A report prepared by California Archaeological
            Consultants, Inc., for the City of Richmond. On file at
            Northwest Information Center, California Archaeological
            Inventory, Sonoma State University, Rohnert Park (S-
            4901).

Thomas, David Hurst
1989   Archaeology.   Fort Worth, Texas: Holt, Rinehart and
            Winston, Inc.

Vita-Finzi, Claudio, and Eric S. Higgs
1970   Prehistoric Economy in the Mt. Carmel Area of
            Palestine: Site Catchment Analysis. Proceedings of the
            Prehistoric Society 36:1-37.

Watts, Diane C.
1984   Bones Along the Bayshore: A Study of Mammalian
            Exploitation and Cultural Taphonomy of Faunal
            Assemblages of Two Bayshore Shellmounds, Ala-328
            and Ala-329. M.A. thesis, California State University,
            Hayward.

Wildesen, L. E.
1969   Ohlone Indian Pre-History. The Indian Historian
            2(1):25-28. San Francisco.

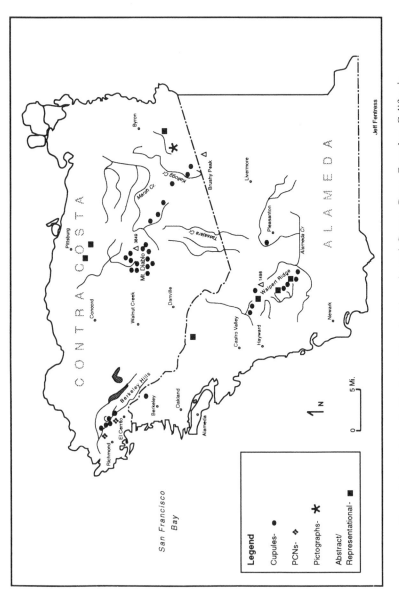

Figure 3.1. Prehistoric Rock Art Sites in Alameda and Contra Costa Counties, California

PREHISTORIC ROCK ART OF ALAMEDA AND CONTRA COSTA COUNTIES

Jeff Fentress

The Bay Area appears as rock art *terra incognita* in standard works on rock art in California (Heizer and Clewlow 1973, Grant 1971). Though it has been recognized since the mid 1970s that rock art forms do exist in the Bay Area (Hotz and Clewlow 1974, Miller 1977), no comprehensive study has been made of rock art in the East Bay.

Four types of rock art will be analyzed in this paper: cupules, PCNs ("pecked curvilinear nucleated" petroglyphs, after Miller 1977), pictographs, and a general category for all other abstract and representational petroglyphs. The forms will be defined and described. The types will be placed into local and regional contexts. Analysis of the forms is based on geographic location, environmental context, ethnographic accounts, relation to other archaeological sites, and ethno-linguistic boundaries.

No ethnographic accounts directly refer to rock art in Alameda or Contra Costa counties. There are no absolute dating techniques applicable to rock art, either. To develop theories about ethnic affiliation of rock art in the area, I have used contextual evidence and evidence from either local or geographically separated ethnic groups to provide possible interpretations of symbolic forms, and for the relation of these forms to specific groups.

The hypothesis has been advanced that members of Proto-Hokan language families may have been the original inhabitants of the Bay Area (Taylor 1961, Moratto 1984), but, at the beginning of the historic period, the local inhabitants were Ohlone (i.e., Costanoan), Miwok and Yokuts, all members of the Penutian language family.

In this case, ethnographic analogy must be made with practices of related groups outside the study area. Ethnographic evidence does exist for rock art practices among Hokan and Penutian language groups outside the study area. Obviously, any extrapolation presupposes both cultural continuity between language groups and cultural conservatism for hundreds of years. The geographic and archaeological contexts of East Bay rock art have distinct patterns that may provide supporting evidence.

Above all, I wish to provide a record of a fragile archaeological resource in a highly urbanized and rapidly changing region. As Moratto states, "the prehistory of the Bay Area is less well known—partly because urban sprawl has destroyed numerous archaeological sites and partly because many of the data from 'salvaged' sites remain unpublished and generally unavailable" (Moratto 1984:218). Sites recorded in the 1950s have already been altered and destroyed. In another 40 years, sites recorded in the 1980s will, undoubtedly, meet the same fate. Land prices and population growth are in direct competition with the conservation of rock art and other prehistoric features. In this contest the short odds are always on conservation.

Finally, it must be noted that the term "rock art" is subject to debate. There is the distinct possibility that these prehistoric forms do not relate in any meaningful way to our conceptions of "art", as they were based in cultures far different from ours. However, the rock art in Alameda and Contra Costa counties was without doubt an effort to communicate with signs. Efforts to understand these signs may advance our understanding of those who came before us and of our own methods of communication.

METHOD

All archaeological site records from Alameda and Contra Costa Counties were reviewed at the University of California, Berkeley Archaeological Research Facility, California State University, Hayward, and at the Northwest Information Center at Sonoma State University. I have visited 38 of 41 possibly prehistoric rock art sites in the project area. The three additional rock art sites recorded in the area are attributed to historic, non-Native American sources. In view of the urbanized environment of this study, some of the purported prehistoric rock art may be modern, as well.

It is likely that more rock art sites will be found in the two counties. Archaeological surveying in the study area has been done primarily by either State Park agencies or by cultural resource management companies to comply with state and federal agency requirements. In both cases, the project focus is site or area specific. This record, then, is geographically arbitrary.

ARCHAEOLOGICAL AND ETHNOGRAPHIC SETTING

Rock art is but one aspect of the archaeological and ethnographic record of the Bay Area. The following summary is provided to serve as a background for the rock art data, and as explanation of some of the archaeological and linguistic terms used in the paper.

In 1949 Robert Heizer proposed that Central California prehistory could be placed in a tripartite matrix: Early, Middle, and Late Horizons. In 1954 R. Beardsley refined Heizer's concept. He added substages, and expanded the scheme to include the Bay Area. In doing so, he codified the Central California Taxonomic System (CCTS). The CCTS became the standard temporal concept for the region.

Eventually, the CCTS was challenged. As Moratto states (1984:185), ". . . it did not permit much cultural variability at any point in time." In 1968 Gerow (with Force) claimed that data gathered at the University Village site on the San Francisco peninsula indicated an early Bay Area culture that did not fit the CCTS framework. In 1972 Ragir suggested that "Culture" be used instead of "Horizon." The use of the term culture indicated the need for a more flexible and adaptive approach than the CCTS which was based on artifact assemblages, primarily found as grave goods.

In 1973-74 Fredrickson proposed the concept of "Pattern." In Fredrickson's view, the Windmiller "culture" (ca. 3000-1000 BC), for example, was not a stratigraphic absolute, nor limited necessarily by region. Instead, it and other archaeological phases could be seen as evidence of a certain mode of socio-economic organization and environmental adaptation. In 1974, Fredrickson introduced a comprehensive chronology for Central California. His terminology will be used in this text.

Linguistic evidence has been used to support archaeological data in the attempt to devise prehistoric models. Two language families are of particular concern in this paper: Hokan and Penutian. The Hokan language family is generally accepted as the oldest language group in California (Moratto 1984:536; Shipley 1978:81). Shipley (1978:81-82) feels the only group possibly older is the Yukian stock (Yuki, Wappo). Historic Hokan speaking groups include the Chimeriko, Achumawi, Pomo, Karuk, Yana, Washo, Shastian, Esselen, Salinan, Chumash and Yuman; however, the concept of a proto-Hokan language stock remains hypothetical (Shipley 1978), and the use of linguistic/ethnic parallels must be correlated with other archaeological data.

The second major language group referred to in this paper is Penutian. Penutian is divided into four subfamilies: Wintuan, Maiduan, Yokutsan and Utian. The proto-historic inhabitants of the East Bay—the Ohlone, Miwok and Yokuts—were all speakers of the Penutian languages. The Miwok and Ohlone (Costanoan) represent "two clearly defined subgroups" (Shipley 1978:84).

In Alameda and Contra Costa Counties the oldest C14 dates are from West Berkeley (Ala-307) ca. 2000 BC (Elsasser 1978:41); and Stone Valley (CCo-308) ca. 2500 BC (Moratto 1984:261). However, there is evidence that the region was inhabited much earlier. Dates from Santa Clara County (SCl-178) and Santa Cruz County (SCr-177) appear to pre-date 7000 BP (Moratto 1984:110). Obsidian hydration dating of Ala-60, near Castro Valley, has indicated the earliest levels could date to 5530-4630 BC (Miller, et al. 1982).

Using combined linguistic and archaeological evidence, Moratto (1984) proposes that the Windmiller pattern may represent the arrival of the Utian groups into Central California. Similarities between Windmiller and the Berkeley pattern (ca. 2500 BC-AD 500) could indicate a date for the Utian entry as early as 2000-1500 BC. If this supposition is correct, it is possible to infer that the early inhabitants of the Bay Area were members of the Hokan or proto-Hokan language group. The dates from SCl-178 and Ala-60 indicate it is quite possible that the East Bay was occupied prior to the proposed Utian arrival.

Archaeological evidence affirms that a distinct cultural change occurred in Central California around 2000 BC. An example of the change comes from data assembled by Archaeological Consulting and Research Services in the Monterey area (Moratto 1984:314). Two distinct patterns seem to have been present: foragers and collectors. The "foragers," who may have been Hokan speakers, utilized a number of bases, gathering their subsistence on a daily basis with little storage. In contrast, the later pattern (possibly the proto-Ohlone) had permanent seasonal bases, food storage patterns (like acorn collecting), food processing stations, and seasonally utilization of both hill and littoral environments.

Fredrickson's "Middle Archaic Period" (ca. 3000-1000 BC, including the Berkeley pattern in the Bay Area) was marked by a subsistence shift from seed collecting to acorn processing. The change is apparent in the archaeological record as manos and metates are replaced (though not universally) by mortars and pestles. Shellfish collecting also gained importance during this period. Fredrickson (1974:46-47) felt this technological/adaptational change could have been the result of "a new population or populations which coexisted with the earlier population ultimately merging with or replacing it culturally."

The Berkeley pattern may represent a proto-Ohlone (Costanoan) population (Moratto 1984:554). The Miwok who occupied the area north of Mount Diablo arrived somewhat later, ca 1350 BC (Moratto 1984:555). The ancestral Yokuts are thought to have entered the northern part of the San Joaquin Valley between 1000 and 1500 BC on the basis of the linguistic reasoning that Yokutsan is less diverse than either Miwok or Utian. By the Emergent Period (ca. AD 500 to Euro-American contact), the Ohlone inhabitants of the East Bay had developed a complex "gatherer" pattern. Large shell middens are found along the bayfront. Substantial settlements were also found inland along major creeks. Seasonal patterns of resource exploitation existed. Salmon runs in the spring, acorn harvests in the fall, and the constant supply of shellfish and deer led to a fairly abundant lifestyle. The same pattern occurred inland as the Miwok fished for salmon and sturgeon in the Sacramento River and went up to the hills for acorns and deer. The Yokuts caught fish in the San Joaquin and Delta and roamed the hills along the edge of the Central Valley. All three groups appeared to have had a patrilineal descent system and an elite group of chiefs and religious specialists. The Miwok and Yokuts shared a totemic moiety system (Wallace 1978:466).

In the East Bay, Mount Diablo was considered the center point in the universe by the Ohlone. According to the Ohlone, the world was once covered by water and the top of Mount Diablo was the only land. Coyote, Hummingbird and Eagle lived on the island. As the waters receded the three explored the world. Humans were then created by Coyote under the direction of Eagle (Kroeber 1925). It is likely that both Miwok and Yokuts shared the Ohlone reverence for the mountain. Unfortunately, the ethnographic record of the original inhabitants of Alameda and Contra Costa is sparse. The influx in turn of Spaniards, Mexicans, and Euro-Americans reduced the native population drastically by the early 1800s. The native culture was nearly obliterated as a result.

CUPULES

(See Figure 3.2)

Cupules are purposefully made depressions on rock surfaces. Ethnographic evidence exists for two functions: as a form of petroglyph, and as a tool for cracking acorns. This combination of the 'sacred and profane', as it were, has led to confusion in the archaeological record. In this paper I will use "cupule" to mean cupule petroglyph.

Compounding the functional dichotomy is an even more basic problem: size. Cupules come in a variety of sizes. They are often found in association with larger depressions: bedrock mortars (hereafter BRMs). BRMs, themselves, come in a variety of sizes. The two forms actually represent opposite ends of a size continuum ranging from ca. 2 cm to ca. 20 cm in diameter. At either end of the scale the forms are obviously different; however, in the middle of the range it is often difficult to tell where a cupule ends and a BRM starts.

The issue of cupule usage primarily refers to situations with horizontal placement. As Elsasser (1985:42) notes, cupules "in association with bedrock mortars has led to speculation that the cupules may have been used as anvils for cracking the outer shells of acorns. However, these depressions often occur on steeply slanting or vertical planes, and could thus have only been used for this purpose with difficulty" (See Figure 3.2).

There are cupules on non-vertical planes in the study area. For example, at CCO-580 in Wildcat Canyon, depressions occur not only on the top surface of the rock but on the shoulders and sides. On the northwest face of a rock at Ala-412, near Castro Valley, three cupules are arranged in a symmetrical triangle.

Figure 3.2. Cupule rock in Wildcat Canyon (CCo-580)

Geographic Location/Environmental Context

Cupule rocks occur throughout the study area. Cupule sites are located in the littoral hills, in the Tri-Valley area, on Mount Diablo, in the Black Hills-Round Valley area, and along or near Kellogg Creek. Only one cupule site has been found north of Mount Diablo.

Cupule rocks are the most prevalent form of rock art in Alameda and Contra Costa counties. Thirty-five of 41 possible rock art sites are cupule rocks. They are also found in association with two other rock art forms; PCNs and incised petroglyphs.

Cupule rocks are generally found near activity centers such as BRM stations or occupation sites (as indicated by the presence of midden). Twenty-two of 35 cupule sites have associated BRMs.

There is a correlation between cupule sites and water courses. In the two counties 23 of 35 (66%) cupule rocks are within 50 meters of water. Of course, occupation sites generally occur near water. There are 13 cupule sites that contain rocks marked only with cupules. There is an even stronger correlation between these "cupule-only" sites and water. Seven of twelve cupule-only boulders in Contra Costa occur on ridges or hillsides above seasonal drainages. The other 5 sites are directly adjacent to ephemeral drainages. Ala-412 is the sole cupule-only site in Alameda county. The rock is on top of a ridge above a creek. The ridge locations may be a pattern as well. Many cupule rocks are located on prominent overlooks.

Regional Context

West and north of the study area, cupule boulders are found in Marin and Sonoma Counties (Miller 1977), Mendocino County (Hedges 1982), (Gary and Foster 1990), and Northern Central California (Nissen and Ritter 1986). To the east, cupule boulders are found in the Sierra Foothills, the Central Sierra (Payen 1959, 1966) and in the Northern Sierra, (Heizer 1953, Heizer and Baumhoff 1962). To the west and south, cupules are found in Stanislaus County (Parkman 1986, 1988), Santa Clara County (Elsasser 1985), Fresno and Merced Counties (Foster, Jenkins and Betts 1990), Tulare County (Weinberger 1982), and in Southern California (Minor 1975; True and Baumhoff 1981).

Cupules are one of the most common rock art forms around the world and are found in locations as culturally and geographically diverse as the Western U.S. and Mexico (Parkman 1990), Siberia (Okladnikov 1971) and Europe (Grieder 1982).

Ethnograph Connections

In California ethnographic accounts concerning cupules come from Hokan, Penutian, Athapascan and Uto-Aztecan language groups. Cupule rocks are connected with fertility rituals, weather control, astronomy, fishing magic, mourning, and in tests of character. The reoccurring theme is that the rocks have power. The power is accessible by ritual.

Barrett lists two specific examples of the use of cupule rocks in fertility ceremonies among the Pomo (an Hokan language group) : ". . . a bluish stone which protrudes from the ground but a few inches. The surface of this is filled with small cuppings and scratches or gashes where the rock has been scraped and pulverized as a medicine for the cure of sterility" (1908:175).

The sterile pair went to one of these rocks and there first a prayer for fertility was made. Then, by means of a pecking stone, some small fragments were chipped from the sides of one of the grooves or cuppings in its surface. These were then ground to a very fine powder which was wrapped in some green leaves and taken to some secluded spot. Here this powder was made into a paste and with it the woman's abdomen was painted with two lines, one running from the top of the sternum to the pubes, the other transversely across the middle of the abdomen. Some of this paste was also inserted in the female. Intercourse at this time positively assured fertility, due to the magic properties of this rock (Barrett 1952:386-387).

An interesting "baby rock" parallel exists among the Kawaiisu, a Uto-Aztecan language group from southeastern California. "Andy Greene, a Kawaiisu man who lives in Tehachapi, told of a boulder which resembles a recumbent pregnant woman near his home which has a cupule like feature on its "navel." He stated that girls who wanted to get pregnant pound on the "navel" with another rock to make a little rock dust which they then eat. He knew nothing of the Pomo "baby rocks" and in fact had never even heard of a tribe named Pomo" (Smith and Lerch 1984:7). This example may show a forgotten cultural diffusion, but also indicates the Pomo analogy may have reverberations outside Hokan language groups.

Rocks were pitted in conjunction with salmon runs among the Hupa (Athapascan):

> Three immortals came into being at Xaslindin. They began to talk about what would be when Indians should come into existence. One of them went away up the Klamath river. The other two remained waiting for him. 'I don't think we better wait for him,' said one of those who remained. He went down to the river. 'Let a stone cup become,' he thought. And it became. And then in it a salmon became. . . He made the Salmon swim down the Trinity and Klamath rivers to the ocean (Goddard 1904:268).

Spier (1930:21) noted the Klamath used to pound on rocks to make the wind blow. Parkman (1990) has advanced the theory that cupules could have been created by the act of pounding. The noise making may have sounded like thunder, signaling the arrival of rain and a change of seasons. Nissen and Ritter (1986) have also made a strong argument connecting cupule and rain rocks with the World Renewal Ceremony of the Hupa, Yurok and Karuk. The change of seasons relates strongly to the replenishing of the earth and the birth, as it were, of new resources: water, fish, plants. These tribes come from different language groups. Shared cultural traditions may outweigh linguistic affiliations.

Other uses of cupule rocks exist. Klamath women pounded rocks during mourning (Nissen and Ritter 1986:70). Cupule boulders have been associated both with astronomical phenomena and the quest for personal power among the Achumawi (Benson and Buckskin 1988).

Ethnographic accounts about cupule use among Penutian groups exist but are limited. Cupule rocks were used in noise making ceremonies among the Yokuts (Latta 1977:196-197) but the purpose is unclear. It may be notable that in the San Joaquin Valley (Yokuts territory), "At the only site where a pitted boulder is relatively isolated from other features, it exists on top of a saddle separating two valleys" (Weinberger 1980:4). This description fits both Ala-412 and CCo-428 in eastern Contra Costa. A Penutian ethnographic account comes from Merriam (1955:11):

> The old Wintoon trail along the Sacramento from Susson down as far as Redding was divided into day's journeys, with regular resting places where the night was spent. At each of these places was a small shallow hole in a rock—a hole apparently not more than a couple of inches in diameter and perhaps an inch in depth. The old Doctor used to go to these holes and pray for strength and success.

A convincing argument has been made (Baumhoff 1980, Nissen and Ritter 1986, Parkman 1990) that cupule rocks are the material remnants of a Hokan or "proto-Hokan" belief system. Baumhoff (1980:180) believed that large, multiple cupule boulders, in the north coast ranges could date to "late Borax Lake and early Houx" (3000-1200 AD). He believed a change to small cupule boulders occurred after ca. 1200 AD. The change related to the growing cultural effect of Penutian culture, in particular the *Kuksu* ceremony. The small rocks may have become the "baby rocks" of historic times.

On the basis of Baumhoff's theory, an early Hokan typology would include multi-cupule rocks. In the Pomo area of Baumhoff's study cupule boulders occur primarily on schist. Three large multi-cupule rocks on schist occur in or near Wildcat Canyon (CCo-125/353, CCo-152 and CCo-580). Nissen and Ritter show that multi-cupule rocks can also occur on other types of rock (sandstone, metamorphic, etc.) within Hokan territories. Sandstone rocks with multiple cupules (Ala-60, Ala-480, CCo-9, CCo-428) are found in various places in Alameda and Contra Costa counties.

The cupule rocks in the East Bay do fit into patterns that are consistent with Baumhoff's hypothesis and with the ethnographic accounts relating to water. Eight rocks have 10 or more cupules. All 8 are within 10 m of water. Multiple cupule rocks indicate repeated ritual use. They may be evidence of a ritual pattern of seasonal and weather control similar to one that occurs farther north in California. Ritual control of salmon runs may have been important to inhabitants of the East Bay. However, the Bay Area is a distinct environment with its own cultural history. Direct correspondence is impossible without local ethnographic evidence.

If we postulate that Hokan people were the creators of multiple cupule rocks, the obvious question is whether the Penutian speakers adopted or continued the use of cupules. Baumhoff (1980:181) believed that "the petroglyphs were retained only as a minor element, a survival: they still existed but with much reduced importance."

The religious practices involving cupules have a recurring connection with fertility cycles, either ecological, or human. The Ohlone celebrated acorn festivals (Margolin 1978) or, at least, acorn rituals (Kroeber 1925:471), signaling the renewal of a life-giving resource. An interesting pattern exists at two of the multiple-cupule sites, Ala-60, and CCo-9. The large cupule boulders are superimposed with mortars, but the cupules have been retained. The boulders with cupules are separate from the largest BRM stations.

It may be that the mortars on the large cupule rocks indicate an incorporation of past beliefs into a new system. Baumhoff's idea that there was a trend towards lesser numbers of cupules over time, may be reflected in the fact that 60% of all cupule rocks in the two county area have less than 10 cupules and 94% have less than 50 cupules.

Obviously, expanding Baumhoff's concentrated and site specific correlation between Hokan (specifically Pomo) sites and cupule boulders to a connection between the Hokan groups and cupules in all regions of California predicates a long period of cultural conservatism and cross regional continuity. As well, an assumption that Penutian speaking people did not use cupule rocks or used them in one manner implies that all Penutian people had the same cultural practices. Undoubtedly, there was assimilation and cultural diffusion between the two language groups. Referring to the conflicts between Heizer's CCTS and Gerow's multilineal models of Bay Area prehistory, Bickel states "there were changes in both areas and separate traditions in each, interwoven with evidence of interplay between them—a complex picture which cannot be portrayed in simple models of parallel or convergent change" (Bickel 1976:338).

Hedges makes the point that "the baby rocks and other petroglyph sites in Pomo territory, like sites in other parts of the state, include various types of cupule occurrences" (Hedges 1982:4). I would like to expand Hedges concept and make the inference that if several forms exist then a variety of possible functions may exist. The possibility of multiple function is supported by locational analysis. Cupule boulders are usually, but not always, found in connection with water resources: in streambeds, and above seasonal drainages. Cupules are often connected with food sources: BRM stations and creeks containing fish. However they are also found in isolation on prominent ridges with overlooks. They are found along aboriginal trails (Vasco Road, Wildcat Canyon). The ethnographic accounts show that a variety of cupule rituals existed. It seems likely that cupule forms and meanings could have changed over time, being incorporated into different belief systems, reinvented, as it were, over and over.

PCNS

(See Figure 3.3)

In 1974 Virginia Hotz and C. W. Clewlow Jr. published an article entitled "A Northern California Petroglyph Site" which described: "a series of 90-95 incisions or scratches of elliptical or oval shape. They are smooth and somewhat weathered, but, nevertheless, are clearly distinct in

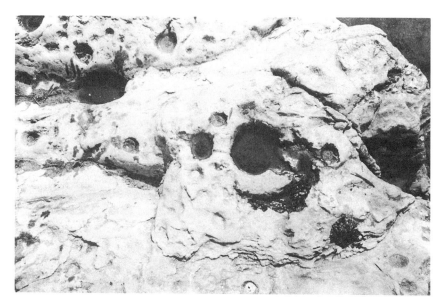

Figure 3.3.   Pecked curved nucleated (PCN) petroglyphs and cupules at
Canyon Trails Park, El Cerrito (CCo-152)

all but about five cases. The individual incisions range from 1.5-3 cm in
depth and from 8-20 cm in diameter" (Hotz and Clewlow 1974:149).

In her Master's Thesis at San Francisco State University, Theresa
Miller coined the phrase "pecked curvilinear nucleated" to describe this
style of rock art. "The basic elements are circles and ovals, which have
nuclei that appear raised. They seldom occur in any discernable pattern.
The elements [are] pecked into the surface of the rock (generally a
chlorite schist boulder). The size ranges from 5-25 cm in diameter
(exterior measurements), with the nuclei from 2.5-20.5 cm in diameter.
The depth of the pecking and the width vary from 5-6 cm" (Miller
1977:44).

Geographic Location/Environmental Context

There are two PCN sites in the study area, CCo-125/353 and
CCo-152. The sites are less than 2 miles apart.

CCo-125 is located in Alvarado Park in Richmond where Wildcat
Canyon opens up into the flatlands about 5 miles from the bay. Several
midden sites, CCo-274, CCo-349, CCo-373, are located both upstream
and downstream from CCo-125. Midden is also found around the top of
CCo-125. These sites and/or the area around the cupule rocks may have
been encountered by Anza in 1775. Anza "mentions a village of at least
100 persons at what is now Wildcat Canyon in Richmond" (Heizer

1974:6). The main boulder/rock face at CCo-125 is one of the largest schist boulders in the East Bay.

An adjacent petroglyph rock may be an outcrop of the same boulder. There are large circular forms superimposed with cupules and BRMs on all the rocks. Some shallow cupules are visible on the slanting face of the main boulder facing the creek. One PCN occurs on the south facing side about half way up.

CCo-152 is located at Canyon Trails Park in El Cerrito where a creek once debauched into the flatlands (See Figure 3.3). The area is severely altered by the construction of a city park. The original site descriptions by Pilling and Squire (1949) list 7 "worked boulders" at CCo-152 and CCo-154. CCo-154 was farther upstream and has been destroyed. In 1953 only one boulder is described in a *Berkeley Gazette* article. It appears to be the same one that is in the park today. It is possible that other PCN forms were present on the missing rocks. A local resident I talked to in February 1992 said she heard once from "an old man in the park" that the boulder now located in the children's playground had been moved there from "up the creek." A. B. Elsasser was told by a woman who lived in the neighborhood that one of the cupped rocks is located in her backyard (personal communication 1991). At any rate, the original integrity of the sites has been destroyed. The evident destruction of at least some of the boulders represents a considerable loss. The remaining boulder is one of the most significant rock art sites in the two counties.

CCo-152 contains at least 7 PCNs. Four are circular and have the centers drilled out by the superimposition of BRMs. There is one untouched ovoid PCN. There are two ovoid shapes that are grooved in the center.

Regional Context

PCN sites have been found in Marin, Sonoma, Mendocino, Santa Clara, San Benito counties, and as far south as San Luis Obispo county. (Parkman 1992). One PCN site is known on the southern Oregon Coast (Pullen 1982).

Ethnographic Connections

The question of PCN ethnic identification and antiquity has led to some interesting and completely speculative theories. Miller (1977:30) claims Barrett "attributes the PCN to the mythical bird people of Pomo mythology" (Miller 1977:30). Actually, Barrett (1952:386-387) says:

Each of the two sterility rocks here were said to insure only for its own particular sex. They were first used by the bird people of the nearby village of mu'yamuya. The story goes that in these ancient times a young man and his sister went out. . . He then made on the surface of the stone a large carving representing a genital. This, even yet, is the most prominent of many marks upon this rocks. Since that day this, and other similar rocks, have been employed in the cure of sterility.

In Pomo territory, many PCNs have slashes and grooves across the centers. These motifs have been called vulvaforms by Miller (1977), Parkman (1992), Hedges (1982) and others. The interpretation of these forms as vulvas is credible; however, the assumption that the male figure in the story was carving a female sexual organ, and that the design referred to in the story is a PCN is problematic.

Miller found that "the PCN style is always modified or destroyed when other petroglyph styles are placed on the same rocks. The other five styles of the North Coast Ranges are, based on the recorded data, superimposed on the PCN style" (Miller 1977:30). Referring to a site in Mendocino, Hedges (1982:3) states "pecked oval forms are greatly weathered and seem to be the earliest form of rock art on the face."

These observations are confirmed at CCo-152 where PCNs are superimposed with both BRMs and cupules. At CCo-152 the circular forms are superimposed with small cupules in a seemingly random fashion. Also, they are superimposed directly in the centers with BRMs. In Santa Clara and San Benito counties circular PCN-like forms have holes ground into the centers. It is possible that the circular forms at CCo-152 once had small holes in the centers that were enlarged, at some point, into BRMs.

The circle and dot style is defined by Heizer and Clewlow as one of the components of the "North Coast Range" style (1973:29). The circle and dot style is similar, yet distinct from the "concentric circle" form found in Santa Clara, San Benito and Mendocino counties. Since it is impossible to say when these carvings were made, one can only note that both forms are found in close geographic proximity and that they seem to be related stylistically. There may be another tradition of concentric circles that is different from the circular PCN forms (Gary and Foster 1990).

Elsasser believes PCNs have "three variant forms with the principle style oval in shape and the others described as circular with a small cupule or "dot" in the center of nucleus. This latter variant has often been referred to as "circle and dot" in other more well defined styles" (1985:42).

PCNs can also be interpreted technologically. Certain types of PCNs were evidently used as quarry blanks in Sonoma, Marin and San Benito counties where the PCN forms appear to have been slabbed off. In the original report on SBn-12 (Pilling 1950), the site was referred to as a steatite bowl-quarry site that was similar to a quarry site on Catalina Island. Pilling (1949) referred to the rocks at CCo-152 as steatite and Squire (1949) described a "grooved area, possibly, where a steatite bowl was removed." Elsasser has disputed this interpretation because 1) many PCNs are ovoid and no ovoid bowls are found in use, 2) quarried ovals are too close together to permit full removal, and 3) the ovals are too small to make bowls from (Marymor 1984:5).

Though bowl quarrying, in particular, may be unlikely, other forms of quarrying and retouch do exist at some PCN sites, e.g., SBn-12 (Mark and Newman 1989:49; Parkman 1988). However, this is not a universal pattern as other PCN sites remain virtually untouched (e.g. Mrn-427).

Parkman (1992) has presented a speculative chronology for PCNs. As noted, PCNs consistently appear as the lowest petroglyph "strata" in Central California and the North Coast Ranges, superimposed by cupules and other forms. Heizer and Baumhoff (1962) felt that cupules could date to 5-3000 BC in Nevada and Eastern California. Parkman feels that cupules may have existed as early as 7000 BC "in the northern Great Basin" (cf. 1992) and could have been brought into Central California during the Lower Archaic Period (ca. 6-3000 BC) by proto-Hokans. If this is true then the PCNs could have been superimposed by cupules during the time when proto-Hokans occupied Central California and thus, the form was created by proto-Hokans.

Parkman feels that PCN manufacture stopped with the spread of Utian groups out of the Delta during the Middle Archaic Period. The variety of the forms makes the picture more complex. The flat circular type of PCN appears to have been used consistently as quarrying blanks. Parkman (cf. p. 12) believes this form may have been part of a Penutian quarrying technique while the ovoid form became archaic. If Parkman is correct, then the PCN sites in the East Bay would be evidence of pre-Utian populations, e.g. proto-Hokan.

However, the greatest concentration of PCNs occurs in Sonoma and Marin counties. There is the possibility of a shared tradition involving groups around the Bay Area and farther north. There may have been a cultural diffusion into the East Bay and farther south. Considering that the accounts concerning cupules are historic, the PCNs and cupules could be of a much later period. Since this project was originally completed in 1992, I visited a PCN site near Port Orford, Oregon. This site has not been mentioned in the reviews of PCN sites (Miller 1977, Parkman 1992) and indicates diffusion of this style may extend farther north than previously believed.

The evidence from CCo-125 and CCo-152 indicates that several processes have occurred. Both ovoid and circular PCNs are present. Only one form, an ovoid, has an untouched appearance. The untouched ovoid and the "vulvaforms" could be entirely different forms. While none of the forms have been completely removed the slashes could have occurred during a quarrying process.

It is evident that these rocks were used for several cultural traditions. The fact that normally technological implements like acorn grinding holes were placed on these rocks, in what appear to be special places, seems to present a mixture of ritual and subsistence. There may be a parallel here with the seemingly opposite functions of cupules. If we suppose that chlorite schist rocks had a connection with fertility or fecundity during the proto-Hokan period, it is conceivable that the Ohlone transferred this belief, in some modified form, to their main food source.

CCo-125 and CCo-152 provide clear evidence that chlorite schist became, at some time in the past, a targeted medium, used for both rock art and artifacts. It has been shown that several rock art forms are present at these sites. However, not only rock art was connected with schist. "Also valued was a fine schist from Wildcat Canyon, Contra Costa County, which appears archaeologically as ornaments and charmstones" (Moratto 1984:221). Evidence exists that schist use for sacred purposes existed cross-culturally in Central California for, at least, 2,000 years. Bickel (1976) delineated changes in charmstone manufacture from schist to sandstone at Ala-328, 12, 13 beginning ca. 300 BC-AD 300.

Bickel's analysis of material recovered from Ala-328 shows that schist charmstones occur in the upper unit of Component III. Component III is the lowest level at Ala-328 (230-270 cm.) and may be as old as 2300 BP. Moratto (1984:255) feels the site may actually be 4-3000 BP. Schist artifacts at Ala-328 have been traced to CCo-125 (Bickel 1976). If Moratto is correct, the manufacture of schist charmstones would have begun shortly after the Utian entrance into the East Bay. Ala-328 was evidently abandoned for periods starting ca. AD 300.   The schist charmstones are replaced by sandstone ones in the upper levels. Could the sandstone cupule rocks have been part of this cultural change?

Charmstones have been used in religious practices throughout Central California (Kroeber 1925, Latta 1977). The Ohlone may have "hung long, smooth charmstones over the river, magic to draw the fish closer" (Margolin 1978:38). Whether PCNs were a proto-Hokan or a later cross-cultural religious symbol, the people of the East Bay seem to have identified the schist boulders as sacred. An identification of schist with power may have begun with rock art and continued with mobiliary artifacts.

Due to the lack of rock art dating techniques identification of PCNs with specific groups remains speculative. However, PCNs provide evidence that in prehistoric Central California a tradition existed that identified schist rocks with power. It is quite apparent that chlorite schist, perhaps because of its special look and feel, attracted several forms of religious interest.

PICTOGRAPHS

(See Figure 3.4)

Pictographs are representational or abstract forms painted on rocks. In contrast, petroglyphs, such as cupules or PCNs, are made by pecking or incising the rock.

Geographic Location/Environmental Context

Two pictograph loci exist in the study area. One is located in Tilden Park in the Berkeley Hills. The site is described in a *Berkeley Gazette* article (June 17, 1953), and was called "Tilden Park 2" by Elsasser and Contreras (1958). The Tilden Park 2 site contains two red hand prints colored with hematite. An adult sized right hand print is placed directly above a child's left hand print. The two prints occur on a volcanic outcrop. They are not in association with any known prehistoric sites. The initial "M" is pecked into the center of the adult hand. Near the handprints were found a variety of incised figures including swastikas. In their study of "Modern Petrography" Elsasser and Contreras (1958) classified these as historic period petroglyphs.

The second site is CCo-434, which contains 9 separate pictograph loci and is, perhaps, the most spectacular of all the rock art sites in the two counties. Known as *Los Vaqueros* or the Vasco Caves, the site is located north of Highway 580 and the Altamont Pass, where numerous sandstone outcrops stand amidst the rolling hills. At an elevation of 500-900' a central California panorama unfolds with a view of the Sierra, the San Joaquin Valley, Mount Hamilton and Mount Diablo.

The pictographs are found in wind and water eroded caves and rockshelters. They are part of an extensive archaeological complex including midden, BRMS, lithic scatters and possible housepits. The

Figure 3.4. Pictograph panel at the Vasco Caves (CCo-434)

designs include red, black and yellow abstract figures, anthropomorphs, animal and bird figures.

Regional Context

The Tilden Park pictographs, if prehistoric, may have a very remote connection with the "Cave of the Hands" (Mnt-44). However, the prints at Mnt-44 are mainly executed in white and black and are stylistically different than the Tilden Park prints.

A regional context for CCo-434 is more complex. About 70 miles to the northeast, around Lake Comanche, and in historic Miwok territory, are several painted sandstone caves. None have representational elements (i.e. bird figures and anthropomorphs), but there are red and black linear and crosshatch motifs that could be related to the red and black figures at CCo-434.

The pictographs closest to and most closely related to CCo-434 are located at Sta-33 along Salado Creek about 30 miles south. Both CCo-434 and Sta-33 are located in the first line of hills west of the San Joaquin Valley and contain pictographs in sandstone caves. Red ochre elements occur at both sites as do mortar holes containing red pigment. It is interesting to note that two "rain rocks" were recorded at Sta-33 by Bennyhoff in 1956. Both sites have BRMs and midden areas in direct proximity. Further south, in San Benito County, a limestone cave with red and black elements was recorded but has since been obliterated (Elsasser 1985:42).

Beyond a 100 mile radius possible parallels occur in the southern San Joaquin Valley in Tulare County, around Hunter Liggett Military Reservation, in the Carrizo Plains, and in Chumash coastal areas around Santa Barbara.

Ethnographic Connections

Tilden Park is located in the traditional territory of the *Huchiun* group of Ohlone Indians. "'These hand prints,' Dr. Heizer said, were 'typically Indian'" (*Berkeley Gazette* June 18, 1953). Elsasser and Contreras noted that "There is a strong possibility that these prints were made prehistorically by Indians, and were not associated with the other petroglyphs" (1958:14). They noted that a prehistoric hematite quarry existed about 4 miles away (Ala-9). The limited elements present in Tilden Park and the proximity of historic petroglyphs make it difficult to identify them definitely as prehistoric.

In the historic period CCo-343 was located in a border zone between Northern Yokuts, Ohlone, and Miwok territories. The main east-west pass from the central valley into the Bay Area, Altamont, is just south of these hills. Latta (1977) lists Altamont as one of the "Most prominent of these old routes" (i.e. aboriginal trails). Davis (1961) shows this route as trail # 102 in his study of trade routes and trails. Not surprisingly, considering the crossroads location, the Vasco Caves were a meeting spot for a variety of local tribes into historic times (Lee Davis, Lowell Bean, personal communication 1992).

Because of the friable nature of the sandstone, it is likely that the rock art at CCo-434 is of the Emergent Period and therefore Miwok or Yokuts. There is no documented tradition of pictographs among the Ohlone. The Ohlone occupied areas south of the Altamont Pass.

A possible case could be made relating the black lines and the red "U" shapes outlined in black with Payen's "Type 4 Simple Abstract Monochrome" or "Type 5 Abstract Polychrome" (Payen 1966). These styles occur primarily on the east side of the San Joaquin Valley and in the Sierra foothills, but Style 5 extends as far west as Lake Comanche. Payen identifies this area as ethnographically Miwok. Bay and Plains Miwok groups occupied areas north and east of Mount Diablo. The Plains Miwok occupied the area around Lake Comanche. Northern Yokuts may have occupied the Comanche area at some period (Latta 1977).

A case can be made for identification of some of the art as Northern Yokuts. The Vasco Caves themselves may have been in Yokuts territory. Of the three ethnic groups, pictographs are most closely identified with Yokuts culture. "The most prevalent and best known form of Yokuts rock art is pictographs" (Weinberger 1982:72).

Stylistic and contextual similarities exist with Northern Yokuts sites, such as Sta-33 and Southern Yokuts sites in Tulare County. According to Grant, "The Southern Sierra Style proposed by Heizer and Clewlow can be typified by the Exeter Rocky Hill polychrome paintings with the most significant subject matter: the split head figure" (Grant 1981:24). Pictographs from CCo-434 show Grant's "split head" motif (See Figure 3.4). Other Yokuts pictographs feature anthropomorphs and fairly realistic animal figures. Both forms are present at CCo-434.

The split tailed figure is reminiscent of figures found at Cueva Pintada in the lower Salinas Valley and Chumash figures in the Santa Barbara area. Trade existed between Salinans, Chumash and the Yokuts who lived in the Southern Valley. Shared rock art elements are present at sites in the Carrizo plain and elsewhere (Hyder, Lee, and Oliver 1986). Grant noted the connection between the Yokuts and Chumash rock art traditions (1981:34).

CCo-434 is in a raptorial breeding area. Eagles and a variety of hawks are commonly seen. The Yokuts were divided into two primary moieties: Eagle and Coyote (Kroeber 1925:494). Two prominent panels depict raptorial figures.

Weinberger has defined public and private rock art sites among the Yokuts (Doktor 1983:63-71). A public site is open, accessible, and "in direct association with bedrock milling features." Public ceremonies could be held in such locales and the very presence of pictographic symbols may have served as a boundary marker and/or reminder of clan and totemic affiliation. Weinberger's "private" rock art locale have no BRMs, are hard to get to, and "relatively enclosed." The pictograph caves at CCo-434 fit this pattern. Caves are near ground level and directly adjacent to BRMs and/or midden or they are located high up in rock formations, with commanding views of the area.

According to Latta's informants pictographs were "*tripne*" (supernatural) and "added prestige" to a place (Latta 1977:600). Several factors combine to mark CCo-434 as a possible ritual center. It is close to a border zone between three ethnic groups. The setting is spectacular, with huge rock formations, a spring, and panoramic views of two sacred mountains, the Delta, and the Sierras. There are more pictographs at this location than at any other area within hundreds of miles. Among the Yokuts, cave painting marked sites where habitation and ceremonies occurred (Latta 1977:600). Pictographs were also used to mark Yokuts shaman's "private caches" containing ritual paraphernalia (Gayton 1948:113).

... the paintings were generally placed at an important village site, one permanently inhabited, or at some place where Indian ceremonies were performed. . . The idea furnished was that the paintings added prestige to the spot and served to awe the lesser characters of the tribe and instill in them a respect for the equipment concealed there (Latta 1977:600).

ABSTRACT AND REPRESENTATIONAL
PETROGLYPHS

(See Figure 3.5)

A variety of incised lines, grooves, and possibly representational figures occur in Alameda and Contra Costa counties. It is quite possible that some of the glyphs recorded as prehistoric are actually historic, or that historic elements have been added to once prehistoric panels. Because of the questionable nature of these petroglyphs, this section is primarily descriptive.

Figure 3.5.   Incised rock, eastern Contra Costa County (CCo-9)

Geographic Location/Environmental Context

Abstract grooves and non-representational incisions are found in association with cupules and PCN's at CCo-125 and CCo-152. In our study area these are also the only petroglyphs occurring on schist rocks. Scratches and grooves occur at both sites. It is difficult to say whether the marks are historic or prehistoric in these cases. Deep grooves do exist on CCo-152, but seem to extend primarily from BRMs or from the circular PCNs forms which are superimposed with mortars. BRMs with associated grooves occur on sandstone rocks at CCo-578, and Ala-60. All four sites are located adjacent to drainages in either the Berkeley or Hayward Hills.

A stone with vertical grooves is found at CCo-9 (See Figure 3.5). It is within 5 m. of a cupule boulder. Several BRM stations are also located at the site. CCo-9 is directly east of Vasco Road, north of the Altamont Pass. The incisions occur on a sandstone rock.

At Ala-410 is a rock with a series of incised lines on a sandstone boulder with one cupule. Another cupule rock and a grinding slick boulder are present. The site is found on a ridge in the Hayward Hills. Incised boulders were found near cupule rocks in heavily used areas of Mount Diablo State Park at CCo-382 and CCo-395.

Possibly representational incised or pecked lines occur at Ala-418, Ala-481, CCo-500, CCo-577, CCo-597, and CCo-609. Ala-418 is a sandstone boulder located in proximity to BRM boulders. The "incised" rock is located in a residential district in Hayward, next to a trail in a public easement between two dead-end streets. There are obvious graffiti on the rock. The origin of the incisions is impossible to ascertain.

Ala-481 is located near the headwater of Kaiser Creek above the San Leandro Reservoir. A concentric circle element is carved into sandstone. There is another surface with a rectangular carving. Several other surfaces with abstract lines look like they were caused by brush or cattle. The site contains both historic and prehistoric elements.

CCo-500 has what appear to be the remnants of an abstract rectilinear petroglyph on a sandstone outcrop. Two cupules are present on the panel. The site is on a hill west of Kirker Pass Road. Midden and a lithic scatter were found directly below the hill. CCo-577 is a fish-like pecked design located in Wildcat Canyon on a schist rock. CCo-597 is a representational glyph with circular lines and a sun figure pecked into a sandstone rock on the east side of the Brushy Peak hills. CCo-609 is a sandstone outcrop which has been heavily incised with a variety of rectilinear figures and lines. It is located off Bailey Road in the Keller landfill, south of Pittsburgh.

Regional Context

Abstract lines and grooves at PCN sites occur throughout the geographic range of this style. Incised lines on sandstone cupule rocks are found in the Northcoast Ranges, the Sierra, the Sierra foothills (Payen 1966) and in Southern California (Minor 1975).

Representational and abstract petroglyph panels occur in the North Coast Ranges, the Sierra, Sierra foothills, San Joaquin Valley, and in Southern California.

Ethnographic Connections

The "Pit-and-Groove" style petroglyph was first described by Heizer and Baumhoff in 1962. Hedges (1982:4) believes that grooves are the defining element of the style. The slashes themselves have been associated with weather control (Heizer and Clewlow 1973:29, Heizer 1953:35) and fertility (Barrett 1908:175) among a variety of ethno-linguistic groups in Northern California. In view of the modern context of CCo-125/152, association with this style is probable but must remain uncertain.

Along with the schist rock art sites cupules with incised lines are also found on sandstone. It is possible that these designs are an extension of the schist or talc "pit and groove" tradition to another medium. Payen noted that while Pomo "pit-and-grooves" occurred on soft "steatite-like stone," "those in the Sierra are found on a variety of rock types" (1966:86). Also, "the Sierran examples are placed where they would have been in view of the community at large" (Payen 1966:86). Payen felt that the Pomo ritual analogy could be applied to Maidu and Miwok areas.

If CCo-9 and Ala-410 are indeed pit-and-groove sites they would actually fit the "public" pattern described by Payen. The grooves or lines at Ala-410 occur on the same rock as cupules. CCo-9 is unusual. As noted, the incised/grooved rock is in the vicinity of several mortars and a cupule boulder. However, the grooved rock is separate.

The concentric circle at Ala-481 is an anomaly. As noted in the PCN section, concentric circles are one of the reoccurring schist boulder elements. The Hokan analogies don't seem to apply here. The concentric circle is on sandstone and is quite large (73 x 61 cm). There are no cupules. There is another possible petroglyph in a rectangular form. The site has prehistoric elements, BRMs and a grinding slick. There are historic remains in the vicinity, including a stone foundation, apple trees and stove parts, and a bottle base dated to 1882.

At CCo-577, there is a fish figure located next to one of the largest streams in the area. CCo-577 is in an area containing two large cupule boulders and several small ones. All the petroglyphs in this area are located directly in or near the creek. However, the ethnographic accounts of rock art and fishing magic in Northern California center on cupules, incisions, and pounding.

CCo-500 and CCo-609 occur within the historic boundaries of the Miwok. Carved petroglyphs are found within Miwok territory east of Sacramento and into the foothills and Sierra. Heizer and Clewlow called these the "Central Sierran Petroglyph Style" and felt the motifs were related to Great Basin styles. However, the origin of the "Central Sierran" glyphs is uncertain. They may have even been made by visitors from the Great Basin and not the Miwok (Moratto 1984:314). Payen places Sierra petroglyphs within Miwok territory but found no ethnographic evidence to support identification with the tribe.

There is a tradition of petroglyphs among the Yokuts (Foster, Jenkins, and Betts 1990; Weinberger 1982). It is possible that CCo-500 and 609 could have been made during a tribal influx by the Yokuts. CCo-597 occurs within Yokuts territory and is close to one of the natural accesses to the hills containing CCo-434. The site could be a trail marker leading to a significant gathering place. The sun figure invites classification as a solstice site. A rayed sun figure appears as a pictograph at Sta-33 about 50 miles to the south. The petroglyphs may be Yokuts, but, considering the movement of tribes through the area, no solid connections can be made.

It is unfortunate that the modern overlay of so many of these possible petroglyphs makes a final determination difficult. However, the possibility still exists that there is a petroglyph "tradition" in the East Bay. A defining attribute could be the use of a pecking technique. The historic glyphs at Ala-19, Ala-51, Tilden Park 1 and 2, the carvings at the sites on Mount Diablo, and most of the marks at CCo-609 are incised. The designs at CCo-500, 577, 597 and Ala-481 are all pecked and possibly abraded. Also, CCo-500, 577, and Ala-481 are all close to prehistoric elements. It is hoped that this report will provide background information if other petroglyphs are discovered.

CONCLUSION

Three prehistoric rock art styles are found to be present in Alameda and Contra Costa counties: cupules, PCNs, and pictographs. Some of the abstract and representational petroglyphs may be prehistoric. However, the presence of historic petroglyphs and graffiti makes this determination uncertain, at the present time.

This survey indicates that parallels with regional styles exist. The presence of cupules on both schist and sandstone fit the East Bay into a regional and worldwide continuum. The cupule and PCN rock art forms on chlorite schist boulders in northwest Contra Costa County relate to similar forms found in Marin, Sonoma, Mendocino, and Santa Clara counties.

The presence of cupules and PCNs may indicate a pre-Penutian occupation of the East Bay. This conclusion is based on the identification of cupules with Hokan groups and the fact that cupules are superimposed on PCNs. To prove the Hokan/cupule connection True and Baumhoff suggested "that where Hokan peoples survived ethnographically the pitted boulders should exist both early and late while in areas occupied ethnographically by non-Hokan peoples they should be early but not late" (1981:266).

Unfortunately, the shell mounds in Wildcat Canyon have never been conclusively dated (A. B. Elsasser personal communication 1992). Ala-60, which contains three multiple cupule boulders, is associated with a midden datable (by obsidian hydration) to as early as 5530-4630 BC. The termination date is suggested as AD 1536 by the California State University at Hayward (1982) or AD 1463 by Basin Research Associates (1989). The 3 large cupule rocks at Ala-60 could date to the estimated Hokan presence in the East Bay. However, it is impossible, at this point, to determine if their creation stopped during the "late" occupation.

The ethnographic literature does indicate that cupule making continued into the historic period, not only by Hokan language groups, but also by Penutians, and Uto-Aztecans. I think it is important to note that language groups aside, cupule rituals are found in a variety of environmental settings and adaptations. California tribes living in North Coast rainforests, Northeastern high deserts, Sierra foothills, tule marshes and coastal bayfronts all had cupule rituals. This environmental variation is also found in Alameda and Contra Costa. Cupule rocks are found near and in streams, on high ridges, on valley floors and on the sides of Mount Diablo. It is likely that cupule rituals were more varied and idiosyncratic than the limited ethnographic literature indicates.

The pictographs at the Vasco Caves have links to pictographs in the San Joaquin Valley and southern Salinas Valley. Stylistically, certain of the paintings have links to Yokuts pictographs. Geographically, the area was in or near Yokuts territory. The pictographs are likely to be of the Emergent Period because of the fragility of their natural context; however, as noted, the Vasco Caves were also accessible to the Miwok and Ohlone. The situation at Vasco Caves may not be an either/or proposition.

The abstract and possibly representational petroglyphs may relate to Northcoast, central Sierra or San Joaquin Valley styles, but the sample is too small and/or too altered by modern man to be positively defined.

The rock art of Alameda and Contra Costa presents a variety of form and context. No one set pattern emerges. Instead, we are presented with a multifaceted picture, which, like the rock art forms themselves, appears deceptively simple at first glance, but grows in complexity as we look closer.

REFERENCES CITED

Barrett, Samuel
1908   The Ethnography of the Pomo and Neighboring Indians. University of California Publications in Archaeology and Ethnology 6(1). Berkeley.

1952   Material Aspects of Pomo Culture. Bulletin of the Public Museum of the City of Milwaukee 20:1-508. New York: AMS Press.

Baumhoff, Martin
1980   The Evolution of Pomo Society. Journal of California and Great Basin Anthropology 2(2):175-185.

Beardsley, R. K.
1954   Temporal and Areal Relationships in Central California Archaeology. University of California Archaeological Survey Reports 24. Berkeley.

Bennyhoff, J. A.
1956   Sta-33. Site report on file at the University of California, Berkeley Archaeological Research Facility.

Benson, Arlene and Floyd Buckskin
1988   Achumawi Jumping Rocks and The Concept of the Test. Paper presented at the Annual Meetings of the American Rock Art Research Association. May 1988. Ridgecrest, California.

Berkeley Gazette
1953a   Fabulous Historical Find Here. June 17.

1953b   Indian Rock in "Cerrito." June 24.

Bickel, Polly McWhorter
1976   Toward a Prehistory of the San Francisco Bay Area: The Archaeology of Sites Ala-328, Ala-12, and Ala-13. Ph.D. Thesis. Harvard University, Cambridge.

Davis, J. T.
1961   Trade Routes and Economic Exchange Among the
              Indians of California.   University of California
              Archaeological Survey Reports 54. Berkeley.

Docktor, Desiree
1983   The Significance of Rock Art Setting in the Interpreta-
              tion of Form and Function: Preliminary Investigation of
              Two Yokuts Rock Art Sites in California. American
              Indian Rock Art 9:63-71. American Rock Art Research
              Association, El Toro, CA.

Elsasser, Albert B.
1978   Development of Regional Prehistoric Cultures.   *In*
              Handbook of the North American Indians Vol 8:
              California. Robert F. Heizer, ed., pp. 37-57. William C.
              Sturtevant, gen. ed. Washington, D. C.: Smithsonian
              Institution.

1985   Review of the Prehistory of the Santa Clara Valley
              Region. Basin Research Associates, Hayward, Califor-
              nia.

Elsasser, Albert B. and E. Contreras
1958   Modern Petrography in Central California and Western
              Nevada. University of California Archaeological Survey
              Reports 41:(65):12-18. Berkeley.

Foster, Daniel, Richard C. Jenkins, and John Betts
1990   Rock Art in the Coalinga Backcountry. Rock Art Papers
              7:53-68. San Diego, California: San Diego Museum of
              Man.

Fredrickson, David A.
1974   Cultural Diversity in Early Central California: A View
              from the North Coast Ranges. The Journal of California
              Anthropology 1(1):41-53.

Gary, Mark and Dan Foster
1990   Mendocino County and Rock Art Conservation. Society
              for California Archaeology Newsletter 24(3). Fullerton,
              California.

Gayton, Anna
1948   Yokuts and Western Mono Ethnography. University of
              California Anthropological Records 10:113. Berkeley.

Gerow, Bert with Roland Force
1968   An Analysis of the University Village Complex. With a
              Reappraisal of Central California Archaeology. Stanford,
              California: Stanford University Press.

Goddard, Pliny E.
1904   Hupa Texts. University of California Publications in
              Archaeology and Ethnology 1(2). Berkeley.

Grant, Campbell
1971   Rock Art. *In* The California Indians: A Sourcebook.
              Robert Heizer and M. Whipple, eds.   Berkeley,
              California: University of California Press.

1981   An Introduction to Yokuts Rock Painting. American
              Indian Rock Art 6:21-35. American Rock Art Research
              Association, El Toro, California.

Grieder, Terence
1982   Origins of Pre-Columbian Art. Austin, Texas: University
              of Texas Press.

Hedges, Ken
1982   A Re-examination of Pomo Baby Rocks.   American
              Indian Rock Art 9:10-21. American Rock Art Research
              Association, El Toro, California.

Heizer, Robert
1949   The Archaeology of Central California I: The Early
              Horizon. University of California Archaeological Survey
              Reports 12(1):1-84. Berkeley.

1953   Sacred Rain Rocks of Northern California. University of
              California Archaeological Survey Reports 22:33-38.
              Berkeley.

Heizer, Robert and Martin Baumhoff
1962   Prehistoric Rock Art of Nevada and Eastern California.
              Berkeley, California: University of California Press.

Heizer, Robert and C. William Clewlow
1973   Prehistoric Rock Art of California. Berkeley, California:
              University of California Press.

Heizer, Robert, ed.
1974   The Costanoan Indians. California History Center.
              DeAnza College, Cupertino, California.

Hotz, Virginia and C. William Clewlow
1974   A Northern California Petroglyph Site. The Masterkey
              4:148-152.

Hyder, William D., Georgia Lee, and Mark Oliver
1986   Culture, Style and Chronology: The Rock Art of the
              Carrizo Plain. American Indian Rock Art 11:43-58. El
              Toro: American Rock Art Research Association.

Kroeber, Alfred L.
1925   Handbook of the Indians of California.   Bureau of
              American Ethnology.   Bulletin 78.   Reprinted by
              California Book Company. Berkeley, California.

Latta, F.
1977   Handbook of Yokuts Indians. Santa Cruz, California:
              Bear State Books.

Margolin, Malcolm
1978   The Ohlone Way: Indian Life in the San Francisco-
              Monterey Bay Area. Berkeley, California: Heyday
              Books.

Mark, Robert and Evelyn Newman
1989   Cup and Ring Petroglyphs in Northern California and
              Beyond. Paper delivered at Australian Rock Art
              Conference.

Marymor, Leigh
1984   SBN 12. Bay Area Rock Art News II(2). Bay Area
              Rock Art Research Association.

Merriam, C. H.
1955   Studies of California Indians.   Berkeley, California:
            University of California Press.

Miller, George, et. al.
1982   Final Report of Archaeological Test Excavations of CA-
            Ala-60.   George Miller, ed.   Report prepared for
            CALTRANS by the Institute of Cultural Resources,
            California State University, Hayward. Pp. 133-174.

Miller, Theresa
1977   Identification and Recording of Prehistoric Petroglyphs
            in Marin and Related Bay Area Counties. M. A. Thesis.
            Department of Anthropology.   San Francisco State
            University.

Minor, Rick
1975   The Pit and Groove Petroglyph Style in Southern
            California. Ethnic Technology Notes 15. San Diego,
            California: San Diego Museum of Man.

Moratto, Michael J.
1984   California Archaeology. Orlando: Academic Press.

Nissen, Karen and Eric W. Ritter
1986   Cupped Rock Art in North-Central California: Hypothesis
            Regarding Age and Social/Ecological Context. American
            Indian Rock Art 11:59-75. American Rock Art Research
            Association, El Toro, California.

Okladnikov, A.
1971   Art of the Amur. Ancient Art of the Russian Far East.
            Abrams, New York.

Parkman, E. Breck
1986   Cupule Petroglyphs in the Diablo Range, California.
            Journal of California and Great Basin Anthropology
            8(2):246-259.

1988   Further Notes on Cupule Petroglyphs in the Diablo
            Range, California. Journal of California and Great Basin
            Anthropology 10(1):114-117.

1990   Toward a Proto-Hokan Ideology. Paper presented at the
               Chacmool Conference. University of Calgary, Alberta.

1992   The PCN-Style Petroglyph: An Enigma of the North
               Coast Ranges.   Unpublished manuscript in author's
               possession.

Payen, Louis
1959   The Petroglyphs of Sacramento and Adjoining Counties.
               University of California Archaeological Survey Reports
               48:66-92. Berkeley.

1966   Prehistoric Rock Art in the Northern Sierra Nevada,
               California. M. A. Thesis. Department of Anthropology.
               California State University, Sacramento.

Pilling, A. R.
1950   SBn-12. Site report in author's possession.

Pilling, A. R. and Bob Squire
1949   CCo-152. Site report on file at Northwest Information
               Center. California State University at Sonoma.

Pullen, Reg
1982   35CU142. Site report on file at State Office of Historic
               Preservation. Salem, Oregon.

Ragir, S. R.
1972   The Early Horizon in Central California Prehistory.
               Contributions to the University of California Archaeolog-
               ical Research Facility Number 15.

Shipley, William
1978   Native Languages of California. *In* Handbook of the
               North American Indians, Volume 8: California. Robert
               F. Heizer, ed., pp. 80-90. William C. Sturtevant, gen.
               ed. Washington, D. C.: Smithsonian Institution. Pp. 80-
               90.

Smith, G. A. and Michael K. Lerch
1984   Cupule Petroglyphs in Southern California.   San
               Bernardino Museum Quarterly Vol. 32.

Spier, Leslie
1930   Klamath Ethnography.   University of California
              Publications in Archaeology and Ethnology 30.
              Berkeley.

Taylor, Walter W.
1961   Archaeology and Language in Western North America.
              American Antiquity 27(1):71-81.

True, Donald and Martin Baumhoff
1981   Pitted Rock Petroglyphs in Southern California. Journal
              of California and Great Basin Anthropology Vol. 3.

Wallace, William
1978   Northern Valley Yokuts. *In* Handbook of the North
              American Indians, Volume 8: California.   Robert F.
              Heizer, ed., pp. 462-476. William C. Sturtevant, gen. ed.
              Washington, D. C.: Smithsonian Institution.

Weinberger, Gay
1980   Cupules and Their Context, Some Southern Valley
              Yokuts Examples.   Paper presented at Society for
              California Archaeology Meeting.

1982   Four Forms of Yokuts Rock Art from Tulare County,
              California. American Indian Rock Art Vol. IX.
              American Rock Art Research Association, El Toro,
              California.

CHOCHEÑO AND *RUMSEN* NARRATIVES: A COMPARISON

Beverly R. Ortiz

With Old California Spanish Translations by
Alex O. Ramirez

Chocheño narratives, presented here for the first time, and *Rumsen* narratives, synopsized here, provide a window into the sacred and secular world of the two groups, hitherto a window closed to the outside world. *Chocheño* and *Rumsen* fall within what has been variously designated as the Ohlone or Costanoan language area, which extends from San Francisco and Richmond, California, south to Monterey, San Juan Bautista and environs, and inland toward the San Luis Reservoir.

Some scholars have identified eight distinct dialects within this area (Levy 1978:485-486; Beeler 1961:191-197). Recent mission register research by Randall Milliken (1992, personal communication) suggests a gradual language cline from north to south, with the languages to the extreme north and south being, Milliken speculates, comparable to a cline from modern Dutch to modern English, or modern Italian to modern Portuguese. In the context of this paper, *Chocheño* refers to the language of the Mission San Jose area, and *Rumsen* to the language of the Mission San Carlos Borromeo (Carmel) area.

Ohlone/Costanoan is a modern designation based upon language relationships, rather than political boundaries. About 45–50 politically independent, multi-village tribes spoke Ohlonean languages. In the northerly portions of the language area each tribe had between 150 and 250 members, and in the south 200 to 400. The population totalled between 15,000 and 20,000 people (Randall Milliken 1994, personal communication).

Forty-five to 50 tribes suggests a much more diverse cultural tradition within the Ohlone/Costanoan language area than generally recognized. The extant narrative traditions of *Chocheño* and *Rumsen* speakers illuminate the nature of this diversity.

A comparison of *Chocheño* and *Rumsen* narratives with those of other California Indian language and tribal groups, particularly groups in West-Central California, will show that *Chocheño* and *Rumsen* narrative traditions, far from existing in a cultural vacuum, share certain motifs and traits with neighboring groups. At the same time, it will show that important differences exist on a micro-level which challenge the notion that Ohlonean speakers were a monolithic entity with a uniform cultural identity.

Most Ohlone/Costanoan narratives fall into the folkloristic category of myth, i.e. sacred narratives describing events which occurred in the remote past in an earlier world. Others fit the classification of legends, i.e. sacred or secular narratives describing events which occurred in the recent past. Mythological characters are non-human, while those of legends are human (Bascom 1965:3-20). Because most people generally associate the words "myth" and "legend" with quaint, unbelieveable stories, I use the more general term "narrative" in their place.

SECTION I: THE *CHOCHEÑO* NARRATIVES

Historical Context

Linguist John Peabody Harrington recorded a number of narratives handed down from Indian people of the Mission San Jose area in the 1920s when he worked with speakers of *Chocheño* at Alisal. Alisal, also known as the Pleasanton Rancheria because of its location on the western outskirts of the town of Pleasanton, was home to a multi-ethnic community of native peoples descended from former Mission San Jose residents, including individuals of Plains Miwok, Northern Valley Yokuts, and Ohlone/Costanoan heritage (Ortiz [1991]:32-34; Mills 1985:81; Gifford 1927:220).

While cataloguing field notes at the University of California at Berkeley Linguistics Department in the summer of 1962, linguist Catherine Callaghan noticed a packet containing 512 loose-leaf pages in Harrington's large script. Inauspiciously labelled "CHOCH," these field notes included the narratives highlighted in this report. They also featured the most extensive study of the San Jose dialect of the

Ohlone/Costanoan language ever made, and information about area culture, history, place names, songs, and family relations.

In the 1970s Callaghan made a thermofax copy of the notes. Later in the same decade, the original notes disappeared. Although Callaghan eventually located about 3/5 of the originals at the U.C. Berkeley Emeritus Office, the other 2/5 remain missing (Callaghan 1986, 1987, 1992, 1993, personal communication).[1]

In 1986 Callaghan shared a copy of the thermofax with me. Later, she sent me a copy of her typescript of the section of the notes that featured the narratives. Harrington had recorded these in a mixture of English and Old California Spanish, the speaking style of his cultural consultants. In 1992 I shared the notes and typescript with Alex Ramirez (*Rumsen*), who grew up in the Carmel Valley. On the basis of his first-hand knowledge of Old California Spanish, Alex made a full translation of the narratives.

For ease of comparison, I've assigned each narrative a title that conforms, whenever practical, to catch-word designations suggested by Gayton (1935:582-599), Barrett (1933:454-464), Kroeber (1908:222), and Lowie (1908:24-27). In the one case that Harrington assigned his own title, "The Man and the Wasps," that title has been maintained.

The *Chocheño* Consultants

María de los Angeles Colós and José Guzman told the *Chocheño* narratives to Harrington. As Colós and Guzman's life histories attest, the survival of the *Chocheño* narratives is all the more remarkable because neither person was from a *Chocheño*-speaking tribe by birth.

María de los Angeles Colós, Harrington's principal *Chocheño* consultant, was the daughter of Joaquina Pico, *Tamaleño*, who lived in the San Lorenzo area, and Gregorio Colós, a Koriak/Russian. The Koriak are the native people of northeastern Siberia. *Tamaleño*, as Colós used it, very likely referred to one of a number of tribes, probably Coast Miwok, and possibly Southern Pomo, who resided at Mission San Rafael (Randall Milliken 1993, personal communication; Harrington [n.d.]:24, 99, 131). Joaquina had been raised by the Picos, a Mexican family living in San Jose.

Born at the ranch of Don Agustín Bernal, María Colós' first language was Spanish, and her parents never spoke to her in "Indian." She told Harrington she learned to speak *Chocheño* from her step-father Santiago Piña and her "grandparents."

---

[1]The Smithsonian Institution has a hand-written copy by either Marta Herrera, Ascencion Solorsano's granddaughter, or Henry Cervantes, Solorsano's grandson, of about 1/3 of the notes (Callaghan 1987, personal communication; Mills 1985:88-89).

Santiago Piña was born on July 11, 1819 and raised by the Piña family. The grandparents from whom Colós learned *Chocheño* were most likely Santiago's parents, Bruno and Fermina. Mission San Jose baptismal records identify Bruno's tribal heritage as "Este," *Taunan* from the Alameda Creek and Del Valle Creek area, and Fermina's as *Luecha* (Corral Hollow near Livermore). Bruno was born in 1796 and Fermina in 1801 (Randall Milliken 1993, personal communication; Harrington [n.d.]:48, 131, 241; Kroeber [1904-1909]:79; Merriam [1905]; Merriam [1904]).

María Colós, whom Harrington called Angela, was a young girl of five or six years of age when the "Yankees came." She witnessed the tragedy of the once widespread practice of kidnapping and enslaving Indian children, describing one such incident to Harrington.

> Angela tells a long story in detail of how she saw a wagon filled with Indian children coming from Martinez. Doña ----- was on the seat. They were bringing them como [like] animals to be brought up by Span. [Spanish] Californians. After they got out of the wagon inf. [consultant] was watching and listening carefully (gest. [gesture] of hanging head and grinning) to overhear what they would say. They mentioned water as mem, they wanted some water to drink. They were naked (Harrington [n.d.]:223).

On the basis of what we know of Colós' mother Joaquina Pico's life (see above), it seems likely she was a victim of childhood kidnapping.

Life wasn't easy for María de los Angeles Colós and her family. Her younger brother Prudencio, who "worked hard and had learned good English," died of a hemorrhage at age 14 while he and Colós labored at the Moraga Rancho. His "patrones gringos" sent a coffin and money for food. Colós' younger half sister, María Antonia Piña, grew up at the San Rafael ranch of Doña Maria Jesus Briones, and died there (Harrington [n.d.]:47-48).

Colós spent most of her childhood helping her mother earn a living by sewing. Economic necessity precluded the opportunity "to make dolls or sew dolls' clothes like other girls were making" or to "play with other girls or to laugh with them" (Harrington [n.d.]:215).

José Guzman, the other person who shared information about *Chocheño* language and culture with Harrington, was born about 1853 in Dublin, California (Harrington [n.d.]:19). José Guzman's father and paternal grandparents were from various tribes of Northern Valley Yokuts speaking peoples. His *Tamcan* (Byron area) father, Habencio Guzman, was born in 1813 and baptized at Mission San Jose in 1817. Habencio's father Habencio (also *Tamcan*) and mother Habencia (*Passasimi* of the Stockton area), were born about 1773 and 1780 respectively (Randall Milliken 1992, personal communication; Harrington [n.d.]:95), shortly before and after the establishment of Mission Dolores in San Francisco in 1776, and long before Mission San Jose was established in Fremont in 1797.

Guzman's father married a woman named Petra on October 4, 1833 (Mission San Jose marriage #2007). Mission San Jose baptismal records show two Petras, one a *Lacquisumne* from the Ripon area, the other a *Julpun* woman from the northernmost tribe along the Old River of the San Joaquin River. Guzman's mother was most likely the *Julpun* Petra, who was born in the same baptismal group as Habencio. If so, she was a Bay Miwok speaker (Randall Milliken 1992-1994, personal communication). Guzman's mother died when he was too young to remember her (Harrington [n.d.]:19).

Like Colós' family, Guzman's family lived and worked at various ranches. For many years, Guzman lived with his father at Rancho San Antonio above Oakland, California. Some- time in the 1870s or 1880s he married Francisca, with whom he had 8 children by 1900 (Randall Milliken 1992, personal com- munication; Harring- ton [n.d.]:19).

The length of Colós' and Guz- man's residence at Alisal, where Harrington visited them in 1921, 1929, and 1930, remains unknown. Harring- ton wrote that Guz-

Fig. 4.1. José Guzman

man "is one of the oldest timers here. Has lived whole life around here."
Colós and Guzman were interviewed at Alisal by several
individuals. C. Hart Merriam worked with Colós for a short time in 1904
and 1905. Sometime between 1903 and 1906 C. E. Kelsey also worked
briefly with Colós, as did Alfred Kroeber in 1904 and 1909, and Edward
Winslow Gifford in about 1920. Kroeber visited with Guzman in 1909,
and C. Hart Merriam visited him in 1910 (Heizer and Nissen 1973:18,
34, 35; Merriam 1967:368; Merriam [1905], [1904]; Kroeber [1904-
1909]:28, 29, 30, 36, 37, 65, 79, 80).

Difficulties and Opportunities

An examination of the *Chocheño* narratives recorded by
Harrington shows them to be suffused with opportunities, challenges, and
difficulties. As in a puzzle leisurely taking form, details are linked in
disjointed fragments for a number of probable reasons: (1) the narratives
were told to an audience of one; (2) the lack of convenient, high-quality
recording equipment made it necessary for Harrington to write the
narratives in long hand while they were being told; (3) Harrington's
unfamiliarity with the narratives necessitated breaks at certain points for
clarification and questions; and (4) Colós and Guzman probably weren't
practiced in the telling.

Despite Harrington's fastidious recording style, he could not write
as quickly as Colós and Guzman spoke. To keep up, he shortened certain
phrases and sometimes used abbreviations. Occasionally, whole sections
of narratives were represented by a single sentence. Harrington either
neglected to follow these up, or his findings are missing from his field
notes.

Despite these difficulties, the narratives retain their integrity, with
the speaking style of the tellers faithfully replicated. The transcription
skips from Old California Spanish to English, often in the same sentence,
just as, one imagines, Harrington's consultants related the story to him.
As a linguist, Harrington undoubtedly found Old California Spanish as
fascinating as *Chocheño*.

It adds to the meaning of the narratives that they contain
gratifying reminders that Colós and Guzman were as much people of
their own time as scholars of their people's past. Instead of presenting
narratives frozen in some elusive or reconstructed past, they merge the
changes wrought by history into a narrative that features European
honeybees working alongside domestic wasps. Another narrative makes
reference to World War I animosities between Germany and France.
Others highlight concepts of the Devil.

Ethnographic details lend cultural significance to acts that might
otherwise seem unfamiliar or incomprehensible. For example, Guzman

and Colós describe an old-time *Chocheño* women's mourning practice of striking themselves with pestles, equating this with Coyote's journey through a rock face while in mourning for his deceased grandson *Kaknú*.

Harrington occasionally reveals Colós' and Guzman's emotional responses to plotlines. Other significances come from without. As Alex Ramirez stated upon completing his translations, "Little memories that were lost forever were brought back" (1992, personal communication).

Unfortunately, Harrington did not usually state whether it was Colós or Guzman who told him particular narratives. Nor did he apparently ever ask from whom Colós and Guzman learned the narratives they told. As Colós' life history indicates, she probably learned many, if not all of her narratives, from her step-father and step-grandparents. Guzman's life history, however, provides no answers to the question. We know only that his "grandfather" told him about a place featured in one narrative and his father took him to a place featured in another. The combined lack of attribution as to teller and teller's teacher makes it impossible to pinpoint specific tribal origins.

Harrington's lack of specific attribution, the disjointed renderings, and the missed detail point to the caution with which one must approach these narratives. At the same time, these are the only *Chocheño* narratives known to exist. This rarity magnifies their importance.

Content Summary with Background Information

Once part of a much more elaborate tradition, the *Chocheño* narratives focus on the grand and heroic acts of *Kaknú*, a supernatural being with human and animal attributes. Variously referred to as First People or Early People, such supernatural beings were said to exist prior to the creation of people. Sometimes fallible, but generally sympathetic and awe-inspiring, the Early People exhibited both the most elevated and the most degraded aspects of human nature.

In this subsection I will provide texts of the *Chocheño* narratives. I will also elucidate the broader context of particular narratives by elaborating characters, events, and places alluded to, but not explicitly identified in the narratives. The texts, based upon Alex Ramirez's translations, largely consist of verbatim transcriptions of the translated originals. Some alterations have been made for purposes of readability.[2]

---

[2]The narratives, as originally recorded by Harrington, their translations, and the reasons for certain translation decisions, will be published elsewhere.

1. *Kaknú* as culture hero—identification of *Kaknú*.

The small spotted Peregrin Falcon that kills ducks and big things—big birds—is called *Kaknú*. He is much mentioned, that falcon. Not everybody can shoot him.

In Spanish *Kaknú* is called "*gabilan patero*." He never misses a duck. He goes about choosing the fattest, never taking a thin one. *Kaknú* kills them and leaves them dead. He leaves them laying for the turkey vulture, for the poor scavenger bird does not kill. This falcon eats fat things. He discards skinny things.

Kaknú has a spotted breast. José has heard that there are two kinds, one that has a lighter breast and one that has a darker breast. One is of the south and one of the north. The darker one must be of the south, José says. Angela speaks up and says the fiercer must be of the south, for they say that the southerners are brave.

In this set of narrative fragments Harrington attempted, but apparently failed, to identify unequivocably the animal with which the supernatural being *Kaknú* shared characteristics.

Harrington was not alone in seeking to resolve the question of *Kaknú*'s identity. According to Milliken (1987:64), the root for "*kakon*" seems to be associated with predatory bird species. Milliken goes on to note:

> Henshaw (1955) recorded *ka-kun* for "south" from the Carmeleño informant at Soledad, and got an identical translation from an Ohlonean speaker at Mission Santa Clara. He also recorded *Kak-u-nu'-y* for 'sparrow hawk' [American kestrel] at Santa Clara and *Ka-k'nu* for the "red-tailed hawk" at Santa Cruz.

José Guzman described *Kaknú* as a duck eater to Harrington. This fact aligns *Kaknú* with the peregrine falcon, a raptor that eats only birds and, at one time, was widely called "duck hawk." The red-tailed hawk, in contrast, eats mammals, while the American kestrel eats insects, small birds, and rhodents, and the prairie falcon eats birds and mammals (Ira Bletz 1993, personal communication).

In another fragment Guzman cast some doubt on this behaviorally-based identification of *Kaknú*, when he identified *Kaknú* as bird 355, the prairie falcon, in Frank M. Chapman's *Color Key to North American Birds with Biographical Appendix* (1903 or 1912 edition).

Guzman wasn't certain of this, however, because he also stated that *Kaknú*'s tail was similar to that of the Mexican goshawk in Chapman's book. Since the Chapman book contains line drawings that are neither well delineated nor properly colored, *Kaknú* could easily have been misidentified. Guzman's behavioral description is presumed the most reliable.

A comparison of the *Kaknú* narrative cycle with that of other West-Central California Indian groups (see "Comparative Narratives," Section III below) bolsters the peregrine falcon attribution. This comparison shows that *Kaknú* functions as the southern equivalent of *Wekwek*, a culture hero to the north identified as peregrin falcon.

Mission register research by Randall Milliken (personal communication, 1994) reveals something of the extent of *Kaknú*'s distribution. *Kaknú*, written as "*cacnu*," appears in the names of seven individuals, three women and four men, at Mission San Jose, as well as 14 individuals, ten women and four men, at Mission San Francisco de Asís. Of the 21 personal names which use *cacnu*, all belong to members of Bay Miwok and Ohlonean-speaking tribes from the Diablo and Livermore valleys and south to the Fremont Plain (see Table 4.1).

Members of the more northerly Bay Miwok tribes—the *Saclan*, *Chupcan*, and possibly the *Jalquin*—have both *wekwek* and *cacnu* in their personal names. This dual use provides a transition area between those tribes who exclusively used *wekwek* and those who exclusively used *cacnu*.

Kaknú's use disappears in the personal names of those individuals baptized at Mission San Carlos Borromeo, Mission Santa Cruz, and Mission San Juan Bautista. The similar "*cacun*," however, occurs in the names of four persons baptized at Mission Santa Clara (see Table 4.1). Two such names belong to individuals from the Fremont area, one from the San Antonio Valley, and only one outside that area. According to Kroeber's *Rumsen* field notes, "*kakun*" means "chicken hawk," an early-day name for the red-tailed hawk. Kroeber likewise recorded "*kakun*" as the name of a rancheria in his notes (Kroeber [1902]:72).

2. Making the world safe—the killing of Body of Stone and the creation of stone monoliths.

After *Kaknú* killed his wife (see Narrative 5, below) he was alone. Finally, when *Kaknú* didn't want to fight anymore with anyone, he turned into the form of the dove, and he entered into the earth. *Kaknú* went down to the lowest owner in the earth, Body of Stone, called *Wiwe*[h]. Body of Stone was a man with a stone body. The consultant doesn't know

TABLE 4.1. WOMEN'S NAMES WITH "CACNU"

NAME	SEX	TRIBE	LANGUAGE	MISSION	BAP-TISM NO.
Cacnu	F	Tuibun	Ohlonean	San Jose	1044
Cacnum	F	Tuibun	Ohlonean	San Jose	631
Cacnucse	M	Tuibun	Ohlonean	San Jose	438
Cacnute	F	Ssaoam	Ohlonean	San Jose	1315
Cacnuse	M	Patlam (village)	Ohlonean	San Jose	767
Cacnuse	F	Huchiun	Ohlonean	San Fran.	1610
Cacnumtole	M	Yrgin	Ohlonean B. Miwok	San Jose	857
Cacnute	F	Jalquin	B. Miwok	San Fran.	2383
Cacnu	F	Jalquin	B. Miwok	San Fran.	2308
Cacnumaye	F	Jalquin/ Tatcan	B. Miwok	San Fran.	2361
Cacnutole	M	Tatcan	B. Miwok	San Jose	1601
Cacnumayé	F	Tatcan	B. Miwok	San Fran.	3016
Cacnumai	F	Saclan	B. Miwok	San Fran.	1735
Cacnumaie	F	Saclan	B. Miwok	San Fran.	1539
Cacnumaie	F	Saclan	B. Miwok	San Fran.	1574
Cacnute	F	Saclan	B. Miwok	San Fran.	1570
Cacnucche	M	Saclan	B. Miwok	San Fran.	1553
Cacnumtolé	M	Saclan	B. Miwok	San Fran.	1556
Cacnuncia	M	Saclan	B. Miwok	San Fran.	1531
Cacnú	M	Volvon	B. Miwok	San Fran.	3149
Cacnu	F	Volvon	B. Miwok	San Fran.	3361
Cacumute	F	S. Antonio (district)	Ohlonean	Santa Clara	1615
Cacurum	F	Santa Agueda (dtr.)	Ohlonean	Santa Clara	1758
Cacunusi	M	Santa Agueda (dtr.)	Ohlonean	Santa Clara	2793
Cacunucse	M	S. Bernardino (dt.)	Ohlonean	Santa Clara	2296

where *Wiwe*[(h)] lived. The people who reached there never returned. Body of Stone killed all the people that reached his home.

The Body of Stone, the lord of the earth under the earth, had two black servants that lived with him, and when he killed a person, he gave the blood to these two to drink. The servants drank the blood. The servants were black because of the blood that they ate. They only ate blood. They were not Body of Stone's sons. They were only slaves—servants—that Body of Stone had for the purpose of commanding.

Only bones were there from the people Body of Stone had eaten. This is why *Kaknú* said he would see if they would eat his body too. *Kaknú* said he would see how he fared there. "They'll not eat me." He had lots of people down there.

When *Kaknú* wanted to submerge anywhere, he would just double up his wings (consultant makes a gesture of shrugging shoulders), and he could enter anywhere out of sight. He made the ground burst open and cave-in. *Kaknú*, always keeping his bow, dived down.

When *Kaknú* entered the smokehole, the people were all standing like wooden stakes looking on. (It was other people who arrived whom he ate.) *Wiwe*[(h)] told them to add fuel so *Kaknú* would get burnt, but instead they pulled the fire down. The people were under *Wiwe*[(h)], but were friends of *Kaknú* really.

Kaknú dove into the sweathouse through the window in the middle of the roof (the smoke hole), when he received the two arrows, but not a wing was injured. The *Kaknú* was agile with the bow—a good fighter. This falcon fought with Body of Stone. The life that *Wiwe*[(h)] had was in his esophagus and in his navel. With each shot that hit home, he made a groaning sound. He was woundable only in his neck above the breastbone and in his navel. The *Kaknú* shot once at each of these places and killed him. There were five arrows, and the fifth pierced *Wiwe*[(h)]'s throat.

The consultant says there are songs about killing *Wiwe*[(h)], but forgets them. It is a long song—with a part about every arrow. Every arrow shot has a song. *Kaknú* mentions *Wiwe*[(h)], and *Wiwe*[(h)] mentions *Kaknú* in the song. As *Kaknú* shoots at *Wiwe*[(h)], *Wiwe*[(h)] sings, "The *Kaknú* will kill me." Then *Kaknú* sings, "The *Wiwe*[(h)] is going to kill me." Each has a song mentioning the name of the other. And then, seizing all the rest of the arrows in the quiver, *Kaknú* plunged them with his hand into *Wiwe*$^{(h)}$'s navel.

Wiwe$^{(h)}$ lost the rancheria, thus losing his life. He died, and he stayed there bursting—all the mountains, etc., flew asunder. The large stone land features of all the earth are the stones that went from his body when killed. Now the whites call them *peñascos*. They were bursting and whirling in all directions.

Then after killing Body of Stone, he took the two black servants by the legs and swung their brains against the post of the temescal. The temescal, Body of Stone, and the two servants burnt up together, and *Kaknú* left. There were many other people there too, but *Kaknú* did not bother them. He only killed the three. Body of Stone had been a feared man. Who would kill him? He had a stone body. The people, kneeling, asked *Kaknú* what he wanted them to do, and they said for him to stay there. He did not kill the other people there. He told them to live well.

Kaknú was a tall, lean man. *Wiwe*$^{(h)}$ was a short, stout man. *Kaknú* is "the famous one" in all the world.

Just as blood blackens when it jells, in this narrative so too do the servants. Jelled blood was no doubt a familiar sight to Colós and Guzman. Alex Ramirez (personal communication, 1993) remembers a man in the Carmel Valley who drank the warm blood of slaughtered cows. After piercing a cow's jugular vein, he caught its blood in a cup. The man saved some of the blood for Alex's mother, who let it sit until it jelled, then fried it, adding watercress and beans. The family ate this dish in tortillas.

A Wappo narrative features this same foodway:

> The deer were skinned and then both his [Coyote's] daughters-in-law and the young man prepared the fire . . . . Coyote cooked the blood and the old man took it out (himself) and ate it; old man coyote himself ate it (Radin 1924:111).

3. Making the world safe - The killing of Owner of the Salt.

The last time *Kaknú* fought was when he fought with the salt owner, who did not want to give salt to other people. The name of the salt owner was *Hí·wiš*. Owner of the Salt lived in another place.

Owner of the Salt was mostly a hunter—a camper. He went in the sea and all over, wherever he wanted to. Owner of Salt has a moist body. Like salt, his body is moist all the time.

Kaknú arrived where the salt owner was. He told him he came to see him—to see how things were going with him. The owner answered that nobody arrived there. "Well, I came here to see," *Kaknú* replied. They did not talk much. They just challenged each other for the fight and *Kaknú* killed him. After *Kaknú* won over Owner of the Salt, the *Kaknú* was Owner of the Salt. For all this they said that *Kaknú* was king.

After he killed Owner of the Salt, he went under the ground. They say that here (consultant gestures down in ground) people don't have eyes. Don Antonio Suñol used to say that below us are people without sight, and above us seven heavens. *Kaknú* only went down to see. He was thinking to fight, but did not, and went to see his grandfather. When the time came, *Kaknú* always went home at night to where his grandmother was.

4. World fire. A single, unexpanded statement in a narrative fragment reads: "Threat of second destruction by fire" (Harrington [n.d.]:147). This statement reminded Alex Ramirez (1993, personal communication) of a common belief related to him as a child—that a flood destroyed the world the first time, and a fire would destroy it the second time. Every New Year's Eve, Alex's mother predicted the world's end. When the expected end didn't come, everybody celebrated.

5. Wife killed for jealousy. Two *Chocheño* narratives concern the consequences of a wife's unfaithfulness.

KAKNÚ AND HIS WIFE

At last *Kaknú* married. He scolded her, and she said that she did not like it that he treated her so strongly. He angrily told her that she would be turned into water, and she turned into water. Her body was water, and onto this day she is water.

Kaknú killed his wife out of jealousy. When he went away his wife dealt with another man. The other man was perhaps *Kaknú*'s friend and *Kaknú* saw what was going on. *Kaknú* had gone on business to a distance, and he perceived like a psychic, and he said, "The vision is here with me." He had help from Coyote also.

WIFE KILLED FOR JEALOUSY

There was a man. He was the husband of the woman. The husband was away. The husband was watching that the woman was dealing with the other man, and he put a curse that the paint of the friend would stay—that the body paint of the other man would stay on the woman. The husband arrived, and the woman began to shrug to cover the paint that had come from the other man. She began to squirm. The man told her happily, "Go bring me water. I am thirsty," but he really was beating his breast with anger. He really knew what was the matter. She went to get water from the river, and she brushed away water to get clear water in her jug, but when she returned and offered it to the man, it was riled. He told her, "Throw it out." "Bring me clean water," he said provokingly to look for a fight. He told her again. She went again, but now she went with fear, for she already knew of the paint on her breast. She went and got clean water and brought it, and brushed it before she gave him the water, but as she handed it to him, there was a frog in it. Then he got angry.

And then he told her, "Go get clean water. I am dry." She went. The man followed her. "Let's see how you get water. Let's see. Let's see!" As the woman was brushing with her hand, he pushed her into the water. "Go be a beaver!" And the beaver left. And the man—well, the man went back.

(Consultant thinks that the other man was a single man and he was stealing the other man's wife. This is a fragment of a long story, but consultant cannot recall the rest.)

6. Establishment of material well being—*Kaknú* provides people with food. A curious, unelaborated statement follows the "*Kaknú* and His Wife" narrative: "'This is for the people, who are today, to eat,' he [*Kaknú*] said, as he threw it from his nose. And hence chia patches, and Indians go hunting it."

Plant use information recorded by Harrington from Ohlonean speakers from the Mission Carmel (*Rumsen*) and Mission San Juan Bautista (*Mutsun*) areas, indicates that chia "seeds were a primary food, served in pinole" (Bocek 1984:253).

7. Origin of death—dead mother nourishes child—attempt to revive a dead relative.

The older child carried the younger on his back. The younger was crying, since their mother was dead and buried. The older broke a branch called *siská* and gave it the younger to suck. Each day, the father saw the young one getting fat and wondered, "Where can he be going to?" *Kaknú* said, "I'm going to spy on these to see where they go."

The other day they went. *Kaknú* followed behind them straight to the grave. The older brother carried his little brother to where their mother was buried, and *Kaknú* saw the mother come up and give the little brother a breast to suck. He saw his young son sitting on the grave. *Kaknú* grabbed his wife and held her. As she came out *Kaknú* dived and grabbed her.

"I will not go," she said. *Kaknú* said, "Yes, you have to go. What would your people say to me? You have people there in the rancheria." She said, "No, leave them. You will be better off there." "But you don't do many things here," he said. "I am dead, buried. How can I go? You have killed me. How can I go to your house again?" she pleaded.

At last, the woman yielded. She went in. She thought of mercy for the two children. For that reason she went.

Kaknú ordered his people to bring firewood to sweat in the sweathouse, and *Kaknú* and his wife with them. *Kaknú*'s wife and *Kaknú* went together and entered the temescal for the wife to remove her smell, and *Kaknú* commanded his people to bring wood to sweat.

People were glad for the return of the lady boss. But there was one gossiper, like a madman. They all went to sweat and that gossiper came last after all. The wife of *Kaknú* was already inside—the dead one. All were happy, when *Caliandra* (Meadowlark) arrived, standing there right at the door of the sweathouse. That lark is called *čí·rikmin* in Indian.

"Whew! What smells so bad here," Meadowlark said. Meadowlark sat at the side of the sweathouse door and said, "Whew! How it stinks here. A stink appears here." It was the odor of the dead woman. Well the woman became angry. The woman left right away. Coyote's wife left like she was flying. She went and threw herself in the river. I don't know what she turned into there.

And Gentleman *Kaknú* rushed out and killed the Meadowlark with kicks only. He tore her neck. *Kaknú* tore up

Meadowlark's neck with kicks. Coyote came out. He was a doctor, and he put tar on the wound on her neck to heal it, and it became her well. If Coyote had not come to the rescue, *Kaknú* would have killed Meadowlark entirely.

And she would probably be there yet, but Meadowlark arrived and did *Kaknú* a bad turn. Well, Meadowlark did not know who it was, but he reached the door and the stench of the dead woman reached him.

Although Harrington didn't explicitly identify Caliandra, the description of the application of tar to this being's neck accords with the black "v" on the neck of meadowlarks. The meadowlark's distinctive, trilling song makes this bird an ideal representation of a gossiper. Analysis of comparative texts (see Section III below) confirms that *Caliandra* and Meadowlark are one and the same. According to C. Hart Merriam,

All the Mewan [Miwok] tribes, and many belonging to widely different stocks—including even the Washoo [sic] of Lake Tahoe and adjacent valleys east of the Sierra—class the Meadowlark among the bad birds. They say he talks too much and is a gossip and they do not like him" (Merriam [1910]:2-13).

Harrington also didn't identify *siská*, a branch that *Kaknú*'s older son gave the younger one to suck in this narrative. A cognate *Wipa* or *Guaypem*[3] (Plains Miwok) narrative suggests that this branch may be milkweed:

On the fourth day Wek'-wek asked his little boy where he went every day with the little one. The boy, afraid to tell the truth, said he took the child to give it milk of the milkweed plant (Merriam [1910]:131).

The Old California Spanish name for milkweed is "immortal" (Bocek 1984:252).

---

[3]This revision of Merriam's "*Wipa*" is based on the research of Randall Milliken (1994, personal communication). Merriam's *Guaypem* consultant was probably "Paula," who lived at Alisal.

8. The origin of death by wise foresight—originator of death the first sufferer.

PAINT FOR DANCERS

On his way home, after killing Owner of the Salt, *Kaknú* saw Rattlesnake Woman gathering seed. Old Man Coyote was wise. When he saw *Kaknú* travelling, the reason he said, "Where can he be going?" was Coyote already had the idea that his grandson was going to meet misfortune.

When *Kaknú* saw Doña Rattlesnake, he carressed her. She said for him not to touch her. Then *Kaknú* asked her, "How do you kill? A woman cannot do that." He looked into her face like she was only a woman. He acted as if she was of no importance.

"How do you kill?" he asked again while looking into her face. He took her arm. "Don't do that to me," she told *Kaknú*. Doña Rattlesnake was pounding her breast in disgust. "Why do you touch me? Don't belittle and shame me. Don't mock me. Where will I go now? Where will I go?" She wanted to go anywhere. "Don't make me a subject of abuse." And bang! She bit him, and he died.

The grandfather, Coyote, had said for him to abuse Lady Rattlesnake so there would be paint for the dancers. When they cremated *Kaknú*'s body, the earth turned red. The red paint is below Tracy, at a place where there is a hot spring, resort, and lake.

José says that it was his grandfather that told him about the place that *Kaknú* was burnt when they were in that vicinity, but they did not visit the paint deposits. The Indians used to dig the paint out with a bar, but José doesn't know whether the place is a cliff or what. The place is probably obscured now.

THE ORIGIN OF DEATH

The Coyote was *weteš*, the one who commanded. He was our God, and God of all the world. He was the grandfather of *Kaknú*. They were like companions. The old man advised *Kaknú* when *Kaknú* wanted to do a bold act. He said, "No," because he knew more. *Kaknú*'s grandfather used to say, "No, no." Right away he took away from *Kaknú* that which was bad. He advised him well.

The Grandfather himself said, "Do not go to the house. These people that we are creating will have to die for four days. Then they will revive and live again."

Coyote said, "No. No. That will not do, for there will be lots of people and not enough to eat. They will have to go to where the dead go in the north."

Coyote did not want people to revive after death, so *Kaknú* had to take the road to the land of the dead. *Kaknú* might have achieved more with time if he had not died thus. The people followed his example. Not too long after *Kaknú* died, the people began to die and go to that place.

MOURNING

They say that when Coyote was in mourning for his son, he passed through a rock, and he left holes in the rock where he passed through eastward. José's father showed him the place. Beyond that hill now there are some finely built natural stone houses—but these houses are made of rock only— (God made them, Angela adds in explaining). "Here is where Coyote came out when he was crying," they told José when at the place, but they did not say who it was he was mourning for. José and his father slept there in the caves on the other side— same as a house. Coyote made a funeral on the other side of the stone houses, José thinks, but does not know just where. The footprint is still a little further on by a cattle trail. José and his father were there to get Spanish bush, *matorál*, for making soap.

The mountain where the footprint is located is over by Altamont. To one in Livermore, Mount Diablo is much to the left of this small mountain. This mountain is full of oak trees. The great natural rock formations like a house are on the other side of it.

These narratives concern themselves with an explanation of death and red paint. A never identified supernatural being called "Grandfather" opposed permanent death, while *Kaknú*'s grandfather Coyote favored it. The former designation "Grandfather" indicates respect.

These narratives also explain certain geographic features: a "footprint" at Brushy Peak; red mineral paint at Byron Hot Springs; and a windowed outcrop at the Caves of Vasco northeast of Livermore.[4] The latter was said to be created when Coyote was mourning for his "son," or alternately, another unidentified being. Since Coyote's grandson *Kaknú* had just been killed, the use of the word "son" is presumed to be in error.

Descriptive passages make clear the locations, never explicitly named, of the footprint, mineral paint, and windowed outcrop. The location of the footprint is confirmed by a sensationalistic article in the September 14, 1928, *Livermore Herald*.

> The area [Brushy Peak and the Caves of Vasco] played an important part in the Indian legends long before the Spanish explorers set foot on these shores. They were supposed to be the dwelling of a mighty giant feared by all Indians of California. On the top of one of these domes can be seen what appears to be the footprint of a giant that measures nearly eight feet long. Another print of the same size but as if made by the opposite foot is found in a stone near Mt. Diablo. The Indians claim that the distance between them represented one stride of the giant (Anonymous 1928:3).

Circa 1925 Harrington wrote a letter to Pleasanton resident Earnest Schween that validates the identification of Brushy Peak and the Caves of Vasco, the locally reputed, one-time hiding place of hero/bandit Joaquin Murietta (Anonymous 1928:3).

> We will make another attempt to take Joe [Guzman] to Brushy Peak where we can explore the location of footprint number three and the caves of Joaquin Murrietta (Calhoun 1973:30-31).

Livermore resident Merilyn Calhoun was shown Harrington's letter by Schween's sister or cousin, now deceased. Calhoun doesn't know if the letter still exists, but Freddie Arnaudon, whose father once owned property near the Alisal, told Calhoun's husband years ago that Guzman showed him a site on a small hill where Coyote left a footprint. The site, where grass never grew, was destroyed when Highway 680 was built (Merilyn Calhoun 1993, personal communication).

---

[4]This outcrop is associated with a more distant winter solstice observatory (Ortiz [1991]).

9. Origin of death—journey to the land of the dead.

LAND OF THE DEAD

Only one road leads to the land of the dead. There is a man who receives the dead there, at the other side, and shows them where they are to go.

There is like a white foam of the sea and there are two pieces of burning and smoking wood and two hollowed stones where they take water to drink before they plunge into the foam. The burning wood and rocks are near together. One rock has water and the other has *panocha*. The two pieces of burning and smoking wood are to warn them—the children and the adults. And all have to eat, but it never finishes.

Panocha referred to "brown sugar" in Alex Ramirez's youth (1992, personal communication). Here it undoubtedly refers to a native food which is discussed as part of a December 11, 1859 report in the *San Francisco Herald*:

Mr. Daniel Hill has presented us with several memorials of the past, which are, says the *Santa Barbara Gazette*, hastily thrown into the following notes. . . .

Padre Antonio Ripoli, who had charge of the Mission of Santa Barbara between 1816 and 1827, gave our old friend, before he left for Boston in 1828, much information about the customs of the Indians of these parts. It seems they had hereabouts the original California Mint. The Indians of the Tulare country generally came over once a year, in bands of from twenty to thirty, male and female, on foot, and armed with bows and arrows. They brought over *panoche* [sic], or thick sugar, made from what is now called honey dew and the sweet carisa cane, and put up into small oblong sacks made of grass and swamp flags [iris]. . . (Anonymous 1859:1).

Chumash elder Fernando Librado[5] had this to say about *panocha*:

---

[5]Librado, who lived ca. 1805-1915, became Harrington's principal consultant on the language of the San Buenaventura Mission area. He lived in and around Ventura, Las Cruces, Santa Ynez, and Santa Barbara (Librado 1981:3).

The priests also gave out a half a ball of panocha, a thick brown sugar, to some Indian that he wanted to give it to. There was no coffee, but some tea. There was also a dish called champurrado, which was atole, chocolate, and panocha mixed together. The priests were economical, according to their tastes. The panocha was brought over here by the Tulareños [Yokuts]. They made it from what is now called honey-dew and a sweet cane, putting it up in small oblong sacks made from grass and wild iris. Sometimes they carried these products in a carrying-net suspended over the forehead, but some Tulareños also had horses (Librado 1980:4).

Harrington (1942:9) noted that Ohlonean speakers gathered honeydew.

10.   Etiological narrative—why certain birds eat certain things. Told by José Guzman.

Kaknú said to his older son: "Go and bring me a duck." He brought a lizard. "No. That is not it. I want a duck." He named the best kind of duck. He was disgusted. "You will have to eat the kind you brought first." Thus he made this species eat lizards.
Then to the other: "Bring me small birds, etc." That is why that species eats small birds. That species dives for them now in the thickets.

11.   Etiological narratives—why certain birds have certain markings. Told by José Guzman.

They killed an elk and cut up the meat. I don't know who killed the deer, but they dressed it by taking out all the meat. They dressed the meat. Others put it on their shoulders. They must have been red-winged blackbirds. Red-winged Blackbird put the meat on his little wings, for those were his arms. And others put it on their heads. They couldn't do more. Those were woodpeckers. They got their heads all bloody, and so, the head stayed bloody. That is why these birds have red there now.
Woodpeckers and blackbirds are of one party, and the hawk tribe another party. They were like the French and Germans. The blackbirds were on one side, and the hawks were on the other side. It was a dispute, that was. I don't

know why that was, but they didn't like each other. The animals didn't like each other.

They had a war together. This is why the hawks strike the blackbirds now.

12. Insects take revenge: The Man and the Wasps.

This is the good version, taken down from José Guzman's dictation.

He was feeding his two children (José doesn't know whether the children are male or female). He was feeding his family by getting honey and larvae thus. He would reach the home of the honeybees and stamped two or three times, and then the honeybees started to sing inside, and he was glad. He would say, "What a lot of people there were. There are many here. That is good." And he killed the old ones with smoke and took the honey and larvae. And he killed the wasps with his paw one by one as they came out, until all were killed.

José saw people kill wasps thus, but saw them kill honeybees with smoke. They rubbed dry *estafiate* (wormwood) with their hands into balls the size of a potato. (Consultant shows how by gestures). Lighting these, they smoked well. They had fans made by attaching a hawk tail to a stick seven inches long (as a little handle) to use as a fan. The tail was well spread out flat and the stick was the handle. The opening of the nest of honeybees is one inch across. They put the ball in, and lit it and fanned. They call *estafiate hí·šen* in Indian, Angela says.

When the honeybees finally became irritated, and the wasps began to miss their young and adults (for the man killed them clean, not leaving one alive), they began to gather. "What shall we do? We have to get him. We will capture him. He has to come with us."

They began to gather from everywhere to make a place to catch him and decide where to set the trap. They worked day and night, they say, to make the hole. When they finished, they told the boss, "We have finished." Then they said to two messengers, "Be alert."

"When he comes. You come quickly," he told his two workers. They called them coyotes. They were like servants. They were dark grayish and very ugly. These little workers were grayish, while the others were black. These were looking out, as they had been told by the chief, to see when that killer would come.

In the morning he hunted them—that killer did. Then they saw him walking. The two at once entered and reported to the captain that he had come. Then a certain few others (not all the nest and not the two workers) kept going out and in, going out and in, to make a show so as to attract the attention of the killer. The captain told all those not honeybees to go out and in thus while the wasps kept inside. All those not killed from far away had gathered there and had been digging the pit.

When the man saw them, he came happily, and they also were happy, for they saw him coming. As soon as he came, right away they threw two kicks to the man, and right away he went down. And they got him inside.

Then they told him, "You came. We were waiting for you." They put a mat down for him, and told him to sit. "What it must have been like!" Angela uttered suddenly in a tone of sympathy. She imagines seeing him sitting in the midst of the swarm of insects. And the wasps all sang, "Hmmm," singing like so.

Soon they started to ask, "Do you know that you are killing us? We cannot raise children." What could he say? He had to go. Then they said to him: "You must come with us now. Here, you will come with us." So what did he have to say? Then they told the others, and they started to work. They started to eat him. They extracted all the flesh. And they left only skin and bones—nothing else. They cleaned all of the flesh from him.

When they finished cleaning him out, they told the others, "Go and bring feathers, and put feathers wherever there was flesh." They had taken out all of the meat, not leaving one little piece inside. "You will leave," they told him as soon as they got through cleaning him and filling him with feathers. "You will leave. Go and tell your family—and your people—tell everyone that you will no longer live. Say goodbye. Tell them that they will see you no more." He did so, and he went there, and told them to gather wood. He was dancing, and others too. In the morning he told them, "I will leave now." He jumped up. He no longer weighed anything. He was only feathers. He said that it was time to leave. He had to leave. His time had come.

He told the people to gather wood—that he was to sweat and dance the last time. He started to dance (consultant

doesn't know at what hour of the night) and in the early
morning he rose up and burst into the wind.

The time had come to give up his life. He just jumped
up and made a thunder-clapping sound. He burst. He was
dead. He threw his bones close by. I don't know, but he did
burst.

The man (being) to which this narrative refers may be Bear. Of
particular interest is a detailed description of the method for smoking
bees out of their nest with wormwood (*Artemisia douglasiana*)—*hí·šen*
in *Chocheño* and *estafiate* in Old California Spanish. While working
with *Rumsen* and *Mutsun* cultural consultants, Harrington was told that
people burned *estafiate* branches to smoke bees from their nests. The
Mutsun name for *estafiate* was given as *hiisen* (Bocek 1984:254). Alex
Ramirez (personal communication, 1993) recalled the yellowish salve his
mother made from *estafiate*, which she rubbed on her children's chests
and backs whenever they had a cold or cough. Ramirez has vivid
memories of this plant's pungent odor. Since *estafiate* repells
mosquitoes, Alex's mother hung it from their porch, allowing the family
to sit there in comfort at night.

13. **Triumph over great odds**. Told by José Guzman.

There was a man who was striving to make a living at
a certain place by paying certain people to climb a tall pole for
the purpose of getting down for him a single big condor feather
that was hung at the top of the pole like people nowadays have
a flag hanging. It was a scheme for killing people.

He had the ordinary woodpecker (evidently the kind
that Angela calls *párá·tat*) try. He walked only a little way up
when the northwind blew hard (the man arranged with the
winds to do thus). When the woodpecker was not so far up the
northwind blew the pole over. It was made of sinew so that
when it fell, it whipped over and killed the one on it.

Then the small woodpecker that has a white head tried.
It walked every way, including with his little head bowed
down, but only got halfway up the pole when the winds made
the pole fall and killed it too.

(There may have been others of the woodpecker tribe
try as far as José knows.) At last, the measuring worm—they
are green or of other colors—wanted to try. He started at the
bottom and went straight up in spite of the wind that the man
had blown. He crawled as they do and also had his thread to

help him. He went to the very top with all the people looking, took the feather, and started down. In coming down he made use of his thread to hang from and came down thus even quicker and safer than he had gone up. Thus he won all the pay.

14. Encounters with the Devil.

There is a dug up place at a rocky hill located Oaklandward of the San José mission. The Devil entered there. When they tried digging the Devil out, he kept going deeper. They did not get him out. Where he went down, a tule thicker than a man's arm grows at a spring the Devil started. This happened three miles from Niles.

After they had dug the Devil, the hill where this happened remained defaced. You can see the hill well from the mission.

Water came after they had dug. Before there was none. After a while, the water burst from the ground. The big tule grew there. The tule is still there and renews itself every year. The consultant has never seen the place, except from a distance.

DEVIL AT MISSION SAN JOSE

They say the Devil became a donkey once at San Jose Mission. "There comes the donkey," they said and all got on his back. And someone to one side saw a cloven foot: "Look! He has a rooster's foot. He has three feet of his own and one of a rooster." The burro threw them all on the ground there and disappeared at that moment. He had been making himself longer, so they said, "Oh! Here we go sitting on the donkey." This happened in the mission yard.

Circa 1925 Harrington wrote about the spring where the Devil dug to Earnest Schween: ". . . when we reached the old spring we found a hole in the ground which Joe said must be where the Devil dug down years ago" (Calhoun 1973:31). Harrington did not specify the location of the spring, but the rocky hill is undoubtedly Mission Peak.

The Devil as recognized by his cloven or rooster's foot is a widespread motif (see Section III below). When Alex Ramirez (1993 and 1994, personal communication) was growing up in the Carmel Valley in the 1930s, his mother Mary showed him a picture of a "rooster's foot,"

which she clipped from a book or magazine. Mrs. Ramirez warned her
son that if the Devil appeared, he'd have just such a rooster's foot, and
so, whenever someone came to visit whom Alex did not recognize, he
sneaked a look at their feet. Alex's grandfather often told stories. When
he began a telling session with the phrase, "And the man came. . .,"
someone invariably asked, "Did he have rooster feet?"

SECTION II: *RUMSEN* NARRATIVES

In this section extant *Rumsen* narratives will be summarized and
catalogued according to catch word designations. These narratives were
recorded by Alfred Kroeber in 1902, J.P. Harrington in the 1920s, and
Alex Ramirez in 1991. The narratives will be considered in subsections
according to the person who recorded them. Each subsection will include
background information about the historical context in which the
narratives came to be recorded, and about the tellers. These will be
followed by content summaries.

RUMSEN NARRATIVES RECORDED BY ALFRED KROEBER

Historical Context and Kroeber's Consultants

On January 2 and January 3, 1902, Alfred Kroeber went to
Monterey, where he interviewed María Viviena Soto, her niece Jacinta
Gonzalez (Pedro Gonzalez's wife), and her nephew Tom Torres. Kroeber
identified the women as *Sureños* from Sur. Although he did not provide
any background information about his consultants, Kroeber did write
down a compelling statement: "Maria Soto said she would dream of me
because she had talked to me in the old language" (Kroeber [1902]:41).

Kroeber's work with *Rumsen* and other California Indians
resulted from his conviction that "an immediate, systematic survey,
however rapid, of the entire state of California, more especially for
language" was in order. His goal was the "gathering and study of
material with a view to determining as briefly as possible the structure of
all the languages in the parts of the state not covered by Dr. [Roland]
Dixon" (Kroeber [[1902]; [1902a]). In 1902 Kroeber wrote a report
about his work with *Rumsen* speakers or, as he recorded it, *Rumsien*, and
other nearby Indian groups. As this report reflects, his interest lay in pre-
contact cultures, rather than people's historically determined, cultural
present.

From Dec. 24 to Jan. 4 I visited Monterey, San Luis Obispo, and Santa Barbara counties. The conditions throughout this section are pretty uniform. The Indians are very few and completely Mexicanized. The young people speak English but no Indian; the old people in part know Indian, but no English. Therefore all linguistic work, to be accurate, must be done in Spanish.

Ethnological information can still be gathered in fragments, but not very well except in connection with language. At Monterey I found a few old people of the Rumsien tribe, which I took as representative of the Costanoan stock. I obtained both linguistic and general ethnological material, but my informant's recollection of both was imperfect. . . .

In April I went to Monterey for a few days to secure with a phonograph certain songs and other material of the Rumsien Indians, which on the previous visit I had been unable to record (Kroeber [1902a]).

During his 1902 visit, Kroeber obtained several narrative fragments, which he published in 1907 in English, and in 1910 in *Rumsen*. A review of these publications reveals inconsistencies between the creation narrative he published in English and the one he published in *Rumsen*. Kroeber's field notes, however, clarify these inconsistencies, revealing that he wrote down more versions than he published.

As the field notes show, the *Rumsen* account of "The Beginning of the World" published in 1907 is a composite based upon a version told in English by Jacinta Gonzalez and another told in *Rumsen*, also by Gonzalez (Kroeber [1902]:42, 54-60). The narrative entitled "Origin of the World" in the 1910 publication is likewise a composite, primarily based on Jacinta Gonzalez' version in the language, with some additions from a separate version in the language by María Soto (Kroeber [1902]:36).

Content Summary with Background Information

1. Origin of the world—the deluge. After the world was flooded, Eagle, Hummingbird, and Coyote took refuge on Pico Blanco.[6] As the waters rose, the trio left for the higher ground of the Sierra de Gabilans (Kroeber [1902]:36, 42, 54).

---

[6]According to Beviana Torres and Jacinta Gonzalez, white stones with blue patches found at Pico Blanco were used as an item of exchange.

2. Origin of the world—procreation with swallowed louse.
Once the flood waters receded, Coyote found a pretty girl, whom Eagle
said would be Coyote's wife.[7] Coyote instructed her to eat one of his
louses (also called flea and wood-tick), and his wife became pregnant.
She fled from Coyote and transformed into a *camaron* (shrimp or sand-
flea) (Kroeber [1902]:36-40, 42-45, 54-60).

**3. Establishment of material well being—Coyote provides
people with food and implements**. Coyote gave the people weapons to
hunt with (bows and arrows) and implements to gather with (pack nets,
burden baskets). He instructed the people how to gather and prepare
several food items: acorn bread, acorn mush, rabbits, abalone, mollusks,
buckeye, and wild oats (Kroeber [1902]:67-70).

4.   Peopling of the world—establishment of rancherias.
Coyote sought, and eventually received, permission from his wife to
marry other women, thereby peopling the world. His children established
five "rancherias": (1) *Ensen*, a tribe in the Salinas area; (2) *Rumsien*, the
Rumsen of the Carmel Valley and Monterey; (3) *Ekheya*, the last Esselen
speakers to go to Mission San Carlos: (4) *Kakonta*, the same as
Sahenteroch, a tribe near Big Sur; and (5) *Wacharones*, the "River
People" of the Castroville area (Milliken 1983, personal communication;
Kroeber [1902]:67, 73-75).

5. The *Makewiks*. Another fragment describes a trip to the
ocean by Coyote and his wife. Coyote taught his wife about her
relatives, the ocean creatures, but he neglected to teach her about the
Makewiks. When one made an appearance, she died of fright. Coyote
righted the situation by raising her from the dead (Kroeber [1902]:73).
John Peabody Harrington shared this narrative with *Rumsen* elder Isabelle
Meadows, who told him the creature was probably a "*lobo del mar*," a
harbor seal or sea lion (Linda Yamane 1993, personal communication).

6. Hoarded game. A greedy Coyote kept his children from
partaking of salmon by hiding it in ashes. Thinking Coyote was eating
fire, the children expressed concern for his well-being. Coyote still
would not let them eat (Kroeber [1902]:74)..

---

[7]Alternately, Viviena Soto's creation account states, "She told eagle she would be his [Coyote's]
wife."

7. Coyote tricks a woman. Coyote intentionally placed a small stick beneath his eyelid, then tricked a woman into removing it. He seized and married her (Kroeber [1902]:78).

8. The Trickster tricked. This fragment reveals Coyote's intense jealousy of Hummingbird, who knew more than he did. Coyote tried to kill Hummingbird several times, but each time Hummingbird outwitted him (Kroeber [1902]:87).

RUMSEN NARRATIVES RECORDED BY HARRINGTON

Historical Context

In January of 1922 John Peabody Harrington began recording *Rumsen* vocabularies with Tomás de la Torre (Tom Torres), with whom he reheard Kroeber's 1910 "Origin of the World." He also visited other *Rumsen* individuals: Tomasa Cantua and Trinidad Ranjel in Seaside, and Laura Ramirez, Cantua's older sister, that same month in Carmel.

In 1929 and 1930 Harrington returned to his *Rumsen* studies, working extensively with Laura Escobar Ramirez. During this time, he also worked with Laura's husband Alfonso Ramirez, their son Pete, Tom Torres, Torres' wife Juana Maria, Marcela Díaz, Bernabel "El Sordo," Merced Gonzales, Lupecina, and María "Mary" Onesimo Ramirez, Alex Ramirez's mother.

In 1932 Harrington began work with Isabelle Meadows, his primary *Rumsen* consultant. He continued to collaborate with Meadows until 1939, the year she died. Harrington also worked in 1932 with Flugenio Cantua, Claudia Corona, Julia Díaz and her brother Saturnino, Andrés Goméz, Joe Hitchcock, and Laura and Alfonso Ramirez. In 1933 he worked with Tom Meadows, Isabelle's brother (Alex Ramirez 1992-1993, personal communication; Mills 1985:82-85,99-113).

While Harrington engaged most of his *Rumsen* consultants in linguistic work, he obtained some *Rumsen* narratives from Isabelle Meadows, Tom Meadows, Laura Ramirez, and Tom Torres. Angel Sánchez provided historical narratives (Mills 1985:112-113).

Harrington's *Rumsen* Consultants—Reminiscences of Alex Ramirez

Alex Ramirez, born December 1928 in Carmel, recalls Harrington's visits with his paternal grandfather Alfonso Ramirez, half *Rumsen* and half Mexican, and his paternal grandmother Laura Escobar Ramirez, also half *Rumsen* and half Mexican. These visits took place when Alex was four years old, but he vididly remembers Harrington's gifts of bananas: "Maybe he bribed everyone with bananas, because that's the reason I liked him."

Alex also remembers the convertible Harrington drove, recalling his astonishment that someone would drive a car without a roof. Whenever Harrington or, as the family called him, "El Alto" arrived, everyone hastened to don their Sunday best (Alex Ramirez 1991-1992, personal communication).

It was no accident that Harrington's research interests would bring him to the Alfonso Ramirez home in Carmel:

Fig. 4.2. Alex Ramirez and his mother Mary Onesimo;
Meadows ranch, Carmel Valley, 1929

> We lived with my grandfather on my father's side in Carmel on Santa Rita Street. It was a gathering place for everybody. The Indians who lived in Carmel Valley, when they came down to Monterey, they would come by that house in Carmel, and stop and have coffee. My mother would give them water and food. It was during the depression so my father used to make beer, and all the beer drinkers would gather around the house . . . . It was a place for Harrington to come and be, because everybody would hang out there (Alex Ramirez 1993, personal communication).

At his grandfather's house, Alex saw traditional dancer José Goméz dance in buckskin regalia. Goméz wore a domed hat over his long braid. The swirlings of coffee can lids saved by Alex's mother dangled from Gomez's outfit (Alex Ramirez 1991, personal communication).

Eventually, Alex's family moved to the Loreta and Domingo Peralta property, then owned by Loreta's son Roy Meadows. The Peralta property had been the only land granted to a *Rumsen* family after the secularization of Mission San Carlos Borromeo (Carmel) in the 1830s. Although continually threatened with expulsion from their property by civil administrator Antonio Romero, who reportedly "resented the ownership of such an extent of land by a native family," the Peraltas, with the intervention of local resident Juana Boronda, were able to keep the land.

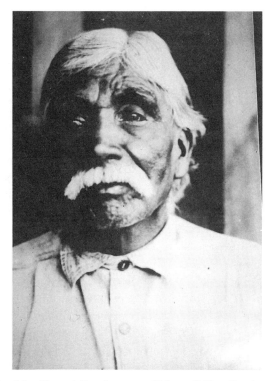

In 1842, following Domingo's death, Loreta, the sister of Alex's maternal great-grand-father Juan Onesimo, married James Meadows, an English whaler who had jumped ship at Monterey Bay in 1835. The Peraltas had hidden Meadows until his ship sailed away, but in 1840 he was arrested and jailed in Mexico. Meadows returned to Monterey in 1841, after his release from prison (Temple 1980:86-87; Tim Thomas, personal communication 6/13/94).

Fig. 4.3. Manuel Onesimo, grandfather of Alex Ramirez, circa 1900; Onesimo lived on the Meadows ranch

When Harrington visited the *Rumsen* community, few *Rumsen* wanted to admit their Indianness because of the prejudice they endured and the discrimination they faced. Harrington's consultants, however, not only maintained their pride, but were willing to share what they knew with outsiders (Alex Ramirez 1991-1993, personal communication).

Isabelle Meadows, the daughter of Loreta and James Meadows, was particularly well-known for her kindness and forthrightness. Unafraid to describe the hardships her people endured, Meadows told Harrington about how, with the closure of Mission Carmel, her people were forced off the mission lands that had been promised to them. She talked about the demoralization that led to diseases, drunkenness, and fights.

Because so few *Rumsen* would talk about the past, Alex remembers many writers, anthropologists, and historians seeking information from his family. While the family considered some of those who came "fly by night," and others "a nuisance," they always welcomed El Alto (Alex Ramirez 1993, personal communication).

Content Summary with Background Information

In recent years Linda Yamane (*Rumsen*) has worked on the translation of the *Rumsen* narratives that Harrington recorded. The summaries that follow are based upon Yamane's work (1993-1994).

1.   End (origin) of the world—the deluge—etiological narration—why certain birds have certain markings. This narrative, called "*cuando se acabó el mundo*" by Harrington's consultants, like those told to Kroeber, opens with a deluge. Unlike Kroeber's version, this version doesn't mention Coyote. Eagle, alone this time, flew above the flood waters until he spied the dry top of Pico Blanco. He landed there to rest, and Hummingbird, Crow, Raven, and Hawk eventually joined him. When Crow and Raven ate the people who drowned in the flood, they turned black. (Consultants: Isabelle Meadows, as learned from "*El Viejo*" Roman Alvarez; possibly others.)

2. End (origin) of the world—earth diver. Unlike the Kroeber versions, this narrative has an earth diver motif. Eagle instructed Hawk to dive into the flood waters until he reached earth. Although Hawk failed to reach earth on his first attempt, he tried again the next morning. During this second attempt, Hawk, at Eagle's behest, held a feather plucked from the center of Eagle's head. The feather grew longer, helping Hawk reach the earth below the deluge. The water subsequently receded. (Consultant: Isabelle Meadows; version by Manuel Onesimo.)

3. Coyote tricks a woman—procreation with swallowed louse. At a dance, Coyote desired the pretty Deer Girl. Coyote put a *huichuta* (wood sliver or small stick) into his eye so she would come near. He ordered her to delouse him, then forced her to eat a *garrapata* (tick, literally "leg grabber") she found on his body.

According to Harrington, Isabelle Meadows volunteered that she thought "the *garrapata* was his *pilliw*" (probably penis). He also wrote:

Isabelle doesn't n. [know] how she got it [the sliver] out of his [Coyote's] eye. Isabelle breaks over into the garrapata story all the time. When the girl ate the garrapata, she got knocked up.

Isabelle told Harrington this narrative "was *bonita* when one knew how to tell it well." Such a telling included a song.

Another version explains how Coyote originated the custom of stealing girls. To engender sympathy, Coyote put a little stick in his eye, which he represented as a big stick. He began wailing to catch Coyote Girl's attention. When his wailing attracted other people to him, Coyote refused to let them near.

Coyote later left for his house, singing to his sweetheart as he went. Attracted by the beautiful song, Coyote Girl followed.

Tom Meadows, who identified the girl as Coyote Girl, and his sister Isabelle Meadows, who called her Deer Girl, told Harrington these versions. Isabelle learned the narrative from Omesia, a *Wacharone* woman who worked for and lived with the Meadows family when Isabelle was young.

4.   Theft of fire—etiological narration—why certain birds have certain markings. Eagle instructed Hummingbird to obtain fire for cooking from the Badger people. Although the Badgers initially thwarted the theft, Hummingbird successfully completed his mission on a second try.   After grabbing the fire from its hiding place with his beak, Hummingbird got a red throat. (Consultants: Unidentified, but probably Isabelle Meadows and Manuel Onesimo.)

5.   Traversing the world. Two bears set out to learn about the world.   One travelled toward the sun, the other north, all the while naming the places they saw.   Eventually they re-met in the Carmel Valley. (Consultants: Unidentified, but probably Isabelle Meadows and Manuel Onesimo.)

6.   Coyote hunts squirrels. Coyote's second wife was Bear. Bear hadn't wanted to marry, and Coyote, angered by her inattention and scolding, decided to go hunting.   Upon finding a dead tree filled with holes, and inhabited by squirrels, Coyote schemed to catch the squirrels without having to work.   He trapped the squirrels in his belly.   On his way home, Coyote had to rest several times.   Each time he did, the squirrels mocked him with song.   Upon reaching home, Coyote relieved himself of the squirrels one by one. (Consultants: Isabelle Meadows as learned from Omesia; possibly one other.)

7. Children's revenge of relative's death. Bear wasn't a fastidious acorn cook. Disgusted by the resulting acorn bread, Coyote pretended to take it to relatives, but instead discarded, then danced upon it. Bear, who had followed her husband, became so angry when she witnessed this that she killed her husband. When Bear's children found out about the killing—in one version she told them, "Don't think you have a father, because I just killed him"—they killed her. Later, people identified a rock in the mouth of the Carmel River as Bear's head. (Consultants: Isabelle Meadows, whom the tragedy of the story reduced to tears; Tom Meadows.)

8. Coyote punished with thirst. This narrative, recorded by Harrington in several versions, describes a fiesta attended by the Early People. While there, Coyote, entrusted to care for some women's babies (alternately children), killed them. In one version Coyote ate so much he couldn't dance, so the women brought him their babies to watch over while they danced. In another version Coyote involved Mountain Lion in the killing.

After finding their babies dead, the women cursed Coyote to be always thirsty. Everywhere Coyote went to drink, the water dried up. He ended up drinking sand (Consultants: Isabelle Meadows as learned from Roman Alvarez; Tom Meadows).

RUMSEN NARRATIVES WITH MEXICAN ORIGINS RECORDED BY ALEX RAMIREZ

Summary with Background Information
1. Coyote and Fox. In 1991 Alex Ramirez published a narrative he learned as a child from his grandfather Manuel Onesimo. This narrative relates two tricks Coyote played upon an unwitting, trusting Fox. Coyote tricked Fox into holding up a cliff to keep it from falling over. Then Coyote enticed Fox to swim toward a round, yellow cheese in the river. Fox won attention and friends in his effort to secure the non-existent cheese, a mere reflection of the moon on the water. Meanwhile, Coyote was left alone and howling.

In his youth, Alex saw many such cheese-like reflections while walking along the Carmel River on moonlight nights (Alex Ramirez 1993, personal communication).

OTHER OHLONE/COSTANOAN NARRATIVES

In addition to recording *Rumsen* and *Chocheño* narratives, Harrington recorded narratives told by Ascencion Solorsano, a speaker of *Mutsun*, the language of the Mission San Juan Bautista area. Harrington first worked with Solorsano in 1922. He next worked with her in 1929, when she was near death (Mills 1985:82). Solorsano, who was born in 1855, learned *Mutsun* from her mother Barbara (Mason [1916a]:1-2). The narratives Harrington recorded with Solorsano have not been analyzed for the present work.

In 1916 John Alden Mason had also visited Ascencion Solorsano. Apparently not wanting to talk with Mason, Solorsano left him with the impression that she remembered "very little" (Mason [1916a]:1-2).

Solorsano referred Mason to Josefa Velasquez, with whom he visited that October. Mason's comments about Velasquez also tell something about Mason.

> I am inclined to think that with a few days experience the old woman could be induced to tell many myths and songs, possibly in text, but as they came too slowly at the beginning I decided it was not worth while [sic] trying again.
>
> She insisted that Ascencion in Gilroy knew more than she, but claimed, like all others, that these two were the only living persons who remembered anything of the language and customs. Refugio Castillo spoke it well, and so did Barbara Solarson [sic], the mother of Ascencion, but these two died not more than 3 years ago. I could learn of no other old or middle-aged Indians in the whole country (Mason [1916a]).

Mason further noted of Ascencion and Josefa:

> Neither of them knew either the myth of the beginning of the world or of the theft of fire . . .
> [They said] . . . the eagle, hummingbird and owl were worshipped" [Mason [1916a]).

Mason indicated that Josefa shared a single sacred narrative with him. This narrative has not been located.

Captain F.W. Beechey published the earliest known reference to the narrative tradition of an Ohlone-speaking tribe, the "*Olchone*," about whom he wrote: "Like most other nations, these people have a tradition of the deluge . . . . (Beechey 1831:II,78).

Beechey described the *Olchone* as inhabiting "the seacoast between San Francisco and Monterey," making it clear that he was referring to the *Oljon*, who "controlled the lower drainages of San Gregorio Creek and Pescadero on the Pacific Coast west of the Santa Clara Valley" (Milliken [1991]:445).

SECTION III: COMPARATIVE NARRATIVES

In this section the *Chocheño* and *Rumsen* narratives will be compared with each other, and with the narratives of other California Indian groups, especially those of West-Central California. Such a comparison will show that *Chocheño* and *Rumsen* narrative traditions, like those of other areas, did not exist in a cultural vacuum, but shared certain motifs and traits. It will also reveal the existence of localized differences that make clear the inherent danger in characterizing the narrative tradition of a given language area by a single corpus of material.

A Comparison of *Chocheño* and *Rumsen* narratives with each other
As shown above, few *Chocheño* and *Rumsen* narratives have been recorded. Those that have are mere fragments of narrative traditions once more extensive. While the dearth of overlapping motifs in what remains makes all but the most cursory comparison impossible, some general points of intersection do exist, and within these some specific differences.
Etiological explanations of animal coloration appear in both *Chocheño* and *Rumsen* narratives: Meadowlark's black neck "v," Woodpecker's red head, and Red-winged Blackbird's red wing patches in those of the *Chocheño*; Hummingbird's red neck in those of the *Rumsen*. In the *Rumsen* Crow and Raven turned black after they ate the people who drowned in the deluge, while in the *Chocheño* the servants of "Body of Stone" turned black from eating blood.
The reason for certain, local geographical features is also explained: a windowed sandstone outcrop and barren ground (Coyote's footprints) in the *Chocheño*; a rock feature at the mouth of the Carmel River in the *Rumsen* (Bear). Violence between husbands and wives likewise occurs in both. In the *Chocheño* narratives, *Kaknú* killed his wife for jealousy; in the *Rumsen*, Bear killed her husband because he failed to respect her acorn.
Another point of intersection results from a single statement in the *Chocheño* corpus: "'This is for the people, who are today, to eat,' he [*Kaknú*] said, as he threw it from his nose. And hence chia patches, and Indians go hunting it." A more elaborate accounting of the provision of

food, this time by Coyote, exists in the *Rumsen* corpus, which does not mention chia.

While extant *Chocheño* and *Rumsen* narratives have little in common, the *Rumsen* narratives recorded by Kroeber and Harrington share three motifs: "End (Origin) of the World," "Coyote Tricks a Woman" and "Procreation with Swallowed Louse." The three motifs, although cognate, have some noticeable discrepancies. For example, in the "End (Origin) of the World" variants recorded by Kroeber, Coyote, Eagle, and Hummingbird are featured; the Harrington variants feature Eagle, Hummingbird, Hawk, Raven, and Crow. Harrington's versions have an earth diver motif, while Kroeber's do not. "Coyote Tricks a Woman" and "Procreation with Swallowed Louse" are separate narratives in the variants recorded by Kroeber, while those recorded by Harrington combine these motifs into a single narrative. The latter variants include different characters—Deer Girl versus Coyote Girl—and somewhat divergent plotlines. Divergence also evidences itself in two versions of "Children's Revenge of Relative's Death" recorded by Harrington.

Such variations may result from differences in the day to day telling, how well the tellers remembered the narratives, or in subtle tribal or regional variations among *Rumsen* speakers (oicotypes or the local form of a given narrative). In the case of "Children's Revenge of Relative's Death" the differences result from the telling of decorous and bawdy versions.

A Comparison of *Chocheño* and *Rumsen* Narratives with those of other California Indian groups

A comparison of *Rumsen* and *Chocheño* narratives with those of other California Indian groups, mostly from West-Central California, uncovers many cognates. Distinctive traits within these cognates can serve as important markers of ethnic identity, both within and without language areas.

Chocheño Narratives compared with those of other areas

1. *Kaknú* as culture hero. The geographical delimitation of character use provides one important marker of ethnic identity.

Kaknú (Peregrine Falcon), Coyote's grandson, is a culture hero in *Chocheño* narratives. *Wekwek*, another name for Peregrine Falcon, is Coyote's grandson and a culture hero in those of the "*Hool-poom'-ne*" (the *Chupumne* and alternately *Gualacomne*, Plains Miwok speakers of the Walnut Grove/Sacramento area). The "*Hoo'-koo-e'-ko*" (an appellation that Catholic priests at Mission Sonoma assigned four Coast

Miwok tribes)[8] also recognized *Wekwek* as Coyote's grandson, as do other Miwok groups (Merriam [1910]:60, 66-90; Barrett 1919:6-7). Some Valley Nisenan, River Patwin, Plains Miwok, and Northern Miwok speakers described Peregrine Falcon as an important personage (Merriam [1910]:48-53, 134-136, 138-151; Kroeber 1932:304; Kroeber 1929:276).

Prairie Falcon appears as a culture hero in *Gashowu* (Southern Valley Yokuts) and Salinan narratives—both the San Antonio and San Miguel dialect (Kroeber 1907:204, Mason 1918:60-64, 67-69, 85-86, 105-108, 110-112). The *Rumsen* culture hero(s) is uncertain, but may have been Hawk, Crow, or Raven.

2. Making the world safe—the killing of Body of Stone and the creation of stone monoliths. Difference and similarity permeate narrative cycles in which the world is made safe for people, and stone monoliths created. While *Kaknú* made the world safe in *Chocheño* narratives by killing "Body of Stone," Prairie Falcon and Raven accomplished the task for the San Antonio Salinan by dispatching such killers as Pelican, Woodpecker, and Xui (Mason 1918:63-64,78-79,85,86,92-93).

Kaknú killed Body of Stone with arrow shots and thrusts to the throat and navel, whereupon "Body of Stone" burst, creating large stone monoliths. In a Marin Miwok parallel Gray Tree Squirrel cut Old Man Rock's "strings." As Old Man Rock rolled along the ground, he formed rocks on hilltops with his sweat. In another Marin Miwok parallel two twins killed *Loo'-poo-oi'-yes*, the Rock Giant of Tamalpais, with an arrow shot to his abalone-covered throat. *Loo'-poo-oi'-yes* shattered, and his pieces became rocks scattered across the countryside (Merriam [1910]:232-235). A Bodega Miwok variant features the Elk Brothers, who caused Old St. Helena Mountain to come "rolling out" by opening a nest of yellowjackets. When the wind momentarily separated the four large abalones at Mountain's neck, an Elk Brother shot him there with an arrow. Mountain promptly burst, thereby forming the rocks now donning the countryside (Collier and Thalman 1991:438-439; Kelly 1978:32-33).

The *Chocheño* Body of Stone lived below the ground. The Merced River region's (Southern Miwok) Rock Giant ate people, then retired into a cave at night. The people, with Fly's assistance, killed this giant by causing him to step upon stone splinters, then burned him up (Merriam [1910]:169-172). A Southern Miwok variant excludes the cave and burning, but includes the same cannibal giant. Again the people

---

killed the giant with Fly's assistance, but this time they caused him to step upon a long awl, which pierced his heart (Barrett 1919:2-3).

A Northern Miwok Rock Giant captured the *Mewuk* (people) and various animals, and took them to his caves, where he continues to live. As in the *Chocheño* version, he kept his victim's remains (Merriam [1910]:231-232). The *Olayome* of Putah Creek also had such a cave dwelling Rock Giant:

> He used to roam about nights, catching Indians and carrying them off to his cave to eat. He has not done this for some time" (Merriam [1910]:236).

3. Making the world safe—the killing of "Body of Salt". See previous discussion for general parallels to the Making the World Safe cycle.

4. World fire. A single sentence in the *Chocheño* narratives alludes to the second destruction of the world by fire. Fire likewise serves as an agent of world destruction and, generally by implication, renewal among the *Chupumne* or *Gualacomne* (Merriam [1910]:75-89), Southern Miwok (Barrett 1919:8), Lake Miwok (Angulo and Freeland 1928:232-233,242; Merriam [1910]:139-146), and Central Yana (Sapir 1910:34-35).

5. Wife killed for jealousy. Two *Chocheño* narratives feature the killing of a wife as a result of her infidelity. In the first, Coyote killed his wife after she slept with another man. He later tried to revive her when he observed her breast feeding their young son from her grave (also compare with "Origin of Death—Attempt to Revive a Dead Relative" below). The second describes a husband who, when he realized his wife was sleeping with another man, marked her with the man's paint. Later, at her husband's request, the wife went several times to bring him water. Each time she returned to her husband, the water had become riled, once by a frog. Finally, her husband angrily pushed her into the water and told her to become a beaver.

A cognate *Guaypem* (Plains Miwok) narrative accords in most details with these two *Chocheño* narratives, if considered in combination.[9] In this version Falcon (*Wekwek*) observed that his wife Gray Goose was having an affair with White-headed Eagle. Upon returning home, Falcon

---

[9]Merriam most likely learned this narrative from Paula, a *Guaypem* woman who lived at Alisal. It is unknown whether Colós or Guzman learned their versions from Paula or someone else.

asked his wife to fetch him clean water, but five times, by the time
Falcon's wife reached their house, the water "had turned into snakes and
frogs and other water animals." Angrily, Falcon killed her, the telltale
black marks White-headed Eagle "had painted" on the wife remaining on
her dead body. For four days the dead woman came to the roundhouse
to "give milk to her young child." When Falcon saw her rise out of her
grave, he seized her and, although she didn't want to go, said he would
cure her. Falcon took his wife to his people's roundhouse, but
Meadowlark complained of the smell, and the dead woman disappeared.
Falcon killed Meadowlark, then tore Meadowlark's mouth, causing a
black mark "where his mouth was torn down, and the marks on his head
where the skull was crushed" (Merriam [1910]: 126-132).

In a Lake Miwok narrative, the male consort, rather than the
wife, suffered the consequence of their indiscretion. When Hawk Chief's
wife Lady Pelican slept with Hawk's little brother Falcon, Hawk Chief
wounded his brother in the eye. Falcon, who flew away, was said still
to cry bloody tears onto a rock where he perched (Angulo and Freeland
1928:242-243).

In a *Wobonuch* (Central Hills Mono) narrative, after Coyote
determined that upon completion of their work men and women "would
gather together to have a good time," *Kaneo* slept with her sister's
husband." When *Kaneo* went to gather onions, the sister's husband
followed. *Kaneo* then killed, cooked, and fed him to the people. In
retaliation the people tried to kill her, but she escaped into water, where
it's said she keeps a man (Gayton and Newman 1940:40).

**6. Establishment of material well being—*Kaknú* provides
people with food**. For comparative material see "*Rumsen* Narratives
Recorded by Kroeber Compared with Those of Other Areas" below.

**7.   Origin of death—attempt to revive a dead rela-
tive—etiological narratives—why certain animals have certain
markings**. The attempt to revive a deceased relative has widespread
distribution in West-Central California "origin of death" narratives.
Meadowlark commonly thwarts this attempt by commenting on the dead
person's smell.

In the *Chocheño* version *Kaknú* tried to revive his dead wife in
a sweathouse, but she fled when Meadowlark commented upon her
stench. In a *Guaypem* cognate, Falcon tried to revive his wife, but
Meadowlark commented on the woman's smell (Merriam [1910]:132).
In a Yosemite Miwok/Paiute variant, as told by a *Chukchansi* (Yokuts)
individual, Meadowlark didn't like the smell of a dead person Coyote

wished to revive. Coyote acquiesced to permanent death, and instituted cremation (Kroeber 1904:203).

A *Gashowu* (Yokuts) parallel relates how some people wished to put a dying person outside the house for three days, then have him revive. Meadowlark, a newly married man, objected to the smell, and persuaded the people to cremate the dead person (Kroeber 1907:205).

In one Eastern Pomo variant Coyote revived Falcon, who had been blown to pieces at a magic tree. Meadowlark commented on the smell, and Falcon, realizing he was unfit, left. In an etiological twist on the *Chocheño* version, an angered Bluejay cut off Meadowlark's tail with a firebrand (Barrett 1933:319-322). In another Eastern Pomo narrative of unknown tribal origin, Pelican, a bear doctor, killed Falcon, who replaced him as chief. After Falcon revived, Meadowlark commented on his smell. Meadowlark's tail was half-way cut off with a mush paddle (Barrett 1933:370-371). A third Eastern Pomo variant has a Bullfrog woman die as the result of eating too many squirrels. After the woman came back to life, Meadowlark commented on her foul odor. Bluejay shovelled coals onto Meadowlark in response (Barrett 1933:249-50).

8. The origin of death by wise foresight—originator of death the first sufferer. Boas (1917:486-491) analyzed origin of death narratives throughout native North America. His research revealed two often concurrent themes: (1) the supernatural being who created death came to regret that decision when a relative died; and (2) the decision to create permanent death, whether for wise or frivolous reasons, was irreversible.

The *Chocheño* origin of death narrative reflects these themes, as do other California Indian origin of death narratives. In a *Wobonuch* (Western Yokuts) narrative Eagle argued for impermanent death. Coyote objected that the world would become too crowded, so the people arranged for Coyote's son to be killed by Owl (Gayton and Newman 1940:40-41). In a *Yana* parallel, Lizard proposed that people would live again, but Coyote objected that they would become too numerous. In response the people decided to make Coyote cry by arranging for his son's killing by a rattlesnake (Sapir 1910:91-93).

In both Lake Miwok and Southeastern Pomo variants, Old Man Moon killed Hawk Chief, and Coyote doctored him back to life. When Meadowlark objected that people should stay dead due to the smell, Coyote put a rattlesnake in the path of Meadowlark's boys, who died. Afterward, Coyote directed that his house, located beyond the ocean, would become the land of the dead (Angulo and Freeland 1928:240-242). In a Central Pomo variant the chief's daughter, at Coyote's instruction, went so close to a rattlesnake hole that she was bitten and died. When the chief wanted her to live again, Coyote objected, saying that without permanent death there would be too many people in the world and not enough food to go around. The chief poisoned Coyote's daughter in retribution (Barrett 1933:92).

The originator of death likewise suffers in two Nisenan narratives. In one, *Híkaht* ("the great chief"), thought the dead "should come to life on the fourth day," but Meadowlark thought the people "were no good and by and by would smell." Coyote agreed with Meadowlark, so *Híkaht* arranged for Coyote's daughter to die from a rattlesnake bite. As a result, Coyote changed his mind about permanent death, but it was too late (Merriam [1910]:55-56). In the other, only Coyote opposed "*Haikat*," a weather doctor. This version's other details accord with those of the former (Kroeber 1929:275-276).

9. Origin of death—journey to the land of the death. The *Chocheño* journey to the land of the dead includes a stop to drink water and eat *panocha* (native sugar). A road leads to a sea foam which the dead pass through. The Chumash soul's journey to the land of the dead, although different in some ways, includes a road and several stopping points (Blackburn 1980:98-100).

10. Etiological narrative—why certain birds eat certain things. As defined by Barrett, etiological narratives "explain the reasons why many things are as they are in the world today." These explanations include the "present condition of things, color or shape of animals, and the like." Barrett found such narratives to be "abundant" in Central California (Barrett 1933:12, 465, 493). In a *Chocheño* fragment *Kaknú*, provoked by the actions of his sons, commanded them to eat certain things. A Central Pomo version tells how Coyote, provoked by the actions of the Early People, turned them into the various birds and other animals of today, commanding where they should live and what they should eat:

> You people do not try to do as I tell you to. You do not seem to care to do the proper things and try to be somebody. You might as well be animals and go and do the way you like best (Barrett 1933:106-107).

11. Etiological narratives—why certain birds have certain markings. As with other etiological explanations, the reasons cited for the markings of certain birds and other animals varies widely. See "Origin of Death" above and "Theft of Fire" below for some examples.

12. Insects take revenge. In a *Chocheño* narrative bees and wasps killed a man who destroyed their relatives. A Chumash narrative relates the stinging of Centipede by mosquitoes, until he became only bones (see "Triumph Over Great Odds" below). Another Chumash narrative tells how Skunk tricked Coyote into watching over a wasp nest, which Skunk had previously plugged with a rock.

> . . . Coyote began to dig with the stick. In a short time he had opened the hole, and the wasps poured out and settled all over him and began to sting him. He cried, "What can I do?" He saw a patch of brush nearby, and he threw himself into it and began to roll around. The wasps finally left . . . (Blackburn 1980:306-307).

A Chemehuevi narrative turns the table when Earth-Wasp, said to be "like the yellow jacket but larger," packed away the Mountain Sheep which Coyote and his Company hunted. After tracking Earth-Wasp to his adobe home, Coyote and the others made stick steps to climb up the side of it, then made a hole to enter. Earth-Wasp, appropriately named Owner of the Stone Pestle, attacked, then killed all but Blue Hawk. After Blue Hawk killed Earth-Wasp, he brought his companions back to life (Laird 1984:115-123).

13. Triumph over great odds. In a *Chocheño* narrative a man schemed to kill Early People by paying them to climb a tall pole and retrieve a condor feather. The man arranged for the north wind to blow each climber off the pole. Only Measuring Worm managed to scale the sinew pole and bring the feather down without getting killed.

A Chumash narrative likewise features a pole climb, but Centipede has replaced Measuring Worm:

> When animals were still people, the boys used to spend all their time trying to climb a smooth pole in order to see who could do it best, and Centipede always won for he was very good at it.

The boys complained about Centipede to Coyote, who bewitched the pole so that it would grow taller as Centipede climbed. Strong winds nearly blew Centipede off the pole twice, but he persevered.

> Just then a swarm of mosquitoes arrived, but they weren't little like they are here on earth; they were gigantic. They began to sting him and suck his blood, and soon there

nothing left of him but bones—just bones, and nothing else
(Blackburn 1980:202).

Coyote regretted what he had done, and climbed up to rescue
Centipede. He found Centipede's bones singing and revived him, then
Eagle began to fly the pair down. On the way, Coyote, who fell off,
became dashed to pieces, but Centipede managed to jump back onto the
pole before falling to the ground. Once Centipede reached the ground,
he revived Coyote's pieces (Blackburn 1980:202-204).

A Wappo variant has *Wekwek*, at the behest of his evil brother-in-
law, climb atop a short tree to capture two young eagles. When *Wekwek*
grasped a branch, the tree flung him "all around the world," but he
managed to hold on until his grandfather Coyote could rescue him (Radin
1924:117-119).

Most West-Central California parallels highlight Measuring
Worm's triumphant climb to the top of a rock which had grown, trapping
early people atop (see Gayton and Newman 1940:27, Barrett 1933:307-
309, and Barrett 1919:22). In these versions Measuring Worm either
rescues the trapped people or returns with their remains. The growing
rock motif has widespread distribution:

> The "Growing Rock" story of Kechayi [Northern
> Foothills Yokuts], Northfork Mono, Miwok, and Pomo form a
> unique nucleus. Wintu, Yauelmani, and Tübatulabal variants
> merge with another tale, that of an old man who tricks his son
> in order to marry his daughters-in-law, which in varying forms
> is distributed from Puget Sound to the Southwest (Gayton and
> Newman 1940:75).

14. Encounters with the Devil. The motif in which the Devil
is recognized by a deformed foot or feet has European origins, and is
now known in many parts of the world. In New Mexican legendry the
Devil's feet take on the appearance of cloven hoofs and claws (Thompson
1955:G303.4.4 and G303.4.5.3.1); versions describe the foot or feet as
having the appearance of a cock, goat, pig, or other animal (Thompson
1955:G303.4.5.9, G303.4.5.4, and G303.4.5.5 respectively). Commonly,
the Devil's feet betray him at a dance hall or card game. Modern
cognates situate the incident at a discotheque (Ortiz [1994]:1-23; Herrera-
Sobek 1988:151; Brunvand 1981:180; Robe 1980:151, 169, 179, 185-188,
190, 192-193, 196, 199, 213).

Rumsen Narratives Recorded by Kroeber compared with those of other areas

1. Origin of the world—the deluge. West-Central California Indian creation narratives commonly begin with a pre-existing supernatural being who, accompanied by various assistant(s), created the earth from a world covered with water. In extant *Rumsen* narratives the flood waters resulted from a deluge, as in Salinan and Bodega Miwok variants, rather than pre-existing (primeval) water, as appears to be the case among the Marin Miwok and *Gashowu* (Yokuts) (Collier and Thalman 1991:435,440; Kelly 1978:28-29; Mason 1916:82); Kroeber 1907:204).

Many groups recognized certain mountains as standing above the water, serving to localize this widespread narrative cycle: the Sierra Gabilans and Pico Blanco for the *Rumsen*; Mount Diablo for the *Chupumne* or *Gualacomne*; Mount Diablo and Reed's Peak for an unspecified group,[10] and Santa Lucia Peak for the San Antonio Salinan (Merriam [1910]:66-90; Mason 1916:82; H.B.D. 1859:326). A Bodega Miwok variant situates a boat above the water (Collier and Thalman 1991:435, Kelly 1978:30). A Chumash cognate places the tallest tree in the world above the floodwaters (Blackburn 1980:94).

2. Origin of the world—procreation with swallowed louse. Louse, alternately Flea and Wood-tick, acts as an agent of procreation in a *Rumsen* narrative—an apt metaphor considering the creature's prolificacy. A Chemehuevi narrative features Body Louse Woman. While Coyote slept with the woman, her mother wove a basket which, when finished, she presented to Coyote, then sent him home. When Coyote opened the basket, people "just boiled out," and became various tribes (Laird 1984:39-48). In a Chumash narrative, Coyote locked two girls in his house by pretending to be one girl's fiancé. Gopher, flea, then louse, were all sent to try and find out what Coyote was hiding (Blackburn 1980:194-196).

> Louse crept in and tasted the two girls. Fox had a salty taste and Wildcat tasted bad. When he saw them he observed that they were already big with child (Blackburn 1980:196).

---

[10]Kroeber (1907:189) speculated that this narrative, which features Coyote and Eagle, "is perhaps from the northern part of the Costanoan territory." This remains conjecture, with Northern Valley Yokuts and other attributions possible.

Mountain Lion eventually rescued the girls, each of whom gave birth to 12 children by Coyote (Blackburn 1980:196).

A *Yaulamni* (Yokuts) narrative likewise mentions Bed Louse:

> While Coyote was repairing his arrows he lasciviously ogled his wife, Bed Louse. When she commented sarcastically upon his burning his arrows, he killed her. Remorseful, Coyote cut his hair and abstained from meat (Gayton and Newman 1940:84).

3. Establishment of material well being—Coyote provides people with food and implements. The *Rumsen* narrative in which Coyote provided the people with food and implements has many cognates. In a *Yokayo* Pomo version, Coyote provided plant and animal foods, food restrictions, bows, arrows, string, snares, fish nets, and rope to catch deer (Barrett 1933:84-85). A lonely Coyote created people, according to a River Patwin variant. At the same time he made "all the animals and plants," food preparation methods, a fire drill, and towns (Kroeber 1932:305).

A *Dumna* (Yokuts) narrative states that God, after creating people and establishing intertribal marriage,

> . . . dropped acorns, manzanita, and all the seeds that were needed. In the spring the salmon came; they were dried and taken home . . . (Gayton and Newman 1940:28).

Following a world flood, according to the Kato, World Maker fixed the world as it is today. He made people, natural phenomenon like clouds and weather, everything the people would eat, plants, animals, seafood, salt, blood, natural features, and water (Goddard 1909:183-188).

4. Peopling of the world—establishment of rancherias. As with the *Rumsen* version, which relates how Coyote's children peopled the world and established five rancherias, according to a *Dumna* (Yokuts) variant, "God made one man and one woman for each tribe and put them where their home is now" (Gayton and Newman 1940:28). According to the *Michahai* (Central Hills Yokuts):

> "Now," said Eagle, "we have to be different kinds of people. We will give them names and tell them where to live. There will be one couple for each kind of tribe."

Then he named over every kind of people and mentioned their home locality—Michahai, Waksachi, Wukchumni, Choinimni—all. He was just telling how it was going to be (Gayton and Newman 1940:32).

According to the River Patwin, Falcon made towns from feathers plucked from birds that had flown into the sky when the world flooded (Kroeber 1932:305). A Marin Miwok account relates how Coyote set four bundles of feathers into the ground in four different places.

Next morning all had turned into people, each bundle becoming a distinct tribe, speaking a language wholly different from the languages of the others (Merriam [1910]:203-205).

A *Túleyome* (Lake Miwok) variant describes Coyote's placement of two feathers wherever he wanted a rancheria, and his naming of each locale.

Next morning they again went out and found that all the feathers had turned into people; that each pair of feathers had become two people, a man and a woman, so that at each place there were [sic] a man and a woman. This is the way all the rancherias were started.

By and by all the people had children and after a while the people became very numerous (Merriam [1910]:148-149).

In a Southern Miwok variant Coyote and Falcon placed a single buzzard and a single crow feather on every hill they came to.

As Coyote deposited the feathers he named each place, and on the following day there were people living in all these localities (Barrett 1919:8-9).

5. The *Makewiks*. Comparative data not located at publication.

6. Hoarded game. A *Rumsen* narrative describes the manner in which Coyote prevented his children from eating his salmon by pretending to eat the hot ashes in which the fish roasted. A Chumash narrative likewise describes Coyote's stinginess. After Coyote killed half a flock of geese by trickery, he had his sons prepare and cook the birds. But Coyote refused to share any of the game with either his sons or his wife Frog (Blackburn 1980:204-206).

7. Coyote tricks a woman. In a *Rumsen* narrative Coyote
tricked a girl into removing a splinter he had placed into his own eye,
then seized and married her. In Kato, Shasta, and Chumash narratives,
Coyote tricked women into intercourse with various disguises—as a baby,
a woman's fiancé, and a steelhead trout, respectively (Blackburn
1980:194-196; Dixon 1910:34; Goddard 1909:219).

8. The trickster tricked. Coyote finds himself outwitted and
deceived in widely variant ways throughout West-Central California. The
tricks often occur as retaliation for Coyote's bad deeds. Central and
Eastern Pomo narratives find him tricked into such acts as eating offal,
breaking his own leg, burning his own hair, poking out an eye, and
jumping into water. Owl, Sapsucker, Woodcock, Osprey, Mink, the
Skunk Brothers, and Blue Jay, among others, all have a hand in the tricks
(Barrett 1933:242-243, 257-258, 260-270, 280-283, 285, 288).

Rumsen Narratives Recorded by Harrington compared with those of other areas

1. Origin of the world—the deluge. For comparative material
see "*Rumsen* Narratives Recorded by Kroeber Compared with Those of
Other Areas" above.

2. End (origin) of the world—earth diver. This common
motif involves a dive beneath the floodwaters by various Early People in
an effort to find land. At times, more than one dive and more than one
diver were required for success. The diver(s) commonly returned nearly
dead or unconscious, with soil or sand beneath their nails which was
variously talked, dropped, or otherwise made into land.

While the *Rumsen* narratives told to Kroeber, like those of the
Bodega Miwok told to Kelly, lack an earth diver, Hawk dove for earth
in the *Rumsen* narrative told to Harrington (Collier and Thalman
1991:435; Kelly 1978:28-29, 30). Duck(s) dove in extant Salinan,
Ytuhohi (Yokuts as told by a Tachi Yokuts individual), *Gashowu*
(Yokuts), *Dumna* (Northern Foothills Yokuts), *Wukchumne* (Central
Foothills Yokuts), *Wasachi* (Western Mono), and *Wobonuch* (Western
Mono) variants (Gayton and Newman 1940:20, 28, 39-40; Kroeber
1929:275; Mason 1916:82; Kroeber 1907:204, 209-210). Nisenan and
River Patwin narratives designate Frog as the diver (Kroeber 1932:304-
305; Kroeber 1929:275). Turtle acted as earth diver in a *Wukchumne*
Yokuts version related by a *Yaudanchi* Yokuts individual (Kroeber
1907:218).

3. Coyote tricks a woman—procreation with swallowed louse. For comparative material see "*Rumsen* Narratives Recorded by Kroeber Compared with Those of Other Areas" above.

4. Theft of fire—etiological narratives—why certain animals have certain markings. The theft of fire occurs in both Northwest California and Central California, but not in the south (Gayton 1935:538). The goal of the theft variously revolves around acquisition of fire for warmth, light, and/or cooking. The identity and number of the thieves, and the circumstances of the theft vary from group to group. Sometimes the perpetrator(s) already knows who has fire; other times the fire is noticed from a distance. At times, more than one attempt at theft must be made. Commonly, the original owner or owners unsuccessfully track the thief or thieves. The thieves, a helper, or helpers secrete the fire in various plants and stones following the theft. These plants and stones correspond to common and uncommon fire making materials in each group.

In *Rumsen*, Bodega Miwok, and *Chupumne* or *Gualacomne* cognates Hummingbird's chin was marked by the fire he stole (Merriam [1910]:89-90; Collier and Thalman 1981:436; Kelly 1978:30-31). According to a Lake Miwok variant, the Shrew Brothers stole sparks from Crow, then Coyote put the fire into the buckeye tree. Coyote told the people how to rub a buckeye fire drill to make fire come out (Merriam [1910]:149-151). A Northern Miwok narrative describes how White-footed Mouse stole fire from the Red-Breasted Robin, its keeper for the Valley People of the San Joaquin Plain, by putting it in his elderberry flute. Coyote later caused some of the fire to become the Sun. The people stored what remained in buckeye and incense cedar trees (Merriam [1910]:48-53).

The Central Miwok near Bald Rock told Merriam how White-footed Mouse stole fire from the Valley People by lulling them asleep with music from his elderberry flute. When Hail and Shower pursued the thief, Mouse hid the coals in a buckeye tree (Merriam [1910]:60-64). In a Central Miwok parallel, Mouse, the flute player, stole fire and hid it in his four flutes. His Early People pursuers eventually quit, and Rain could not put the fire out. Once home, Mouse started a fire in the roundhouse where, depending on how close people sat to the fire, they developed different languages (Berman 1982:76-77). Mouse used four flutes to steal fire in another Central Miwok variant, defeating his Wind, Rain, and Hail pursuers. Upon Mouse's return, the people met him in their assembly house for the fire's distribution. When Coyote prevented everyone from receiving the same amount of fire, they developed different languages (Gifford 1917:284-286). A fourth Central Miwok variant varies in few details. Mouse took only two flutes this time, placing one of them, with its stolen coals, beneath a buckeye tree. The other flute was "taken" by Rain (Gifford 1917:332-33).

According to the *Wukchumne* (Yokuts), after stealing fire, Jackrabbit hid some coals in his ear, giving this animal its present scorched look. To thwart his pursuers Jackrabbit created a hailstorm. Once safely home, he instructed the people how to make fire drills from buckeye. He also showed them how to make fire by striking white rocks of a certain type together. A third *Wukchumne* variant relates that the pursuers, rather than Jackrabbit, made the rainstorm in the hopes of extinguishing the stolen fire (Gayton and Newman 1940:20-21).

The *Dumna* (Northern Foothills Yokuts) state that Jackrabbit hid a coal underneath his tail, then put the fire in rocks and buckeye so it wouldn't be lost again (Gayton and Newman 1940:28). In a *Truhohi* (Yokuts) narrative, as told by a Tachi Yokuts individual, Coyote, Crow, Roadrunner, and Fox cooperated in the theft (Kroeber 1907:211). In a *Michahai* (Central Hills Yokuts) account Bat, a powerful dream helper, stole fire from the killers who controlled it by secreting it in his anus:

> Bat's clothes are of rubber, that's why he didn't get burned. But he was blackened by the charcoal, and has been so ever since (Gayton and Newman 1940:32).

In a *Wobonuch* (Central Hills Mono) narrative, Bat stole fire from the water snakes who lived near the ocean, then invented the fire drill (Gayton and Newman 1940). Kangaroo-rat stole fire in a Salinan (San Antonio dialect) narrative, thereby burning his once-bushy tail (Mason 1918:82-83). A Nisenan narrative relates the exploits of mice, who travelled across the sea, where they stole fire from its condor protectors. *Híkaht*, the weather shaman, put the fire into trees, wood, and stones (Kroeber 1929:276).

In a Shasta version Coyote stole Pain's fire, then passed it on through helpers (Dixon 1910:13-14). In a Kato variant Hummingbird stole fire while Coyote danced to distract its Spider protector (Goddard 1909:195-197). A Central Yana narrative describes how Fox and a bird stole fire while its owners slept. Later Coyote carelessly started a world fire with it (Sapir 1910:31-35). Several Early People with torches stole fire in an Achumawi version. Dog, who secreted the fire in his punk-filled ear, was the only thief to save it from a dousing by rain (Dixon 1908:165).

5. Traversing the world. As part of the Origin of the World cycle, some West-Central California Indian groups describe a world tour.

According to the *Rumsen* version, two bears travelled across the world in opposite directions, naming all the places they came to.

The *Wobonuch* (Central Hills Mono) describe world inspections by Coyote, Elk, and Mountain Sheep. Wolf sent Coyote on two tours of inspection after Coyote instituted a deluge and the world was remade. After the second tour, Coyote reported that the world was large enough. Later, Elk and Mountain Sheep travelled the world in separate directions making mountains. They met up at Wolf's place before going to new homes, Mountain Sheep to the "rough country" and Elk to the valley.

> Coyote now was sent off on another tour of the land, this time to name every place, creek, hill, and so on that he came to. He started down in the valley. He worked very hard and at last returned. Wolf asked him if all was finished. Coyote said it was (Gayton and Newman 1940:39-41).

6. Coyote hunts squirrels. Although differing greatly in details, both the *Rumsen* and Eastern Pomo versions of Coyote's squirrel hunting exploits focus on his trickery. In the latter, Coyote attracted the squirrels by placing abalone shell ornaments on his fingers and holding his arm down their hole. The squirrels retaliated for Coyote's greed in taking more than he needed for food by pulling off his arm. After his arm healed, Coyote tried another method. While the squirrels slept in a dancehouse, Coyote tied their hair together, then roasted them by setting fire to the house. Eventually, the squirrels revived (Barrett 1933:247-249, 251-254).

7. Children's revenge of relative's death. In a *Rumsen* narrative, Bear killed her husband Coyote, who failed to respect her acorn. Bear's children killed her to avenge their father. Perhaps not coincidentally, in Chemehuevi narratives "the Bear People are Coyote's adversaries" (Laird 1984:241).

Cognate Bear and Fawn narratives occur in several versions throughout West-Central California. Typically in these, a mother bear kills a mother deer. After Deer's children discover the killing, they avenge their mother's death by killing Bear and/or her cub or cubs.

In Central Miwok versions, Grizzly Bear killed Deer while removing Deer's head lice. Later, Deer's two fawns, with the help of their grandfather, killed Bear with heated stones (Berman 1982:92-101; Gifford 1917: 286-292; Merriam [1910]:110-112). In a Northern Miwok variant, Grizzly Bear bit Deer's neck and killed her. Deer's fawns realized what happened when they saw their mother's liver in Bear's basket. On the pretense of playing a game, the fawns suffocated Bear's cub in a sealed cave, which they filled with smoke. When Grizzly Bear found out what the fawns had done, she pursued them, but they killed Grizzly Bear with a heated stone (Merriam [1910]:102-109). The Valley Nisenan Bear and Fawn narratives differ in only a few details, featuring Antelope and her two boys rather than Deer and her fawns (Kroeber 1929:277).

8. Coyote punished with thirst. In a *Rumsen* narrative, after Coyote killed some women's babies, he was punished with thirst. In a Chumash variant, as punishment for stinginess, Coyote's wife Frog arranged that he would go thirsty. (Blackburn 1980:206-207).

Rumsen Narrative with Mexican origins Recorded by Ramirez compared with those of other areas

Holding Up the Rock - Moon as Reflected Cheese. The holding up the rock or cliff motif (Aarne-Thompson 1961:1530; Hansen 1957:72U; Robe 1973:1530; Thompson 1919:XIX-I, 24, 25, 26) came in from Mexico through Spain. It also occurs in Africa, Argentina, Chile, Peru, Cape Verde Islands, Croatia, Denmark, Dominican Republic, England, France, Germany, Hungary, Ireland, Latvia, Poland, Puerto Rico, Rumania, Serbia, Slovenia, Turkey, and other parts of the United States (American Indian and non-Indian versions). Characters include humans and various animals—coyote, fox, rabbit, tiger, and lamb (Paredes 1970:56; Robe 1970:74-77, 99-101; Wheeler 1934:509-511; Thompson 1919:420, 425-426; Boas 1912:206, 237).

The version recorded by Alex Ramirez accords well with the California Indian notion of Coyote as a trickster character. As such, it demonstrates an exception to the rule in cognate, California Indian versions, which maintain the original's characterization of Coyote as the tricked. In two cognate Chumash narratives Fox fools Coyote into holding up a rock, and Rabbit fools him into holding up a ravine wall (Blackburn 1980:303, 314). A cognate Wappo narrative fixes Cottontail as the trickster who convinces Coyote to hold up a rock (Radin 1924:11).

The moon as reflected cheese motif (Aarne-Thompson 1961:34 and 1336; Ashliman 1987:34; Boggs 1930:29; Hansen 1957:34; Robe 1973:23, 34, 34B, 34B*, Thompson 1919:XXIVE) also has non-Indian origins, but today is known in many parts of the world. Coyote, and to a lesser extent Fox, are common characters in Mexican and New Mexican versions. As with holding up the rock or cliff, Coyote is the tricked, rather than the trickster where he appears as a character in these (West 1988:90; Espinosa 1976:181-183, 219; Paredes 1970:57-58; Robe 1970:

67-69, 74-77, 90-91, 99-101; Wheeler 1934:511-518, 524-526; Boas 1912:206, 238).

In a *Chukchansi* (Yokuts) version, Stink Beetle fooled Coyote into seeking the cheese, while Skunk and Fox fooled him in Chumash variants, and Cottontail in a Wappo narrative (Blackburn 1980:303-304,306; Rogers and Gayton 1944:199-200; Radin 1924:13). In a Marin Miwok fragment, Coyote dived for the cheese, but Marin Miwok consultant Juanita Carrio did not mention a trickster (Catherine Callaghan, personal communication 8/13/1993).

CONCLUSION

Chocheño and *Rumsen* narratives share motifs and traits with those of groups from other areas, but they have distinctive elements as well. In this study I have sought to highlight the similarities as well as the dissimilarities as a means of clarifying the complexities of California Indian narrative traditions.

Several authors have commented on the similarities and dissimilarities of cognate narratives both within and without California Indian language families and areas. Gayton and Newman (1940:15) had this to say about narrative variances when assessing Yokuts affiliations:

> [Yokuts mythology] is finely enmeshed in the fabric of contiguous western mythology by means of common elements and incidents. But in contrast to their neighbors, who toward the north participate more and more in the mythology of the Southern Plateau and Basin, and toward the south in that of the Southern Basin and Yumans, the Yokuts are the focus of a small area with limited affiliations. The contrast is particularly acute when we envisage the sweeping distribution of cognate tales from Plateau, through the Basin, and into the Southwest, which are absent from the Central California mythologic area.

After comparing numerous California Indian narratives, Gayton (1935:596-597) concluded with the following:

> It must be remembered that in this attempt to envisage intra-California differences in terms of broader cultural wholes, the picture is based on the grosser and more obvious likenesses. However, it seems probable to the writer that an examination of local miscellaneous tales and elements would show cleavages along the same general lines . . .

In any group of tales under consideration, the concepts upon which they are based extend far beyond the horizon, and as attention is turned upon plots, incidents, and elements the view narrows until only local details are in focus. Yet none of the constituents have identical distribution. As in any other phase of culture, the variable provenience of its components makes areal delimitations of mythology a matter of arbitration.

The present study, although limited in scope, has sought to balance "the grosser and more obvious likenesses" of *Chocheño, Rumsen,* and West-Central California Indian narratives against the "cleavages" of difference which provided markers of cultural identity for the members of individual tribal groups.

A statement by Milton Lucas (Kashaya Pomo/Bodega Miwok) helps bring this matter into focus. Commenting on the difference between the way Kashayans told a certain narrative, and the way his Miwok grandfather told it, Lucas had this to say:

> It was told before many, many times in Kashaya people. But I told it according to the way I heard [my Miwok grandpa]. They're a little different. I find out the [Kashaya] people said, "No. It's not that way. It's this way." But that's the only way I heard it (Milton Lucas 1988, personal communication).

When one begins to focus on local "plots, incidents, and elements," as Gayton suggests, the view indeed "narrows until only local details are in focus." There can be no doubt that such details, whether solely the result of different characters within the same plot sequence, or more broadly the result of a complex of divergently nuanced actions, added tremendously to the sense of identity of the members of each tribe. The characters named, the reasons for an animal's markings, the context for the jealousy—these become the salient traits which define local oicotypes.

The association of specific features on the landscape with specific narrative incidents seems particularly telling. Such narratives, by preserving the sacred history of geographical features, undoubtedly brought a heightened sense of identity with and reverence for one's homeland, resulting in a strong sense of place in the world.

As the comparative material suggests, language areas, while useful, don't correspond to cultural realities as recognized and experienced by the people themselves. Within West-Central California Indian narratives, characters, incidents, themes and subthemes converge, diverge, and reorganize themselves in ways that highlight the unique tradition of each tribe. They reveal the extent to which each group's narrative tradition was interwoven with and distinguished from that of their neighbors, and their neighbors' neighbors in turn.

In like fashion, the disparate *Chocheño* and *Rumsen* narrative traditions belie an undoubtedly much more diverse narrative tradition among the 50 to 60 tribes inhabiting the Ohlonean language area. The paucity of extant Ohlonean narratives, however, makes it impossible to discern the level of distinctiveness that would enable one to reach definitive conclusions about the nature of this diversity. Because the identity of the teller is often unknown, as is the identity of the teller's teacher, the tribal origin of given narrative remains elusive. In the few *Rumsen* cases where more than one version of a narrative exists, it hasn't been possible to ascertain with certainty whether the variation results from differences in the day to day telling, from differences in how well the tellers remembered the narratives, or in oicotypes.

What is certain, however, is that knowing *Chocheño* or *Rumsen* narrative traditions does not accord with having knowledge of the narrative tradition of all Ohlonean speakers. In this sense, the current study underscores the peril of characterizing the narrative tradition of an entire California Indian language family or language area on the basis of one small corpus of narratives from a single individual or a few individuals. It also underscores the need to elucidate the tribal backgrounds of tellers, not just their language affiliations, as well as who they learned a given narrative from, to facilitate the identification of oicotypes which can amplify the diversity of narrative traditions.

This study suggests that a wider comparative reexamination of the unity, diversity, and meanings of California Indian narrative traditions is in order, work that was begun by Demetracopoulou and Du Bois (1932), Barrett (1933:465-490), Demetracopoulou (1933:101-128), Gayton (1935:582-599), and Gayton and Newman (1940:11-17, 53-105). Such work is needed on the level of the individual narrative, and on a tribal, regional, and extra-California basis.

Acknowledgements

Special thanks to Catherine Callaghan, Malcolm Margolin, Randall Milliken, Alex Ramirez, and Linda Yamane, who all reviewed and commented on portions of the manuscript; to William S. Simmons for calling my attention to the non-Indian origins of the Ramirez narrative; Dorothea Theodoratus for providing access to her copy of the C. Hart Merriam journals; Alan Dundes for calling my attention to the 1917 Boas article; and to Mary Praetzellis for calling my attention to the *Livermore Herald* article.

REFERENCES CITED

Aarne, A., and Thompson, Stith
    1961   The Types of the Folk-tale. Folklore Fellows Communi-
                    cations 184. 2nd revision. Helsingfors.

Angulo, Jaime de, and Freeland, L.S.
    1928   Miwok and Pomo Myths.   The Journal of American
                    Folklore 41(160):232-252.

Anonymous
    1859   The Indians of Santa Barbara and the Original California
                    Mint. The San Francisco Herald 10(176):1/2. December
                    11.

Anonymous
    1928   Beauties of Brushy Peak Attract Interest.   Livermore
                    Herald, 3/8-9. September 14.

Ashliman, D. L.
    1987   A Guide to Folktales in the English Language Based on
                    the Aarne-Thompson Classification System. Biographies
                    and Indexes of World Literature. New York: Green-
                    wood Press.

Barrett, Samuel A.
    1919   Myths of the Southern Sierra Miwok.   University of
                    California Publications in American Archaeology and
                    Ethnology 16(1):1-28. Berkeley.

    1933   Pomo Myths. Bulletin of the Public Museum of the City
                    of Milwaukee 15.

Bascom, William
    1965   The Forms of Folklore: Prose Narratives. The Journal
                    of American Folklore 78:3-20.

Beechey, Captain F.W.
    1831   Narrative of a Voyage to the Pacific and Beering's Strait
                    to Cooperate with the Polar Expeditions Performed in his
                    Majesty's Ship Blossom, Under the Command of Captain

F.W. Beechey, R.N. F.R.S. & C. in the Years 1825, 26, 27, 28. London: Henry Colburn and Richard Bentley.

Beeler, Madison S.
1961   Northern Costanoan. International Journal of American Linguistics 27(3):191-197.

Berman, Howard, ed.
1982   Freeland's Central Sierra Miwok Myths. Survey of California and Other Indian Languages Report 3:1-135. Berkeley.

Blackburn, Thomas C., ed.
1980   December's Child, A Book of Chumash Oral Narratives Collected by J.P. Harrington. Berkeley: University of California Press.

Boas, Franz
1912   Notes on Mexican Folk-Lore. Journal of American Folklore 25(48):204-260.

1917   The Origin of Death. The Journal of American Folk-lore 30(68):486-491.

Bocek, Barbara
1984   Ethnobotany of Costanoan Indians, California, Based on Collections by John P. Harrington. Economic Botany 38(2):240-255.

Boggs, Ralph S.
1930   Index of Spanish Folktales. Folklore Fellows Communications 90.

Brunvand, Jan Harold
1981   The Vanishing Hitchhiker, American Urban Legends and Their Meanings. New York: W. W. Norton and Company.

Calhoun, Merilyn
1973   Early Days in the Livermore-Amador Valley. Hayward, CA: Alameda County School Department.

Chapman, Frank M.
1903   Color Key to North American Birds.   New York:
               Doubleday, Page and Company.

1912   Color Key to North American Birds.   New York:
               Doubleday, Page and Company.

Collier, Mary E. T., and Sylvia Barker Thalman, eds.
1991   Interview with Tom Smith and Maria Copa, Isabel
               Kelly's Ethnographic Notes on the Coast Miwok Indians
               of Marin and Southern Sonoma Counties, California.
               San Rafael, CA: Miwok Archeological Preserve of
               Marin.

Demetracopolou, Dorothy
1933   The Loon Woman Myth: A Study in Synthesis. Journal
               of American Folklore 46(180):101-128.

Demetracopolou, Dorothy, and Cora A. Du Bois
1932   A Study of Wintu Mythology.   Journal of American
               Folklore 45(178):375-500.

Dixon, Roland B.
1908   Achomawi and Atsugewi Tales.   Journal of American
               Folklore 21:159-171.

1910   Shasta Myths. Journal of American Folklore 23(87):8-
               37(89):364-370.

Espinosa, José Manuel
1976   Spanish Folk-Tales from New Mexico.   Millwood, New
               York: Kraus Reprint Company. Originally published,
               1937.

Gayton, Anna H.
1935   Areal Affiliations of California Folktales.   American
               Anthropologist. 37(4):582-599.

Gayton, Anna H. and Newman, Stanley S.
1940   Yokuts and Western Mono Myths.   Anthropological
               Records 5(1):1-109.

Gifford, Edward Winslow
1917   Miwok Myths. University of California Publications in American Archaeology and Ethnology 12(8):283-388. Berkeley.

1927   Southern Maidu Religious Ceremonies. American Anthropologist 29(3):214-257.

Goddard, Pliny E.
1909   Kato Texts. University of California Publications in American Archaeology and Ethnology 5(3):65-238. Berkeley.

Hansen, Terrence Leslie
1957   The Types of the Folktale in Cuba, Puerto Rico, the Dominican Republic, and Spanish South America. Folklore Studies 8. Berkeley: University of California Press.

Harrington, John Peabody
[n.d.]   [Linguistic and Ethnographic Field Notes of Chocheño, 1921, 1929, 1930.] (Copy in possession of author.)

[n.d.a]   [Linguistic and Ethnographic Field Notes of the Rumsen, 1922, 1929-1939.] On file at the Smithsonian Institution; microfilm copy at San Jose State University.

1942   Cultural Element Distributions: XIX Central California Coast. Anthropological Records 7(1):1-44.

H.B.D.
1859   Tradition of the California Indians. Hesperian Magazine 3:326.

Heizer, Robert F., and Karen M. Nissen
1973   The Human Sources of California Ethnography. Berkeley: Archaeological Research Facility, Department of Anthropology, University of California.

Henshaw, Henry W.
1955   California Indian Linguistic Records: The Mission Indian Vocabularies of H.W. Henshaw. University of California Anthropological Records 15(2):85-202.

Herrera-Sobek, Maria
1988   The Devil in the Discotheque. *In* A Semiotic Analysis
               of a Contemporary Legend, Monsters with Iron Teeth,
               Perspectives on Contemporary Legend Volume III,
               Gillian Bennett and Paul Smith, eds., pp. 147-157.
               Sheffield Academic Press.

Kelly Isabel T.
1978   Some Coast Miwok Tales.   Journal of California
               Anthropology 5:21-41.

Kroeber, Alfred
[1902]   [Linguistic and Ethnographic Field Notes of the
               Rumsen.]   Field Notebook on file at Linguistics
               Department, University of California at Berkeley.

[1902a]   [Correspondence to the Honorary Advisory Committee,
               Department of Anthropology, University of California,
               from New York, November 8, 1902, Report for
               September 1901 - 1902.] Correspondence and Papers on
               file at The Bancroft Library.

[1904-1909]   [Moquelumnan/Costanoan/Yokuts Linguistic and
               Ethnographic Field Notes.] Field Notes on file at The
               Bancroft Library, Carton 6, Book 52, University of
               California at Berkeley.

1904   The Languages of the Coast of California South of San
               Francisco.   University of California Publications in
               American Archaeology and Ethnology 2(2):29-80.
               Berkeley.

1907   Indian Myths of South Central California. University of
               California Publications in American Archaeology and
               Ethnology 4(4):169-249. Berkeley.

1908   Catch-Words in American Mythology. The Journal of
               American Folklore 21:222-227.

1910   The Chumash and Costanoan Languages. University of
               California Publications in American Archaeology and
               Ethnology 9(2):237-271. Berkeley.

[1914]   [Linguistic and Ethnographic Notes on the Costanoan.]
                Field Notes on file at The Bancroft Library, University
                of California at Berkeley.

1929   The Valley Nisenan. University of California Publica-
                tions in American Archaeology and Ethnology 24(4):253-
                290. Berkeley.

1932   The Patwin and Their Neighbors. University of
                California Publications in Archaeology and Ethnology
                29(4):253-423. Berkeley.

Laird, Carobeth
1984   Mirror and Pattern, George Laird's World of Chemeh-
                uevi Mythology. Banning, CA: Malki Museum Press.

Levy, Richard
1978   Costanoan. *In* Handbook of North American Indians,
                Volume 8, Robert F. Heizer, ed., pp. 485-495. William
                C. Sturtevant, gen. ed. Washington D.C.: Smithsonian
                Institution.

Librado, Francisco
1980   Breath of Sun: Life in Early California as Told by a
                Chumash Indian, Fernando Librado, to John P.
                Harrington, Travis Hudson, ed. Banning: Malki
                Museum Press and Ventura County Historical Society.

1981   The Eye of the Flute, Chumash Traditional History and
                Ritual as Told by Fernando Librado Kitsepawit to John
                P. Harrington, Edited with Notes by Travis Hudson,
                Thomas Blackburn, Rosario Curletti, and Janice
                Timbrook. Banning: Malki Museum Press and Santa
                Barbara: Santa Barbara Museum of Natural History.

Lowie, Robert H.
1908   Catch-Words for Mythological Motives. The Journal of
                American Folklore 21:24-27.

Mason, J. Alden
1916   The Mutsun Dialect of Costanoan Based on the
                Vocabulary of De La Cuesta. University of California

Publications in American Archaeology and Ethnology 11(7):399-472. Berkeley.

[1916a]   [Reports on Trips Made by J. A. Mason, October 1916 to San Juan Bautista and Watsonville to See Costanoan Informants and to Valley to Obtain Suisun and Wintun Vocabularies.] (Typescript report on file at The Bancroft Library, University of California at Berkeley.)

1918   Language of the Salinan Indians. University of California Publications in American Archaeology and Ethnology 14(1):1-154. Berkeley.

Merriam, C. Hart
[1904]   Ethnography, Material Culture, and Vocabularies of the Ohlone/Costanoan Indians. Manuscript on file at The Bancroft Library, University of California at Berkeley.

[1905]   Ethnography, Material Culture, and Vocabularies of the Ohlone/Costanoan Indians. Manuscript on file at The Bancroft Library, University of California at Berkeley.

[1909a]   Journals, California, November 15, 1909, page 7. On file at Manuscript Division, Container numbers 6-21, Library of Congress, Washington D.C.

[1910]   The Dawn of the World, Myths and Tales Told by the Mewan Indians of California. Cleveland: Arthur H. Clark. Republished as The Dawn of the World, Myths and Tales of the Miwok Indians of California, 1993 by University of Nebraska Press, Lincoln, Nebraska.

1967   Ethnographic Notes on California Indian Tribes, Part III. Robert F. Heizer, editor. University of California Archaeological Survey Reports 68. Berkeley.

Milliken, Randall
[1991]   An Ethnohistory of the Indian People of the San Francisco Bay Area from 1770 to 1810. Unpublished Ph.D. Dissertation, University of California, Berkeley.

1987   Ethnohistory of the Rumsen. Papers in Northern
                California Anthropology 2. Berkeley, CA: Northern
                California Anthropological Group.

Mills, Elaine, ed.
1985   The Papers of John Peabody Harrington in the Smithso-
                nian Institution 1907-1957, Volume Two, A Guide to the
                Field Notes, Native American History, Language and
                Culture of Northern and Central California. White
                Plains, New York: Kraus International Publications.

Munz, Philip A.
1973   A California Flora with Supplement. Berkeley:
                University of California Press.

Ortiz, Beverly R.
[1991]   An Ethnohistory and Sacred Geography of Mount
                Diablo. Manuscript in possession of author.

[1994]   The Devil's Deformed Feet: A Study in Symbolism.
                Manuscript in possession of author.

Paredes, Américo, ed.
1970   Folktales of Mexico. Chicago, London: The University
                of Chicago Press.

Radin, Paul
1924   Wappo Texts. University of California Publications in
                American Archaeology and Ethnology 19(1):1-47.
                Berkeley.

Ramirez, Alex O.
1991   Tjatjakiymatchan (Coyote), A Legend from Carmel
                Valley. Carmel Valley, CA: Carmel Valley Indian
                Cultural Center.

Robe, Stanley
1970   Mexican Tales and Legends from Los Altos. Folklore
                Studies 20. Berkeley: University of California Press.

1973   Index of Mexican Folktales Including Narrative Texts
                from Mexico, Central America, and the Hispanic United
                States. Berkeley: University of California Press.

Robe, Stanley, ed.
1980   Hispanic Legends from New Mexico. Berkeley: Univer-
                sity of California Press.

Rogers, Barbara Thrall, and A. H. Gayton
1944   Twenty-Seven Chukchansi Yokuts Myths. Journal of
                American Folklore 57(225):190-207.

Sapir, Edward
1910   Yana Texts, Together with Yana Myths Collected by
                Roland B. Dixon. University of California Publications
                in American Archaeology and Ethnology 9(1):1-235.
                Berkeley.

Shipley, William
1963   Maidu Texts and Dictionary. University of California
                Publications in Linguistics 33. Berkeley.

Taylor, Alexander S.
1860   Indianology of California. The California Farmer and
                Journal of Useful Sciences. First Series. February 22,
                1860-June 29, 1860.

Temple, Sydney
1980   The Carmel Mission. Santa Cruz: Western Tanager
                Press.

Thompson, Stith
1919   European Tales Among the North American Indians, A
                Study in the Migration of Folk-Tales.   Colorado
                Springs: Colorado College Publication.

1955   Motif Index of Folk-Literature.   Bloomington and
                Indianapolis: Indiana University.

West, John O., ed.
1988   Mexican-American Folklore, Legends, Songs, Festivals,
                Proverbs, Crafts, Tales of Saints, of Revolutionaries, and
                More. The American Folklore Series. Little Rock:
                August House.

Wheeler, Howard T.
1934   Tales from Jalisco, Mexico. Memoirs of the American Folklore Society 35.

THE COSTANOAN-YOKUTS LANGUAGE
BOUNDARY IN THE CONTACT PERIOD

Randall Milliken

In this article I will discuss the historic Costanoan (Ohlone) tribelets of Central California's easternmost Coast Range valleys. Modern scholars have assumed that the rough dry hill country that drained eastward into the San Joaquin Valley was the homeland of Yokuts-speaking tribelets at the time of the Spanish arrival. Such was not the case. Costanoan-speaking tribelets inhabited the eastern Coast Range hills from Kellogg Creek near Mount Diablo south to Panoche Creek.

Figure 5.1 illustrates my current understanding of contact-period Costanoan tribal locations. Few of the groups shown on the map were documented by the early twentieth century ethnographers, A. L. Kroeber, J. P. Harrington, or C. Hart Merriam. Most of the tribal locations shown on the map were discovered through analysis of information in Spanish period mission records. In this article I will discuss in detail only the eastern Coast Range Costanoan-speaking tribelets, reserving discussion of the greater part of the Costanoan-speaking area for a later article. As a preface to the discussion, I will first discuss previous scholarly publications pertinent to the matter.

TWENTIETH CENTURY COSTANOAN ETHNOGEOGRAPHY

In 1925 A. L. Kroeber published the first ethnographic study of the part of west Central California in his landmark *Handbook of the Indians of California*. Kroeber's (1925:465) map of the area showed hypothetical Costanoan dialect areas. Regarding the eastern boundary of the Costanoan-speaking tribelets, he wrote:

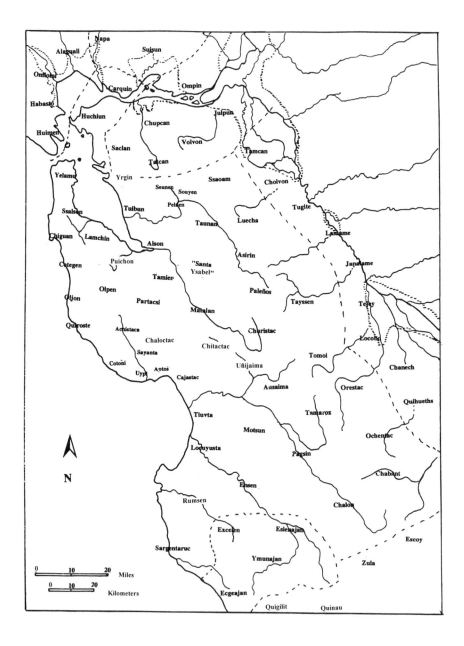

Figure 5.1. Contact-period Costanoan tribal locations

The Costanoan limits inland are not precisely known. They have sometimes been asserted, or loosely assumed, to have been formed by the San Joaquin River, but it is far more probable that the boundary was constituted by the interior chain of the coast ranges, the Mount Diablo Range of the maps (Kroeber 1925:462).

Kroeber's 1925 map placed the eastern boundary along the Coast Range spine. Although he acknowledged in his text that he was guessing, the mapped boundary set a precedent for the interpretation of Costanoan tribal distribution that has been followed to this day.

Richard Levy (1978:485), following Kroeber, placed the Costanoan-Yokuts boundary along the central Coast Range ridge in his "Costanoan" chapter in the *California* volume of the *Handbook of North American Indians*. And in the "Northern Valley Yokuts" chapter in the same volume, William J. Wallace (1978:462) duly assigned the eastward-facing slopes of the Coast Range to Yokuts-speaking peoples. Neither author offered any solid information for his determination.

Frank Latta (1977:122) also agreed with Kroeber that the eastern side of the Coast Range was held by Yokuts-speaking tribelets. In his *Handbook of Yokuts Indians* he flatly states that specific Yokuts-speaking tribelets held various creek drainages of the eastern Coast Range. For instance, he wrote that the *Cholbumne* tribelet "occupied Livermore Valley and controlled the trails over Altamont, Patterson and Corral Hollow passes, Crane Ridge and through Mocho Canyon" (Latta 1977:82). He stated that eastern Coast Range lands further south were also held by Yokuts-speakers.

The Hoyumne and Miumne ranged from the San Joaquin River west to the summit of the inner Mount Diablo range of the Coast Mountains. They controlled the great basin of Orestimba Creek, also San Antonio Valley and the country immediately north of that area (Latta 1977:127).

Latta's information about the Coast Ranges came from Tony Aguila, a cowboy who had been born in 1848 (Latta 1977:130-136). Aguila had heard stories from Indian cowboys during his youth. None of Aguila's informants ever claimed to be Yokuts speakers. Mission San Jose registers show that two of them, José and Lupe, were descended from *Pascasio*, a Costanoan-speaking *Ssaoam* (SJO-B 1238, 6169, 7380). Latta merely assumed, as had so many others, that the eastern Coast Range flanks had been held by Yokuts speakers.

RECONSTRUCTING TRIBAL GEOGRAPHY

The tribal areas shown in Figure 5.1 were reconstructed from vague, occasionally contradictory, information found in entries in the registers of baptisms, marriages, and deaths of Missions San Jose, Santa Clara, Santa Cruz, San Juan Bautista, and Soledad. The missionary priests at Missions San Jose, Santa Cruz, San Juan Bautista, and Soledad wrote down the names of the village or tribelet of each of their converts. Unfortunately, the missionaries seldom provided any direct clues about the whereabouts of such villages or tribelets.

I determined tribelet locations from mission register clues organized on the basis of two key assumptions.

1.   Tribelets that first appeared in the mission record entries lived closer to the missions than tribelets that followed them in the mission record entries.

2.   Tribelets that were heavily intermarried with one another lived adjacent to one another.

On the basis of these assumptions, a lattice-work of probable spatial relations was reconstructed for the groups named in the mission registers (see Milliken 1991).

Mission Santa Clara information presented a special problem for this type of geographic reconstruction. During the 1777-1804 period, the missionary priests at that mission failed to identify the village or tribelet homelands of their new neophytes. Instead, they divided the landscape into arbitrary territories, to which they assigned Spanish names. All people from the hills directly east of the Santa Clara Valley were noted in the Mission Santa Clara Baptismal Register as being from the district of "San Antonio," irrespective of their tribal affiliation.

Fortunately, more explicit home tribelet identification was provided for new neophytes baptized in the Mission Santa Clara registers from 1805 forward. The newly arriving *Luechas* from the northeast and *Tayssens* from the southeast were explicitly identified in their baptismal entries from 1805 through 1811. Some "San Antonio" people continued to be baptized through 1811. But another mission register source helps us understand which tribelets were represented under the rubric "San Antonio." "San Antonio" district people who died during the 1810-1830 period were identified in the death registers as being members of three groups, *Paleños*, *Juñas*, and *Bolbons*. By application of the distance rule, it becomes clear that the *Paleños* were the westernmost of the "San

Antonio" groups, the *Bolbons* the easternmost. The *Bolbons* themselves were intermarried with the *Luechas* to their north and the *Tayssens* to their south. Thus the tribelet relations east of the Santa Clara Valley become clear.

IDENTIFYING TRIBAL LANGUAGE AFFILIATIONS

The language affiliations of the mission period tribelets must also be determined by indirect means. In letters and reports, the missionary priests often mentioned the bewildering mixture of languages and dialects in Central California. But they did not provide systematic lists of tribelets identified by language group. We do have a note written by Father Felipe Arroyo de la Cuesta at Mission San Juan Bautista which indicates that *Chabant* and *Orestac* tribelets of the eastern Coast Range spoke dialects of the same language as that spoken by the *Motsuns* of Mission San Juan Bautista, i.e. Costanoan.

Father Arroyo's note was in the form of an addition to his list of the first ten numerals in the *Motsun* idiom. I provide here the list and note as presented in the published version of Father Arroyo's 1815 *Gramatica Mutson* (Arroyo de la Cuesta [1815] 1861:16).

Hemetcha	*uno*	
Utsgin	*dos*	
Capjan	*tres*	
Utsit	*cuatro*	
Parue	*cinco*	
Naquichi	*seis*	
Tsaquichi	*siete*	
Taittimin	*ocho*	
Pacqui	*nueve*	*Guatsu (Orestacos: Chapantines)*
Tancsegte	*diez*	*Matsu (" ")*

I assume that the "*Chapantines*" were the *Chapanas* of Mission San Juan Bautista baptismal records and the *Chabants* of the Mission Soledad records. No such direct clues regarding language affiliation are available for the other eastern Coast Range tribelets.

The language spoken by the other eastern Coast Range groups has been determined through an indirect method, analysis of female personal name sound elements. Just as Swedish personal names are constructed from sound elements very different from those in Italian personal names, so too were Costanoan personal names very different from Yokuts

personal names. The most consistent and easily analyzable differences
are in the suffixes of female personal names (see Bennyhoff 1977:38-41).
    Costanoan-speaking populations can be identified by the presence
of the suffix constellation "{vowel}+m/n" on at least ten percent of their
female names. Example names are *Ajuan, Pugam, Lotchem, Pispin,
Attiom*, and *Saicúm*. The "{vowel}+m/n" suffix occurred on 73% of the
female names among the *Sayanta, Chaloctac*, and *Partacsi* groups who
lived in the mountainous country between the Santa Cruz and the Santa
Clara Valley. The signature "{vowel}+m/n" suffix became less common
as one proceeded to the east and south from the Santa Cruz Mountains.
Table 5.1 contrasts core area Costanoan-speaking tribelets, eastern Coast
Range tribelets (Costanoan), and western San Joaquin Valley tribelets
(Yokuts-speakers), with respect to the percentage of female names ending
with "{vowel}+m/n."

**TABLE 5.1. PERCENTAGE OF FEMALE PERSONAL NAMES
ENDING WITH THE SUFFIX "{VOWEL}+M/N" AMONG
SELECTED COSTANOAN-SPEAKING TRIBELETS AND
YOKUTS-SPEAKING TRIBELETS AT THE BEGINNING OF THE
NINETEENTH CENTURY**

Sample Coastal Area and Central Area Costanoan Tribelets		Eastern Coast Range Costanoan Tribelets		West San Joaquin Yokuts Tribelets	
Tuibun (Fremont)	25%	*Ssaoam*	28%	*Tamcan*	3%
Ssalson (San Mateo)	50%	*Luecha*	27%	*Cholvon*	0%
Tamien (Santa Clara)	53%	*Bolbon*	17%	*Tugite*	6%
Oljon (San Gregorio)	67%	*Tayssen*	21%	*Lamame*	0%
Uñijaima (Gilroy)	53%	*Tomoi*	22%	*Locobo*	0%
Uypi (Santa Cruz)	38%	*Orestac*	31%	*Chanech*	5%
Pagsin (Paicines)	29%	*Ochentac*	18%	*Quihueths-*	
Rumsen (Carmel)	17%	*Chabant*	10%	*Cutocho*	3%

    There is no doubt that the westernmost San Joaquin Valley
groups spoke dialects of the Yokuts language, although I cannot
demonstrate that fact at this time through female personal name analysis.
I have yet to differentiate signature suffix constellations specific to the
Northern Valley Yokuts groups. But there are other clues about the
distribution of Yokuts in the San Joaquin Valley. Alphonse Pinart
([1894] 1955) recorded a Northern Valley Yokuts "*Tcholovone*"
vocabulary in Pleasanton, California in 1880 from a descendent of the

Cholvon tribelet of the western edge of the San Joaquin Valley in the present Tracy vicinity.   Farther to the south, Arroyo de la Cuesta explicitly identified the *Quihueths* and *Cutocho* people of the western edge of the San Joaquin Valley in present Fresno County as speakers of *Lathruunun*, his name for the Yokuts language (Arroyo de la Cuesta [1821-1837]: November 1827 entry).

Thirty-one percent of the *Orestac* women baptized at Mission San Juan Bautista between 1798 and 1807 had names which ended with a "{vowel}+m/n" suffix, while only 5% of the women's names from their San Joaquin Valley neighbors, the *Chanech (alias Yeurata)*, ended with a "{vowel}+m/n" suffix.   The contrast between hill and plains groups is not so strong in other areas.   Only ten percent of the *Chabant* female personal names ended with "{vowel}+m/n".   This is not surprising, since they were the most distant Costanoan-speaking group from the core area of the "{vowel}+m/n" suffix distribution.   Note that the "{vowel}+m/n" suffix appeared on only seventeen percent of the female names among the Costanoan-speaking *Rumsens* of the Carmel Valley.   I interpret the presence of occasional Costanoan personal name suffixes among the *Tugite*, *Chanech*, and *Cutocho* to intermarriage out onto the San Joaquin Plain by women from Costanoan-speaking hill groups.

THE EASTERN COSTANOAN TRIBELETS

Ssaoam

The *Ssaoam* tribelet lived in the dry hills and tiny valleys around Brushy Peak and Altamont Pass, hill lands which separated the Livermore Valley from the San Joaquin Valley.   They went to Mission San Jose from 1802 through 1805, eighty-seven between October of 1804 and February of 1805.   Only one *Ssaoam* went to Mission San Francisco, a man married into a large group of Bay Miwok-speaking *Tatcans* (SFR-B 2989).   The *Yuliens*, a small group of nineteen people who went to Mission San Jose from 1803 to 1808, seem to have been a sub-group or alias name of the *Ssaoams*.   Of six young *Yuliens* baptized in February of 1804, four had parents baptized a year later and identified as *Ssaoams* (SJO-B 1094,1095,1101, 1102), while two had parents baptized just six months later and identified as *Yuliens* (SJO-B 1095,1096).   The latter two had grandparents who were *Ssaoams* (SJO-B 903,1263,1279).

Most documented pre-mission marriages of the *Ssaoam/Yuliens* were with other Coast Range groups, two with the *Luechas* to their southeast, one with the *Taunans* to their south, one with the *Souyens* to the southwest, one with the *Tatcans* to the west, and one with the

Volvons to the northeast. Additionally, two intermarriages to San Joaquin Valley groups were noted, one with the *Cholvons* to the east, and one with the *Julpuns* to the northeast.

Luecha

I place the *Luechas* at Corral Hollow and Arroyo Mocho in the rough lands southeast of the Livermore Valley, overlooking the San Joaquin Valley, on the basis of their intermarriage pattern with surrounding groups (cf. Cook 1957:144). The placement is substantiated by information provided by José María Amador during the 1860s. He reported that they had lived "four or five leagues" (twelve miles) east of Livermore (1957:144). That would place them in the Patterson Pass area just north of Corral Hollow.

The *Luechas* have a special place in the history of native resistance to western expansion. They are the only Coast Range group to have killed a Spanish invader in their territory. In early February of 1805 they attacked a small party of Spaniards and Mission San Jose Indians who were passing up Arroyo Mocho in search of an *Asirin* village. They killed Mission San Jose steward Ygnacio Higuera and three Mission San Jose Indians, dismembering their bodies (SJO-B 537-540). The event led to a series of Spanish retaliatory expeditions in the spring of 1805. Most of the *Luechas* went in to Mission Santa Clara over the two years following battles in the spring of 1805. A smaller number went to Mission San Jose.

The *Luechas* at Mission Santa Clara were intermarried with *Taunans* (one marriage), *Asirins* (two marriages), and *Bolbons* (two marriages) of the hills, as well as the *Pitemes* (one marriage), a sub-group of either the *Josmites* or *Tugites* of the San Joaquin River. The *Luechas* who went to Mission San Jose were intermarried with the *Ssaoams* to their northeast (two marriages) and the *Cholvons* of the San Joaquin Plain.

Bolbon

The *Bolbon* tribelet held the steep canyons of the Del Puerto Creek drainage to the east of the Santa Clara Valley, the most rugged landscape in the entire Costanoan language area. They migrated from 1806 through 1811 to Mission Santa Clara, where they were designated "San Antonio" in the baptismal register. Most of them went to the mission in the summer of 1810, making them the last Coast Range group to move to the missions.

The *Bolbons* may actually have been two tribal groups, or a number of small bands not bound together at a tribal level. It is very difficult to judge, because they were identified only as "San Antonio" at baptism, part of a group of 125 married couples and their children from numerous groups lumped together under that designation between 1781 and 1817. Most Central California tribelets sent between twenty and thirty couples to the missions. This suggests that four or five tribelets were represented by the "San Antonio" converts at Mission Santa Clara.

Cross references from other records allow us to isolate three tribal groups within the "San Antonio" district. Beginning in 1811, the San Antonio converts who died at Mission Santa Clara were identified by tribal group. Thirty-nine of them were listed as *Bolbons*, forty-two as *Juñas*, and three as *Palas*. Others continued to be identified at death as San Antonio. The *Paleños*, other types of information indicate, were the nearest San Antonio people to the Santa Clara Valley, absorbed between 1799 and 1803. The next eastern group were the *Juñas* of San Antonio Valley in the midst of the inner Coast Range. The death record cross-references indicate that the last cluster of San Antonio couples baptized at Mission Santa Clara, thirty couples over 1809 and 1810, were the *Bolbons*.

The *Bolbons* at Mission Santa Clara must not be confused with two other Central California tribelets that were also called *Bolbon* by one or another Spanish scribe, the *Volvons* of the Mount Diablo area and the *Cholvons* of the San Joaquin River. On October 22, 1811, a Spanish expedition led by Father Ramón Abella of Mission San Francisco visited at "the village of *Pescadero*, called also of the *Bolbones*" along a fork of the San Joaquin River north of the present city of Tracy (Argüello [1811] 1960:262). They were actually in the territory of the Yokuts-speaking *Cholvons*, a tribelet that appears in the Mission San Jose records.

The confusion between the *Bolbons* of Mission Santa Clara and the *Volvons*, Bay Miwok-speakers of the hills east of Mount Diablo, is more difficult to resolve. The letters "b" and "v" were used interchangeably in many words by Spanish writers of the early eighteenth century. Clearly the spellings *Bolbon* and *Volvon* were alternatives of a single native word. Intermarriage patterns of the *Volvons* at Mission Santa Clara and the *Bolbons* of Mission Santa Clara were so different from each other that the only doubt about their separateness resided in the fact that they were both Coast Range groups and they had the same names. However, three "*Volvon del Sur*" people were baptized with *Luechas* and *Cholvons* at Mission San Jose, the home of the Mount Diablo *Volvons* (SJB-B 1360,1657,1935). Those "*Volvons del Sur*" at Mission San Jose were certainly from the Del Puerto Creek *Bolbons*.

The Mission Santa Clara *Bolbons* of Del Puerto Creek were intermarried with *Juñas* of San Antonio Valley (three marriages), *Tugites* (one marriage), and *Lamames* of the San Joaquin River.

Tayssen

The *Tayssens* inhabited a large area centered on the Orestimba Creek drainage. The *Tayssens* converted at Mission Santa Clara between 1803 and 1811, most of them in 1805 and 1806. A small number of them went to Mission Santa Cruz in 1806 and 1807 under the group name *Sumu* (SCR-B 1287, father SCL-B 5236; SCR-B 1302, father SCL-B 4746).

The number of *Tayssen* married couples baptized at Mission Santa Clara, seventy-two, is far more than would be expected for a single tribal group. Typically, west Central California tribelets sent from twenty to thirty couples to the missions. The name *Tayssen* is probably a cover term used by the missionaries for all people from the Crow Creek, Orestimba Creek, and Garzas Creek drainages. Whether they were a cluster of two or three tribelets, or a loose network of nomadic bands is not known.

Tayssens who went to Mission Santa Clara had pre-existing marriages with *Juñas* and *Paleños*. Those who went to Mission Santa Cruz were intermarried with *Tomoi* people. No *Tayssen* converts can be shown to have been married to any San Joaquin River groups at the times of their baptisms. However, large numbers of *Tayssen* widows, widowers, and unmarried young people married *Lamames* and *Janalames* from the San Joaquin at Mission Santa Clara during the 1812-1820 period.

Tomoi

The *Tomoi* tribelet held the valley of San Luis Creek to the east of Pacheco Pass. Most of its members moved to Mission Santa Cruz between 1803 and 1807. This is initially surprising, considering the fact that their homeland was much closer to Mission San Juan Bautista than to Mission Santa Cruz. Their migration to Santa Cruz may have been the result of an antagonism with one of their neighbors who had gone to San Juan Bautista. On the other hand, they may have been routed to Mission Santa Cruz by the missionary priests.

A few *Tomoi* people went to Mission Santa Clara during the 1805-1809 period, and perhaps even earlier. Telesforo of Mission Santa Clara, baptized in 1807 from the "*San Carlos*" district (SCL-B 5252), was identified with *Tomoi* through the later baptism of his mother (see below). According to notes taken by Chester King, Telesforo was himself identified in a later mission padron as being from *Tomoi*. Telesforo's daughter Quarta (SCL-B 5265) was the namesake of Quarto and Quarta, baptized at Mission Santa Clara a month after the last Spanish military sweep through the Coast Range in July of 1805 (SCL-B 4871-4873). The second to last "San Carlos" district convert at Mission Santa Clara, the boy Oton baptized in 1811, was specifically noted to be from "the *ranchería* of Quarto" (SCL-B 5762). He transferred to Mission Santa Cruz, where he was listed as being from "*Tomoy*" at his marriage in 1824 (SCR-M 718).

The last *Tomoi* baptisms at Mission Santa Cruz were in 1808 and 1811. In March of 1808 a *Tomoi* woman was baptized with a group of *Locobos* and *Sachuens* from the San Joaquin River (SCR-B 1397). Two years later a lone fifty year old *Tomoi* man was baptized on June 23, 1811. By that time large groups of Yokuts-speaking *Tejeys* and *Yeuratas* (probably an alias for *Chanech*) from the Gustine-Los Banos areas had moved to Santa Cruz. The very last known *Tomoi* convert was baptized at Mission Santa Clara in 1817. She was a seventy year old woman baptized with San Joaquin River groups, *Pitemes*, *Chipeyquis'* and *Janalames* (SCL-B 6553, indicated both as "*San Carlos*" and "*rancherías de Tomoi*"). The woman was the mother of Telesforo, the "*Tomoy*" man baptized at Mission Santa Clara in 1807.

The *Tomoi* people at Mission Santa Cruz were intermarried with people from the unlocated Coast Range villages of *Acastac* (SCR-B 1086-1112,1097-1200) and *Sitectac* (SCR-B 1080-1106,1084-1110). It should be noted that those two village names may have been references to specific *Tomoi* villages. *Tomoi* people were also intermarried with *Sumus* and *Uclis*, who seem to have been *Tayssens* at Mission Santa Cruz (SCR-B 1314-1315, 1320-1321). And finally, they were intermarried with the *Locobo* tribelet, Yokuts-speakers from the western edge of the San Joaquin Valley, probably where San Luis Creek leaves the hills (SCR-B 1229-1248, 1297-1310).

Orestac

The *Orestac* group lived in the Los Banos Creek drainage and possibly part of the Ortigalita Creek drainage. They went to Mission San Juan Bautista between 1801 and 1807. They sent only 18 married couples to Mission San Juan Bautista, so cannot be projected to have held a very large piece of land (see Figure 5.1). They were heavily intermarried with the *Tamarox*, so much so that I initially considered them to be a single people. Five nuclear family genealogies reconstructed from Mission San Juan Bautista baptismal register cross-references include siblings from both of the groups (parent sets SJB-B 934-316,

1493-1615, 1493-1258, sibling groups SJB-B 807/931, 1054/1743). Also, in a padron kept over the years 1814 to 1821, Father Arroyo de la Cuesta identified eight people as *Orestac* who had been identified as *Tamarox* by other priests at their baptisms years earlier.

Other evidence shows that they were separate groups, although strongly intermarried. In the summer of 1802 a 40 year old man, *Catchupap*, was baptized "of the *ranchería* of the *Orestacos*, in that of the *Tamaroxes*" (SJB-B 934). The statement clearly indicates that *Orestac* and *Tamarox* were two different places. With that statement in mind, I re-examined the genealogies of the five families with siblings from both places. In all five cases the siblings were adults who had probably moved back and forth between the two groups after marriage.

The *Orestac* people who moved to Mission San Juan Bautista were intermarried with *Ochentacs* (three marriages), *Tamaroxes* (three marriages), and *Pagsins* (one marriage). They had no pre-missionization marriages to any San Joaquin Valley groups. However, many of the young unmarried people, widows, and widowers of the *Orestacs* married San Joaquin Valley people from *Nopchinche*, *Eyulahua*, and *Chausila* (SJB-M 564, 609, 700, 870).

Ochentac

The group that I here call *Ochentac* held the Little Panoche and Ortigilata Creek drainages. They went to Mission San Juan Bautista from 1798 to 1807. Individuals from the group were identified by a variety of locational terms, including *Millanistico*, *Guachirron de la Sierra*, *Guachurron-Pagsin*, *Tulareño Guachirron*, and *Ochentac*. Numerous Mission San Juan Bautista family genealogies show that the "*Guachirron de la Sierra*" at that mission are the same people as the *Millanistaco* (sibling set SJB-B 249/276/738/830/1113; parent set SJB-B 1491-1492). Other genealogies show that the "*Guachirron de la Sierra*" are also the same people as the *Ochentac* (sibling sets SJB-B 178/1302, 1795/1796/1996; parent sets SJB-B 1800-1752, 1803-1804, 1805-1640). And other family genealogies indicate that the *Ochentac* and *Millanistaco* people are one and the same (sibling set SJB-B; parent set SJB-B 1491-1492, 1516-1517; family group SJB-B 1508/1509/1518).

The bewildering mix of aliases used for this single *Ochentac* group is a result of alternative names given by a variety of Franciscan missionaries. Between 1797 and 1804 Fathers Gil, Martiarena, Martínez, and Yturrate referred to group members only as "*Guachirrones de la Sierra*." From the summer of 1804 through 1807 Father Dulanto applied "*Ochentac*" and "*Millanistaco*" to separate families, while Father Yturrate applied both terms to siblings within nuclear families. Father Jacinto

López called some members of this group "*Tulareño Guachirrones*" (SJB-B 626-630). In the margin of one entry he noted a man as "*Orestacos o Tamarox*" while in the text of the entry he wrote that the man was from "*la ranchería Mirianixtác*" (SJB-B 635). Finally, Father Arroyo de la Cuesta, who arrived in 1808, soon after the group was absorbed into Mission San Juan Bautista, noted some of these people in later death records and padrons as "*Guachirron Sierra;*" others as "*Ochentac;*" and still others as *Orestacs*.

It is clear that the *Ochentacs* held lands to the south of the *Orestacs*. They were the last Coast Range group to keep a large segment of their population away from Mission San Juan Bautista, an indication that they lived at a relatively great distance from that mission. And many of their members re-aggregated to Mission Soledad within a few years of their baptism, indicating that they lived in an area from which that more southerly mission also drew converts (SJB-B 244, 1014, 1113, 1432, 1505, 1507, 1512, 1516, 1565, 1576).

Ochentacs were intermarried with *Pagsins* (three marriages), *Orestacs* (two marriages), and *Tamaroxes* at the time that they moved to Mission San Juan Bautista. No marriages to *Chabant* can be identified, but such may have occurred among people who moved to Mission Soledad.

Chabant

The *Chabant* tribelet seems to have held the valley of Panoche Creek. They went to Mission Soledad from 1798 through 1806. Three individuals from the group were baptized at Mission San Juan Bautista (spelled *Chapana*). And one man at Mission Santa Cruz was listed as a "*Chapantac*" person in his second wedding, although he was elsewhere said to be from *Tomoi* (SCr-1343). Little more can be mentioned about the group at this time because detailed genealogical relationships have not been carried out for individuals listed in the Mission Soledad vital registers.

CONCLUSION

Costanoan-speaking tribelets inhabited the hill country of Central California's Inner Coast Ranges just west of the San Joaquin Valley at the time of the Spanish invasion in the late eighteenth century. Mission baptismal registers kept by Spanish Franciscan priests provide a record of the numbers of people from the various tribelets and the time periods over which each tribelet migrated from its home area to one or more missions. The information from those registers provides enough evidence to place each tribelet in a general area, but not enough information to delineate specific boundary lines between them.

Mission baptismal register entries also give us the necessary information regarding the language spoken by each of the tribelets. Most Spanish priests wrote down the native personal names of their new neophytes. Large numbers of Costanoan-speaking women had names ending with -am, -em, -im, -om, -um or -an, -en, -im, -om, and -m. The female personal names of Yokuts speakers seldom end with such suffixes. The differences in suffix distributions among the Costanoan-speaking groups suggest that there were only minor dialect differences from one group to the next.

Most of the eastern Coast Range groups sent 18 to 25 couples to the missions. These numbers were similar to multi-village tribelets around San Francisco Bay. On the other hand, territorial areas of eastern Coast Range groups averaged 50% larger than the territories of San Francisco Bay Area tribelets, 100 to 150 square miles. Most individuals found spouses within their own group. Exogamous marriage seems to have been restricted to neighbors from contiguous tribelets. The eastern Coast Range groups made occasional marriages to their Yokuts-speaking neighbors on the plains.

An important area for future consideration is the nature of political organization in the eastern Coast Range area. I have discussed groups with the assumption that they were tribelets, coalitions of unrelated extended families who defended clearly bounded territories against encroachment from neighbors. However, some of the named groups may not have been tribelets. In some rugged areas with limited summer water supplies, people may have dispersed over the landscape in tiny hamlets. Under such circumstances each extended family in a group like the *Tayssens* may have been entirely independent of any higher political authority. It is not likely that new data will be uncovered in the future to resolve this question. But it is important to keep in mind that there are alternative interpretations regarding the nature of social-political life among eastern Coast Range inhabitants at the time of the Spanish invasion of California.

REFERENCES CITED

Mission Register Sources

SCL-B
n.d. *Libro de Bautismos.* Mission Santa Clara. Volume 1. Original on file at the Orradre Library Archives, University of Santa Clara, Santa Clara, California.

SCR-B
n.d. *Libro de Bautismos.* Mission Santa Cruz. Volume 1. Manuscript on file at the Pastoral Office of the Monterey Archdiocese, Catholic Church, Monterey, California.

SJB-B
n.d. *Libro de Bautismos.* Mission San Juan Bautista. Volume 1. Manuscript on file at the Pastoral Office of the Monterey Archdiocese, Catholic Church, Monterey, California.

SJO-B
n.d. *Libro de Bautismos.* Mission San Jose. Volume 1. Original on file at the San Francisco Archdiocese Archives, Colma, California.

SO-B
n.d. *Libro de Bautismos.* Mission Soledad. Manuscript on file at the Pastoral Office of the Monterey Archdiocese, Catholic Church, Monterey, California.

Other Sources

Argüello, Gervasio
[1811] 1960 *Diario de un registro de los ríos grandes* (translated and edited by Sherburne Cook). Pp. 261-265 in Colonial Expeditions to the Interior of California: Central Valley, 1800-1820. University of California Anthropological Records 16(6):239-292. Berkeley.

Arroyo de la Cuesta, Felipe
[1815] 1861   Grammar of the Mutsun Language of Alta California.
               Shea's Library of American Linguistics 8. New York:
               Cramoisy Press. (Translated from the 1815 manuscript
               titled *Gramatica Mutsun*.)

[1821-1837]   *Lecciones de Indios*. (Notebook of grammars and
               vocabularies, recorded between 1821 and 1837 at several
               missions.) 50p. H. H. Bancroft Collection (C-C 63:1).
               Bancroft Library, Berkeley.

Bennyhoff, James A.
1977   The Ethnohistory of the Plains Miwok. Center for
               Archaeological Research at Davis. University of
               California, Davis.

Cook, Sherburne F.
1957   The Aboriginal Population of Alameda and Contra Costa
               Counties, California. University of California Anthropo-
               logical Records 16(4):131-156.

Kroeber, A. L.
1925   Handbook of the Indians of California. Bureau of
               American Ethnology Bulletin 78. Washington, D. C.

Latta, Frank
1977   Handbook of Yokuts Indians. Second Edition. Bear
               State Books: Santa Cruz, California.

Levy, Richard
1978   Costanoan. *In* Handbook of North American Indians:
               Volume 8 (California). Robert F. Heizer, ed., pp. 485-
               495. William C. Sturtevant, gen. ed. Washington:
               Smithsonian Institution.

Milliken, Randall
1991   An Ethnohistory of the Indian People of the San
               Francisco Bay Area from 1770 to 1810. Ph.D. disserta-
               tion at the University of California, Berkeley.

Pinart, Alphonse
[1894] 1955   *Etudes sur les Indiens Californiens. In* Studies of
               California Indians by C. Hart Merriam, edited by the
               staff of the Department of Anthropology. Pp. 133-138.
               University of California Press, Berkeley.

Wallace, William J.
   1978   Northern Valley Yokuts.   *In* Handbook of North
               American Indians: Volume 8 (California).   Robert F.
               Heizer, ed., pp. 462-470. William C. Sturtevant, gen. ed.
               Washington: Smithsonian Institution.

RUMSEN SEASONALITY AND POPULATION DYNAMICS[1]

Gary S. Breschini and Trudy Haversat

Seasonality in archaeological sites along the Central California coast is usually explored by evaluating the physical remains found in those deposits. Indicators such as otoliths (cf. Breschini and Haversat 1988, 1989) or carbonized plant remains, and the presence or absence of particular vertebrate remains or artifacts may provide a reasonable estimate of seasonality.

There is another line of evidence, however, that may contribute corroborating data towards determining the seasonal round during late prehistoric times. This involves the analysis of mission records and other historical accounts. Combined with the archaeological data, these accounts may also contribute significant insights into the validity of theoretical models of past population dynamics.

This paper applies these data to the exploration of seasonality and past population dynamics among the *Rumsen* Costanoan of Central California.

RUMSEN BAPTISMAL RECORDS

At the missions, baptism records contain details on the individual being baptized; frequently included are the person's Indian name, home village or district of residence, and the date. At Carmel Mission, the first aboriginal group encountered was the *Rumsen* Costanoan, as *Rumsen*

[1] Paper presented at The Ohlone Indians of the Bay Area: A Continuing Tradition conference, C.E. Smith Museum of Anthropology, California State University, Hayward, November 14, 1992.

territory was situated in and around the Monterey Peninsula and the lower Carmel Valley.

We have examined *Rumsen* baptisms for seasonality data. Our research was based on the first 1,500 baptisms from Mission San Carlos.[2] On the basis of the analysis of 432 *Rumsen* baptisms, there are thought to have been five principal *Rumsen* villages: *Achasta, Ichxenta, Tucutnut, Socorronda,* and *Echilat* (Figure 6.1). We found that the pattern of *Rumsen* baptisms from these villages was not uniformly dispersed throughout the year. By far the greatest number of baptisms (just over 27%) occurred during the month of July (Table 6.1 and Figure 6.2). While there could be several reasons for this, a major clue is provided by the writing of Junipero Serra.

Serra notes that in July of 1774 there was a festival atmosphere around Carmel Mission when surf smelt spawned on the beach. The Christianized *Rumsens* from the mission joined the non-Christian villagers every day to catch the fish, taking time off from the wheat harvest to do so. People even came to the beach from villages of neighboring tribelets many miles inland. As Serra noted:

> . . . After two weeks of fish eating, on the Sunday following, leaving the sardines in peace, they went hunting for the nests of sea birds that live in the rocks and feed on fish. They caught a lot of young birds which were, generally speaking, as big as good sized chickens. And so they passed Sunday camping on the Carmel beach, divided into countless groups, each with its fire, roasting and eating what they had caught [Serra 1748-84/1955-56:2:142].

During this gathering, on July 27-28, 1774, there were 21 *Rumsen* baptisms. Extending this period through August 15 yields a total of 60 baptisms—nearly 14% of all *Rumsen* were baptized in just over two weeks! Most of these baptisms probably occurred on the coast. The reason for this is simple: the *Rumsen* most likely spent several weeks camped on the coast within easy reach of the missionaries. Of importance to this study, however, is the likelihood that the coastal visit was probably a regular, or even an annual practice for the inland *Rumsen* groups.

Following up on this clue led to similar data for other years as well (Table 6.2). This pattern could not be traced beyond 1778 as there

---

[2] The baptismal data was procured by Randy Milliken for one of our recent projects.

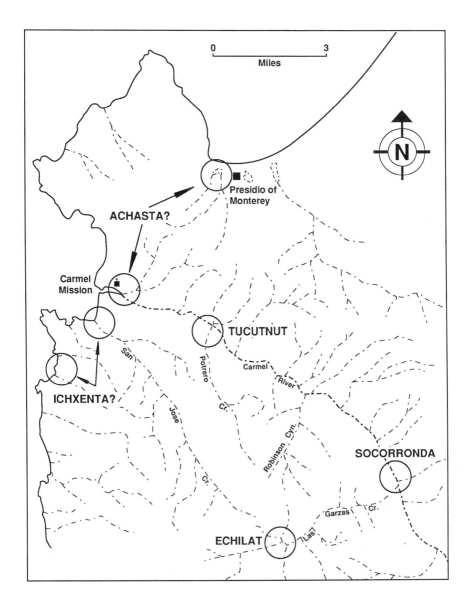

Figure 6.1. *Rumsen* village communities (after Milliken 1992)

TABLE 6.1. *RUMSEN* BAPTISMS BY VILLAGE AND MONTH

	Tucutnut	Achasta	Echilat	Ichxenta	Socorronda	Totals
Dec.	4	6	11	2	5	28
Jan.	19	13	10	7	3	52
Feb.	22	16	7	9	13	67
Mar.	12	11	18	6	8	55
Apr.	9	6	10	2	2	29
May	13	13	0	0	0	26
June	11	1	0	2	1	15
July	41	10	25	10	23	109
Aug.	10	3	7	3	6	29
Sep.	6	0	0	5	2	13
Oct.	1	2	2	0	3	8
Nov.	1	0	0	0	0	1
	149	81	90	46	66	432

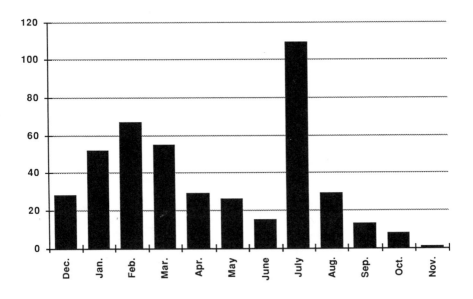

Figure 6.2. Seasonality of *Rumsen* baptisms (n=432)

were no longer enough unbaptized *Rumsens* to continue most aboriginal practices.

Searching the baptismal records for other evidence of seasonality provided additional patterns that, for the most part, apply to the *Rumsen* as a whole and to each of the five *Rumsen* villages individually (see Figures 6.2a through 6.2e).

There is a major drop in baptisms during the months of September, October, and November (only 5% of the baptisms occurred during this quarter of the year). A possible explanation for this parallels the explanation for the increased baptisms during July. During July, the *Rumsens* were camping on the beach within easy reach of the missionaries. During September, October, and November they were probably widely dispersed throughout the hills in search of acorns, and possibly other foods, to store for the winter months. At this time of the year they were much harder for the missionaries to find, and much less likely to sit still long enough to receive the training the missionaries considered necessary for baptism. This pattern appears to apply to all five villages. The month of September has the most baptisms during this quarter, suggesting that the move to the hills began during or late in the month.

During the winter months, approximately December through March, the *Rumsens* were more likely to be sedentary, residing in winter villages where the missionaries could more easily find them and provide the training they considered necessary for baptism. This pattern appears to have applied to all five villages.

An additional period when fewer baptisms occurred was in May and June. While this pattern is not as clearly seen, it is possible that this was another time when populations were more dispersed and mobile, and consequently harder for the missionaries to find and baptize. May and June probably represented an intense gathering period for edible, as well as medicinal and utilitarian plants. During this time of year a number of favored edible plants become available, including clovers, goosefoot, wild peas, lupines, and other species. Some were eaten fresh, while others were stored for future use. This possible pattern did not apply to all villages equally. The data for *Tucutnut* do not appear to exhibit any changes during this period, and the reduction in baptisms at *Ichxenta* applies only to May.[3]

---

[3] The use of baptismal records to establish patterns of seasonal movement has some inherent dangers. For example, when the missionaries baptised numerous *Rumsen* during the months of July and August of 1774, while they were visiting Carmel Beach, they recorded the village where the individuals originated, not where the baptism took place.

TABLE 6.2.
MAJOR PERIODS OF BAPTISMS DURING JULY OR AUGUST

Period	Number of Baptisms
July 18-26, 1773	23
July 27-August 15, 1774	60
July 2-19, 1777	22
July 9-14, 1778	13
Total	118

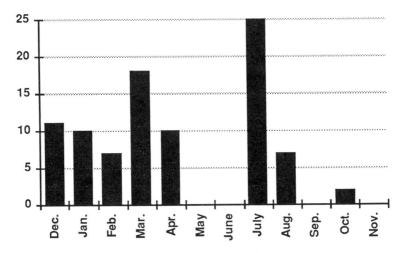

Figure 6.2a. Achasta baptisms (n = 81)

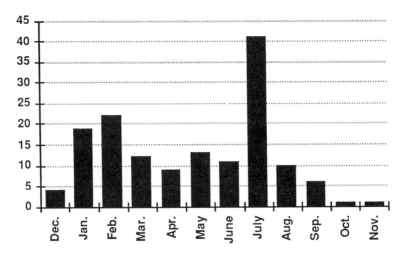

Figure 6.2b. Tucutnut baptisms (n = 149)

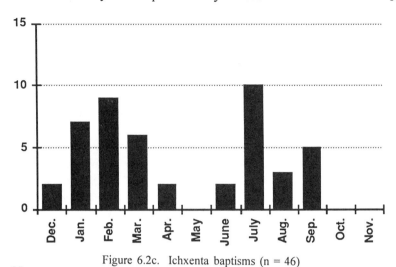

Figure 6.2c. Ichxenta baptisms (n = 46)

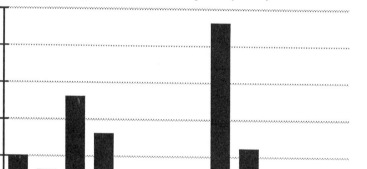

Figure 6.2d. Socorronda baptisms (n = 66)

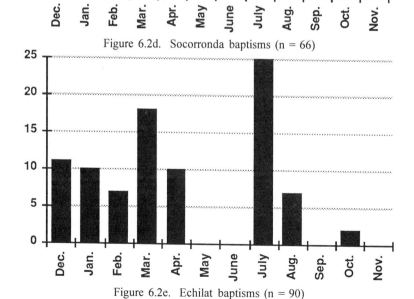

Figure 6.2e. Echilat baptisms (n = 90)

Additional Evidence

We know from recent archaeological research that the inhabitants of *Echilat* had more direct contact, and more exploitation rights, to the coast than previously realized.

However, when the inhabitants of *Echilat* journeyed to the ocean for the annual coastal visit, it would have been natural for them to take suitable gifts for the coastal groups with them. Certainly the Spanish explorers and missionaries mentioned that the Indians always brought gifts of food to them. For example, Culleton (1950:34) notes that the Portolá expedition was camping along the ocean in the area of San Jose Beach on November 30, 1769. The explorers were very hungry, and had little luck in obtaining food until the Indians (almost certainly *Rumsens*) brought gifts of pinole and seeds, which they undoubtedly had stored from earlier in the year. The local Indians "never came to visit the Spaniards without bringing them a substantial present of game, which as a rule consisted of two or three deer or antelopes, which they offered without demanding or even asking for anything (in return)" (Costansó 1769/1910:65-67). On the basis of this, we can expect that the large amount of food that was imported to the *Echilat* area from the coast was only half of a two-way exchange system which also transported food and other resources to the coast.

Given the population movements noted above, it would be logical to assume that some of the *Rumsens* living on the coast or along the Carmel River would travel to *Echilat* or one of the other upland villages during the acorn or seed harvests, and that the inhabitants of *Echilat* would have traveled to the Carmel River for annual salmon or steelhead runs.

Finally, the diaries of both the Vizcaíno (December 13, 1602-January 3, 1603) and Portolá (November 28-December 10, 1769) visits attested that the exposed coast around Monterey and Carmel was deserted during those months of the year. The Vizcaíno expedition mentioned a deserted village on the north bank of the Carmel River about one league (2.6 miles) from where they camped near the mouth of the Carmel River. This village most likely was *Tucutnut*. Diarists on both expeditions mentioned that there were no inhabited villages along the coast in the Carmel and Monterey areas; from this we can conclude that *Achasta* and *Ichxenta* also were deserted during this time of the year. It is likely, then, that the inland villages of *Socorronda* and *Echilat*, and perhaps *Tebityilat* and other villages, were home to a disproportionate number of people during the coldest winter months.

Late Period Coastal Sites

If the *Rumsen* tradition of an annual coastal visit persisted for any significant length of time, a considerable number of distinctive archaeological sites should be found on the coast.

There are two archaeological sites in the Carmel Highlands area which may have functioned as residential bases either during the summer coastal visit or during more extended parts of the year: CA-MNT-156 and CA-MNT-436. CA-MNT-436 has not been dated, but CA-MNT-156 has produced radiocarbon dates of 1100, 1275, and 1370 BP, all on shell (uncorrected).

The activities at these two sites included intensive processing of shellfish as well as exploitation of marine mammals. Some terrestrial resources also were exploited. What is not clear is whether these sites were occupied by inland groups, such as the residents of *Echilat*, during an annual coastal visit, or whether they were used exclusively by local groups, such as the residents of *Ichxenta*. Given the extensive mobility that village groups appear to have enjoyed within *Rumsen* territory, it may be theorized that all of the *Rumsen* groups would have had some access to these sites for at least part of the year.

As noted in Breschini and Haversat (1991), there are numerous Late Period Coastal Shellfish Processing sites extending from Fisherman's Wharf on the north almost to the Little Sur River on the south. It is likely that the coastal visit of the *Rumsen* groups made temporary use of many of these sites. Archaeological sites which have been radiocarbon dated and which appear to meet the criteria for Late Period Coastal Shellfish Processing sites (Breschini and Haversat 1991) are listed in Table 6.3.

The Problem of the
Missing Late Period Villages

On the basis of mission records, there are thought to have been five principal Late Period *Rumsen* villages (*Achasta, Ichxenta, Tucutnut, Socorronda*, and *Echilat*). However, the identification of these villages archaeologically has been a problem. There are a number of likely candidates which have been examined, but in most cases archaeological data suggests a Middle Period date. No single large Late Period villages are known. The closest is a cluster of five or ten sites which together probably constituted the Late Period village of *Echilat*.

The available information suggests that there may have been five principal *Rumsen* villages during the Middle Period. During the Late

TABLE 6.3. RADIOCARBON DATED LATE PERIOD COASTAL SHELLFISH PROCESSING SITES (all dates in this table were obtained from *Haliotis r.* shell, and are uncorrected). Source: Breschini et al. (1992).

Site	Location	Oldest date*
CA-MNT-17	Carmel	1055
CA-MNT-98	Carmel Highlands	770
CA-MNT-108	Monterey	940
CA-MNT-117	Pacific Grove	1040
CA-MNT-118	Pacific Grove	590
CA-MNT-129	Pacific Grove	1220
CA-MNT-148	Pebble Beach	480
CA-MNT-152	Pebble Beach	1080
CA-MNT-160	Pebble Beach	1160
CA-MNT-170	Pebble Beach	880
CA-MNT-240	Pebble Beach	720
CA-MNT-242	Pebble Beach	1080
CA-MNT-438	Carmel Highlands	1020
CA-MNT-445	Carmel Highlands	110
CA-MNT-690	Carmel Highlands	330
CA-MNT-998	Monterey	785
CA-MNT-1084	Pebble Beach	1240
CA-MNT-1331	Carmel Highlands	600
CA-MNT-1348	Carmel Highlands	790
H-418	Pebble Beach	855
AC-1119C	Pebble Beach	610

* This represents the oldest date known for the Late Period component. Several of these sites also contain an unrelated Early Period component.

Period, when the population was larger and much more dispersed, virtually all of the large Middle Period villages appear to have been abandoned. The traditional village names persisted, but were applied to districts by the time the missionaries arrived in 1790.

To date, only one model has been formulated which explains this transition from the Middle to the Late period. This is explored in the following section.

Models of *Rumsen* Culture History

The standard archaeological model of Central California culture history was developed largely by R.F. Heizer and others in the late 1930s and 1940s. Little elaboration or expansion occurred after the mid-1950s. This model, called the Central California Taxonomic System, was based largely on research conducted in the Lower Sacramento Valley, and was initially thought to apply to all of Central California. However, one after another of its major tenets and assumptions have been found to be inaccurate or inapplicable (Gerow 1968; Breschini 1983), and this model has generally fallen into disuse.

This has left the field without any single dominant model, and a series of more specific regional models have been proposed to account for one or more aspects of Central California cultural development.

One provocative way of looking at the prehistory of Central California has been proposed by T.F. King and P.P. Hickman (1973). This model, which was advanced for the San Felipe area of the southern Santa Clara Valley, had earlier been advanced in the form of comments on the evolution of cultural complexity in prehistoric California in general, and in the San Francisco Bay in particular (T.F. King 1970, 1972). This model suggests the following general progression:

1) Nonagricultural societies will become sedentary when a) the variety and seasonal availability of natural foods within the catchment of the occupational site are sufficiently great to obviate the need to travel from place to place to obtain food, or b) social interaction systems are sufficiently developed to move large quantities of food between villages. Other things being equal, sedentary village life will develop in areas where many food resources are available in all seasons.

2) When a hunter-gatherer society becomes sedentary, its population increases, because sedentarism permits a relaxation of population-control systems. When the population reaches a level at which the carrying capacity of the local environment is approached, it becomes necessary for subpopulations to "bud off" and establish new communities.

3) The establishment of new communities in less rich and/or varied environments creates a stressful situation in which readaptation is selected for. Establishment of such communities on lands adjacent to or near those of the parent community (and of one another) creates a condition of social circumscription; under such a condition not only is stress between the growing populations likely to result in conflicts, but such conflict is likely to result in the development of hierarchical rank

systems, both because conquered groups and individuals cannot be expelled but must be integrated into the dominant society as lower classes and because the need to be prepared for warfare selects for highly organized social systems.

4)   An alternative of supplement to warfare as a means of reallocating resources is the development of trade systems among populations occupying varying and complementary environments. Such trade systems, like warfare, require considerable organization both within and between communities.

5)   As organization increases, it becomes possible to widen the circle of interaction to take in more and more groups occupying more and more types of environments and exploiting more and more resources, including non-food resources that facilitate banking and exchange. The operation of the trade system makes possible the support of large sedentary populations in areas whose natural resources may be insufficiently rich, varied, or stable to support such populations by themselves [King and Hickman 1973:72-73].

Researchers in Central California have traditionally expected that connections between the Delta/Bay Area in the north and the Channel Islands/Southern California in the south should be found in the South Coast Ranges. The prehistory of this area has been little known until recently, and in the absence of specific data, researchers have frequently relied on theoretical models.

King and Hickman, for example, provided a series of general theoretical explanations for cultural transmissions during different periods. These are provided as a series of testable propositions "about the possible forms of interaction that went on across the area in prehistoric times, and about the socio-economic concomitants of these kinds of interaction" (King and Hickman 1973:v-3). These testable hypotheses amplify their model of the evolution of cultural complexity cited above. Only those portions dealing with the Middle and Late Periods are included below:

The Middle Horizon: 4000-1500 BP. The Middle Horizon is a time of considerable culture change in both the north and south, but the nature of this change is difficult to generalize about. The establishment of many new villages in new portions

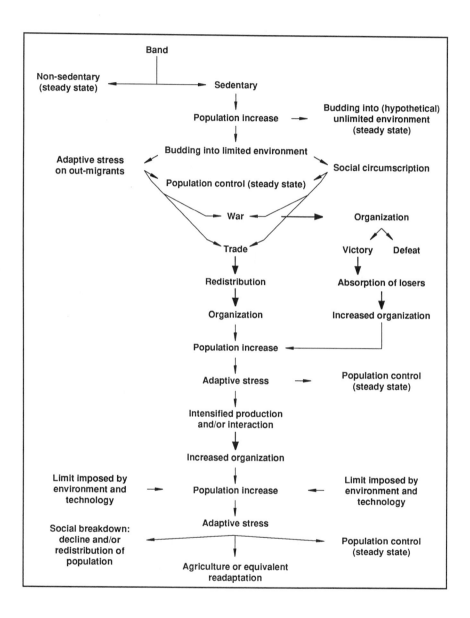

Figure 6.3. Organizational Trajectories of Hunter-Gatherer Societies (adapted from King and Hickman 1973:74). Thickened arrows indicate tendency toward increased political differentiation.

of the state suggests population dispersal, but the size and apparent organization of some Middle Horizon villages suggests nucleation. An expansion of trade is indicated by the widespread dispersal of obsidian from the various eastern and northern California sources, and of shell beads from the coast into the interior, but there is also evidence of considerable specificity in the adaptation of local populations to local environments. Mortuary populations show evidence of both widespread violence and complex political organization.

To place these apparent changes in an interpretive framework, we can propose that the Middle Horizon represents a period when maritime/littoral adaptation along the California coast permitted and impelled a large-scale population increase in sedentary coastal villages, culminating in periodic population pulses into the interior. Populations moving into the new environments would have been under pressure to experiment with methods of readaptation, to interact with other groups, and to maintain trade and other ties with coastal villages. This process . . . may be responsible for the Middle Horizon as we know it.

If this reconstruction is accurate, we should find on the central coast that the Middle Horizon is a time of large, centralized village formation. There should be evidence of the use of many environmental niches, and there should be considerable evidence of contact—amical and enmical—with the interior.

The Protohistoric: 1500-400 BP. During the protohistoric period in northern and southern California, there is evidence for rapid socio-economic change. The clam disc bead economy appears, and clam discs are adopted as currency across broad parts of the north, while in the south a proliferation of *Olivella* money beads occurs. There are suggestions of shifts in coast-interior trade patterns; for example, the use of obsidian from the east of the Sierra Nevada drops sharply in the Chumash area after the Middle Horizon.

A possible means of accounting for these changes is to propose that, in some major parts of the state at least, the protohistoric period is one of social breakdown, in which inflation and individual economic initiative characterizes the socio-economic system. This breakdown might have been impelled by an insupportable imbalance between population and resources resulting from the adoption of subsistence strategies (such as trade itself) that permitted further population growth during and after the Middle Horizon, rather than establishing equilibrium.

If this proposition were to hold on the central coast, during the protohistoric we should find evidence of egalitarian-type social institutions such as age-grades, etc., rather than hierarchical organizations. There should also be evidence of the disintegration of large organized groups, reflected in the denucleation of the settlement system and a tendency for community and mortuary organization to become less structured [King and Hickman 1973:v-3—v-5].

King and Hickman's model provides the best explanation currently available for the presence of large centralized villages during the Middle Period and the lack of such villages during the Late Period. The accuracy of this model is surprising, as it was constructed in the early 1970s, before much archaeology had been conducted in the central coast region.

SUMMARY

Analysis of the baptismal records and other historical accounts has yielded information which helps our understanding of seasonality and past population dynamics of the *Rumsen* Costanoan. As the examples show, this information may be used in association with data gleaned from the excavation of archaeological sites to provide new insights and more accurate assessments of the past.

REFERENCES

Breschini, G.S.
1972   Archaeological Investigations at MNT-436, the Kodani
                Site. Monterey County Archaeological Society Quarterly
                1(4).

1980   Esselen Prehistory. Paper presented at the Annual
                Meeting of the Society for California Archaeology,
                Redding.

1981   Models of Central California Prehistory. Paper presented
                at the Annual Meeting of the Society for California
                Archaeology, Bakersfield.

1983   Models of Population Movements in Central California
                Prehistory.   Doctoral dissertation, Department of
                Anthropology, Washington State University, Pullman.

Breschini, G.S., and T. Haversat
1985   Linguistic Prehistory of South-Central California. Paper
                presented to the Symposium on Central California
                Prehistory, San Jose State University, San Jose.

1988   Archaeological Excavations at CA-SLO-7 and CA-SLO-
                8, Diablo Canyon, San Luis Obispo County, California.
                Coyote Press Archives of California Prehistory 28.

1989   Archaeological Excavations at CA-MNT-108, at Fisher-
                man's Wharf, Monterey, Monterey County, California.
                Coyote Press Archives of California Prehistory 29.

1991   Archaeological Investigations at Three Late Period
                Coastal Abalone Processing Sites on the Monterey
                Peninsula, Monterey County, California. Coyote Press
                Archives of California Prehistory 33:31-44.

Breschini, G.S., T. Haversat, and J. Erlandson
1992   California Radiocarbon Dates. Seventh Edition. Salinas:
                Coyote Press.

Breschini, G.S., T. Haversat, and R.P. Hampson
1983   A Cultural Resources Overview of the Coast and Coast-Valley Study Areas [California]. Submitted to the Bureau of Land Management, Bakersfield.

Broadbent, S.M.
1972   The Rumsen of Monterey: An Ethnography from Historical Sources. *In* Miscellaneous Papers on Archaeology, pp. 45-93. Contributions of the University of California Archaeological Research Facility 14.

Costansó, Miguel
1769/1910   The Narrative of the Portolá Expedition of 1769-1770 by Miguel Costansó. Edited by Adolph van Hemert-Engert and Frederick J. Teggart. Academy of Pacific Coast History Publications 1(4). Berkeley: University of California Press.

Culleton, J.
1950   Indians and Pioneers of Old Monterey. Fresno: Academy of California Church History.

Engelhardt, Z.
1934   Mission San Carlos Borromeo (Carmelo): The Father of the Missions. Mission Santa Barbara, Santa Barbara. Reprinted in 1973 by Ballena Press, Ramona, California.

Gerow, B.A. (with R.B. Force)
1968   An Analysis of the University Village Complex with a Reappraisal of Central California Archaeology. Stanford: Stanford University Press.

Haversat, T., and G.S. Breschini
1984   New Interpretations in South Coast Ranges Prehistory. Paper presented at the Annual Northern Data Sharing Meeting of the Society for California Archaeology, Aptos.

King, C.D.
1971   Chumash Intervillage Economic Exchange. The Indian Historian 4(1):31-43.

1981   The Evolution of Chumash Society: A Comparative Study of Artifacts Used in System Maintenance in the Santa Barbara Channel Region Before A.D. 1804. Ph.D. dissertation, Department of Anthropology, University of California, Davis.

King, T.F.
1970   The Dead at Tiburon. Occasional Papers of the North-west California Archaeological Society 2.

1972   New Views of California Indian Societies. The Indian Historian 5(3).

King, T.F., and P.P. Hickman
1973   The Southern Santa Clara Valley: A General Plan for Archaeology. San Felipe Archaeology I. Submitted to National Park Service, San Francisco. Ms. on file (E-4 SBN), Northwest Regional Information Center of the California Archaeological Inventory, Rohnert Park.

Kroeber, A.L.
1925   Handbook of the Indians of California. Bureau of American Ethnology Bulletin 78.

Levy, R.
1978   Costanoan. In Handbook of North American Indians, Vol. 8 (California). Pp. 485-495. Robert F. Heizer, ed. W. Sturtevant, gen. ed. Washington, D.C.: Smithsonian Institution.

Margolin, M.
1978   The Ohlone Way: Indian Life in the San Francisco-Monterey Bay Area. Berkeley: Heyday Books.

Milliken, R.
1981   Ethnohistory of the Rumsen: The Mission Period. In Report of Archaeological Excavations at Nineteen Archaeological Sites for the Stage 1 Pacific Grove-Monterey Consolidation Project Regional Sewerage System, S.A. Dietz and T.L. Jackson, eds., Four volumes. Submitted to State Water Resources Control Board, Sacramento.

1987   Ethnohistory of the Rumsen. Papers in Northern
               California Anthropology 2. Berkeley: Northern
               California Anthropological Group.

1991   Ethnography and Ethnohistory of the Big Sur District,
               California State Park System, During the 1770-1810
               Time Period. Submitted to Department of Parks and
               Recreation, Sacramento.

1992   Ethnographic and Ethnohistoric Background for the San
               Francisquito Flat Vicinity, Carmel Valley, Monterey
               County, California. Appendix 2 *in* Baseline
               Archaeological Studies at Rancho San Carlos, Carmel
               Valley, Monterey County, California by Gary S.
               Breschini and Trudy Haversat. Submitted to Rancho San
               Carlos Partnership.

Pritchard, W.E.
1968   Preliminary Excavations at El Castillo, Presidio of
               Monterey, Monterey, California. Central California
               Archaeological Foundation, Sacramento.

1984   Preliminary Archaeological Investigations at CA-MNT-
               101, Monterey, California. Coyote Press Archives of
               California Prehistory 3:1-42.

Serra, Junípero
1748-84/   The Writings of Junípero Serra, 4 volumes. Antonine
1955-56   Tibesar, ed. Washington: Academy of American
               Franciscan History.

CENTRAL OHLONE ETHNOHISTORY

Chester King

The San Carlos Group

The area between San Jose and San Juan Bautista and extending from Santa Cruz to the San Joaquin Valley has proven to be difficult to map by village or tribe. At Santa Clara Mission only the closest villages were given separate names. The more distant villages were grouped by region.

The closest villages to the mission were given the names "our mother Santa Clara" (north San Jose), "our father San Francisco" (downtown San Jose), San Juan Bautista (San Jose south of Hillsdale), San Jose Cupertino (Cupertino), Santa Ysabel (east San Jose), and San Francisco Solano (Milpitas-Alviso) (King 1978, Milliken 1991).

The next four groups recognized in the Santa Clara Mission registers are very large and include people from villages located in particular directions from the mission. The four groups were Santa Agueda (villages north of Milpitas), San Bernardino (villages west of Cupertino), San Carlos (villages south of San Jose), and San Antonio (villages east of San Jose), northeast of San Antonio were the *Luechas* and southeast of San Antonio were the *Tayssen* (King 1977, Milliken 1991).

The San Carlos group was probably so named because Mission San Carlos was the closest mission to the south at the time of first application of the name. The San Carlos baptism and death entries at Santa Clara Mission seldom contained information concerning specific villages. The registers do contain scattered information concerning villages and internal regularities provide clues concerning the distribution of people from the region. The registers of Santa Cruz and San Juan

Bautista Missions provide information concerning the villages or tribal groups included in the San Carlos group at Santa Clara Mission.

Transfers between Santa Clara and Santa Cruz and San Juan Bautista Missions are mentioned in the registers of missions they transferred from and the missions they transferred to. Transfers are identified in padrons, death, and marriage registers and as parents of children in baptismal entries. Some groups of people baptized at the same time lack death entries and or contain death entries stating that people died at other missions. These groups of people were probably all from areas controlled by surrounding missions.

Parents of children baptized at Santa Clara Mission were sometimes baptized at other missions. Some parents can be identified as transfers to the other missions. In other cases, they can be identified by the native names of parents listed in the Santa Clara Mission registers.

When all the information concerning village designation at other missions, village designations at Santa Clara Mission, and kin ties between individuals with village designations is pooled, it is possible to discern patterns of baptism within the group designated San Carlos.

San Carlos included all the Ohlone groups baptized at Santa Cruz Mission except the San Rafael-Mutune group, which was part of the group called San Bernardino at Santa Clara Mission. Groups of people baptized on the same day at Santa Clara Mission sometimes have few death entries at Santa Clara Mission. Often some of the people in these groups can be identified as transfers to Santa Cruz Mission. A sequence of recruitment from the San Carlos group can be identified, with most early ties being with *Chaloctac* (Los Gatos-El Rancho or San Carlos of the Sierra), *Somontac* (Almaden Valley-La Laguna Seca), *Sayanta*, and *Achistaca*. There were many baptisms from Santa Cruz area villages in 1791 who transferred to Santa Cruz Mission after it was founded. Later ties were with *Pitac*, *Chipuctac-Ausaima* and the latest ties were between *Tomoi* people. It appears that most people baptized as from San Carlos after 1802 were from *Tomoi*. At Santa Clara Mission, most San Carlos people baptized between 1789 and 1802 were from La Laguna Seca. Many of the people baptized between 1781 and 1789 were from the mountains, apparently the Los Gatos area and the Almaden Valley. Figure 7.1 indicates the distribution of groups subsumed under the term San Carlos at Santa Clara Mission.

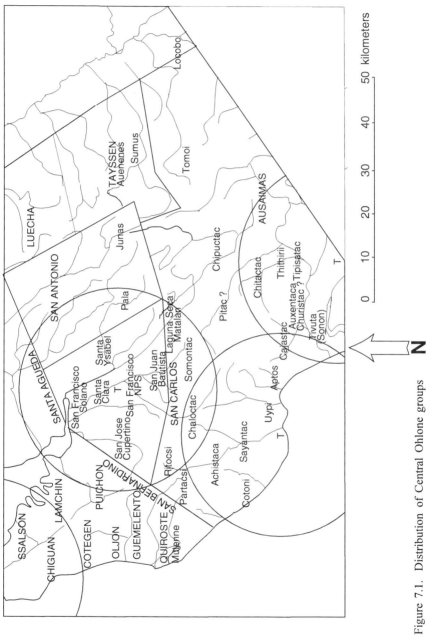

Figure 7.1. Distribution of Central Ohlone groups

Reconstruction of the Size of the Pre-colonial Population

To reconstruct the general size of the pre-colonial population it is necessary to determine the effects of introduced diseases on what is normally described as an age pyramid.   A normal age pyramid for a given population includes more individuals in young age groups and fewer in older age groups. This distribution is due to reductions in size of older age groups caused by death. The age structures of populations baptized at California missions look more like Christmas trees than pyramids (Figure 7.2). After 1790, it appears that there were few births and there was high child mortality. Apparently these changes were the results of syphilis. Other irregularities in population were apparently caused by an influenza epidemic in 1777. It appears that villages furthest away from Spanish settlements and missions suffered less from syphilis than those close to Spanish soldiers and citizens. Figure 7.2 indicates the years individuals baptized at the missions were born in parts of the San Carlos area.   The figure includes children born at the mission whose fathers were from the villages. Further studies are necessary to accurately determine the populations which were present prior to European contact. In Table 7.1, the group labeled NW refers to settlements in the vicinity of the San Lorenzo River drainage described in detail in the next section.

TABLE 7.1.   SUMMARY OF AGE DISTRIBUTIONS FOR GROUPS SHOWN IN FIGURE 7.2

Year of Birth	NW	S San Carlos	Ausaima	Unijaima	Tomoi	Orestac	Total
1715-1719	1	3					4
1720-1724	1						1
1725-1729	6	1	1	1	4	1	14
1730-1734	3		5	1			9
1735-1739	13	8	1	1	3		26
1740-1744	6		5	1	3		15
1745-1749	16	12	9	3	7	12	59
1750-1754	12	4	4	7	5	1	33
1755-1759	24	18	7	3	10	4	66
1760-1764	31	10	14	15	10	3	83
1765-1769	28	20	12	7	26	20	113
1770-1774	28	25	16	10	17	11	107
1775-1799	15	13	21	8	34	11	102
1780-1784	51	19	24	9	19	11	133
1785-1789	101	33	24	13	23	9	203
1790-1794	54	65	40	21	25	18	223
1795-1799	25	34	72	32	19	9	191
1800-1804	7	31	54	18	20	23	153
1805-1809	5	22	22	20	22	14	105
1810-1814	8	10	18	8	4	8	56
1815-1817	6	9	21	3	5	4	48
Total	441	337	370	181	256	159	1744

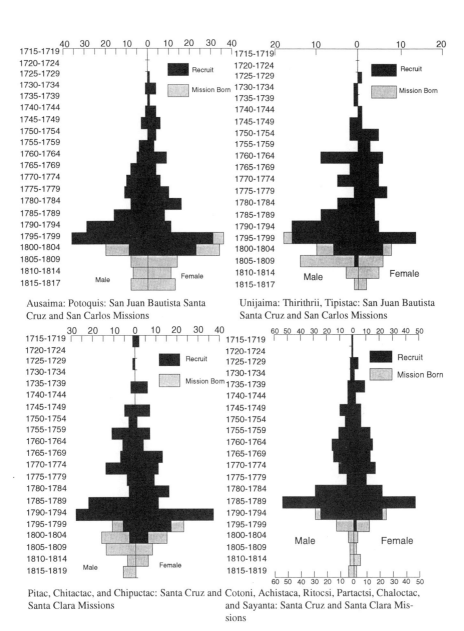

Ausaima: Potoquis: San Juan Bautista Santa Cruz and San Carlos Missions

Unijaima: Thirithrii, Tipistac: San Juan Bautista Santa Cruz and San Carlos Missions

Pitac, Chitactac, and Chipuctac: Santa Cruz and Santa Clara Missions

Cotoni, Achistaca, Ritocsi, Partactsi, Chaloctac, and Sayanta: Santa Cruz and Santa Clara Missions

Figure 7.2. Age structures of selected Central Ohlone groups

Charts of Recorded Kinship Relations of People from the Northwestern San Carlos Settlements of *Somontac* **(Santa Clara),** *Chaloctac* **(Jesus, El Rancho),** *Sayanta* **(San Juan Capistrano)** *Achistaca* **(San Dionisio),** *Cotoni* **(Santiago),** *Ritocsi* **(San Jose) and** *Partacsi* **(San Bernardo).**

The following twelve figures (Figures 7.3-7.14) indicate kinship relationships between individuals baptized from villages located in the Santa Cruz Mountains in the San Lorenzo Creek drainage and adjacent areas.   Information listed under triangles or circles is given in the following order: baptism number, native name when given, Spanish name given at time of baptism, relationships stated in baptism entries, village or tribe name, death entry number and additional information given in death or padron entries. The following abbreviations are used in these charts: Ca for San Carlos Mission, Cr. for Santa Cruz Mission, B. for San Juan Bautista Mission, and Cl for Santa Clara Mission. "b" indicates baptism register number, "m" indicates marriage register number, "d" indicates death register number, a "p" indicates padron entry. The year following "p" indicates the year the padron was started. Age at the time of baptism is indicated by the number inside the triangle (male) or circle (female) indicating people. A number with a "d" following it indicated days, one with an "m" following it indicates months, and numbers alone indicate years. Abbreviations for kin ties include "fa" for father, "mo" for mother, "bro" for brother, "sis" for sister, and "cnl" for carnal. Table 7.2 indicates the years individuals were baptized at Santa Clara and Santa Cruz Missions between 1777 and 1804. This information is useful in interpreting the relative ages of individuals included in Figures 7.3-7.13.

TABLE 7.2. BAPTISM NUMBERS BY YEAR AT SANTA CLARA AND SANTA CRUZ MISSIONS

Year	Santa Clara	Year	Santa Clara	Santa Cruz
1777	1-70	1791	1836-2006	1-87
1778	71-130	1792	2007-2219	88-161
1779	131-155	1793	2220-2414	162-242
1780	156-250	1794	2415-2923	243-371
1781	251-322	1795	2924-3226	373-622
1782	323-424	1796	3227-3365	623-733
1783	425-606	1797	3366-3502	734-767
1784	607-697	1798	3503-3709	768-857
1785	698-820	1799	3711-3882	858-897
1786	820-982	1800	3883-4024	898-949
1787	983-1134	1801	4025-4173	950-975
1788	1135-1261	1802	4174-4407	976-1031
1789	1262-1508	1803	4408-4548	1032-1062
1790	1509-1835	1804	4549-4665	1063-1135

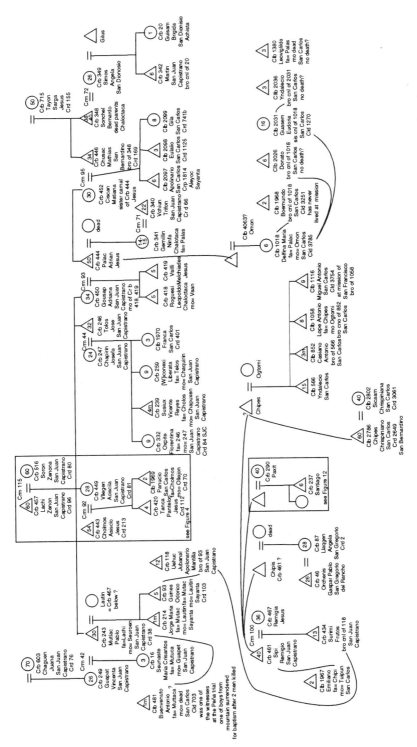

Figure 7.3. Kinship ties indicated for villages in the vicinity of the San Lorenzo drainage (one of 12 charts)

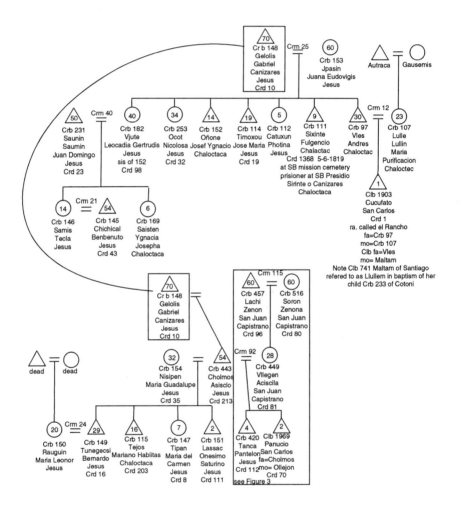

Figure 7.4. Kinship ties indicated for villages in the vicinity of the San Lorenzo drainage

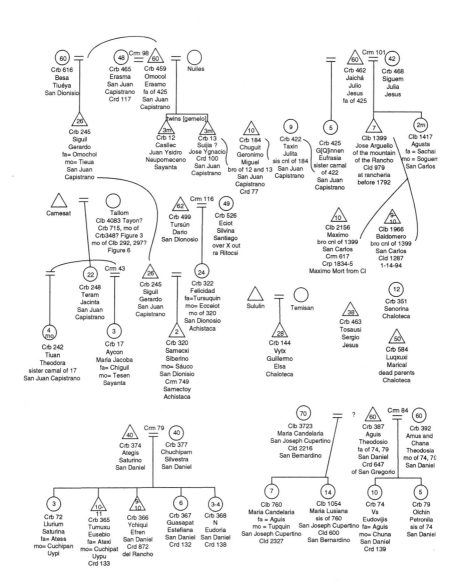

Figure 7.5. Kinship ties indicated for villages in the vicinity of the San Lorenzo drainage

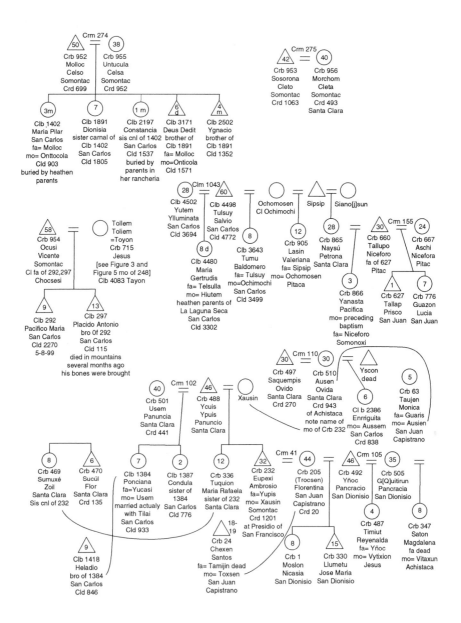

Figure 7.6. Kinship ties indicated for villages in the vicinity of the San Lorenzo drainage

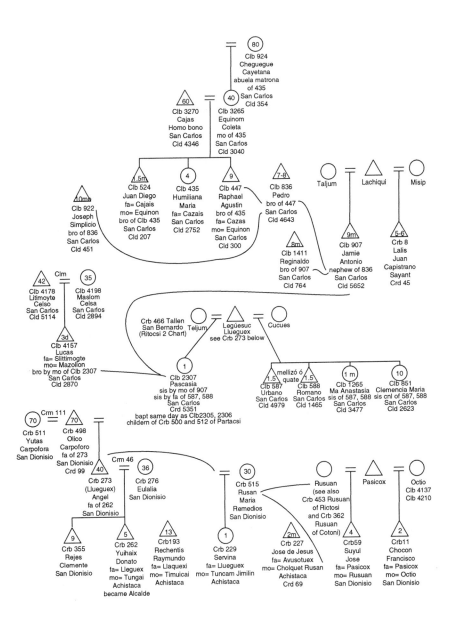

Figure 7.7. Kinship ties indicated for villages in the vicinity of the San Lorenzo drainage

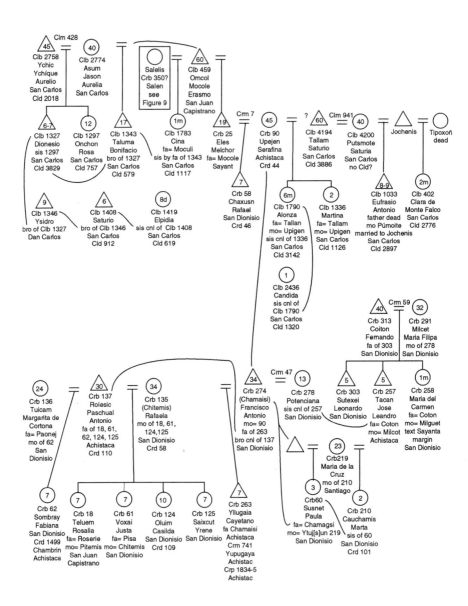

Figure 7.8. Kinship ties indicated for villages in the vicinity of the San Lorenzo drainage

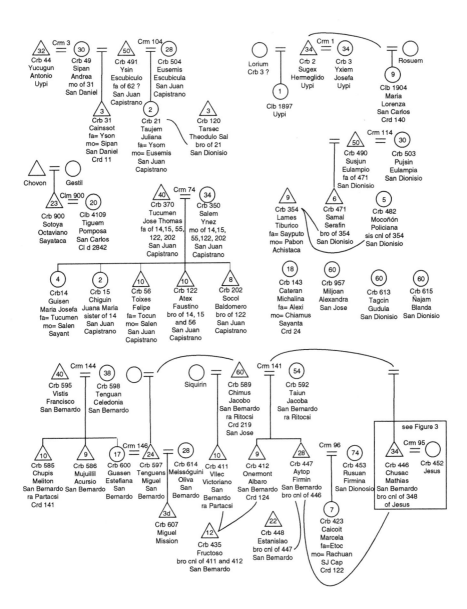

Figure 7.9. Kinship ties indicated for villages in the vicinity of the San Lorenzo drainage

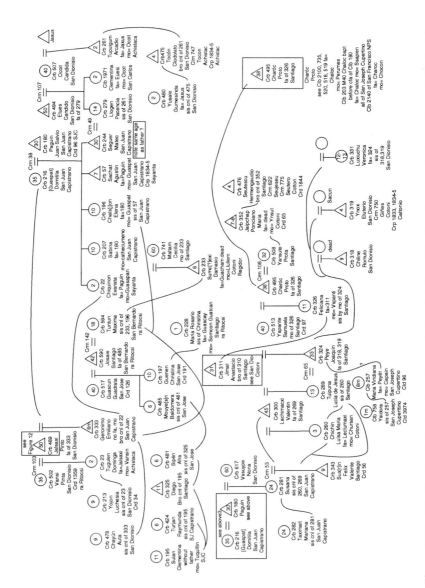

Figure 7.10. Kinship ties indicated for villages in the vicinity of the San Lorenzo drainage (one of 12 charts)

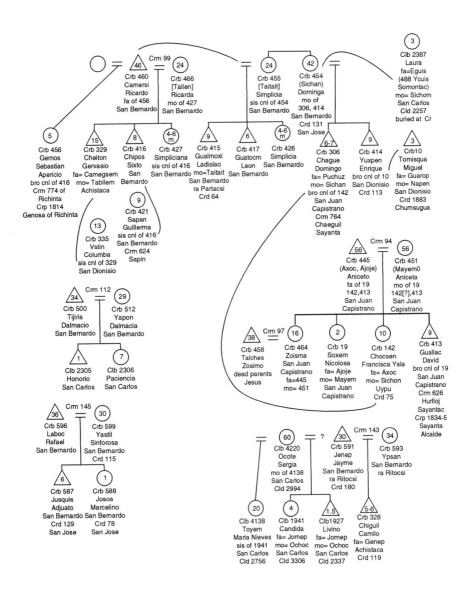

Figure 7.11. Kinship ties indicated for villages in the vicinity of the San Lorenzo drainage

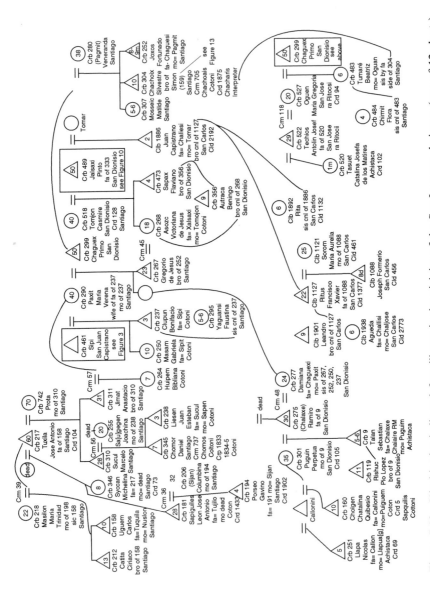

Figure 7.12. Kinship ties indicated for villages in the vicinity of the San Lorenzo drainage (one of 12 charts)

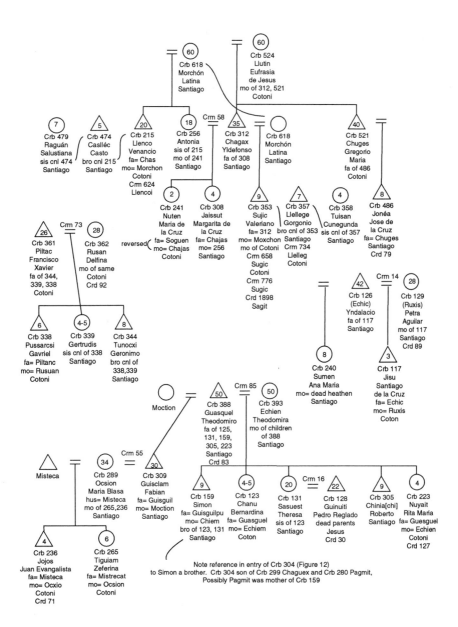

Figure 7.13. Kinship ties indicated for villages in the vicinity of the San Lorenzo drainage

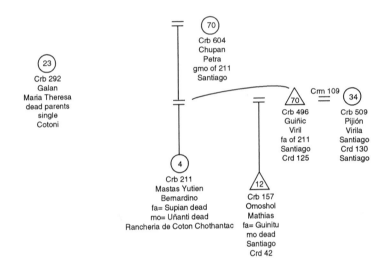

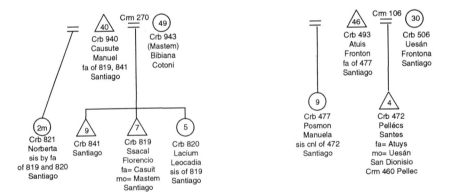

Figure 7.14. Kinship ties indicated for villages in the vicinity of the San Lorenzo drainage

The kinship charts can be used to reconstruct the histories of recruitment of families into the missions. The history of recruitment aids in interpretation of native political systems and provides insight of the procedures used to recruit people into the missions. The patterns of marriage provide insights to the native political organization and the degree of ties between settlements can be discerned. The following discussion relies on information contained in the charts.

Wife Stealing

As indicated above in Figures 7.3-7.14, the kinship data for San Lorenzo Creek in the Santa Cruz Mission area are very detailed. There are many half sib ties recorded for this area. These ties result in close integration of families within a region. The presence of half sibs seems most intense within "tribal areas," but is also documented between "tribes." In reconstructing kinship ties, it was often necessary to use entries for parents' native names to determine relationships.

Marriages are the basis of bonds of alliance in all but the most modern political systems. Examples include recent European royalty, Helen of Troy, and the marriages of Henry the VIII. In European tradition the plays of Shakespeare and other tales of palace intrigue involve the changes in alliance brought about by the actions of rulers.

Concerning warfare among the Salinan, Fages noted in 1775:

> They are continually at war with their neighbors; for purpose of going out on any of these expeditions, the men and women first gather to take counsel in the house of the capitan in command, whence the soldiers set out for the engagement, bearing the proper orders. The affair is limited to setting fire to this or that village of the adversary, sacking it, and bringing away some of the women either married or single [Priestley 1972:58].

When Governor Neve ordered the priests to give the Indians self government in 1779, the men who were elected *alcaldes* at several missions stole other men's wives and ran away from the missions. This included an *alcalde* from San Carlos Mission and one from San Luis Obispo Mission.

Argüello wrote to Fages concerning a fight between Indians on April 30, 1788.

. . . informs that the heathen of the village next to Mission Santa Clara had fought with the hill people. Some Christians of the mission joined the skirmish. Because of that he sent sergeant Amador, who upon arrival at said Mission found that the priests had punished two or three Christians who had gone to see the encounter, according to his investigation. He immediately went among the neighboring villages to reprove the ringleaders and [tell them] that if in the future they invite some Christians to their rumbles, they will be punished; and the same was done with the Christians.

On this occasion he verified that a heathen named "the Rooster," a worker at the Pueblo, was moving to put together a group to go make war with other heathen over a woman. He was seized and given some lashes. After three days under detention he was put at liberty [Argüello 1788].

Fages instructed Macario Castro on January 2, 1790:

When some non-Christians are being persecuted by others who have taken their women, you ought to persuade them they ought to return them and to make them see the wrong in what they have done, and tell them that if I know, it will make me angry and I will come with many soldiers to punish them; the same approach is to be used if the distant Rancherias steal women of their neighbors. They should be sent to petition the chiefs with the same council. But on the other hand, if the women have already been captured for some time and are with children, leave them as they are, since it is desired that the non-Christians be free [Fages 1790].

In 1807, three *Tatcan* couples fled San Francisco Mission to live with relatives among the *Chupcans*.

The pagans kidnapped the wife of one of them, who returned alone to tell his relatives about it. On February 3 the one who returned, whose name is Octaviano (and who has now run away again), and a friend of his got a number of people from his homeland ... [Milliken 1991:311].

The themes of starting wars by stealing wives and of taking women captives during wars can be found in archival sources for many areas of pre-colonial California. The bonds established by marriages between important families were important for the maintenance of traditional political systems. Stealing of wives resulted in decreased bonds to the group which suffered losses and increased bonds by groups which successfully took wives. In addition to wars, many half sib relationships were due to changing marriage partners and polygamous marriages. Several statements in answers to information requests of 1813 indicate this was the case.

Mission San Juan Bautista—"They were readily satisfied, even in the case of adultery of one of the parties or both, to come together again even if the man had two or three wives if it was feasible to keep them all for they looked more to the procreation of children than to the stability of the marriage bond" (Geiger and Meighan 1976:68).

Mission San Carlos—"While pagan conditions held sway unfaithfulness on the part of a woman led to many wars and killings, wherefore self-restraint was observed" (Geiger and Meighan 1976:26).

Mission San Francisco—"If the partners separate the children generally follow the mother" (Geiger and Meighan 1976:27).

Women Married to More than One Man Still Living

Several women can be identified in the registers of Santa Cruz Mission from the Lorenzo Creek drainage and vicinity who had children by more than one man; in each instance, two or more men were alive at the woman's baptism.

Paxit

Crb 290 *Paxit* 40 yrs of *Cotoni* was apparently a wife of *Sipi* before baptism and was married (Crm 57) to an ex-husband at time of baptism (Figure 7.12).

TABLE 7.3. HUSBANDS OF *PAXIT*

Bapt #	Age	Birth Year	Native Name	Village	Children	Other wives
Cr 299	50	1744	Chaguex	Achistaca	2	2
Cr 461	40	1755	Sipi, Chipi	Sayanta	2	4 ?
Cr 311	31	1763	Jimat	Cotoni	1	0

TABLE 7.4. CHILDREN OF *PAXIT* (FIGURE 7.12)

Bapt #	Age	Birth Year	Village	Father
Cr 277	24	1770	Achistaca	Chaguex
Cr 267	23	1771	Cotoni	Chaguex
Cr 250	10 (20)	1784 (1774)	Cotoni	Sipi
Cr 264	7	1787	Cotoni	Jimat
Cr 237	3	1790	Cotoni	Sipi

TABLE 7.5. OTHER WIVES OF *SIPI* (FIGURE 7.3)

Bapt #	Native Name	Age	Birth Year	Village	Children
Cr 467		36	1757	Chaloctac	Crb 434
-	dead			Chaloctac	Crb 87
?	Tulpun			San Carlos	Clb 1967
?	Ogtomi			San Carlos	Clb 566, 852, 1058, 1116

TABLE 7.6. OTHER WIVES OF *CHAGUEX* (FIGURE 7.12)

Bapt #	Native Name	Age	Birth Year	Village	Children
Cr 280	Pagmit	38	1756	Cotoni	Crb 252, 304, and 307
Cr 527	Oguen	20	1775	Ritocsi.	Crb 483, 484

Sipan

Crb 49 *Sipan* 30 years of *Uypi* was married (Crm 3) to Crb 44 at the mission; she had a younger child by *Yson* (Figure 7.9).

TABLE 7.7. HUSBANDS OF *SIPAN*

Bapt #	Age	Birth Year	Native Name	Village	Children	Other wives
Cr 491	46	1749	Yson, Ysin	Sayanta	Crb 31	Crb 504
Cr 44	32	1759	Yucugun	Uypi		

Guaspat

Crb 216 *Guaspat* 35 yrs of *Sayanta* was married (Crm 38) to Crb 180 *Paguin*. She had a young child by Crb 489 *Jalsaxi* (Figure 7.10).

TABLE 7.8. HUSBANDS OF *GUASPAT*

Bapt #	Age	Birth Year	Name	Village	Children	Other wives
Cr 180	30	1763	Paguin	Sayanta	Crb 22, 57, 196, 207, 244	Crb 617 Achistaca
Cr 489	50	1745	Jalsaxi	Achistaca	Crb 333	Crb 502, 518, Cl Tomar, Chaljose

Upejen

Crb 90 *Upejen* 45 yrs of *Achistaca* was married (Crm 7) to Crb 25 *Eles*. She also apparently had children at Santa Clara mission by Clb 4194 *Tallam* (Figure 7.8).

TABLE 7.9. HUSBANDS OF *UPEJEN*

Bapt #	Age	Birth Year	Name	Village	Children	Other wives
Crb 25.	19	1766	Eles	Sayanta	Crb 58	
Clb 4194	60	1742	Tallam	San Carlos	Clb 1336, 1790	Clb 4200

Yspante

     Crb 513 *Yspante* 40 yrs of *Cotoni* had a daughter Crb 326 by Crb 495 *Charoc*. Her daughter Crb 326 was sister by her mother of Crb 324 *Peye* of *Cotoni* (Figure 7.10).

TABLE 7.10. HUSBANDS OF *YSPANTE*

Bapt #	Age	Birth Year	Name	Village	Children	Other wives
Cr 495	30	1765	Charóc	Cotoni	Crb 326	Crb 508, Cl Perumes, Ssapien, Chocon
?			?	Cotoni	Crb 324	

     In the selection of people presented above, many of the husbands had more than one wife. It is probable than these women were the daughters of important families. Changes in husbands may have been most common among the upper classes.

Conclusions

     The registers of Santa Clara and Santa Cruz Missions provide important information concerning the size and distribution of Ohlone people at the time of historic contact.   The registers also provide information which can be used to provide insight concerning Protohistoric socio-political organization. The comparison of information concerning kinship relationships recorded in the registers of Spanish missions will result in a more detailed understanding of native Californian political organization.

REFERENCES CITED

Argüello, José
1788   Argüello al Gobernador Pedro Fages sobre pelea de Indios. San Francisco Presidio. April 30, 1788. [Abstract of destroyed original]. Archives of California (CA 4:261-262). Bancroft Library, University of California, Berkeley.

Fages, Pedro
1790   Fages a Macario Castro. Monterey. January 2, 1790. [Abstract of destroyed original]. Archives of California (CA 44:27-29). Bancroft Library, University of California, Berkeley.

Geiger, Maynard and Clement Meighan
1976   As the Padres Saw Them: California Indian Life and Customs are Reported by the Franciscan Missionaries 1813-1815. Santa Barbara Mission Archive Library, Santa Barbara.

King, Chester
1977   Matalan Ethnohistory. Chapter 4 of Final Report of Archaeological Test Excavations for Construction of Freeway 04-SCI-101 Post Miles 17.2-19.4., submitted by Archaeological Consulting and Research Services Inc., July, 1977. Manuscript on file with Caltrans District 04, San Francisco.

1978   Historic Indian Settlements in the Vicinity of the Holiday Inn Site. Chapter 15 in Archaeological Investigations at CA-SCI-128, The Holiday Inn Site. Edited by Joseph C. Winter. San Jose.

Milliken, Randall
1991   An Ethnohistory of the Indian People of the San Francisco Bay Area from 1770 to 1810. Ph.D. Dissertation, Anthropology, University of California, Berkeley.

Priestley, Herbert L.. trans.
    1972   A Historical, Political, and Natural Description of
                  California by Pedro Fages. Ramona: Ballena Press.

THE DEVELOPMENT OF SAN JOSE
MISSION, 1797-1840

Robert H. Jackson

The quincentenary of the encounter between the Old and New worlds has focused attention again on the impact of European colonization on the native peoples of the Americas. The Spanish people who first settled North America in the early sixteenth century, implemented policies to integrate Indians into an emerging colonial order that relied on the exploitation of their labor and skimmed off surpluses from the peasant community economy. On the frontiers of Spain's New World empire the mission was the most important colonial institution. Under the supervision of missionaries, the Indians were to be converted to Catholicism, and prepared for their role in the new colonial order as laborers and tribute payers.

The study of the Spanish frontier mission has undergone considerable change. "In recent years," states an article discussing the quincentennial and the role of Jesuit missionaries in the New World,

> scholars have devoted increasing attention to the acculturative impact of Catholic religious orders in the encounters. Departing from the earlier approaches of scholars like Robert Ricard and Herbert Eugene Bolton who emphasized a European perspective, researchers in an emerging school of "New Mission History" have employed methodologies from ethnohistory and anthropology to derive a more balanced assessment which also incorporates Amerindian perspectives. The mission historians are currently debating such issues as the extent to which religious orders modified the culture of American natives and conversely the way in which they promoted exchange between

cultures and borrowed from what they experienced in the Americas (Gagliano 1992:32).[1]

Focuses of the "New Mission History" include the colonial aspect of the missions in relationship to the goals of Spanish officials, and native responses to mission programs. It also reevaluates the historiography of the missions—how historians have interpreted the development of the missions and their impact on native peoples.

In this essay, I evaluate, from the perspective of the "New Mission History," the Spanish colonization of Alta California, a frontier region in northern New Spain, through a discussion of the development of one mission, San Jose, established in 1797 among the Ohlone/Costanoan. Using this perspective, I attempt to show the development of the missions as an element of a larger colonial policy, and the ways that Indian responses to the mission program modified the development of San Jose Mission. The organization of agriculture and ranching, the construction of the complex of buildings at the mission as related to social control, and the implementation of the *congregacion* policy; i.e. the resettlement of dispersed Indian populations into large communities to be modeled on the corporate indigenous communities of central Mexico.

Recent historiographic views of the missions, particularly the interpretations of the mission economies of historical geographer David Hornbeck and archaeologist Julia Costello, published in volume one of *Columbian Consequences* edited by David Thomas are worthy of comment (Hornbeck 1989: 423-431; Costello 1989:435-449).[2] Hornbeck and Costello attempt to evaluate the development of the Alta California mission economies, but ignore the role of the Indian converts living in the mission as actors in the community that they themselves created through their labor. Hornbeck understands the development of the mission economies as a transition from self-sufficiency to commercially oriented production of hides and tallow for export. According to him, the Franciscans de-emphasized *congregacion* and evangelization in favor of commercial agriculture, an interpretation based on the decline in the number of converts being brought into the missions. Costello re-enforces

---

[1]The concept of the "New Mission History" comes from a volume of edited essays I co-edited with Erick Langer that is currently being reviewed for publication by the University of Nebraska Press.

[2]For a critique of the Hornbeck-Costello model see Jackson 1991b, and Jackson 1992b.

Hornbeck's interpretation on the basis of a flawed analysis of data on the amount of grain planted and harvested. The amount of grain planted appears to have dropped in the 1820s. Costello interprets this as signifying a conscious decision on the part of the Franciscans to shift labor from agriculture to ranching, and to the slaughter of cattle for hides and tallow (Hornbeck 1989).

A closer analysis of the record of agricultural production at San Jose Mission disproves the main contentions of the Hornbeck-Costello model (see Tables 8.1-8.4). The amount of grain planted and harvested varied from year to year, as did productivity, measured here by the ratio of grain sown to grain harvested. There clearly were years of poor grain production, due primarily to weather conditions or the paralysis of the labor force by severe epidemics. In 1806-1807, 1822, and 1824, for example, the return on corn was very low; in 1821-1822, 1824, and 1827-28, that of barley; and in 1826 to 1829, that of wheat. The average amount of grain planted at San Jose actually increased during the 1820s, the period that Costello hypothesized as evidencing an actual decline in agriculture. Between 1800 and 1829, the average amount of wheat planted increased from 76.6 fanegas during the decade 1800-1809, to 110.2 fanegas during the following decade, and to 210.6 fanegas from 1820 to 1829. The average wheat harvest declined from 1820 to 1829 because of weather conditions, soil erosion, and other factors. The amount of barley and corn sown increased during the decade 1820-1829, as did the average harvest. The productivity of all three crops was down. Clearly, Costello's interpretation is incorrect.

What role did the Indian converts living at San Jose Mission have in the development of the mission economy? Costello argued, as noted above, that labor released from agriculture went to the tending and slaughter of cattle for the hide and tallow trade, and in some instances the over-killing of cattle led to the depletion of the herds. The basic assumption of both Hornbeck and Costello is that Indians were passive actors. Hornbeck attributed the drop in the number of converts entering the missions only to a de-emphasis of agriculture. He completely ignored the growing ability of interior tribes to resist Franciscan recruitment, which, more than any other factor, contributed to the drop in the number of recruits entering the missions. Similarly, Costello assumed that the over-culling of herds was the only cause for the short-term decline in the number of cattle. There is another explanation for the decline in the cattle herds at San Jose Mission (see Table 8.5).

Cattle dispersed over pasture were herded by Indian *vaqueros* using horses from the mission horse herds. Raids after 1811 by hostile Indians from the Central Valley allied with fugitives from the missions

TABLE 8.1. GRAIN PRODUCTION AT SAN JOSE MISSION IN FANEGAS, 1798-1834

	Wheat		Barley		Corn	
Year	Sown	Harvest	Sown	Harvest	Sown	Harvest
1798	34	330	-	-	1	250
1799	60	610	-	-	2	300
1800	62	750	-	-	1 3/4	200
1801	90	1180	4	40	3	400
1802	84	1200	6 1/2	108	2 1/2	230
1803	75 3/4	1109	18	580	3	200
1804	103	2800	40	1600	1	200
1805	64	3700	17	920	1	110
1806	71	2513	14	756	9	150
1807	78	1400	4	80	5	80
1808	88	1500	4	80	1/2	30
1809	50	1088	4	50	3/4	100
1810	63	2300	3	140	1/2	50
1811	61	1668 1/2	3	45 1/2	2	138
1812	100	2160	7	127	1	300
1813	145	3820	20	333	1/2	150
1814	140	2550	7	200	1/4	20
1815	45	2854	7	134	1/2	100
1816	61	3000	5	107	2	170
1817	179	4150	5	137	2	260
1818	137	3620	19	178	2	300
1819	171	4605	22	224	5	800
1820	180	5210	10	135	7	800
1821	369	6000	18	123	9	1000
1822	200	2350	10	30	7	20
1823	288	3383	20	242	5	300
1824	160	2500	20	150	5	40

1825	180	3200	26	300	6	600
1826	207	1700	30	700	6	200
1827	230	2000	40	200	5	19
1828	200	1700	27	30	4	400
1829	92	300	12	0	17	200
1830	150	4000	37	964	6	1000
1831	100	4000	20	1100	4 1/2	1000
1832	100	4000	20	1100	4	1000
1833	80	760	25	302	3	200
1834	90	1180	20	150	4	350

Source: Annual Reports, Archivo General de la Nacion, Mexico, D.F., Santa Barbara Mission Archive-Library, Santa Barbara, California; Ms. "Mission Statistics," The Bancroft Library, University of California, Berkeley.

TABLE 8.2. RATIO OF GRAIN HARVESTED TO GRAIN SOWN, 1798-1834

Year	Wheat	Barley	Corn
1798	9.71	-	250.00
1799	10.17	-	150.00
1800	12.10	-	114.29
1801	13.11	10.00	133.33
1802	14.29	16.62	92.00
1803	14.64	32.22	66.67
1804	27.18	40.00	200.00
1805	57.81	54.12	110.00
1806	35.39	54.00	16.67
1807	17.95	20.00	16.00
1808	17.05	20.00	60.00
1809	21.76	12.50	133.33
1810	36.51	46.67	100.00
1811	27.35	15.17	69.00
1812	21.60	18.14	300.00
1813	26.34	16.65	300.00

1814	18.21	28.57	80.00
1815	63.42	19.14	200.00
1816	49.18	35.67	85.00
1817	23.18	27.40	150.00
1818	26.42	9.37	150.00
1819	26.93	10.18	160.00
1820	28.94	13.50	114.29
1821	16.26	6.83	111.11
1822	11.75	3.00	2.86
1823	11.75	12.10	60.00
1824	15.66	7.50	8.00
1825	17.78	11.54	100.00
1826	8.21	23.33	33.33
1827	8.70	5.00	3.80
1828	8.50	1.11	100.00
1829	3.26	0	28.57
1830	26.67	26.05	166.67
1831	40.00	42.31	222.22
1832	40.00	42.31	250.00
1833	9.50	12.08	66.67
1834	13.11	7.50	7.96

Source: Table 8.1.

TABLE 8.3. MEAN GRAIN SOWN AND HARVESTED AT SAN JOSE MISSION, 1800-1829

	Wheat		Barley		Corn	
Years	Sown	Harvested	Sown	Harvested	Sown	Harvested
1800-1809	76.6	1724.0	12.4	468.0	2.8	170
1810-1819	110.2	3072.7	9.6	162.6	1.6	228.8
1820-1829	210.6	2834.3	21.3	191.0	7.1	357.9

Source: Table 8.1.

TABLE 8.4. MEAN RATIO OF GRAIN HARVESTED: SOWN AT SAN JOSE MISSION, 1800-1829

Years	Wheat	Barley	Corn
1800-1809	22.51	37.74	60.71
1810-1819	27.88	16.94	143.00
1820-1829	13.46	8.97	50.41

Source: Table 8.1

TABLE 8.5. NUMBERS OF LIVESTOCK REPORTED AT SAN JOSE MISSION, 1797-1834

Year	Cattle	Index (1810=100)	Sheep	Index (1810=100)	Horses	Index (1810=100)
1797	100	2	130	2	20	2
1798	150	3	180	3	39	3
1799	224	4	200	3	79	7
1800	300	5	1600	23	60	5
1801	351	6	2000	29	238	21
1802	620	10	3500	50	322	28
1803	900	15	4600	66	338	29
1804	1844	31	5800	83	560	49
1805	3162	53	8000	114	1123	98
1806	4000	67	5600	80	1199	104
1807	4000	67	6000	86	1060	92
1808	4000	67	5000	71	1150	100
1809	5000	83	5500	79	1150	100
1810	6000	100	7000	100	1150	100
1811	5000	83	8000	114	1000	87
1812	4000	67	8000	114	860	75
1813	4500	75	8000	114	480	42
1814	5000	83	7800	111	500	44
1815	5000	83	8000	114	280	24
1816	5000	83	7680	110	320	28

1817	5000	83	7000	100	670	58
1818	5500	92	7049	101	690	60
1819	5500	92	9000	129	700	61
1820	6000	100	12000	171	850	74
1821	6000	100	12000	171	900	78
1822	7000	117	15000	214	850	74
1823	7000	117	13000	186	650	57
1824	9000	150	15000	214	650	57
1825	10000	167	15000	214	650	57
1826	15000	250	20000	286	560	49
1827	18000	300	15000	214	1000	87
1828	15000	250	15000	214	1000	87
1829	15000	250	13000	186	1000	87
1830	12000	200	13000	186	1200	104
1831	12000	200	13000	186	1200	104
1832	12000	200	13000	186	1200	104
1833	11870	198	13540	193	1350	117
1834	12990	217	13970	200	1425	124

Source: Annual Reports, Archivo General da la Nacion, Mexico, D.F., Santa Barbara Mission Archive-Library, Santa Barbara, California; Ms. "Mission Statistics," The Bancroft Library, University of California, Berkeley, California.

depleted the horse herds of San Jose Mission. Fewer horses meant that fewer *vaqueros* were available to round up cattle. Between 1810 and 1815, the number of horses at San Jose Mission dropped from 1,150 to a mere 280. Moreover, not all of the horses were broken. The number of cattle dropped during the same years, from 6,000 in 1810 to 4,000 in 1812, and 5,000 in 1815. The figures for the number of cattle are given in round numbers which indicate that they are only estimates, and in the mid-1810s did not change for several consecutive years. The figures either indicate that the Franciscan missionaries did not have an accurate count of the number of cattle on the open range, or are simply the number of cattle rounded-up each year.

The construction of the building complex at San Jose Mission was a third major activity that required large amounts of labor. The

Franciscans recorded, in varying degrees of detail, major building projects, including the use of the buildings. Adobe buildings also required frequent maintenance, including plastering and white-washing to protect the adobe walls of the mission structures, and periodic adjustment of roof tiles. However, the record of building construction at San Jose is incomplete. No annual reports have survived for the years 1799 to 1809, the period during which the main quadrangle took shape and a large church was completed. Other sources provide some information on the structures erected during the ten years for which there is an information gap (see Table 8.6).

In 1797, following the establishment of the mission, the Franciscans directed the construction of temporary buildings described as *jacales*, palisades chinked with mud, and roofed with tule. The temporary buildings included a chapel, quarters for the missionaries, and an office. The first permanent structure, a granary, was built in 1798. Over the next decade a large adobe church was added to the complex. The main quadrangle was completed with two additional granaries, workshops, and a wing of fifteen rooms containing, among other things, quarters for the missionaries. Construction of permanent Indian housing may have begun prior to 1810.

After 1810, additional structures were added to the mission complex. In 1810, 1811, and 1826, barracks-style apartments for Indian families were built. The missionaries directed the construction of a new soldiers' barracks and guard house. A water powered mill was completed in 1820. The growing volume of hide and tallow sales in the 1820s, following the legalization of the trade, prompted the construction in 1827 of facilities to process and store hides and tallow products. The new facilities included a tanning vat, soap works, and storage room for hides.

The change in Mexican politics after 1810 modified the San Jose Mission economy. The outbreak of civil war in central Mexico in 1810 cut off funds and supplies for the military garrisons in Alta California. The missions picked up the slack by providing growing quantities of grain, clothing, and leather goods to the garrisons (Jackson 1991a:387-439). At San Jose the Franciscans increased production after 1810 to help supply the presidios. They especially increased the production of wheat, the preferred grain of Spaniards, and in the decade 1810 to 1819 wheat harvests were up considerably from the previous decade. The dependence of the presidios on supplies from the missions placed pressure on the missionaries to maintain the labor supply in the face of adverse demographic patterns.

The Franciscans were not only carrying out the mandate to evangelize the Ohlone/Costanoan and interior groups, they were also replenishing the labor supply. In a recent article (Jackson 1992a:141-

TABLE 8.6. BUILDING CONSTRUCTION REPORTED AT SAN JOSE MISSION

1797: Temporary buildings described as *jacales* (palisade and mud roofed with tules) were built, including quarters for the missionaries, an office, and a chapel. Other projects included corrals for the livestock, and a fence built around an orchard.

1798: A granary with a loft was built. The chapel was enlarged. Irrigation ditches were built for the corn fields.

1799-1809: No annual reports for this period survive. However, data from other sources, including an 1837 inventory, give an indication of building projects undertaken during the decade. A new church was built between 1805 and 1809, and completed the main quadrangle. The wing adjoining the church, measuring 100 x 17 varas and containing 15 rooms, was built. It housed the quarters for the missionaries. Two granaries were added to the one built in 1798, and apparently formed one whole wing of the main quadrangle measuring 100 x 10 varas. Workshops and storage rooms were also built, and construction on adobe apartments for Indian families probably began.

1810: Ten apartments were built for as many Indian families, as well as a dovecote and room to house looms.

1811: Twenty-four apartments were built for Indian families, and a room was added to the soldier's barracks.

1812: The roof on the church was raised by 3 varas.

1813: One wing of the quadrangle was roofed with tiles.

1814: A new soldier's barracks was built, all roofed with tile. The barracks consisted of six apartments for the soldiers and their families, each with a kitchen on the side, a guard house, and a storage room.

1815: No construction reported.

1816: No construction reported.

1817: No construction reported.

1818: No construction reported.

1819: No construction reported.

1820: A water powered mill was built.

1821: No construction reported.

1822: No construction reported.

1823: An orchard was enclosed with an adobe wall.

1824: No construction reported.

1825: Twenty-two apartments were built for as many Indian families.

1826: Twenty-three apartments were built for as many Indian families.

1827: A tanning vat, storage room for hides, and a soap works were built.

1828: No construction reported. Existing structures maintained.

1829: No construction reported. Existing structures maintained.

1830: No construction reported. Existing structures maintained.

1831: No construction reported. Existing structures maintained.

1832: No construction reported. Existing structures maintained.

Source: Annual Reports, Archivo General de la Nacion, Mexico, D.F., Santa Barbara Mission Archive-Library, Santa Barbara, California; Stephen Dietz, et al, Final Report of Archaeological Investigations at Mission San Jose, unpublished manuscript, Pp. 17-18, 23-24.

156), I outline demographic patterns in the five San Francisco Bay Area missions. Mean life expectancy at birth at San Jose Mission was extremely low, a mere 1.7 years. Death rates were consistently higher than birth rates (see Table 8.8), and, as indicated by the low life expectancy, rates of infant and child mortality were extremely high.

Despite the adverse demographic patterns, the number of Indians living at San Jose Mission increased for most years in the nineteenth century. The Franciscans repopulated the mission by resettling thousands of converts, often using force to bring Indians to live at the mission. There was a big push after 1810 to resettle converts from the Central Valley at greater distances from the mission. In the twenty-four years between 1811 and 1834, the Franciscans stationed at San Jose baptized 5,185 converts, an average of 216 per year. The mission population reached a maximum of 1,886 in 1831 (see Table 8.7). In the first fourteen years following the foundation of the mission, 1797 to 1810, the Franciscans baptized an average of 108 converts per year. As the missionaries looked further afield for converts to replace the Indians who died at the mission, they drew upon a larger population living in the Sacramento River Delta and Central Valley. I think there is no question that the need to replenish the labor force was an important factor in the post 1811 drive to resettle Indians to the mission.

TABLE 8.7.   POPULATION, BAPTISMS, AND BURIALS RECORDED AT SAN JOSE MISSION, 1797-1840

Year	Baptism of Converts	Births	Burials	Population
1797	33	0	0	33
1798	130	8	8	154
1799	58	9	32	
1800	119	16	88	275
1801	221	22	63	
1802	233	15	91	622
1803	180	36	110	
1804	216	14	174	779
1805	171	32	174	
1806	28	14	198	662
1807	11	27	71	
1808	16	11	97	544
1809	78	11	62	
1810	14	17	58	545
1811	473	26	83	961
1812	288	60	137	1172
1813	38	55	116	1151
1814	48	33	84	1149
1815	215	35	107	1298
1816	323	39	157	1508
1817	202	56	195	1576
1818	246	55	176	1675
1819	98	56	164	1670
1820	234	47	163	1754
1821	114	54	166	1754
1822	19	39	193	1620
1823	222	46	143	1746

1824	300	32	195	1806
1825	155	43	211	1796
1826	190	25	230	1783
1827	158	33	178	1800
1828	194	21	259	1766
1829	27	36	186	1641
1830	191	30	118	1745
1831	514	33	196	1886
1832	1	26	203	
1833	43	49	209	
1834	892	42	225	
1835	56	51	180	
1836	67	44	165	
1837	8	58	140	
1838	12	40	252	
1839	9	39	136	
1840	171	61	163	

Source: Robert H. Jackson, Gentile Recruitment and Population Movement in the San Francisco Bay Area Missions. Journal of California and Great Basin Anthropology 6:2 (1984), p. 238; Ms. Mission Statistics, The Bancroft Library, University of California, Berkeley.

TABLE 8.8.   CRUDE BIRTH AND DEATH RATES PER THOUSAND POPULATION AT SAN JOSE MISSION, 1799-1835

Year	Crude Birth Rate	Crude Death Rate
1799	58	208
1800		
1801	80	229
1802		
1803	58	177
1804		
1805	41	223

1806		
1807	41	107
1808		
1809	20	114
1810		
1811	48	152
1812	62	143
1813	47	99
1814	29	73
1815	31	93
1816	30	121
1817	37	129
1818	35	112
1819	33	98
1820	28	98
1821	31	95
1822	22	110
1823	28	88
1824	18	112
1825	24	117
1826	14	128
1827	19	100
1828	12	144
1829	20	105
1830	18	72
1831	19	112
1832	14	108
1833		
1834		
1835		

Source: Table 8.7.

CONCLUSION: MISSION SECULARIZATION AND THE LARGER HISTORICAL CONTEXT

By way of conclusion I should like to discuss briefly the impact of the secularization of San Jose Mission. It had been intended that by means of secularization, the missions would be converted into villages populated by acculturated Indians. High death rates in the mission and the rapid turnover in population precluded the acculturation of the Indian converts. The break-down of social control following the secularization of the mission led to the dispersion of the Indians who fled the mission to return to the Central Valley, or looked for work on the emerging cattle ranches or growing towns. In the six years following the secularization of the mission, the Franciscans baptized another 323 converts, many brought to the area from the Central Valley by ranch owners and the military, to obtain new laborers and stop raids on herds of livestock.

By law the corporate property of the missions, lands, buildings, livestock, and equipment, was to have been distributed among the Indians living at the mission. However, the bulk of mission property passed into the hands of the secular administrators placed in charge of the mission, and the local politicians who implemented the secularization law. This law was legislated in Mexico City by liberal politicians as part of an anti-mission program. The main buildings of the mission complex were converted to different uses. The church built between 1805 and 1809 stood until demolished by an earthquake in 1868 (but was rebuilt in the mid-1980s as a monument to the history of missions viewed from the point of view of the missionaries). The Catholic Church obtained title to 28 acres of land surrounding the mission site, and prominent settlers created ranches from former mission lands stocked with animals from mission herds. Rancho Valle de San Jose (Sunol and Bernal), located east of Mission San Jose in an interior valley, covered 48,436 acres. Smaller ranches such as Potrero de los Cerritos (10,610 acres), Arroyo de la Alameda (17,705 acres), and Agua Caliente (9,564 acres) were carved out of mission lands in the plain around San Francisco Bay (Beck and Haase 1974).

How important was the frontier mission in colonial policy? The colonization of Alta California, begun in 1769, coincided with a period of imperial fiscal, military, and bureaucratic reform known to historians as the "Bourbon Reforms." The Spanish government attempted to reassert control over the colonial bureaucracy of the Americas, improve defense, and raise additional revenues while cutting the costs of government. Alta California, a strategic region, was occupied for geopolitical reasons—to prevent an English or Russian occupation of the region (Jackson 1991a:387-439). The Franciscans received control of mission temporalities (labor and economic production) in the 1770s from officials in Mexico City for the specific purpose of reducing the cost of colonizing the province by supplying food, clothing, shoes, and leather products at prices considerably lower than what the cost of shipping food from Mexico would have been. The missionaries also provided labor to the military garrisons for construction projects. Father Narciso Duran, stationed at San Jose Mission for some 27 years beginning in 1806, exploited the labor of the Indian converts at San Jose Mission to supply increasing quantities of food, clothing, shoes and other products to the military, primarily San Francisco Presidio. The guard posted at the mission protected the missionaries and maintained the social controls that the Franciscans implemented to ensure the smooth functioning of the mission economies.

Changing politics in Mexico City following Mexican independence led to the end of the mission regime; however, the missions clearly satisfied the policy objectives of colonial officials. San Jose, which ranked second in terms of population, and produced large surpluses for the military, played an important role in the political economy of colonial Alta California. The missions contributed in the short-run to the successful Spanish colonization of Alta California, but at what cost for the Indian converts brought to live at the missions? Contrary to the romanticized and biased view of the missionaries presented in Franciscan church self-history, the missionaries who staffed the Alta California missions, most of whom, including Duran, were natives of Spain, were pragmatic agents of Spanish colonial policy.[3] Even Junipero Serra, who began his New World career as a hell and brimstone evangelical revivalist preacher in Mexico City, was the pragmatic architect of the policy that granted the Franciscans control over the mission temporalities in exchange for subsidizing the costs to the royal government of providing soldiers to protect the missionaries. In my view, the Franciscans saw no inconsistency in the evangelization and exploitation of Indian converts to further colonial policy objectives. Spanish-born Franciscans stationed in

---

[3]The pragmatism of the Franciscans stationed in the Alta California missions can clearly be seen in their correspondence between themselves, with the Apostolic College of San Fernando in Mexico City that directly administered the Alta California Missions, and civil and religious officials in California itself. The writings of the eighteenth and nineteenth century Franciscans contrasts with the utopian idealism and spiritual mysticism of the sixteenth century Franciscans, products of the reform of the Franciscan order in Castile and Franciscan mysticism that emerged at the beginning of the sixteenth century under the direction of Fray Francisco Ximenez de Cisneros (confessor to Queen Isabella), who spearheaded the first efforts to evangelize Indians in central Mexico. See Lynch (1964:58-67); Kamen (1983:111-121); Phelan (1970).

Alta California for many years, including Duran, were conservative royalist supporters of the Spanish colonial order in the Americas, and viewed the secularization of the missions as the undoing of a lifetime labor on behalf of King and God.

REFERENCES CITED

Beck, Warren and Inez Haase
1974   Historical Atlas of California. Map 30. Norman.

Costello, Julia
1989   Variability among the Alta California Missions: The
              Economics of Agricultural Production. *In* Columbian
              Consequences 1: Archaeological and Historical Per-
              spectives on the Spanish Borderlands West. Pp. 435-
              449. David Thomas, ed. Washington, D.C.

Gagliano, Joseph
1992   Agents of Change: The Jesuits and Encounters of Two
              Worlds. Encounters: A Quincentenary Review 9 (Sum-
              mer):32.

Hornbeck, David
1989   Economic Growth and Change at the Missions of Alta
              California, 1769-1846. *In* Columbian Consequences 1:
              Archaeological and Historical Perspectives on the
              Spanish Borderlands West. Pp. 423-431. David Thom-
              as, ed. Washington, D.C.

Jackson, Robert H.
1991a   Population and the Economic Dimension of Colonization:
              in Alta California: Four Mission Communities. Journal
              of the Southwest 33 (3):387-439.

1991b   The Economy and Demography of San Gabriel Mission,
              1771-1834: A Structural Analysis. Paper presented at
              the symposium, Spanish California, 1522-1822, Santa
              Barbara, California, July 15.

1992a   The Dynamic of Indian Demographic Collapse in the San
              Francisco Bay Missions, Alta California, 1776-1840.
              The American Indian Quarterly 16 (2):141-156.

1992b   The Changing Structure of the Alta California Mission
              Economies: A Reinterpretation.   Pacific Historical
              Review 61(3):387-415.

Kamen, Henry
   1983   Spain 1469-1714: A Society in Conflict. London and
                   New York.

Lynch, John
   1964   Spain Under the Hapsburgs: Empire and Absolutism
                   1516-1598. Oxford.

Phelan, John L.
   1970   The Millennial Kingdom of the Franciscans in the New
                   World. Berkeley and Los Angeles.

TAMIEN STATION ARCHAEOLOGICAL PROJECT

Mark G. Hylkema

In the course of urban redevelopment and the construction of highways, rail lines, and other commuter networks, prehistoric archaeological sites are occasionally encountered prior to or during construction work. Such an event occurred during a joint transportation project between the California Department of Transportation (Caltrans) and Santa Clara County while a multi-modal transportation terminal in the City of San Jose was being developed (see Figure 9.1).

Rapid population growth in the Santa Clara Valley of Central California has resulted in the need for expanded transportation systems. State transportation projects using federal funds are required to comply with federal environmental laws that define a process that either protects archaeological sites or leads to the recovery of information through excavation that would otherwise be lost through project development. Section 106 of the National Historic Preservation Act of 1966 (NHPA) establishes the guidelines for this process in order to satisfy the legal requirements for environmental assessments under the National Environmental Protection Act (NEPA).

The Tamien Station archaeological project represents the successful integration of environmental law, archaeological investigation, Native American self-determination, and public benefit. By going beyond the standard programmatic approach of cultural resource mitigation, which focuses on meeting the demands of state and federal agencies with respect to archaeology, this project provided opportunity for Native American consultants to assist in the decision making process. Their participation reflected the cultural vitality of the Ohlone descendants, who

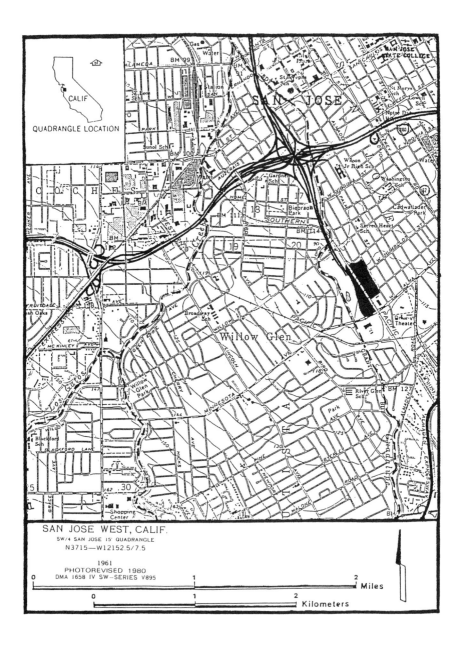

Figure 9.1. Project location

ultimately documented their own contemporary ethnography for inclusion in the final archaeological report.

Archaeological reports usually contain a section that consists of an ethnographic overview of the indigenous people of a given area. Unfortunately, the recent history of contemporary Native Americans is seldom a component of such discussions. This has occasionally alienated the Native American consultants from the archaeological process. Being aware of this, Caltrans asked the Ohlone consultants to write a section for the report documenting their history from the mission period until their involvement with the project. In response they supported the scientific goals developed for the archaeological site identified as CA-SCL-690.

By sharing the responsibility of legal compliance, concern for ancestral Ohlone remains, and ultimately the analysis, documentation, and reinterment of the remains, Caltrans was able to construct a complex transportation terminal without compromising the historic and ethical values attributable to a site of this nature. A permanent museum exhibit documenting the archaeological investigation has been built by Caltrans and dedicated to the ancestral Ohlone whose bones remain at a place called Tamien Station.

PROJECT DESCRIPTION

In 1976, a Light Rail Feasibility Study and Alternatives Analysis sponsored by the Urban Mass Transportation Administration (UMTA) and the Santa Clara County Transit District (SCCTD) identified the need for a major new transportation terminal and transfer facility near or within downtown San Jose. The study indicated that the proposed Light Rail System (LRT) and express bus routes should connect efficiently and effectively with the existing and soon-to-be-upgraded Southern Pacific/Caltrans peninsula railroad operation (Caltrain). This upgraded heavy railway line would extend commuter services, which ran from San Francisco to San Jose, further south to the City of Morgan Hill. Existing railway stations were to be expanded and new ones built. Tamien Station, the topic of this paper, is one of these stations. The station was originally going to be called the Alma Avenue Station but was changed to Tamien after the place name used by the Ohlone people at Mission Santa Clara for the lower Guadalupe River area.

Tamien Station is on AMTRAK's "Coast Starlight Route." At that time Caltrans owned and operated Caltrain, while SCCTD owned, operated, and continued to build segments of the LRT. In addition to the merging of the heavy and light rail system at Tamien Station, a new freeway extension of Route 87 converges at this location (see Figure 9.2).

In fact, the LRT tracks have been set within the median divider of Route 87. In summary then, Tamien Station is the point for the LRT; Caltrain and Route 87 intersect and form the transfer station. Intercity buses also meet at the station creating a highly integrated mass transportation system.

BACKGROUND

Prior to 1989, the project location was the site of an enormous fruit cannery, and a major archaeological site had been covered by the asphalt, concrete and structures of the facility. The cannery was first established in 1918, and continued to enlarge until the demise of agriculture in the Santa Clara Valley that began to accelerate in the 1960s as a result of urban expansion and industrial development. The archaeological site remained covered until Santa Clara County and Caltrans preparations to develop the cannery into a semi-subterranean parking lot for the station were well under way.

Prior to the construction of projects of this magnitude a public hearing must be held so that residents of the area to be affected and other concerned individuals can have an opportunity to comment on the proposed work. In the spring of 1989, Mr. Victor Merlino, a retired cannery foreman, attended the public hearing and began a series of events that resulted in the discovery of an important prehistoric ancestral Ohlone village with over 124 human burials. Mr. Merlino reported finding human bones and artifacts over a period of forty years whenever work at the cannery required subsurface excavations. Aside from Mr. Merlino's report, there were no other clues that this site existed. The requisite surface survey for such finds was conducted by Caltrans back in 1985, but did not find evidence of this site—not surprising since the entire area was covered by asphalt, concrete, railroad tracks, pumps, sumps, wells, and massive cannery structures. Mr. Merlino's report was made well after the environmental studies had been approved and just prior to executing the contract for demolition of the extant buildings and construction of the parking lot. The 106 compliance process is appropriately implemented at the beginning of project planning, not when a project is about to be built. This was not the best time to begin the process of federal compliance for archaeological sites. Given the legal procedures involved in the finding of sensitive cultural remains, specifically human burials, the potential for very costly construction delays was great.

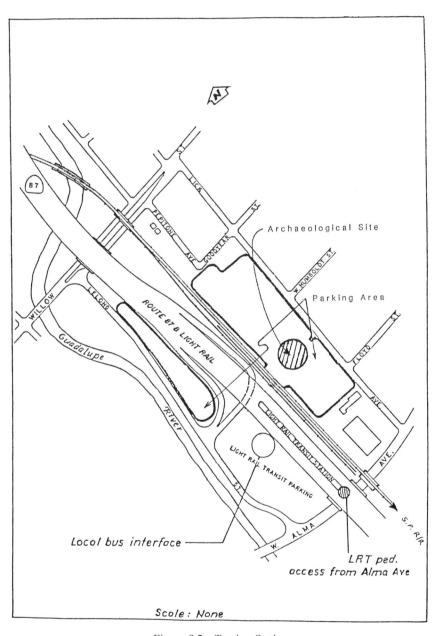

Figure 9.2. Tamien Station

PLANNING FOR ARCHAEOLOGICAL DISCOVERIES

Planning for the proposed transportation terminal project was required to comply with Section 106 of the National Historic Preservation Act of 1966 because federal funds were involved. Compliance procedures normally involve three steps that include: 1) identification of archaeological sites through surface surveys and literature reviews, 2) excavation to determine if there are any significant data that qualify the site as eligible for listing on the National Register of Historic Places, and 3) a full-scale archaeological excavation of areas affected by the project if the site is eligible, and if the project cannot be changed to avoid impacting it. For the last stage a treatment plan that specifies the research objectives and methodology must be reviewed by the State Historic Preservation Office (SHPO) and the Advisory Council on Historic Preservation (ACHP); moreover, for sites with the potential for human burials, a Memorandum of Agreement (MOA) must be signed by the agency, SHPO, and ACHP. The MOA is a legally binding document that, in this case, defines procedures for exhumation and disposition of human remains. Native American consultation prior to the drafting of the MOA is required in order to determine the optimal approach for handling the recovery, analysis and reinterment of the skeletal remains and, typically, the associated grave artifacts as well. The 106 process can take up to two or three years when major archaeological sites are discovered. Failure to comply with the 106 process can subject the lead agency to lengthy and costly delays resulting from litigation. Further, compliance with Section 106 is typically carried out well in advance of the approval of the environmental studies.

The scheduled date for awarding the demolition contract at Tamien Station was approximately five months after Victor Merlino had notified Caltrans of the potential archaeological site. In short, Caltrans had a problem to solve in a very limited time period.

Generally there are two approaches for the treatment of archaeological sites found late in the project development process that meet the conditions of the laws. Each situation involves a set of risks that must be evaluated.

The first approach is an emergency-oriented process. Members of the Native American community monitor project demolition and construction (specifically, all ground breaking activity). If archaeological resources are found, then project-related activities that disturb the find are suspended until (in negotiations with the regulating agencies) a plan to excavate the site is developed. This process may be the most expedient if there is strong evidence that a minor site or a very disturbed archaeological deposit will be encountered. However, for sites with a potential for significant remains, there is a risk that construction delays will be extensive and costly while negotiations with the regulatory agencies and the Native Americans take place. This situation may delay the contractor, which in turn causes the public agency to pay the contractor penalties for delaying construction. In the case of very large projects these fees can cost several hundred thousand dollars if delays extend beyond a couple of weeks and the contractor is unable to work.

Careful and controlled archaeological recovery techniques are frequently compromised because heavy equipment is being used to retrieve important data as quickly as possible. The most important aspects of artifact recovery, the provenience of items *in situ*, which is the basis for archaeological interpretation, is lost. Finally, the removal of sensitive skeletal remains with a backhoe damages the fragile bones and may be considered disrespectful by Indian people who have become increasingly concerned about the disposition of their ancestors' remains. The agency archaeologist, caught in the middle, must consider the economic concerns of the agency, the scientific value of the archaeology, and the spiritual concerns of the Indians.

The second approach requires planning for sensitive and significant archaeological remains by developing an excavation plan and completing the bureaucratic process before the archaeological and construction field work begins. Essentially, the entire 106 process described above is completed in a single document, the Treatment Plan, and is subsequently reviewed by the regulating agencies. An MOA accompanies the Treatment Plan if there is a potential for unearthing human remains. This approach, as compared to the first approach, requires extensive planning prior to the field work. From a management perspective, the dedication of labor for a project where the potential for an archaeological site is unknown may seem inefficient and wasteful. Indeed, if nothing of archaeological value is found after investment of staff time, the agency has taken a risk and has lost. Conversely, these conservative measures may ultimately avoid costly construction delays.

In response to Victor Merlino's information, Caltrans adopted the second approach and assumed that a major archaeological site lay beneath the cannery and, therefore, a fully conceived archaeological field and lab investigation was developed and presented in the treatment plan. An agreement for the presence of Native American Monitors, and, of course, a plan for reburial of human skeletal remains (should any be found) was formulated. These conservative methods seemed most appropriate given the circumstances: Mr. Merlino had provided precise information on the locations of the past discoveries, the types of archaeological remains uncovered, and indeed, exact months and years of his finds. Large prehistoric burial sites are not uncommon in the Santa Clara Valley, and there was no reason to believe that this site would be an exception.

The treatment plan described a research design based on local archaeological investigations and defined the following procedures: 1) monitoring the demolition of the cannery by an archaeologist and a Native American of local descent, 2) contingency plans requiring that if burials were found during demolition, the contractor would be directed to work away from the find while archaeologists excavated the burial, and 3) the implementation of a controlled archaeological excavation after demolition identified locations where burials or other important archaeological elements were discovered. The treatment plan also outlined specific research objectives to be addressed by the analysis of the recovered data and specified excavation techniques to be used.

The goals of the archaeological program were: 1) to remove sensitive cultural elements from the Area of Direct Impact; 2) to conduct a thorough analysis of the remains and other cultural constituents; 3) to document the results in a final report; and 4) to reinter the human skeletal remains.

The treatment plan was reviewed by the Native American consultants. It was agreed that analysis of the human remains could be carried out if the archaeologist could identify specific needs and goals of such investigations for their consideration, and guarantee the reinterment of the burials as close to their point of origin as possible.

THE FIELD WORK

During the demolition of subsurface cannery foundations and related structures, we observed and recovered numerous isolated human bones from the central portion of the 24 acre parcel. The removal of a very large fuel tank in this area led to the initial discovery of 23 mostly intact burials. There was no midden-like soil between them to denote an area of archaeological sensitivity; however, the deep open pit left by the removal of the fuel tank provided a useful soil profile of stratigraphic relationships to a depth of over four meters. The profile revealed a surface layer of historically disturbed soils to a depth of 40 cm. This dark brown clay layer rested upon a light brown colored clay matrix, which was approximately 60 cm. thick, at 40 to 100 cm. below ground surface. Both of the clay layers in turn rested upon a thick gravel bed that was formerly the stream channel of the ancestral Guadalupe River. This gravel bed was two meters thick and was deposited over a light brown to blue mottled clay deposit of undetermined depth.

The burials found during the monitoring phase (most of which remained *in situ* for later controlled excavation) were all within the upper two clay layers and indicated that the site had been established on slightly raised ground surrounded by marshy wetlands near the river.   The consultants on geomorphology have identified episodic deposits of silt along the river banks that created natural levees, or high spots. These locations were attractive to prehistoric settlement.   Knowledge of the stratigraphy for this site enabled the archaeologist to estimate the depth of the cultural deposit, excavation volumes, and the time involved in the excavation.   Further, this data allowed for the development of an adequate budget for the field and lab work, which was to follow the demolition phase.

Caltrans negotiated an interagency agreement with the San Jose State University Academic Foundation to hire the necessary field and lab personnel.   Physical Anthropologist Dr. Robert Jurmain supervised the osteological research and university coordination.   Ohlone Families Consulting Services was contracted to provide Native American monitors to assist with the recovery work.

The controlled excavation, which began in the middle of January and ended in May 1990, accomplished the hand excavation of 269 cubic meters of the site in 75 working days.   A grid system of 2 x 2 meter excavation blocks was established, radiating out from the area of the fuel tank excavation pit and the first finds.   A total of 89 burials was found within the hand excavated 2 x 2 meter units.   Soils from the site were sifted through 1/4 inch mesh screens in order to process large volumes from the units rapidly.   When bone was encountered, soil from within a 10 cm radius of the find was wet screened through either 1/8 or 1/16 inch mesh to recover small bones and beads that might otherwise be overlooked by dry screening through larger mesh screens.   The wet screening was accomplished by hooking up a water meter to a street sidewalk fire hydrant and connecting several garden hoses to it.   Water was then passed over the screens containing the excavated soils, removing the overburden, and the remaining constituents were then dried and sorted.   Over 35,000 shell beads were recovered in this way, along with small human and faunal bone fragments, shell pendants, debitage, and a range of other elements.

A large number of burials was found clustered near where the fuel tank had been removed. As the excavation units worked increasingly farther away from the main cluster the number of finds began to diminish.   A backhoe was then used in an attempt to find burials that were isolated at various distances away from the primary concentration. The backhoe operator was directed to excavate long lineal trenches as well as large square blocks similar in size to the 2 x 2 meter units.   The backhoe bucket had a straightedged steel plate welded over the teeth that originally formed the lip of the bucket. By covering the teeth with a plate the operator could scrape the soils from the blocks in nearly 10 cm levels without tearing up chunks of earth. Approximately fifteen blocks were excavated by backhoe with the units in rows, leaving a 30 cm soil baulk between them. The backhoe testing exposed 10 burials.

During the course of hand excavating the large 2 x 2 meter units towards the northwestern quadrant of the site, burial finds decreased and gave way to an extensive thermally affected rock cobble layer. This layer rarely exceeded 40 cm in thickness and was divided into several Feature areas. Both wet and dry screening techniques through 1/4 and 1/8 inch mesh facilitated the recovery of a greater abundance of artifactual and faunal elements. Approximately 18 cubic meters of feature soil was screened from hand excavated units composing an area measuring nearly 10 x 14 meters. Several intact hearths were identified and from these several soil samples were taken for macro-floral analysis. Charcoal and baked earth were observed in large concentrations throughout the features. Unlike the matrix between the burial area, the features contained a great deal of debris relating to the processing of foods, tool construction and use, as well as the numerous cooked cobbles that generally defined the extent of the deposit.

After the features had been investigated and the exploratory trenching failed to encounter additional finds, the field crew was dismissed and the artifact analysis started. Construction of the parking lot was scheduled for the following fall season.

An additional 26 burials were found between October 1990 and February 1991, when construction of the parking lot was begun. These last individuals were very far away from the main cluster and had survived the demolition and eluded our backhoe probing. The construction phase was also monitored by archaeologists and Native Americans. The same recovery techniques were used, although the 1/4 inch rapid recovery method no longer applied. Several of these later burials were damaged by either heavy equipment or historic construction events at the cannery.

The osteological research had been progressing concurrently with the excavation so that most of this work was done shortly after construction ceased. After the field work had been completed, Caltrans employed the services of Biosystems Analysis Inc. to organize the analysts' reports and interpret the significance of the mortuary complex under the direction of Dr. Thomas Jackson.

ANALYTICAL RESULTS

The archaeological report for this project is currently in progress. Information from the various specialists' studies has led to additional research questions as the data builds on itself. The following description is a brief summary of findings, the greater detail of which is reserved for the final report.

The Tamien Station archaeological site, CA-SCL-690, produced a wide variety of artifact types in relative abundance. Social distinctions between individuals within the cemetery complex were evident and, using *Olivella biplicata* shell beads as a measure of economic viability, many burials exhibited considerable wealth. Of the 124 flexed burials over 2/3 retained some type of artifact other than beads in association. Temporally diagnostic artifact types, radiocarbon dating, and obsidian hydration studies have shown that the site represents a single component assemblage dating to the Middle/Late Transitional Period. This time has been defined as the Upper Archaic Period (Fredrickson 1974). Uncorrected dates range from 800 to 1200 AD, the majority of which cluster between 900 to 1100 AD.

Over 35,000 shell beads were recovered and typed by Randall Milliken using the scheme developed by Bennyhoff and Hughes (1987). A little over 95% were in association with burials, with the total averaging approximately 270 beads per individual. These types included Ala, Alb, Alc, C2, C7, D1, G1, F3, M1/F3, and M1 beads (see Figure 9.3). In addition to these, over 160 abalone pendants (*Haliotis rufescens* and *Haliotis cracherodii*) were found, most of which were intact enough for identification by type. The dominant pendant form was circular, ranging in size from a quarter to a silver dollar, with one or two perforations near the edge that frequently exhibited patterns of incised lines and grooves around the circumference (types CA3a, CA3g, CA3h, and CA3j using the Bennyhoff and Hughes nomenclature). Some of these types are presented in Figure 9.4.

Thirteen samples of organic materials were submitted to Beta Analytic Inc. for radiocarbon dating analysis. These samples included charcoal, shell beads, and human bone in direct association with features or burials. The first batch of dates came from materials other than human bone. The bead types had already provided a general chronological framework for the assemblage; however, the possibility that the bur-

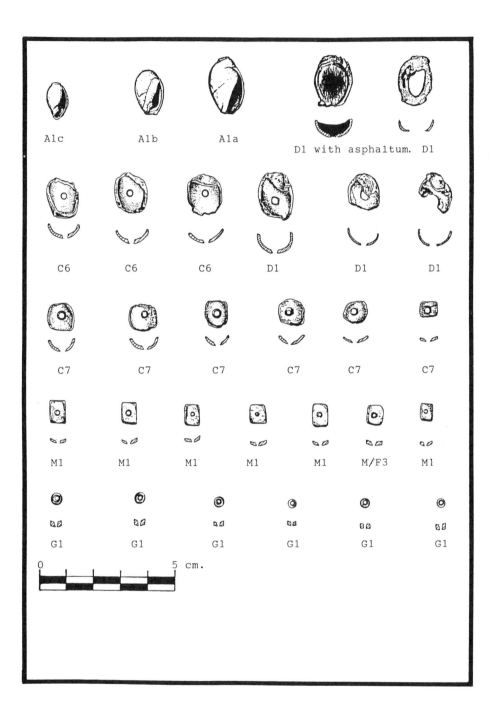

Figure 9.3. *Olivella* bead types, CA-SCL-690

**Table 9.1.   UNCORRECTED RADIOCARBON DATES FROM
CA-SCL-690**

Cat. #	Sample #	Item	C-14 Years B.P.
B-44244	0150	Olivella Ala, Burial 24	840 ± 60
B-44245	0228	Olivella Gla, Burial 31	1230 ± 70
B-44246	0232	Charcoal, Burial 31	900 ± 70
B-44247	0308	Olivella M1, Burial 41	1160 ± 50
B-44248	0581	Olivella Ala, Burial 92	870 ± 60
B-44249	1381	Charcoal, Feature 3	680 ± 50
B-44250	1591	Olivella D1, Burial 39	1050 ± 60
B-46641		Bone- Burial 31	940 ± 80
B-44642		Bone- Burial 39	1100 ± 60
B-46643		Bone- Burial 41	720 ± 60
B-46644		Bone- Burial 55	700 ± 60
B-46645		Olivella Ala, Burial 55	1040 ± 50
B-46646		Bone- Burial 78	840 ± 60

ials without associated artifacts might represent another temporal component remained a possibility. Further, potential correction factors needed for correspondence between dated shell and the other materials still had to be developed. This led to the conclusion that human bone would provide the most accurate means of dating the site and establishing correction ratios for the other organic materials. Also, we were not absolutely sure that the extensive rock features were contemporaneous with the mortuary complex, although temporally diagnostic artifact types similar to those associated with the burials pointed to a coeval relationship.

After we described the nature of our investigations and shared our questions with the Native American consultants, they voted to allow the limited sampling of human bone for radiocarbon assay. This was not an easy decision and considerable discussion took place among them before they decided to permit it. Once permission had been granted, five bone samples were processed for a total of thirteen radiocarbon dates. The results are given in Table 9.1.

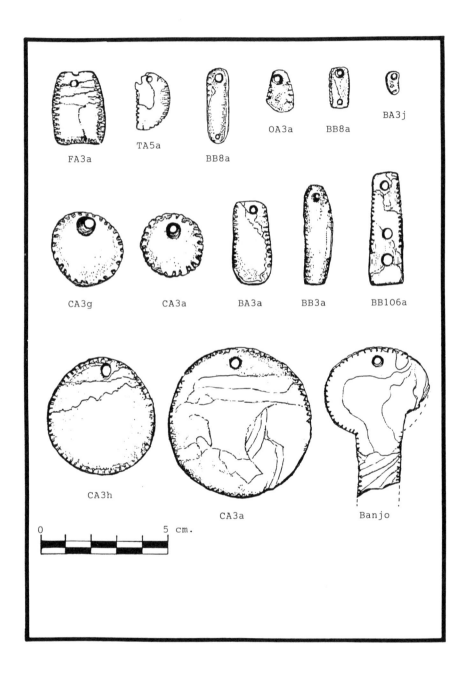

Figure 9.4. Abalone pendant types, CA-SCL-690

Dated shell samples weighed over 30 grams each, charcoal from Feature 3 weighed 100 grams; charcoal from Burial 31, 35 grams; and all of the human bone samples, over 120 grams. The bones tested were complete tibiae.

The single date from the feature complex along with diagnostic artifact types show that it is contemporaneous with the mortuary complex. Other artifacts, other than beads and radiocarbon dates, reflect a Middle/Late Transitional Period affiliation. These include several obsidian stockton serrated types as well as slightly serrated lanceolate forms (see Figure 9.5). One burial retained a very large obsidian blade with a deeply concave base and wide neck width, and was the exception to the general trend in projectile point forms. This same individual also had a very large chert biface and many *Olivella* type Ala beads. Overall, the total number of points was low. Despite the well represented presence of Franciscan chert debitage, only three points were found to be made of this material. Nearly all of the obsidian originated from the Napa Valley source with hydration readings clustering between 1.8 and 2.4 microns.

The rest of the assemblage consisted of bird bone whistles, awls, hairpins, scapula saws, antler wedges, bone types, bowl mortars, pestles, handstones, non-stemmed tubular tobacco pipes, plummets, drills, and other assorted items (some of which are illustrated in Figures 9.6 and 9.7). These were found in direct association with burials and in the features. Many of the pestles exceeded 30 cm in length, and several were twice as long. A few of the burials were found with bowl mortars inverted over their heads. Many of the bone artifacts and plummets retained asphaltum stains from its use as an adhesive, as did a number of the shell beads and pendants.

A wide variety of faunal bone elements were recovered, the majority of which came from the feature complex. Identified species included fish, birds, mammals, and reptiles. Fish bone, identified by Dr. Kenneth Gobalet of California State University, Bakersfield, consisted of both fresh and salt water species such as splittail, hitch, thicktail chub, minnow, Sacramento sucker, steelhead, Pacific herring, Pacific sardine, rockfish, and leopard shark. The other faunal bone was identified by Dwight Simons of Biosystems Analysis Inc. Bird remains from the site represented geese, ducks, hawks, falcons, California quail, heron, curlews, band-tailed pigeons, barn owls, flickers, and crows. Mammals represented included pronghorn, tule elk, deer, bobcat, striped skunk, spotted skunk badger, longtailed weasel, raccoon, grizzly bear, gray fox, wolf, coyote, rat, squirrel, gopher, mole, jackrabbit, and cotton tail rabbit. The reptilian remains were from the Pacific pond turtle.

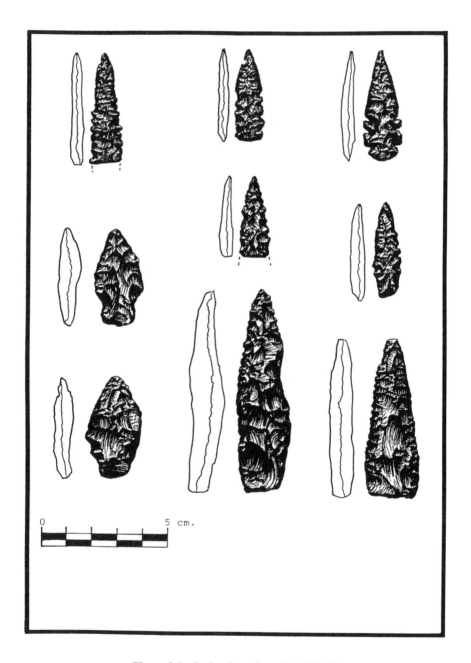

Figure 9.5. Projectile points, CA-SCL-690

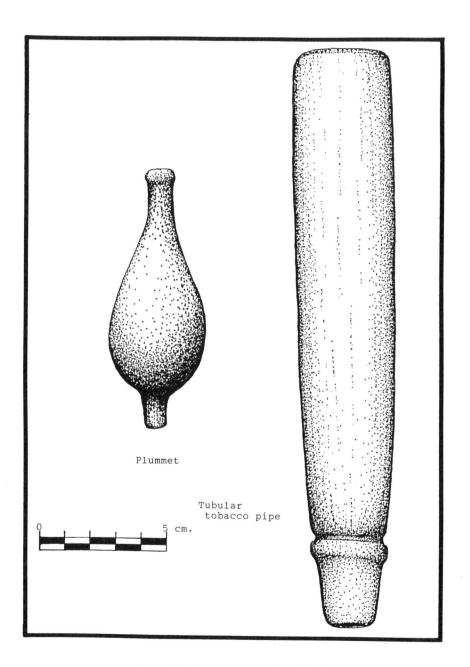

Plummet

Tubular
tobacco pipe

0   1   5 cm.

Figure 9.6. Stone artifacts, CA-SCL-690

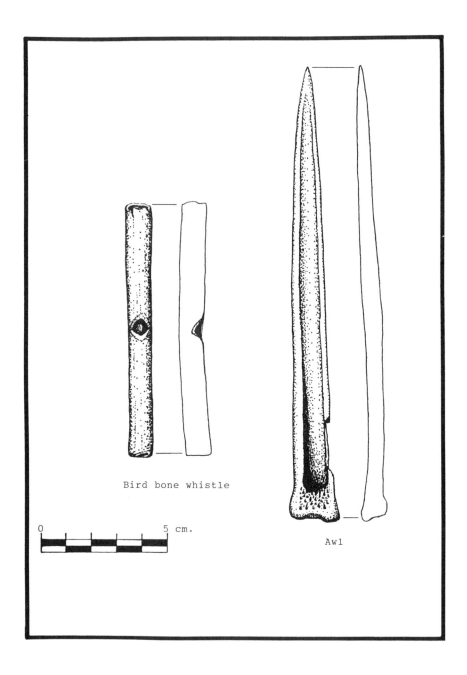

Bird bone whistle

0   5 cm.

Awl

Figure 9.7. Bone artifacts, CA-SCL-690

Soil samples from within the feature complex were examined for the presence of plant remains by pouring them in buckets of water and filtering out the seeds and charcoal. Charlie Miksicek of Biosystems Analysis Inc. examined the recovered seeds and stems, which served as an indicator of the local habitat as well as species used in the diet. Trees identified from the sample included willow, cottonwood, sycamore, pine, and others which were nearby and represented by the charred nuts that were used as food. These included acorns and hazelnuts. Plants edible as seeds consisted of Indian buckwheat, tarweed, fescue grass, rye grass, hair grass, bentgrass, bromegrass, maygrass, and reed grass. Plants that were edible as both seeds and greens consisted of pigweed, large goosefoot, and goosefoot. Finally, plants edible just for their greens included lupine, deer vetch, and miner's lettuce. Also present were cattails (of which rhizome, greens, and pollen were edible), filaree, and bedstraw.

The osteological investigation was thorough. A complete inventory of the remains was constructed, paleopathologies noted, sex and ages determined, anthropometrics tabulated, and X-rays taken. A dental surgeon has examined the teeth of most of the individuals. Several of the burials retained evidence of projectile point fragments imbedded in the bone as well as other traumatic evidence. Infants were found to be unusually underrepresented at SCL-690 when compared to other regional sites. Currently the organization of individuals and their associated artifacts within the cemetery is being examined for information regarding social relationships.

PUBLIC BENEFIT

Although funding for state and federal archaeological investigations is primarily generated by the public through taxes, most people are not even aware that such research is going on. There has been little opportunity to transfer the results of archaeological research into a form that is understandable, interesting or available to members of the public. Native Americans have also pointed out that much of what they read in the reports fails to satisfy their quest for greater understanding of their cultural heritage. There are several reasons for this situation. Archaeologists are employed to conduct intensive scientific investigations and frequently must budget their activities to focus on the salient points of their tasks. Agencies typically do not have the resources to spend extra funding beyond the need for environmental clearance obligations. Furthermore, because of the persistent problem of amateur artifact collecting and the looting of sensitive sites, archaeologists must be very

careful about the information they disseminate. The value of the research
is related to the location from where it came, but it is difficult to describe
the results of such research without compromising the location's integrity.

The field work for the Tamien Station project provided a good
example of the importance for agencies to take a conservative approach
towards archaeology. This fact was conveyed to the Santa Clara County
Transit District and Caltrans planning staff through a series of lectures
and slide shows. The purpose of these presentations was to expose
management to the work that their specialists do. As a result, the
agencies realized the potential benefit of this work to the public and
decided to construct a permanent exhibit at the station. Further, a
memorial plaque dedicated to the ancestral Ohlone people has been
placed on the structure.

In this instance it was safe for the location of the site to become
public knowledge without fear of vandalism—after all, it had already
been cleared for the construction of the station. It was cleared; but not
emptied. All of the human skeletal remains and their associated artifacts
were reinterred back on the property in November, 1991, after the
analytical goals had been met. Many of the Ohlone descendants
supervised the interment which was done in such a way as to retain the
individual order of each burial. They were placed very deep into the
ground near their point of origin and will not likely be disturbed again.

Caltrans has constructed a permanent exhibit structure within the
heavy rail station which describes the story of the archaeological recovery
at Tamien Station. Artifacts not associated with burials are included in
the display. Photographs, sketches, and some replicated artifacts made
by contemporary Native Californian artists enhance the story, which
begins with the discovery of the site, and ends with a discussion of the
reinterment. Because of the large number of commuters using the station
this publicly funded project will expose people to the prehistory and rich
cultural heritage of Santa Clara Valley.

Acknowledgements
        I should like to thank Marcia Kelly and Mara Melandry of the California
Department of Transportation, for managing the 106 compliance prior to the field work.
I especially wish to thank Rosemary Cambra, Chairwoman of Ohlone Families Consulting
Services, for coordinating Native American concerns by meeting regularly with many of
the descendants and seeking their input as a council. Rosemary also provided the Native
American monitors who assisted in the recovery work. The council members are to be
thanked for their consent to the dating of human bone—a painful decision that required
extensive explanation on the part of the archaeologist as to the reasons why such analysis
would address specific research questions.
        Also, I would like to thank the research specialists, specifically Michael Amrine,
Joe Carrol, Rick Fitzgerald, Dr. Kenneth Gobalet, Charlane Gross, Jeffrey Hall, Dr.

Thomas Jackson, Dr. Robert Jurmain, Alan Leventhal, Muriel Maverick, Charles Miksicek, Dr. Randy Milliken, Dwight Simons, Cherie Walth, Sandy Weldon, Jerry Weber, Brian Wickstrom, just to name a few. Finally, I want to thank the many crew members who did the archaeological field work.

REFERENCES CITED

Bennyhoff, J. A. and R. E. Hughes
    1987   Shell Bead and Ornament Exchange Networks Between
                California and the Western Great Basin. Anthropological
                Papers of the American Museum of Natural History, Vol.
                64: Part 2. New York.

Fredrickson, D. A.
    1974   Cultural Diversity in Early Central California: A View
                from the North Coast Ranges. Journal of California
                Anthropology 1(1):41-53.

THE LANGUAGE
OF RACE HATRED

Edward D. Castillo

The International Columbian Quincentennial has over the last few years focused a considerable amount of national attention on the current status of our understanding concerning the nature of the encounter between Native Peoples of the Americas and Europeans in the past. In the Far West and Southwest, relations between Indians and Spanish missionaries have received unprecedented attention. Borrowing from anthropology, demography, and related humanities, a new generation of historians has produced startling new perspectives on the relationships between the Spanish missionaries and Indians, especially with respect to California (Axtell 1982:35-41; Fontana 1987:55-59; Heizer 1978:121-139; Phillips 1989:83-90; Sandos 1985:109-133; Shipek 1985:480-491; Weber 1990:429-48; Wiget 1982:181-199). These works have given pause to thoughtful readers, and have brought about a healthy skepticism of earlier works that argue that missionization for Indians was some kind of uplifting experience.

The restored missions in California have become places of considerable interest. Thousands and thousands of tourists and virtually every fourth grade public school class visit the various missions for a mandatory look. These visitors, both adult and children, are presented with what David Hurst Thomas, curator of anthropology at the American Museum of Natural History, calls "California's Mythical Mission Past" (Thomas 1991:119-157). Not only are the majority of physical reconstructions of the missions inaccurate, so too are the tales of intents, practices, and the outcomes of missionization on the Indians who were supposed to be the beneficiaries of these institutions.

The recreated mission past was concocted in the late 19th century, in part to sell California real estate and in part to provide historical justification for the Franciscan order's participation in the destruction and dispossession of thousands of California Indian men, women, and children as part of a scheme of world conquest devised by the Roman Catholic Church and the empire of Spain.

The principal tool in the historic rehabilitation of the Franciscan order's empire building enterprise was an elaborate reconstruction of the histories of the missions, beginning in the last quarter of the 19th century. Ironically, it was in part the misguided reformist zeal of Helen Hunt Jackson that helped inaugurate a "fantasy" past for the California missions and the Indians who were subjected to their labor and Christianization programs. In an attempt to whip up support for the badly abused southern California Indians with whom she came in contact, she wrote the romantic novel, *Ramona*, which did serious damage to the historical facts of the Indian experience in the missions (Mathes 1990).

Jackson's romantic tale was followed by Franciscan writer Zephyrin Engelhardt's series of mission histories (ca. 1908-1933). In these works, Engelhardt consistently attacked secular historians like Hubert Howe Bancroft and Theodore Hittell, whose works occasionally revealed aspects of the coercive nature of the Franciscans' baptismal, labor, and family-destroying practices (Engelhardt 1908-1915). Those secular historians' occasional mild criticisms of the Spanish padres' treatment of the Indians came under further attacks by the founder of a new school of Borderlands historians led by Herbert Eugene Bolton. Bolton focused upon counteracting what he considered the "Black Legend." In the course of his revisionist reevaluation of the Spanish colonial empire and its various personalities, Bolton became so absorbed in his subject that he ignored the negative impact that the empire's policies had had on native peoples. Bolton in turn trained several generations of borderland historians who eventually erected an equally flawed "White Legend." Together Engelhardt and Bolton and others of their school of thought shaped many of the public school texts, academic materials, and popular writings about the California missions and those of the greater Southwest (Weber 1988[1]).

Here in California, Engelhardt's polemics established a strategy that became the centerpiece of a policy of arguing against any criticism whatsoever of the Spanish padres and their institutions. California

---

[1]See especially Chapter 3, "Turner, the Boltonians, and the Spanish Borderlands." Here historian Weber criticizes earlier generations of borderland historians because they ignored the Indians in their descriptive narrative histories. On page 41, he writes, ". . . an understanding of the frontier process must take into account peoples and their motives on both sides of a frontier."

Indians were to be systematically denigrated with respect to intelligence, culture, and race. There was nothing original about this approach. Indeed, it was common practice during the mission period, and was viewed sympathetically by most Euro-Americans until recently. About 1910, Engelhardt wrote, "All accounts agree in representing the natives as among the most stupid, brutish, filthy, lazy and improvident aborigines of the Americas" (Engelhardt 1908-1915, II:262). That mean-spirited and heartless racism set the tone for many of this century's Franciscan historical writings, which in turn have dominated much of the published material on the Mission Indians of California. It is important to keep in mind that the purpose of racist language is to dehumanize people of other races and demean their culture.

Preventing American Indians from using their traditional languages was part of a larger intellectual exercise by European newcomers to the Americas that attempted to redefine the aboriginal peoples of this land in order to justify treating them as less than human (Drinnon 1980).[2] As thoughts affect our language, so does language affect our thoughts. Eventually our behavior and actions are similarly affected. In his famous essay, "Politics and the English Language," the late George Orwell observed that language becomes ugly and inaccurate because our thoughts are foolish, and then, "the slovenliness of our language makes it easier for us to have foolish thoughts." He further maintained that, "the decadence of our language is probably curable," and that "silly words and expressions have often disappeared, not through any evolutionary process, but owing to the conscious action of a minority" (1971:88). The historical abuse of native peoples of Alta California by the late 19th and 20th century church writers serves a perfect example of Orwell's axiom.

Scholars, political leaders, and church authorities of the early Spanish empire were in fact divided on this issue of the Indians' humanity. It was the church that originally argued in favor of the humanity of the aboriginal peoples of the place they called New Spain (Hanke 1959)[3]. But in the aftermath of the disastrous missionization policy's effect on the Indians of the Americas, the Franciscan order seems to have embraced the opposite philosophy in order to explain why and how things went wrong during the half-century or more when they

---

[2]Drinnon, in this powerful book, studies popular literature in analyzing race hatred aimed at American Indians, and links it to colonization.

[3]Hanke, in this pioneering study, documents the debate between those Spaniards who supported the idea of declaring Indians human beings against those who wished to have them labelled "natural slaves."

controlled the land resources and the very lives of many California Indians.

The history and culture of the Costanoan Indians has been more grossly distorted, misinterpreted, and ignored than those of almost any other Indians in California, as the native peoples themselves and most scholars who have chosen to address the issue have long recognized. The Indians of the area are not even mentioned in most of the written works on San Francisco Bay history.

An inherent problem with Indian history is that with few exceptions only the conquerors left written records.[4] Unfortunately, even where rare written accounts of Costanoan experiences in the California missions exist, they are contemptuously dismissed by some writers and church activists as anti-Catholic lies, largely because of the narrow Euro-centric vision of Franciscan and Catholic church self-histories. For example, after my translation of Costanoan Indian and Mission Santa Cruz neophyte Lorenzo Asisara's narrative about the assassination of Padre Andrés Quintana[5] was published in *California History* (1989a:116-125), I was subjected to severe criticism in subsequent "Letters to the Editor" from church activists and historians in the Bolton/Engelhardt tradition, and the veracity of Asisara's account was unsuccessfully assailed.

Beginning in 1936, the Catholic priest Francis Florence McCarthy began writing a history of Mission San Jose, Engelhardt having never completed the history of that mission. The book he produced (McCarthy 1958),[6] aimed at a general audience, from the first page to the last is racist, and constitutes one of the most virulent attacks on American Indians by a Catholic author since World War II.

The first chapter purports to inform the reader of the origins and culture of the Costanoan Indians. According to the author, ". . . the brutish Costanoans arrived on the shores of the San Francisco Bay, to spend the long aeon of intervening centuries in continuous unameliorated savagery, until mercifully lifted up from their degradation by their

---

[4]Martin (1987:28) offers a penetrating criticism of authors who rely solely on colonial records to reconstruct contact history between non-literate Indians and literate colonists, "We should quit deluding ourselves about the significance of and explanatory value of such history, for it is essentially White history, White reality, White thought world. As such it has its place, certainly, but the point is that it has subtly transgressed its explanatory boundaries, to pose as the sole or only valid, or only serious explanation of what transpired when the Indians and Whitemen met."

[5]See below.

[6]Incredibly, the 1977 edition of this book was funded by a grant from the Alameda County Bicentennial Commission!

Franciscan teachers" (McCarthy 1958:11-12).

Other equally ill informed and bizarre theories on the Indian race are expounded. In later chapters McCarthy describes native homes as "huts" and as "sinks of filth" (McCarthy 1977:11-12). In chapter three the author resorts to the term "digger" to express his contempt for the culture of the local Indians. Elsewhere he describes Costanoan Indian culture as "barbarous . . . unprepossessing and uninteresting," and a life in such a situation as "drab existence" (1958:30-31). But that is only the beginning, for he next launches into a denigration of the physical appearance of a Costanoan:

> . . . lumpish, paunch-bellied person standing on ungainly legs. His straight, coarse, matted black hair grows far down over his low receding forehead toward the eyes. From under thick, bushy eyebrows a pair of black, beady, deep-set, dull eyes peer stupidly. The unprepossessing face, framed by rather large ears, is further marred by salient cheekbones, a large mouth with thick prominent lips, and by an unshapely nose depressed at the root and spread wide at the nostrils. A saving feature was a set of large regular teeth, whose whiteness accentuated the olive black color of the face and body (1958:33).

In 1806, the German born physician Georg Heinrich von Langsdorff wrote some complimentary notes on Costanoan Indians as part of a report on the Count Nikilai Petrovich Rezanov's official Russian visit to the San Francisco Bay. Not content to allow any historical data contradict his views, McCarthy goes to great lengths to convince his readers that Langsdorff's praise was "all too extravagant" and argues that the physician was actually describing Wintun, Miwok and Yokuts people, and not the Costanoans at Mission San Jose (McCarthy 1958:32).[7]

It is clear McCarthy has simply followed the lead of Engelhardt and other biased writers of the 19th and early 20th century regarding racial tolerance and acceptance of cultures different than his own.

---

[7] An analysis of baptismal records and other data does not bear out McCarthy's argument that the subjects of Langsdorff's compliments were not Costanoan. See Jackson's and Milliken's articles in this volume, and Milliken 1991:383-386 on the East Bay collapse between 1801 and 1805, and related tables of statistics.

NATIVE VICES

McCarthy focuses considerable attention on the vices and various behaviors of the Costanoans that he finds disgusting, citing the writings of his Franciscan brethren:

> In the 'interrogatorio' [an official questionnaire of 1814] Fathers Duran and Fortuni of Mission San Jose list as 'dominate vices and faults' of the East Bay Indians, anger, immorality, stealing, and lying; they attribute as the principal cause of the low birth rate and crime of abortion—'common among their women' (1958:33-34).

One can only marvel at this self-serving assertion that Indian behavior and alleged vices were responsible for the low birth rate found in the missions. Secular historians, however, will not be surprised by such misinformed opinions. In today's social science terms we call this a philosophy of "blaming the victim."

Russian born artist Louis Choris, who was a member of the official Russian scientific expedition of Otto von Kotzebue that visited the San Francisco Bay in 1816, made this haunting observation of neophytes at Mission San Francisco, "I have never seen one laugh, I have never seen one look one in the face" (Choris 1913:17). While McCarthy actually cites this quote, he has misinterpreted it as proof of the "forbidding" nature of their characters (1958:34). It is worth noting that this observation was made after two decades or more of missionization. In secular historical and anthropological context Choris' observation means something entirely different. It is in fact a damning statement recording the psychological stress of a formerly free hunting and collecting society that has undergone a coerced transformation into a slave society (see Castillo 1993; Archibald 1978:172-181).[8]

Numerous other dehumanizing and invidious words are used by McCarthy to describe alleged California Indian vices, but enough examples have been cited to give a glimpse of the case he has constructed about native peoples and their culture. If one is to follow McCarthy's logic, such a "debased people" must be saved from themselves, and it was

---

[8]Archibald's careful study concludes, "The missions were not agents of intentional enslavement, but rather rapid and therefore violent social change. The results were people wrenched from home, tradition and family, subjugated to an alien culture and contradictory values. Predictably these people did not submit to such treatment voluntarily and force became a necessary concomitant. The result in many cases was slavery in fact although not in intent."

fortunate for them that the Franciscans were willing to spend their lives bringing Christianity and "civilization" to them.

INDIANS IN MISSION HISTORY

McCarthy had done serious violence to the historical realities that made up the history of the Costanoan adaptation and response to Franciscan authority.   For instance, he asserts (1958:72) that the Franciscan padres actually taught the "helpless Indians" to hunt, fish and cook!

His account of the massive fugitivism of a group of Costanoan and Plains Miwok neophytes who staged an escape from the filthy and disease-ridden Mission San Francisco in 1775 provides an interesting example of how Mission apologists explain away such startling events. McCarthy uses this incident as a part of the background for the establishment of Mission San Jose. A careful examination of missionary correspondence and reports demonstrate quite clearly the desperate situation faced by Mission San Francisco's terrified Indian men, women, and children.   For months before the great escape, a huge influx of Saclans [Bay Miwok] had begun to frequent Mission San Francisco, largely because of a severe drought that had significantly reduced their natural food supply at a time when both Costanoan and Saclan villages were experiencing great stress from the new Spanish diseases, and had witnessed an alarming increase in their infant mortality rates. Desperate parents were willing to try anything for survival of their children. Consequently, massive baptisms took place in late 1794 and early 1795. Suddenly, the Mission's population increased by seventy-five percent (Milliken 1991:214-235: H. McCarthy 1988:4-5).

A pattern, all too familiar to demographers, began to unfold. A typhus epidemic erupted at the mission in March of 1795. Terrified Saclans and members of a Costanoan group called Huchiun received permission to visit their homeland across the bay. When they failed to return voluntarily, Christian Indians, according to historian Hubert Howe Bancroft, were "bribed" to bring them back (Bancroft 1963:584). Encountering the fugitives near Napa, the Christian Indians suffered a stinging military defeat from the defiant Saclans and Huchiun, who were described by the Spanish military as "a brave people" (Bancroft 1963:709).   During the rest of that spring and until the end of that summer nearly 300 more Costanoans and Saclans abandoned Mission San Francisco in a mass escape to freedom. Even long-term neophytes supposedly happy in their "vestibule to heaven," joined the "apostates." The military governor was alarmed by the unprecedented request by the

San Francisco padres for presidio personnel to inaugurate military campaigns to return the fugitive neophytes. Instead of granting the request for an armed escort, the governor launched a military investigation into conditions at Mission Dolores. That report documented excessive labor, a lack of food, and the extreme cruelty of the disciplinarian Padre Danti. Padre Presidente Lasuén acknowledged that great forced labor projects had recently been undertaken at Mission San Francisco, and that he had indeed reprimanded both padres and urged them to be more forbearing (Lasuén 1965:401). As a result of the situation, not one tribal couple could be persuaded to be baptized from May 2, 1795 to March of 1800 (Mission San Jose *Libro de Bautismos*). This was an unprecedented effort to resist the physical and social destruction that awaited mission Indians.

Yet McCarthy explains the above extraordinary series of events with this statement:

> Now and then some Indian converts would run away from the Missions, irked at the moral restraints obtaining in civilized society, and seeking to gratify their carnal propensities amongst their loose living pagan people. Sometimes too, when an epidemic might be raging at a mission, numbers of Indians would flee to their former homes in fear of their lives (McCarthy 1958:62).

Thus, while acknowledging one of the major causes of the fugitivism, he at the same time suggests the motive might be better understood as an opportunity for "carnal" behavior, rather than fear. In fact, some intelligence had reached colonial authorities that a plan existed among the East Bay Costanoans to destroy the new Mission San Jose. As might be expected, the mass escape to freedom brought about a series of military encounters in which there was further loss of Indian life. Trenches were dug in the center of some free villages in order to make Spanish forces dismount and fight on foot. Eventually this violent conflict came to an end with the capture of 83 of the fugitives and 19 non-Christians suspected of harboring runaways and resisting Spanish military forays into their territory (McCarthy 1958:66; Milliken 1991:235). The series of armed military forays of 1797 ensured the safety of the newly established Mission San Jose.

McCarthy, in his account of these events, quoted Father Lasuén, who laid the blame on those whose voices have been muted in literature:

> Father Fermin de Lasuén laid full blame for the tragic affair on the Mission Dolores (San Francisco) delegation of

Indians, when he wrote, in a consoling letter to Father Danti, who was grief stricken over the loss of life: "The misfortune is indeed painful in every way; but if your messengers had observed your wise directions and warnings, such a calamity would not have come to pass" (1958:62).

This example of McCarthy's historiographic method follows closely that established by Engelhardt. Later Franciscan writers have continued the trend, blaming Indian deaths, suffering, or resistance on the Indians, either pagan or "Christian," although in fairness to some of them, it must be said that their writings in recent years are for the most part devoid of blatant racist language.

The establishment of Mission San Jose provides us with other examples of the abuse of historical process that aims to serve Eurocentric racial and religious agendas.

Military authorities had received testimony under duress that Costanoan chief *Oiyugma* [whom McCarthy identifies as *Oujugmas*] from the village of *Juquili* near present day Berkeley, had threatened to kill soldiers and those Indians who might assist the Spanish in establishment of Mission San Jose in their territory. Lured into the Spanish stronghold with promises of favorable trade arrangements, the captain and three of his followers were confronted with accusations based on the previously mentioned intelligence. Naturally, *Oiyugma* denied the charges originating from *Saclan* and Costanoan captives. Ignoring the coercive settings from which the accusation and denials emanated, McCarthy argues that the Chief's subsequent "conversion" is a significant example of the peaceful methods used by Franciscans to convert the Indians. Yet no evidence of *Oiyugma*'s baptism is in fact offered. In fact, the baptismal records of Mission San Jose include **no** record of a baptism for *Oiyugma* in that year or in the years that followed (McCarthy 1958:67; Mission San Jose, *Libro de Bautismos*).

McCarthy denies any coercion existed in the recruitment of neophytes to the new mission by disingenuously arguing that it was against mission practice and would, if it occurred, "invite . . . ecclesiastical censure and summary punishment"(1958:66). Such a naive argument suggests that if a law, practice, or rule exists, it follows that everyone will abide by its strictures; an argument clearly failing when the historical record is consulted. So, what brought the Costanoans and others into Mission San Jose? McCarthy argues that the guarantee of social security lured pagans into the arms of the missionaries, alleging that the Indians were naked or ill clad, poorly sheltered, and always on the verge of starvation, and that they came to the mission to enjoy substantial regular meals and the warm clothing and comfortable

dwellings provided by the self-less padres. They, he argues, were
disposed to learn, "the arts of civilization and truths of Christianity"
(McCarthy 1958:67). Such a scenario again demeans native culture and
ignores the complex reasons why in fact the Indians submitted to baptism.
For instance, the introduction of European stock animals—horses, cattle,
pigs, sheep and mules—seriously depleted native foods, and, combined
with the murderous waves of introduced diseases, caused the collapse of
more and more formerly independent villages who could no longer
sustain their functions as economic and civic centers in the face of such
pressures (see Castillo 1989b:333-348; West 1989:333-348).

His description of the "conversion" of the local Indians provides
McCarthy with another opportunity to heap abuse upon the intelligence
and adaptability of the Costanoan Indians. He tells readers that the rote
memorization of a set of prayers (in a completely foreign language) and
their daily recitation was sufficient to prove the Indians "converted."
This is how he believes it worked,

> By this method even the dullest amongst the Indians
> would be able, in the matter of a few months, to recite the
> catechism. This feat of memory by people of a brutish race,
> whose ancestory had remained intellectually stagnate for four
> thousand years, is the more remarkable in face of the
> extensiveness of the catechetical course (McCarthy 1958:70).

The abandonment of traditional non-Christian beliefs and
practices combined with the internalization of Christian doctrine
constitutes actual conversion. However, recent scholarly research has
demonstrated convincingly that it was highly unlikely that such
conversions took place in a broad cross section of Spanish frontier
missionary enterprises of the 18th and 19th centuries. For instance, with
interpreters teaching doctrine it was impossible to borrow native moral
terms with all their culture-bound meanings, and to expect the many
subtle inflections to survive both cross-cultural transfer complicated by
a language translation. Historian Louise Burkhart summarized the
dilemma this way:

> The friars were obliged to accommodate their teachings
> to native thought categories to a greater degree than they—or
> their apologists—dared to admit, and even greater than they
> may have realized. The Indians' inability to become [the]
> model Christians their missionaries hoped for, a failure the
> latter attributed to the Devil's power or the Indians' weakness,
> was in part a result of poor communication. A significant

portion of the Christian doctrine was simply lost in translation (Burkhart 1989:44; see also Matson and Fontana 1977).

The late Sherburne F. Cook, whose pioneering demographic work was the first serious scholarly study to focus on the California Indians' response to foreign invasion and domination, reasonably argued that it was virtually impossible to completely control the minds of the neophytes and prevent parents from passing along traditional beliefs and folkways. He summarized his findings this way: "I know of no competent contemporary authority who vouchsafed the unqualified assertion that the neophytes had to a significant degree given up their primitive customs and superstitions" (Cook 1976:31).

Mexican historian Jorge Klor de Alva, after a study of missionary efforts to convert the Indians of New Spain, concluded that the most common response of Indians to Christianity was incomplete conversion, in which Christian elements were only superficially incorporated into the native culture. Numerous other modern scholars have drawn similar conclusions (Klor de Alva 1982).

A basic contradiction exists when an apologist like McCarthy alleges wholesale conversions took place. Any scholar familiar with documents produced by missionaries and their contemporaries is struck by the habitual complaint of missionaries that their neophytes are dull witted, refuse to speak Spanish, and don't seem to be making much progress abandoning their old ways. Tragically, the realities of the massive neophyte deaths and the questionable nature of their conversions ensured repeated extensions of the missionaries' supposed ten year tenure of both the spiritual and temporal authority over the Indians. Through this combination of developments, the Franciscans were able to delay for nearly seven decades handing over the mission estates to the Indians who were supposed to inherit them after ten years (Servin 1965:133-149).

GENDER AND PUNISHMENT

An especially offensive and inaccurate section of McCarthy's book is its treatment of Indian women. The description of female gender roles at Mission San Jose begins with a denigration of female gender roles in traditional Costanoan society. McCarthy writes, "The women, who in paganism had been condemned to the monotonous daily stints of gathering seeds, roots, berries and acorns and preparing them for the family meal, or to the simple accomplishment of weaving baskets . . . " (1958:71-72).

There follows a glowing description of how the women had

learned new and valuable skills, like candle making and macramé. McCarthy goes to great length to reveal to his readers that when pregnant, women were relieved of harder tasks and given short term assignments at simple tasks like cleaning wheat, washing wool, or pulling weeds. He cites Padre Presidente Lasuén's allegation that Indians make fun of the padres' concern for pregnant women, while noting that pregnant neophytes do as they please knowing they will not be punished.

But Indian women were in fact routinely beaten at the mission. McCarthy explains mission discipline this way:

> The Franciscans normally guided their dull, coarse, and carnally minded charges with gentleness. On occasions, however, they were compelled to punish some of them for transgression . . . the mission employed various forms of punishment, common throughout Mexico at the time, such as the stocks, the pillory, leg chains, extra work, imprisonment, or the lash. When flogging was resorted to, the maximum number of blows was limited by Spanish law to twenty-five, though this number was very seldom given (1958:139-140).

Unfortunately, the real status of females in the missions was considerable less pampered and comfortable than McCarthy, Lasuén, and other apologists would care to recall. In fact, a significant gender status and population decline can be well documented for females in the California missions. Shocked by the partial nudity and what they took to be the "uninhibited native sexuality" of the Indians, the Franciscans inaugurated draconian measures to compel female neophytes to conform to the padres' ideals of proper female decorum and behavior. Immediately following baptism, female children over the age of five and all older unmarried females were separated from their families and locked in barracks called *monjerios*. Russian explorer Otto von Kotzebue, visiting nearby Mission Santa Clara in 1824, described one such barracks housing female Costanoan neophytes as a building resembling a prison, without windows and only one carefully secured door where

> these dungeons are opened two or three times a day, but only to allow the prisoners to pass to and from the church. I have occasionally seen the poor girls rushing out eagerly to breath the fresh air, and driven immediately into the church like a flock of sheep by an old ragged Spaniard armed with a stick. After mass, they are in the same manner hurried back to their prison (Overland Monthly 1869:261).

Military governor Diego de Borica wrote in 1797 of his concern for the health of female neophytes confined in such squalor after visiting the *monjerio* at Mission Carmel, where he was overpowered by the stench of human feces (1797).

In contrast McCarthy describes the *monjerio* as,

> . . . a fine building . . . . Three large windows on one side, and four loopholes on the other gave sufficient light and good ventilation to the spacious quarters. As a precaution against intrusion, the windows were placed high on the walls. Toilette facilities were located in a room adjoining the dormitory. A cheerful fire blazed on the hearth during the winter nights, while candles supplied illumination in the evenings throughout the year (1958:131-132).

Females were issued heavy, ill-fitting wool shirts and petticoats that according to one contemporary observer, left wearers, "diseased with the itch" (Heizer 1968:86). Female neophytes in fact suffered a status decline once they were part of the new mission communities. The male dominated society there provided no opportunities for women to assume leadership positions comparable to the chieftainships, shaman and ritual status available to them in some California native societies. Divorce was denied them, and their role degenerated into producing children, and performing manual labor for the colonists. The Franciscans made no effort to elevate even the most devout neophytes to the status of nuns throughout their nearly 70 year tenure over California Indians (Castillo 1994).

Worse still was a disturbing pattern of wholesale sexual assault on female neophytes (including children), chiefly at the hands of soldiers (Hurtado 1992:370-386), but Costanoan Indian Lorenzo Asisara testified to one of Hubert Howe Bancroft's researchers about Mission San Jose's Padre Luis Gil y Taboada's sexual appetite for Indian females this way:

> He was very amorous. He hugged and kissed the Indian women, and he had contact with them until he had syphilis and skin eruptions broke out. (Don Jose Maria Amador affirmed this, and since they were good friends, he gave him medicines to cure him). Finding himself in this situation, he would celebrate mass sitting in his house. He was not able many times to celebrate mass standing up because he

was all ulcerated (Castillo 1989b:399).[9]

Perhaps most troublesome for apologists to explain away is the coercive nature of the padres' use of beatings, stocks and shackles to control the female children and adults, whose lives, McCarthy alleges, were "easy and pleasant" (McCarthy 1958:139-40). Women at San Jose and elsewhere suffered floggings similar to those inflicted on male adults and children, but French explorer Jean Francois de La Perouse, visiting Alta California in 1786, made this observation about female neophyte punishments at Mission Carmel: "Women are never whipped in public, but in an enclosed and somewhat distant place that their cries may not excite too lively compassion, which might cause the men to revolt" (Margolin 1989:89).

The Frenchman, perhaps imbued with enlightenment ideas, further observed that even by 18th century Catholic standards the punishment of Indians seemed excessive: "Corporal punishment is inflicted on the Indians of both sexes who neglect the exercises of piety, and many sins, which in Europe are left to Divine justice, are here punished by irons and stocks" (1989:82).

Despite these and numerous other documents relating to corporeal punishment, which McCarthy either ignored or was ignorant of, he asserts that the Indians were never chastised without being convinced of their guilt, and not because of some ill will the padres may have harbored against an Indian. According to McCarthy, "the neophytes accept with humility the chastisements and afterward they remain as affectionate toward the father as before" (1958:141).[10]

Some gender unique punishments were reserved for female neophytes suspected of infanticide and abortions, which were associated with pregnancies often resulting from occasional gang rapes by soldiers, or adultery. Asisara described one particularly cruel and bizarre form of punishment at Mission Santa Cruz. Unhappy with a sterile neophyte's inability to conceive children, Padre Ramon Olbes ordered the terrified woman and her husband to perform coitus in his presence. When they refused, the husband was placed in shackles and his wife was taken to another room to "examine her reproductive parts." She resisted and bit

---

[9]Catholic writers relying on the testimony of other padres have categorically denied Asisara's testimony on Taboada's indiscretions. See Geiger (1969:104-106).

[10]A quotation from an outraged Plains Miwok neophyte who had endured a humiliating public flogging at Mission San Jose refutes this assertion. He threw the shirt and blanket given to him at baptism at the feet of Padre Duran and declared, "Padre, take back thy Christianity; I want none of it. I will return a pagan to my country" (Bancroft 1888). Costanoan Indian and ex-neophyte Lorenzo Asisara bitterly recalled, "We were always trembling with fear of the lash" (Harrison 1892:47).

the perverse padre in the arm. Asisara explains:

> Then Olbés ordered that they take her and give her 50
> lashes. After the 50 lashes, he ordered that she be shackled and
> locked in the *monjerio*. Finishing this, Padre Olbés ordered
> that a wooden doll be made, like a recently born child. He
> took the doll to the whipped woman and ordered her to take
> that doll for her child, and to carry it in front of all the people
> for nine days. He obligated her to present herself in front of
> the temple with that [doll] as if it were her child for nine days.
> With all these things, the women who were sterile became very
> alarmed (Castillo 1989b:389).

A remarkably similar punishment is recorded at Mission San
Gabriel, suggesting that these types of punishments may have been more
than the acts of a single deranged padre (Heizer 1968:87).

The onslaught of European diseases was accelerated by
incarceration in unhealthy and filthy *monjerios*. A serious female
population decline throughout the missions of California resulted.
Consequently, after 1800 a growing gender imbalance developed with
few females surviving. A physician touring California in 1832 made
these disquieting observations on the obvious gender imbalance found
throughout the missions:

> It is a very extraordinary fact that their decrease is
> greatly hastened by the failure of the female offspring—or the
> much greater number of deaths amongst the females in early
> youth than among the males—I have not been able to clearly
> determine which, though the latter appears the more probable;
> the fact, however, of their being a much smaller [number of
> women, means that many of the men] cannot find wives
> (Coulter 1951:67).

As a result of a statistical analysis of annual reports from Mission
San Jose and other San Francisco Bay Area missions between 1798 and
1832, historian Robert Jackson concluded: "Mortality rates were higher
among women and young girls and young children than adult men, and
by the 1820s and 1830s the mission populations increasingly were
unbalanced with a majority of men of working age" (1992:151-152).

These sobering data in part explain why after 1810 the
missionaries increasingly sought out healthy Indians living in the Central
Valley to repopulate the alarmingly decreased number of local Costanoans
with Miwok and Yokuts tribesmen.

NATIVE RESISTANCE

The extraordinary resistance of San Jose's neophyte population, made up increasingly of Central Valley Miwok and Yokuts, constitutes the final chapter of a subjected peoples' efforts to oppose the labor demands of the Franciscans. Central Valley Miwok and Yokuts grew increasingly determined to resist Spanish efforts to return fugitive neophyte laborers who habitually attempted to flee the Franciscan labor mills, and escape the grasp of the Franciscans. Predictably, McCarthy saw things differently. He offers this description of such resistance efforts: "The unstable inhabitants of the inland valleys were often guilty of serious offenses against the Missions, so that the government was forced periodically to dispatch punitive expeditions against them" (McCarthy 1958:68).

In the fall of 1828 an unexpected and shocking defection of a trusted and highly respected San Jose *Alcalde*, a Northern Yokuts called Estanislao, joined with disenchanted Santa Clara neophytes in refusing to return to their respective missions. The fugitives openly challenged colonial authorities to try and recapture them. The defiant Estanislao sent a taunting note to Padre Duran of Mission San Jose: "We are rising in revolt . . . . We have no fear of the soldiers, for even now, they are very few, mere boys, and not even sharp shooters" (Holterman 1970:44).

Despite the fact that this note was taken quite seriously by contemporary military authorities, McCarthy characterized Estanislao's declaration as, "childish, puerile boastfulness." Ignoring, or ignorant of the increased labor demands and other intolerable conditions at Mission San Jose, he says of Estanislao's fugitivism: ". . . abandonment of mission life by Christian Indians was motivated generally by a desire to exchange the moral restrictions for the carnal licenses of pagan existence" (1958:201-202).

Thus McCarthy identified the causes of the military, political and economic resistance of fugitive neophytes to a desire on their part for sexual gratification without the "restraint" of the padres. His limited understanding of complex cultural dynamics that were causing such incidents underscores the limited usefulness of his book for those seeking an understanding of what was happening at Mission San Jose.

CONCLUSION

Numerous other examples of McCarthy's errors regarding the Indians and Mission San Jose's history are obvious to the fair-minded reader of the work. The documentation presented here is sufficient to illustrate the themes that characterize this self-serving approach to church history. McCarthy attempts to demonstrate that before contact with the Franciscans, California Indians were dull, sex-obsessed savages whose harsh lives were meaningless, and that their alleged miserable lives were transformed and made meaningful by the efforts of the Franciscans. They were made Christian and were Hispanicized, and at the same time they provided the Franciscans and the secular authorities with a virtually unpaid labor force that profited both the empire and the order. Those who suffered without complaint and died without too much fuss are patronizingly described as good Indians. Those who objected are derided as childish and selfish (Weber 1988:33-34).[11] Anything and everything that went wrong during the missionaries' tenure over the lives of the Indians is generally blamed automatically on governmental authorities, mixed blood *gente de razon*, foreigners, or, better still, on the Indians themselves.

Until the middle of November, 1992, McCarthy's book was still being sold at Mission San Jose's gift shop. It was at that time that I presented a shorter version of this paper at the Scholars' Conference associated with the C. E. Smith Museum of Anthropology's exhibit, "The Ohlone Indians of the Bay Area: A Continuing Tradition." Remarkably, the next day the book was reported no longer available. Although I am gratified at this evidence of having made my point, I am not in favor of banning this book, or any other. I think books like this can serve as samples to illustrate the racism that had caused so much grief to many Indian people, to students of history, and to the church itself, whose image has been so badly marred. On the other hand, books that express such racial hatred should be kept off the shelves of public school libraries, to be found by unprepared school children, who may well presume that such works inform them accurately about Indians during the mission period. McCarthy's book and those like it might more usefully be found, alongside less biased and more accurate works, in college libraries and special reading sections in public libraries, where mature and

---

[11]Weber, a Borderlands historian, summarizes such Euro-centric positions this way, ". . . from the Franciscans' viewpoint, and that of historians sympathetic to them, the hard work, self-sacrifice, skill and energy of the missionaries had overcome the resistance of obdurate, slothful and ungrateful savages. Moreover, historians have generally emulated Franciscans in not lingering over disturbing questions about the morality of evangelism."

critical minds can better compare and evaluate their contents.

The availability (until recently) of this racist tract, poorly disguised as history, together with the vigorous attempt to obfuscate the legacy of Padre Junipero Serra among educators and the general public, has its most damaging effect on the children of California, especially American Indian school children. Historian James Sandos, who has conducted award-winning research on the abuses of the historical process in the Serra canonization drive, writes:

> I can see classrooms in California where teaching the full story of Junipero Serra will produce a cry of disbelief from Roman Catholic children and their parents who will claim that a saint could never have abused anyone. I also foresee pressure by school boards on teachers to avoid the controversy. After many years of trying to bring an appreciation and critical understanding of Native American culture into the story of California history, historians and anthropologists now face the challenge of maintaining such progress as has been made in the face of religious exaltation and the oxymoronic claims that history proves Serra was a saint and hence could not be responsible for the abuse of Indians that history also records (Sandos 1989:24).

Having experienced numerous humiliating history lessons and instructional materials in my own public school education, where I was informed that my ancestors were dirty savages and only worthy after surrendering their independence, resources, lands, labor, and lives to non-Indians,[12] I had hoped my young children might be spared those painful "lessons." Such experiences poison the heart and for many crush the spirit. No child of any race or religious background deserves such self-esteem destroying experiences. No student should be subjected to religiously inspired historical distortions that force children to choose either to accept the allegation that their ancestors were little more than animals, or to act out their objection by dropping out intellectually and

---

[12]It is significant that Helen Bauer's *California Indian Days*, which bears considerable resemblance to McCarthy's book in tone, and of which anthropologist Lowell John Bean (1972) wrote a scathing critique more than twenty years ago, is still widely used in California's fourth grade classes. The ignorance and prejudice that infuse Bauer's book are not appropriate for the fourth grade children of this increasingly multicultural state.

socially .[13] It is clear that authors like McCarthy and others still alive and active are not interested in mission history that might ask or answer difficult questions. Ethnohistorian Bernard Fontana responded to one scholar's allegation regarding the success in Texas of Mission San Antonio's actions that resulted in the extinction of Indian groups by asking, "If the Indian cultures are extinct, is that success? And if so, how was that success achieved and by whose rules?" (Fontana 1987:58). McCarthy's book and others like it demonstrate that apologist writers are willing to continue to sacrifice California Indians in a progressively futile effort to protect the Franciscan order's historical image in California.

Knowledgeable Costanoan Indians, other Mission Indian descendants, and indeed all California Indians are gravely offended by such works, which only serve to remind us of the enduring wrong that was done to our ancestors, which is now being denied by those who profited the most. The wholesale theft of our land, resources, and the failure to acknowledge the suffering and death of Indians during the Mission period in California can no longer be categorically ignored. Fortunately, the crude appeals to authority that characterize church self-histories have lost much of their appeal to the general public. Despite declining influence, mission apologists continue to make crude appeals to racism that become less and less palatable to scholars and the public. A new generation of secular scholars using new research techniques and new sources of data provide today's audiences a more sophisticated and evenhanded understanding of what occurred when Indians encountered missionaries in what the father of Borderlands history, Herbert Eugene Bolton, called that "distant rim of Christendom" in 18th and 19th century California.

---

[13]The late founder and president of the American Indian Historical Society, Rupert Costo, testified at Congressional hearings regarding biased textbooks and classroom instruction in 1969, "There is not one Indian in this country who does not cringe in anguish and frustration because of these textbooks. There is not one Indian child who has not come home in shame and tears after one of those sessions in which he is taught that his people were dirty, animal like, something less than human beings" (Costo 1970:9).

REFERENCES CITED

Archibald, Robert
1978   Indian Labor at the California Missions, Slavery or Salvation? Journal of San Diego History 24(2):172-181.

Axtell, James
1982   Some Thoughts on the Ethnohistory of Missions. Ethnohistory 29(1):35-41. Reprinted 1991 in Native American Perspectives on the Colonization of Alta California. Edward D. Castillo, ed. New York: Garland Press.

Bancroft, Hubert Howe
1888   California Pastoral. San Francisco: The History Company.

1963   History of California. Vol. 1:584. Santa Barbara: Wallace Hebberd.

Bauer, Helen
1958   California Indian Days. Doubleday and Co. Revised 1968.

Bean, Lowell John
1972   The Language of Stereotype, Inaccuracy, Distortion. *In* The American Indian Reader: Education. Rupert Costo, ed., pp. 135-136. San Francisco: Indian Historian Press.

Burkhart, Louise M.
1989   The Slippery Earth: Nahua-Christian Moral Dialogue in Sixteenth Century Mexico. Tucson: The University of Arizona Press.

Castillo, Edward D.
1993   Neophyte Resistance and Accommodation in the Missions of Alta California. *In* The Spanish Missionary Heritage of the United States, United States National Park Services Quincentennial Program, San Antonio Missions Historic Park, San Antonio, Texas.

1994   Gender Status Decline, Resistance and Accommodation Among Female Neophytes in the Missions of Alta California. American Indian Cultural Research Journal 18(1).

Castillo, Edward D., ed. and trans.
1989a   The Assassination of Padre Andrés Quintana by the Indians of Mission Santa Cruz in 1812: The Narrative of Lorenzo Asisara. California History 68(3):116-125.

1989b   An Indian Account of the Decline and Collapse of Mexico's Hegemony Over the Missionized Indians of California. American Indian Quarterly 13(4):399.

Choris, Louis
1913   San Francisco 100 Years Ago. Porter Garnet, trans. San Francisco: Am. Robinson Co.

Cook, Sherburne F.
1976   The Conflict Between The California Indians and White Civilization. Berkeley: University of California Press.

Costo, Rupert
1970   Textbooks and the American Indian. San Francisco: Indian Historian Press.

Coulter, Thomas
1951   Notes on Upper California: A Journey From Monterey to the Colorado River in 1832. Los Angeles: Dawson Books.

de Borica, Diego
1797   June 30. Letter located in the Stevens Collection, General Library of the University of Texas, Austin.

Drinnon, Richard
1980   Facing West: The Metaphysics of Indian Hating and Empire-Building. Minneapolis: University of Minnesota Press.

Engelhardt, Zephyrin, O.F.M.
1908-1915   The Missions and Missionaries of California. 4 vols. San Francisco: James H. Barry.

1921   San Luis Rey Mission. San Francisco: James H. Barry.

1922   San Juan Capistrano Mission. Los Angeles: Standard
              Printing Company.

1927   San Fernando Rey: The Mission of the Valley. Chi-
              cago: Franciscan Herald Press.

1933   Mission San Luis Obispo in the Valley of the Bears.
              Santa Barbara, Calif.: Mission Santa Barbara.

Fontana, Bernard
1987   Indians and Missionaries of the Southwest During the
              Spanish Years: Cross Cultural Perceptions and
              Misperceptions. *In* Proceedings of the 1884 and 1985
              San Antonio Missions Research Conferences, pp. 55-59.
              San Antonio: Lebco Graphics.

Geiger, Maynard, O.F.M.
1969   Franciscan Missionaries in Hispanic California, 1769-
              1848. San Marino, California: Huntington Library.

Hanke, Lewis
1959   Aristotle and The American Indian: A Study in Race
              Prejudice in the Modern World.   Chicago: Henry
              Regnery Co.

Harrison, E. S.
1892   Narrative of a Mission Indian. *In* History of Santa Cruz
              County. San Francisco: Pacific Press Publishing Co.

Heizer, Robert F.
1968   The Indians of Los Angeles, Hugo Reid's Letters of
              1852. Los Angeles: Southwest Museum.

1978   Impact of Colonization on Native California Societies.
              The Journal of San Diego History 24(1):121-139.
              Reprinted 1991 in The Spanish Missions of Baja Califor-
              nia. Robert H. Jackson, ed. New York: Garland Press.

Holterman, Jack
1970   The Revolt of Estanislao. The Indian Historian 3(1):44.

Hurtado, Albert
1992   Sexuality in California's Franciscan Missions: Cultural
              Perceptions and Sad Realities.   California History
              71(3):370-386.

Jackson, Robert
1992   The Dynamic of Indian Demographic Collapse in the San
              Francisco Bay Missions, Alta California, 1776-1840.
              The American Indian Quarterly 16(2):151-2.

Klor de Alva, Jorge
1982   Spiritual Conflict and Accommodation in New Spain:
              Toward a Typology of Aztec Responses to Christianity.
              In The Inca and Aztec States 1400-1800: Anthropology
              and History.   George Collier et al., ed.   New York:
              Academic Press.

Lasuén, Fermin F.
1965   The Writings of Fermin Francisco de Lasuen.   Finbar
              Kenneally, ed.   Richmond: Academy of American
              Franciscan History.

Margolin, Malcolm
1989   Monterey in 1786.   The Journals of Jean Francois de La
              Perouse.   Berkeley: Heyday Books.

Martin, Calvin, ed.
1987   The American Indian and the Problem of History.
              Oxford: Oxford University Press.

Mathes, Valerie Sherer
1990   Helen Hunt Jackson and Her Indian Reform Legacy.
              Austin: University of Texas Press.

Matson, Daniel and Bernard Fontana, eds. and trans.
1977   Friar Bringas Reports to the King: Methods of Indoctri-
              nation on the Frontier of New Spain.   1796-1797.
              Tucson: The University of Arizona Press.

McCarthy, Francis Florence
1958   The History of Mission San Jose California 1797-1835.
              Fresno: Academy Library Guild.   Republished in 1977.

McCarthy, Helen
1988   Debunking A Historical Myth, The Saclan Rebellion.
            News from Native California 2(1):4-5.

Milliken, Randall T.
1991   An Ethnohistory of the Indian People of the San Fran-
            cisco Bay Area from 1770 to 1810. Ph.D. Thesis,
            Department of Anthropology, University of California,
            Berkeley.

Mission San Jose
n.d.   *Libro de Bautismos*. Colma, California: San Francisco
            Archdioces Chancery Archive.

Orwell, George
1971   Politics and the English Language. *In* The Borzoi
            Reader, C. Muscantine and M. Griffith, eds., p. 88. 2nd
            edition. New York: Alfred Knopf.

Overland Monthly
1869   Footprints of Early California Discoverers. Overland
            Monthly, p. 261. Found in Bancroft Library, University
            of California, Berkeley.

Phillips, George H.
1989   The Alcaldes: Indian Leadership in the Spanish Missions
            of California.   *In* The Newberry Library's D'arcy
            McNickle Center for the Study of the American Indian,
            Occasional Papers in Curriculum Series, Number 11, The
            Struggle for Political Autonomy. Chicago.

Sandos, James A.
1985   Levantamiento! The Chumash Uprising Reconsidered.
            Southern California Quarterly 67(2):109-133.

1989   Junipero Serra and California History. The Californians
            8(3):24.

Servin, Manuel
1965   The Secularization of the California Missions: A Reap-
            praisal. Southern California Quarterly 47:133-149.

Shipek, Florence
1985   California Indian Reactions to the Franciscans.   The
               Americas, Academy of American Franciscan History
               41(4):480-491.

Thomas, David Hurst
1991   Harvesting Ramona's Garden: Life in California's
               Mythical Mission Past.   *In* Columbian Consequences,
               Vol. 3, The Spanish Borderlands in Pan American
               Perspective, pp. 119-157.   David H. Thomas, ed.
               Washington, D.C.: Smithsonian Institution Press.

Weber, David
1990   Blood of Martyrs, Blood of Indians: Toward a More
               Balanced View of Spanish Missions in the Seventeenth
               Century North America.   *In* Columbian Consequences:
               Archaeological and Historical Perspectives on the
               Spanish Borderlands East, Vol. II.   Washington, D.C.:
               Smithsonian Institution Press.

Weber, David J.
1988   Myth and History of The Hispanic Southwest. Albuquer-
               que: University of New Mexico Press.

Wiget, Andrew
1982   Truth and The Hopi: An Historiographic Study of
               Documented Oral Tradition Concerning the Coming of
               the Spanish. Ethnohistory 23:181-199.

THE OHLONE
BACK FROM EXTINCTION

Alan Leventhal, Les Field, Hank Alvarez and Rosemary Cambra

The quincentennial year, 1992, was commemorated by many peoples throughout the world, for whom the five hundred years had diverse meanings. For the indigenous peoples of the Americas, this year symbolized and highlighted their ongoing struggles for cultural, political, and economic empowerment within the nation-states in which their homelands are now located. In California, the quincentennial commemoration coincided with the historical opening of opportunities for indigenous peoples both to empower themselves politically and to revise the historical and anthropological record that has provided the ideological backbone of their oppressed status.

Among the culturally and linguistically diverse native peoples who inhabited what is now the state of California before the arrival of Europeans, the Ohlone peoples comprised a complex series of cultures that spoke related languages and occupied a large area bounded by the Carquinez Strait and the Golden Gate to the north, and Big Sur and Soledad to the south. Within this region, the Ohlone-speaking societies traded with, allied themselves with, and sometimes battled against one another; they were similarly tied to neighboring societies where very different languages were spoken. Like many other California native peoples, the Ohlone-speakers were subjected to the disastrous experience of missionization under the Spanish Empire and, following the admission of California to the United States, were dispossessed of their remaining lands and denied legal status by the state and federal governments (Hoopes 1975; Rawls 1986; Hurtado 1988; Shipek 1989; Monroy 1990; and others). Early in this century, the Ohlone peoples were declared "extinct" by an influential anthropologist, a powerful figure within the discipline's history (particularly in California), Alfred Kroeber. The

dissenting voices of other anthropologists, such as John P. Harrington and
C. Hart Merriam, provided ample documentation that the Ohlone peoples
had survived into the twentieth century, albeit transformed by the
experience of the missions, and California's annexation to the United
States (Merriam 1967; Harrington 1921-1939); nevertheless, it was
Kroeber's pronouncement that shaped the politics of powerlessness for the
Ohlones for many decades. That situation has only recently begun to
change.

In the early 1980s, the descendants of the *Chochenyo* Ohlone-
speakers of the southern and eastern San Francisco Bay Area re-grouped
and constituted themselves as the *Muwekma* Ohlone Tribe, a process that
may be called "a contemporary revitalization" (see Field, Leventhal,
Sanchez and Cambra 1992a, 1992b). A similar revitalization process has
taken place among the families of the Ohlone peoples in the San Juan
Bautista-Gilroy area, who have formally re-grouped as the *Amah-Mutsun*
Tribal Band; and also among the neighboring Esselen people to the south,
who were also declared extinct by Kroeber and other anthropologists, and
by some historians (Kroeber 1925:544; Underhill 1953; Hester 1978;
Cutter 1990; and others). Documenting and publicizing their cultural and
historical continuity with their pre-contact, Mission and post-statehood
ancestors has been a key strategy in the *Muwekma*, *Amah-Mutsun* and
Esselen Nations' revitalization processes. By laying claim to their history
in both academic and popular media (Field, Leventhal, Sanchez and
Cambra 1992a), by establishing collaborative relationships with federal,
state, county, and city agencies, and by creating their own archaeological
consulting firm, the *Muwekma* have undertaken to counteract the
ideological legacies that justified and maintained their political, economic,
and cultural disenfranchisement. This strategy is aimed at reestablishing
federal acknowledgment of the tribal status for the *Muwekma*, the *Amah-
Mutsun*, and the Esselens, which was terminated in all three cases in
1927. It was in that year that Superintendent L. A. Dorrington of the
Indian Field Service, assigned to evaluate the land needs of homeless
California Indians, asserted that the native communities of Alameda, San
Benito, and Monterey counties were not in need of any land, and failed
even to mention Indians in other Bay Area counties (1927). Thus the
federal government dismissed the needs of these respective communities
as distinctive cultural entities with rights to a land base as defined under
the appropriation acts of 1906 and 1908 (34 Stat. 325, June 24, 1906 and
35 Stat. 70, April 30, 1908; see also Senate Document 131, 58th
Congress, 2nd Session, 1904, pp. 1-16 [reprinted in Heizer 1979]; Kelsey
1913; Hauke 1916; Terrell 1916; and Dorrington 1927). Our task here
is to initiate an assessment of the political, economic, and academic
forces that over the last two centuries have undermined and attempted to

erase the existence of Ohlone civilization in Central California. We do so by tracing the history of the Ohlone peoples through three thematic eras we have called Domination, Fragmentation and "Extinction."

THEORETICAL CONCERNS

It is difficult to undertake our critical review of Ohlone history and disenfranchisement in a completely linear fashion because all such projects are entangled in the historical legacy of anthropological and ethnohistorical representations of the Ohlone peoples. The first anthropologists arrived in California long after Spanish conquest and missionization had transformed Ohlone and other Central California societies, but anthropologists like Kroeber and others undertook to describe and partially reconstruct pre-Hispanic native culture and society (cf. Goldschmidt 1951). We therefore confront the shaping influence of anthropology upon the disenfranchisement of Central California peoples both *before* and *after* anthropologists themselves were physically present in the area, since their descriptions, pervaded by their own theoretical agenda, have constituted our "knowledge" about both pre-and post-contact California native peoples. Understanding how this knowledge has been shaped allows us to trace the relationship between anthropological work and the past and present disempowerment of the Ohlones in concrete ways that show how such a process has been maintained and how it can be challenged.

There are several ways that anthropologists have classified and analyzed native Californians that are immediately relevant to a critical reassessment of Ohlone histories. Alfred Kroeber arrived in California in 1901, concerned to describe "native primitive culture before it went all to pieces" (Kroeber 1948:427), which he believed could be accomplished by treating the surviving descendants of the catastrophes Californian natives had endured as specimens of "timeless, ahistorical cultural type[s]" (Buckley 1989:439). From the point of view of many present-day anthropologists Kroeber did not take sufficient note of the genocidal ventures Europeans and Euro-Americans had conducted against California natives (Buckley 1989). For this reason he persistently confused fragmented societies and cultures he described with the pre-contact condition of those same societies and cultures.

One of the most important legacies of Kroeber's confusion is his description of native California societies as composed of "tribelets" (Kroeber 1955, 1962). This term defined a political and geographical unit comprising several villages, usually including a principal and most powerful central village, tied by relations of kinship, and internally homogeneous with respect to the organization of land ownership, ceremonies, warfare, and resource allocations. Kroeber's emphasis on the small scale of indigenous California social organization led him to attach the diminutive "-let" to the anthropologically normative term "tribe." By his count, over five hundred tribelets existed in California at the time of contact.

This term, almost universally accepted by anthropologists, historians, educators, and cultural resource management (CRM) archaeologists, is considered demeaning by Ohlone, Esselen and other California Indian people, but that is not the only reason to evaluate it critically. In contemporary anthropology, both old and new ethnographies are read to determine their theoretical content, the audiences towards which they are aimed, and the debates they address. Current discourse in anthropology highlights the ethnographer's functions as author and editor, and draws attention to the inclusions and exclusions of data to support certain conclusions. In this light, it is undeniable that Kroeber, his colleagues, and his students collected hundreds of names of indigenous social groups identifiable with particular geographical areas. Clearly, he had found one kind of important social grouping, or, perhaps, a social grouping that was important to California natives in the context of their recent experience of genocide.

It is also clear that Kroeber's interests in small, neatly defined groups, with small scale ethnic diffusion and differentiation, and with salvaging the traits of each small bounded group stemmed from the trajectory of American anthropology and the enduring influence of Franz Boas in the first decades of the twentieth century. The listing of traits of Indian societies and cultures under pre-conceived headings such as material culture, ceremonial systems, social organization and the like, all of which have little to do with the cultural categories and perspectives of the indigenous people "under study," is an enduring problem in anthropology in general and in California ethnography in particular (concerning the latter, see Blackburn 1976). "Tribelet" has been employed by many influential anthropologists and authors who followed Kroeber (Heizer 1974b, 1978a; Levy 1978; Margolin 1978; Milliken 1983, 1990; and many others), maintaining an impression of pre-contact native California as a region of extremely small-scale, provincial cultures that lacked forms of large-scale integration. As we discuss later, the deployment of "tribelet" and other Kroeberian frames of reference has all too frequently blocked a more sophisticated appraisal of the societies and cultures that existed in California and the San Francisco Bay Area before missionization.

In the same vein, the linguistic classificatory systems created by anthropologists (e.g., Latham 1856; Powers 1877; Powell 1877; Dixon and Kroeber 1913, 1919; Merriam 1967; Levy 1978; and others) have also distorted pre-contact realities, and this distortion is well reflected in the case of the Ohlone peoples. The Spaniards called the diverse peoples living on or near the coastline from Monterey to the Golden Gate a generic term: *costeños*, or coast-dwellers, a term later Anglicized to "*costaños*." Anthropologists and linguists (Latham 1856 [who first classified this language group as Costanoan]; Powell 1877; Kroeber 1925; Levy 1978; and others) classified these peoples as "Costanoans," having discovered that their languages could be shown to be closely related, and incorrectly implied that these peoples could be glossed as a single ethnic group (see Underhill 1953; Kehoe 1992, discussed later). Merriam (1967) called these same peoples and their languages "Ohlonean," derived from "Ohlone," a term that the descendants of the varied peoples of this San Francisco Bay Area have used to identify themselves since the early part of this century. In this muddled situation, in which pre-contact identity has been obscured by successive layers of outsiders' labeling, we use "Ohlone" in recognition of and with respect for its usage by the present-day tribes. At the same time, our use of the term Ohlone does not imply that language similarities determined the political and cultural identities of the culturally diverse pre-contact ancestors of the contemporary Ohlone tribal peoples.

There are deeper issues still that have shaped the past and present relationship between anthropology and history on the one hand, and the Ohlone and other native Californian peoples on the other. These groups have been described as "foragers" because they did not herd domesticated animals or cultivate domesticated plants (Salzman 1967; Hunter 1985; Crapo 1987; and others). The textbooks that anthropologists use in their undergraduate courses continue to teach university students their traditional view of world history, a stage theory of human evolution that ranks "foragers" (or "hunter-gatherers") as the earliest, and therefore most primitive, stage in the evolution of society and culture (see Peoples and Bailey 1994 for an excellent example in a recently revised textbook). Foraging peoples inhabiting the most ecologically marginal regions on this planet, such as the !Kung of the Kalahari, are inevitably portrayed as representative of this stage in human history.[1] Mainstream

---

[1]Our critique must leave aside the persistent (and outrageous) depiction of the !Kung and others as timeless relics of the Paleolithic, despite both their brutal transformation by colonialism and, even more important, increasingly convincing evidence that the !Kung were never isolated, but have participated for centuries in a thriving trading system with their pastoral and cultivating neighbors (see Gordon 1992).

anthropology's evolutionary stage theory is not congruent with the dense populations, permanent settlements, ranked social systems, partially monetized economies, regional integration, and cultural sophistication among "foragers" who lived in the ecologically rich habitats of California and the Pacific Northwest. If such peoples are considered at all by textbooks, they are usually treated as "exceptions that prove the [evolutionary] rule" (again, see Peoples and Bailey 1994).

Kroeber's descriptions of native Californian societies as, in effect, "primitive" permits anthropologists and historians to comfortably fit the pre-contact Californians into the "foraging stage" of history. Many contemporary anthropologists and archaeologists, as we show later, have been content to deploy Kroeber's descriptions of Californian native peoples uncritically and not to consider newer descriptions of these peoples. This suggests the profound nature of these anthropologists' internalization of the stage theory view of history, a view that renders reconsideration of the Californian peoples irrelevant, even irritating, in the larger picture.   This use of Kroeber as an authority about native Californian societies, duplicated as we shall see in the uncritical acceptance by many latter-day anthropologists of Kroeber's "extinction sentence" over the Ohlone, cannot, we contend, be separated from the physical conquest and subordination of California by European and Euro-American colonialisms. Under colonial regimes, native Californians were called "primitives," often in much coarser and overtly racist terms (e.g., Hittell 1879). Anthropology's legitimation of the "primitive" (not to mention "extinct") status of native Californians thus plays a role in theoretically mediating the historical powers that have disenfranchised the Ohlones and other native Californians.

SPANISH DOMINATION OF PRE-CONTACT CALIFORNIAN CULTURE AND SOCIETY

Our brief analysis of pre-contact civilization in the Bay Area owes much to the work of Lowell Bean and others (Bean and Blackburn 1976) who have worked to create frameworks that for the most part revise the Kroeberian-derived view that we contend has played a role in the subordination of the Ohlone peoples and other native Californians.

The territory now occupied by the state of California possessed the densest aboriginal population of any region of comparable size north of the Valley of Mexico, and a non-agricultural population that numbered between three hundred thousand and one million people (Dobyns 1966; Cook 1976a, 1978:91). The extraordinary concentration of linguistic diversity in the state indicates that beginning fifteen thousand years ago or perhaps even earlier, California received wave after wave of indigenous peoples, each of which developed its own productive system to utilize the ecological niches that are concentrated on the Pacific littoral (cf. Chartkoff and Chartkoff 1984; Moratto 1984). The ecological bounty of this region facilitated periods of demographic expansion and socioeconomic intensification that featured neither agricultural food production nor the urbanization of population. By the late pre-contact period (AD 900-1500), archaeological data strongly suggest that social stratification, ceremonial intensification, and technological development were accompanied by the expansion of settlement in and around the Bay Area (T. King 1970; Bean and King 1974; Wiberg 1984; Luby 1991; Leventhal 1993; and others).

From the Kroeberian perspective, California Indians including the Ohlone produced their subsistence simply by gathering and hunting in rich ecosystems that offered them easy subsistence. While California natives did harvest readily available wild foods, particularly fish, sea mammals and shellfish from marine and freshwater habitats, newer perspectives have identified complex interactions with, and managing of, the natural environment through which native Californians produced sustained and sustainable food surpluses (Bean and Lawton 1976; Blackburn and Anderson 1993). These quasi-agricultural practices depended largely upon burning as a means of clearing and fertilizing land (Lewis 1973, 1993; cf. Cronon 1983). Native Californians gathered the seeds of useful wild grasses and sowed these seeds in burned areas to produce food for themselves, as well as fodder that attracted herds of herbivorous game. The Ohlones and other Central California natives seasonally relied upon the harvest of acorns from a number of different oak species that thrived in such managed landscapes. The management (through burning) and reliance upon diverse plant communities producing high yields of seeds, nuts and acorns conditioned the development of processing, milling, and cooking technologies that strongly resemble or are identical to technologies other peoples developed for utilizing cultivated grains (Fowler 1971; cf. Struever 1971; Lewis 1973; and others).

In short, the production systems of native Californians provided reliable food surpluses for large populations located in the myriad micro-ecosystems distributed around the Bay Area. These surpluses, in turn, were the basis for trading systems that integrated the diverse ecological regions managed by native peoples (Fages 1937; Goldschmidt 1951; Vayda 1967; Chagnon 1970; Bean 1976; Blackburn 1976; Heizer 1978b; and others). The various Ohlone peoples lived in regions that provided resources for manufacturing what Bean has called "treasure goods," resources such as abalone, Olivella shell, and cinnabar from which ornaments (social badges or markers of distinction) of political and ceremonial significance were crafted (1976:120). The production of food surpluses and of treasure goods gave many Ohlone villages that had access to certain resources an advantageous position in regional trade networks (Davis 1961; Heizer 1978b; Bean 1978; Leventhal 1993; and others).

Based upon such information, our reconstruction of Ohlone societies at the time of contact emphasizes both micro and macro organizational forms, in contrast with Kroeber's tribelet model. Kroeber (1962) defined a tribelet as composed of a central village inhabited by inter-related extended families encircled by smaller, outlying villages also inhabited by inter-related families, which together constituted a territorial perimeter under the exclusive control of each tribelet's hereditary and elected political elites. Each tribelet territory, according to Kroeber, constituted an ethnically and linguistically homogeneous unit. Anthropologists working with both Kroeber's concept of tribelet and the idea that language similarities can be used to describe fictive ethnicities have drawn patchwork maps of the "Native ethnic groups" of pre-contact California (see Heizer 1974a, 1978a; Levy 1978; Margolin 1978; and others).

We do not identify the area composed of a central village and surrounding outlying villages as necessarily an autonomous or discreet socio-cultural unit, and it is unclear whether the village unit functioned cognitively as the most important source of cultural identity for the people who lived in each village. Regional linkages along lines of trade, kinship, and the performance of shared rituals (e.g., *Kuksu*, trade feasts, funerals and mourning anniversaries) likely shaped differently sized and constituted identities for social groups and individuals in native California (Blackburn 1976). Among village elites, for example, the political world clearly did not stop at the boundaries of their own village's territory. Elites from villages all over the territory of Ohlone-speaking peoples depended upon marrying into elite families from other villages, villages in which Ohlone languages may or may not have been spoken. Inter-marriage gave rise to extended networks of multi-lingual elite families or communities, whose wealth and status represented the accumulation of economic surpluses from territories much larger than the village (Bean 1978; cf. Milliken 1990, 1991). Through elite intermarriage, larger regions were integrated which overlapped and crossed linguistic boundaries (Bean and Lawton 1976; Bean 1992).

Elite intermarriage facilitated and underscored other regional integrating forces such as trade. People from different villages, often distantly related, struck up personal trading relationships, called "special friendships," which often lasted whole lifetimes (Bean 1976). Through networks of "special friends," food, tools, and treasure goods were traded from village to village over long distances. Networks of ritual and ceremonial obligation called together large numbers of diverse peoples for particular occasions, such as the funerals of significant inter-village elite personages (Blackburn 1976). On such occasions, trade fairs also occurred, and elites likely arranged the future marriages of their children. Taken all together, the trading of subsistence and treasure goods, the exchanges of marriage partners, and the cycles of ritual and ceremony tied together constellations of kin-based village communities into integrated political, economic and cultural fields led by a small inter-village elite strata (see Bean 1992). We might describe these elite-ruled realms as quasi-chiefdoms or ranked chiefdoms (Service 1962, 1975; Fried 1967; for an archaeological perspective on evidence of social ranking within the San Francisco Bay see T. King 1970, 1974; Wiberg 1984; Luby 1991; and Leventhal 1993).

The paradox of a bountiful environment, large population, and lack of recognizable cultivation confounded the Spaniards, the first Europeans determined to control what is now the state of California. Elsewhere in Latin America, particularly in the Andes and Meso-America (see Salomon 1981; Rappaport 1990; Smith 1990; and many others), indigenous political structures and processes for manufacturing commodities were more familiar to European eyes; therefore, at least for a time following the initial conquest of indigenous civilizations, the Spaniards harnessed indigenous political and economic organizations for their own purposes. Because the Spaniards could not understand a civilization whose productive base, economic surplus, and sources of wealth were fundamentally alien, their domination of Californian natives hinged upon completely re-molding their cultures and societies into forms that were comprehensible to European sensibilities.

The Franciscan missions, by means of which the Spanish Empire lay claim to California, implanted European political and economic systems. The process of implantation required, first, that Native American religions and cultural practices be restricted and eventually forbidden, and, later, that the economic and environmental foundations of native life be destroyed (Cook 1976b; Castillo 1978, 1989; Brady, Crome and Reese 1984). The missionized peoples of the Bay Area and elsewhere in coastal California became a labor force for an emergent agricultural economy that obliged natives to leave aside most indigenous ritual and ceremonial practices, as well as the manufacture of many aspects of aboriginal material culture. As agricultural laborers, missionized Indians were largely separated from the seasonal rhythms of their own food production practices, while the growth of mission farms and rangeland for cattle initiated an environmental transformation of the Bay Area and the entire coast that destroyed much of the resource base of the indigenous economy.

The demographic collapse of the Ohlone populations held captive at Mission Dolores at the tip of the San Francisco peninsula, Missions Santa Clara and San Jose in the South and East Bay respectively, the *Amah-Mutsun* at San Juan Bautista to the south, and the Esselens at Mission San Carlos on the Monterey peninsula occurred because of the horrendous effects of European-introduced diseases, exacerbated by the unhealthy diet and over-crowded living conditions at the missions. Birth rates plummeted from disease, mistreatment of women, and from a psychological phenomenon now recognized as post-traumatic stress (Cook 1976b; Rawls 1986; Hurtado 1988; Jackson 1992; and others). As the populations of Ohlones both inside and outside of the missions decreased, survivors tended to congregate around the missions, seeking solutions to their seemingly unsolveable problems from the missionaries who were causing those same problems. Under the circumstance of socio-cultural holocaust, many Bay Area Ohlones identified with their oppressors, who seemed to have overthrown and taken control of all of the old systems of spiritual and earthly power (see Milliken 1991 for a different interpretation that partly exonerates the missions).

In response to the diminution of their labor force, the Franciscan fathers directed Spanish soldiers to bring in new converts from further afield. The Miwok, Yokuts, Patwin, and Esselen speaking peoples from villages located east, north and south of the Bay Area missions made up the new cohort of neophytes, and they intermarried with the surviving Ohlone-speaking peoples (Milliken 1978, 1982, 1983, 1990, 1991). Such intermarriage was, as we have emphasized, already typical of the intermarriage between Yokuts, Miwok, Patwin and Ohlone speaking elites in the pre-contact era. At the missions, intermarriage apparently continued subtly to reinforce sociopolitical hierarchies and elite families. Even under the triple assault of religious conversion, ecological transformation, and demographic collapse, indigenous political leadership and resistance did not disappear. The missions struggled against frequent desertions by neophytes, and armed rebellions occurred at Missions Dolores and San Jose. Led by Pomponio at Mission Dolores (early 1820s), and by the famous Estanislao at Mission San Jose and Cipriano at Mission Santa Clara, indigenous guerrilla armies combined the forces of both runaway neophytes and natives from villages the Spanish had not yet dominated (see Holterman 1970; Brown 1975; Rawls 1986; Castillo 1989). Yet the Spaniards, for the most part, succeeded in destroying the ecological bases for the indigenous economy, and in transforming the Bay

Area peoples and their close neighbors into an exploited, impoverished working class. It was as a peon working class that the natives of the Bay Area and elsewhere in Hispanic California confronted the next stage of European domination, with the admission of California into the United States.

POST-COLONIAL FRAGMENTATION OF OHLONE SOCIETY AND CULTURE

Elsewhere we have recounted in detail the historical circumstances regarding East Bay Ohlone survival from the middle of the nineteenth century into the early years of this century (Field, Leventhal, Sanchez, and Cambra 1992a). Some of those circumstances played a role in the economic disenfranchisement that conditioned the political fragmentation of the Ohlone people during this period.

Recent historical work stresses the importance of Indian labor in Hispanic and early American California (Rawls 1986; Hurtado 1988; Castillo 1989; Monroy 1990). In California, as everywhere in the Spanish Empire, the conquerors made use of Indians as laborers. This commonality stands in contrast to English and Euro-American colonization regimes extant in the rest of North America, which maintained almost impermeable boundaries between white settlements and native populations, or simply removed native peoples from areas reserved for white settlement. The differences between colonial regimes shaped important changes for Indian labor and laborers, as California passed from Spanish to Mexican to American control.

The influx of Europeans and Euro-Americans into California coincided with the waning years of the Spanish Empire and the independence of Mexico in 1821. Between 1834 and 1836, the Mexican government secularized the missions with the stated intention of dividing mission properties among the neophytes and their descendants. Instead, the *Californios*, the Hispanic families of the Bay Area and elsewhere, established large estates (mostly cattle ranches) on the old mission lands, and many of the former neophytes were hired on as *vaqueros* (ranch hands or cowboys) and as domestic servants. Some non-Hispanic settlers initially followed the Hispanic custom of employing Indians as agricultural, ranch, and household workers, both in the missionized coastal areas and in the newly colonized regions of the interior, the latter exemplified by Sutter's estate in the Sacramento valley (Hurtado 1988).

Not all of the formerly missionized Indians of the Bay Area exchanged a Franciscan father for a *Californio* or Euro-American master.

Some former neophytes abandoned the Bay Area altogether for regions outside of Hispanic settlement, although some of them were soon drawn into the orbit of newer, Euro-American enterprises such as Sutter's. Wherever they went, Indian *vaqueros* and other laborers may have drawn wages from their non-Indian employers, but they seldom stopped making use of whatever native resource bases remained. Often, hunting and gathering wild foods, even in the transformed landscape of post-mission California, enabled native peoples to survive. Some former neophytes and their children attempted to survive by reconstructing indigenous communities in the most remote areas of the Bay Area, relying on the Euro-American economy as little as possible (Brady, Crome and Reese 1984). Indians from Missions San Jose and Santa Clara retreated to the hinterlands of the East Bay, in the Diablo range and Livermore Valley, where they organized new communities, sometimes on or near the sites of old pre-contact villages. Such a reconstitution of indigenous community and identity also occurred near San Juan Bautista in the mid and late nineteenth century.

The expansion of American settlement and political power dovetailed with this indigenous revitalization. With statehood and the decline of Hispanic social and cultural practices, and especially during and after the Gold Rush, the now dominant Euro-Americans reasserted patterns of interaction with native peoples established elsewhere in North America. The politics of Manifest Destiny (see Hoopes 1975; Rawls 1986; and others) justified genocidal policies towards California Indians aimed at removing Indian populations from land that whites coveted. Virulent racism pervaded the attitudes of Euro-American settlers towards California Indians, who were given the derogatory epithet "digger Indian"; such a view was legitimized by the Social Darwinist theory typical of early scholarly authors such as Hubert Bancroft (1874), Lorenzo Yates (1875), John Hittell (1879) and others. In the new state of California, Indians lost their legal rights to bear witness or to defend themselves in court. Indian labor became increasingly marginalized. This occurred most notably in the gold mining areas and the new agricultural heartlands of the Sacramento and San Joaquin valleys, where initially indigenous peoples had adapted themselves to the new conditions and some native miners achieved a degree of financial success (Hurtado 1988; Monroy 1990).

In the Bay Area of the 1860s, the estates of the *Californios* had mostly passed into American hands, both because American laws required that the validity of the *Californios'* land titles be proved in a lengthy and costly process, and because a crippling drought had destroyed production on the estates, obliging the *Californios* to sell out (Pitt 1968; Bean and Rawls 1988). New American landowners tended to discontinue the use of native labor in favor of the large numbers of recently arrived young men of European descent, who seldom had families to support as Indian men did. Under such circumstances, an Indian strategy of withdrawal into hinterlands seemed to make the most sense—for a while. The creation of a large, culturally revitalized Ohlone community in the East Bay, the *Alisal rancheria*, occurred at the same time as the economic degradation of native peoples throughout the state and the steady strangulation of economic opportunities for Indian people (Field, Leventhal, Sanchez and Cambra 1992a).

Alisal extended over a large acreage just south of the town of Pleasanton, land ceded to the Indians by a *Californio* family, the Bernals, who had kept their estate when California became part of the United States, and who undoubtedly employed many Ohlones as seasonal workers and *vaqueros*. Individuals in the Bernal family intermarried with and served as *compadres*, or ritual godparents, to some of the late 19th century Ohlone children whose descendants are now prominent in the contemporary *Muwekma* Ohlone Tribe. For example, Petrus A. Bernal was the *compadre* for Raymonda (Ramona) Marine, born in Alisal in 1893. Ramona was the grandmother of *Muwekma* chairwoman Rosemary Cambra (Book III, Mission San Jose Baptismal Records 1892-1925:17).

When the Hearst family acquired this property in the 1880s, the *Alisal* community's

Fig. 11.1. *Muwekma* elders Henry "Hank" Alvarez and his older brother John "Pop" Alvarez in the 1930s

claim to the land was recognized and respected. Successive landowners' relatively liberal attitudes toward the community, in addition to the relative geographical remoteness of the *rancheria*, made *Alisal* economically possible. Under such circumstances, the cultural and political richness of the intertwined and intermarried families living at *Alisal*, among whom Ohlone, Yokuts, and Miwok languages were spoken, produced a ritually and ceremonially syncretic cultural revival. Fortunately, the linguistic and cultural richness at *Alisal* was recorded by several ethnographers, including J. Curtin in 1884 (Beeler 1961), C. Hart Merriam in 1905 (1967), A.L. Kroeber (1904, 1910), E.W. Gifford (1914), J.A. Mason (1916), and John P. Harrington (1921-1934). The breadth of cultural revitalization was nowhere more evident than in the central role *Alisal* Ohlones played in combining the Ghost Dance religion of the late nineteenth century with indigenous Californian rituals, such as the *Kuksu* Dance and the World Renewal Ceremony, and then in diffusing this religion to other native peoples in Central California (Gifford 1926, 1927; Kelly 1932, 1978, 1991; DuBois 1939).

Although the cultural achievements of the Ohlone people at *Alisal* were inestimable, the *rancheria* eventually waned as the slender economic base supporting the community dwindled, and the surrounding white population enveloped the region. During the early twentieth century, the Ohlone claim to *Alisal* was lost in a paper shuffle in Washington D.C. (Dorrington 1927[2]; Heizer 1978c). Native political leadership faltered without an economic base for the community, use of indigenous (particularly Ohlone) languages disappeared by the third decade of this century, and the family became the only economically viable unit.

The will to survive as Indian people made even this extreme fragmentation a possible cultural survival strategy, as families drifted away from *Alisal* to other parts of the Bay Area. With their sense of community fragmented after *Alisal* was abandoned, the persistence of intermarriage and ritual godparenthood kept the Ohlone families intertwined and in touch with the informal leadership of charismatic individuals (a process that was revitalized during the 1928-1933 enrollment under the California Jurisdictional Act). The contemporary *Muwekma* Ohlone are the direct descendants of the families who lived at *Alisal*. In the same fashion, the *Amah-Mutsun* members descend directly from the Ohlone peoples who were indigenous to the region around

---

[2]In L.A. Dorrington's letter written to the Commissioner of Indian Affairs, dated June 23, 1927 regarding the status of the purchase of land for homeless California Indians, are included statements dismissing the needs of the Verona Band (*Muwekma*) of Alameda County, the San Juan Bautista Band (*Amah-Mutsun*) of San Benito County, and remnants of the Pleyto, Jolon and Milpitas Bands (Esselen Nation and Salinan Nation).

Mission San Juan Bautista and later took refuge in that region again after statehood. The contemporary Esselens descend from the Mission San Carlos neophytes who returned to their old territories following the secularization of the missions.

THE RE-EMERGENCE OF OHLONE PEOPLES
IN THE TWENTIETH CENTURY

While Kroeber, like many of the other ethnographers listed previously, witnessed the linguistic and cultural richness extant at the *Alisal rancheria* (as well as at other Ohlone and Esselen communities), the fragmentation that occurred for the *Muwekma* after *Alisal's* demise led him to write that they were "extinct." In his *Handbook* article (1925), he wrote:

> The Costanoan group is extinct so far as all practical purposes are concerned. A few scattered individuals survive, whose ancestors were once attached to the missions San Jose, San Juan Bautista, and San Carlos, but they are of mixed-tribal ancestry and live lost among other Indians or obscure Mexicans.

In comments made some thirty years later, Kroeber somewhat mitigated the finality of his pronouncement. He served as an expert witness speaking on behalf of native Californians during the California Claims hearings held by the federal government in Berkeley and San Francisco in 1955 (Kroeber and Heizer 1970; Shipek 1989). While the hearings were intended to redress the injustices against California Indians that the federal government had perpetrated, instead they legitimized the native peoples' loss of huge acreage and of federal acknowledgment itself, a loss for which they were paid only a paltry amount (Stewart 1978; see Field, Leventhal, Sanchez, and Cambra 1992a for how the East Bay Ohlones experienced this "settlement."). In defense of the Indians and of peoples pronounced "extinct," Kroeber wrote:

> . . . there is a widespread belief that many Indian groups, especially the smaller ones, have now become extinct . . . Anthropologists sometimes have gone a step farther, and when they can no longer learn from living informants the speech and modes of life of the ancestors of these informants, they talk of that tribe or group as being extinct—when they mean merely that **knowledge** of the aboriginal language and culture has

become extinct among the survivors. The survivors are there;
they may even be full-bloods; racially or biologically the stock
is not extinct; but they can no longer help the anthropologist
acquire the knowledge about the group that he would like to
preserve (Kroeber and Heizer 1970:2-3).

While this qualification might be viewed as a retraction of his
previous position, Kroeber's statement both underscored anthropology's
authority to declare which people are extinct and which are not, and
reinforced the widely held notion that cultural transformations among
native peoples erase their indigenous identity and basically make them
"not Indians anymore." Kroeber seemed to say: "If descendants do not
know the details about traditional culture or practice, then the question
should be asked, 'Are they Indian?'."

Kroeber's authoritative summations have had broad influence
upon four kinds of professionals: anthropologists, popular historians,
cultural geographers, and cultural resource management archaeologists.
The writings of some of these professionals, in turn, have maintained and
reinforced the "fact" of Ohlone extinction. Our treatment of particular
writers within these genres is far from exhaustive, and there have been
many exceptions to the pattern we describe below. Rather, we seek to
describe the conditions under which a people, in this case the descendants
of the Ohlone-speaking peoples of the San Francisco Bay Area, can exist
and yet be invisible both to the general public and the professional
communities whose authority is relied upon by local, state and federal
governmental agencies (especially agencies concerned with and funding
cultural resource projects). Such a discussion does not lay blame on any
particular doorstep. The Ohlone people recognize the subtleties by which
relations of power and disempowerment are mediated and mirrored by
knowledge, authority, and public opinion.

Among the anthropologists who parroted Kroeber's extinction
sentence, many were not powerful or influential in California.
Nevertheless, by uncritically accepting Kroeber's summation in textbooks,
such authors have contributed to the overall impression that there are no
longer any Ohlone people left. This holds true in both older and newer
texts. For example, Ruth Underhill essentially parroted Kroeber in her
book *Red Man's America*:

> Esselen . . . : Possibly a remnant of a larger group; first
> California group to become extinct.
> Costanoan . . . : Now extinct for all practical purposes
> (1953:288, 291).

Lantis, Steiner, and Karinen, cultural geographers teaching at two California universities (Chico State and Long Beach State) wrote in their textbook *California: Land of Contrast* the following excerpted account for the Costanoans and the Esselens of the central coast:

> The *Costanoans* (Spanish for "coastal folk") lived in scattered villages. Kroeber has estimated that their numbers may have reached 7000. Their culture was rude even for California—men went naked when the weather allowed and women wore short skin skirts. . . .

> The *Hokans* were represented by three groups (Esselens, Salinan, and Chumash). The Esselen lived south of the Costanoans in limited numbers. . . . These were the first California Indians to become extinct (1963:266).

Cutter (1990), a historian specializing in California history, commented in his book *California in 1792: A Spanish Naval Visit*, about Kroeber's anthropological position on *Rumsen* and Esselen people:

> The noted California anthropologist would have appreciated the information contained in the 1792 report since he had to excuse his lack of very precise knowledge concerning both of these groups by indicating that they were the first to become entirely extinct "and are as good as unknown" (1990:113, footnote 25).

In a very recent and widely read introductory text to Native North Americans used in many undergraduate courses, Alice Kehoe declares:

> The central coast south of San Francisco and the adjacent Santa Clara Valley across the Coast Range were occupied by the Costanoans, once speaking a language closely related to Miwok, now effectively extinct as a nation (1992:402).

In the Bay Area itself, many anthropologists remain convinced that, if Ohlone descendants exist, they are hardly worthy of attention. Frank Norick, Principal Museum Anthropologist at the Hearst Museum at the University of California, Berkeley, was quoted in a newspaper interview as follows:

. . . there are few Indians left in the Bay Area who have some
vague Native American heritage, but until [a recent book on the
subject] came out, they didn't know who the East Bay Indians
were. We don't know who the East Bay Indians were, and the
few Indians that happened to survive were swallowed up and
exterminated by civilization by the latter part of the last
century. That's not to say that there aren't people around here
who are of Indian heritage, but I'd be willing to bet they
couldn't give you even the semblance of a [lineage] account
that was aboriginal (Norick interview in Express Newspaper
9/21/89:15-16).

The opinions of "experts" are received by those who write
popular histories as authoritative sources. Such popular authors probably
did not read Kroeber, and their notions are far more crude and pejorative
than   the   worst   ethnographic   misrepresentations;   nevertheless,
anthropological concepts of both primitiveness and extinction play into
popular, journalistic sensationalism concerning "dying Indian tribes," and
individuals who are "the last of their kind."   One example of these
popular history tendencies recalled by the *Mutsun* Ohlone descendants
occurred at the death of Ascencion Solorsano de Cervantes, a *Mutsun*
woman who was an accomplished healer and social worker, and who also
was the last fluent speaker of the *Mutsun* language, *Hoomontwash*. When
she died, newspaper journalists romanticized her as "the last full-blooded
San Juan Indian," even though her large extended family continued to
live on in the area (see Field, Leventhal and Mondragon 1994).

More disturbing still is the recent re-issue of a popular history of
the New Almaden Mines area of the Santa Clara Valley entitled *Cinnabar
Hills,* written by Lanyon and Bulmore (1967), the latter a graduate of
Stanford University and a longtime educator at San Jose State. Harking
back to the most invidious racism hurled at California native peoples, the
authors expand upon the notion of the "primitive" California Indian,
writing:

As compared to the other tribes to the South, [the
Ohlones] were inoffensive, mild-mannered, inferior in
intelligence, and existed on a low level of primitive culture.
The native did little hunting and lacked the understanding to till
the soil. . . . Their survival was wholly dependent upon the
most accessible items of food that were available in nature's
garden. . . . The Olhone [sic] were not of a creative nature, and
produced little except some basketry, stone utensils and items
of bone. . . . For lack of any substantial evidence, it is assumed
they were completely satisfied with their meager existence and

completely satisfied with their meager existence and lacked the intelligence to improve their standard of living (1967:1).

Malcolm Margolin's *The Ohlone Way* (1978), is an example of a well intentioned popular history that ends up subtly reinforcing popular cultural and historical stereotypes and anthropological racism. This book is perhaps the most widely read pseudo-ethnohistorical depiction of pre- and post-contact Ohlone culture and society. Despite the author's sympathetic treatment of the limited sources available to him, the book reproduces the popular notion that the Ohlones lived in small-scale, simple, and provincial social and cultural arrangements. While *The Ohlone Way* presents only a historical reconstruction of the pre-contact world which has been strongly shaped by Kroeberian frameworks, the book has been treated in the Bay Area and elsewhere as definitive—"the last word," so to speak, concerning the Ohlones. In this way, the book has buttressed the conceptual barriers between the general public and the contemporary revitalization and regrouping of the *Muwekma* Ohlones.

The influence of the Kroeberian legacy that characterizes native Californian societies and cultures as simple, small-scale, and ultimately primitive, and that declares particular groups "extinct" has been particularly prominent among many of the cultural resource management archaeologists working in the San Francisco Bay Area during the last quarter of a century (this despite the fact that for a quarter of a century other views—views of complexity in cultural sophistication—have been noted in the anthropological literature by several scholars, including Bean, Blackburn, Tom King, Chester King, etc.) The work of this group of professionals has had the most direct influence upon the lives and cultural identity of the Ohlone descendants because of the former's control over Ohlone ancestral skeletal remains, associated grave regalia, and other sites of the Ohlone past. It is therefore in the conflict between certain CRM archaeologists and the Ohlone Tribes that the mediation and maintenance of the power of the extinction sentence is most evident, and, conversely, it is within the context of this conflict that the Ohlone people have regrouped and recovered their sense of collective identity (Leventhal et al. 1992).

The explosion of urban expansion and rural development in the Bay Area since 1970 onto lands previously utilized for agriculture, grazing, or simply as open space has been the forum in which this conflict took shape. During this period, national, state and local legislation in the United States created frameworks that mandated the mitigation of adverse imports on archaeological sites, human remains and artifacts as non-renewable resources. Archaeologists themselves recognized that controls were necessary, and supported the creation of a process for both completing archaeological/environmental-impact reports and for planning the mitigation of adverse impacts on discovered sites. This process, which also accommodated the participation of Native Americans in the monitoring of their ancestors, has directed substantial amounts of money toward contract archaeology firms in the Bay Area. Unfortunately, for many years, both in the Bay Area and elsewhere in the United States, the attempted legal protection of archaeological sites has seldom initiated anything more than token accommodation between the archaeologists excavating ancient Indian sites, and individual descendants of the indigenous peoples hand-picked to collaborate as passive monitors with many of the CRM firms. Such firms often evade, if not subvert, the hard work of responding to the concerns and sensitivities of formally organized Ohlone tribal governments through the manipulation of individual descendants. This process is further exacerbated by the Native American Heritage Commission, which, like the Bureau of Indian Affairs, has lumped all "Most Likely Descendants" in the Bay Area into the generalized tribal classification: Costanoan. When confronted by the need to arbitrate on the question of tribal boundaries all over the state, the Native American Heritage Commission selects individuals it thinks are "most likely descended" from prehistoric occupants of sites where human remains are discovered. This selection process often disregards the existence of formal tribal governments and areas that were aboriginal to their respective tribes. The end result of this process is further disenfranchisement and state sponsored factionalism.

This has been the case even in states where modern Indian tribes are federally recognized and live on reservations. For the Ohlone descendants, the absence of federal acknowledgment has been exacerbated by CRM archaeologists' citation of Kroeber's sentence of extinction as a statement of fact. Most of the interpretive studies that CRM archaeologists publish about their excavations include a small section called "ethnohistory," in which the authors typically discount the existence and/or legitimacy of the Ohlone descendants. For example, in an evaluative report that Garaventa et al. (1991) wrote for Basin Research about their excavations at the Guadalupe River in San Jose, the authors wrote:

> The Costanoan aboriginal lifeway apparently disappeared by 1810 . . . Thus multi-ethnic communities grew up in and around Costanoan territory, and it was these people who provided ethnological data in the period from 1878 to 1933 (Garaventa et al. 1991:9).

The last sentence discounts both the contemporary descendants and the rich sources of data gathered by J.P. Harrington and others early in this century because they are concerned with "multi-ethnic communities," and not with "real" Ohlones. Similar kinds of pseudo-science, often quoting Kroeber as well, can be found in studies published by Munoz (1983); Pastron and Walsh (1988); Cartier (1990); and Basin Research (1984, 1985, 1990) among others. Admirable mission era ethnohistorical studies can be found in Winter (1978a, 1978b); C. King (1974, 1977, 1978a, 1978b); and Milliken (1978, 1981, 1988, 1993). While the former group of studies erases the relationship between the contemporary tribes and their ancestors, and thus reproduces the extinction sentence over and over, we note that these same contract archaeologists, many of whom are paid with public funds, have produced very little published work that sheds light on the complexity of pre-contact Ohlone society and culture.

The implications of this kind of CRM interpretive work for the Ohlone tribes have therefore been threefold. First, if no culturally significant tribal people of the pre-contact Bay Area natives survive, then the ethnographer's tools—oral history, intensive interviewing, participant observation—are no longer relevant and no anthropological research need

Figure 11.2. *Muwekma* Chairwoman Rosemary Cambra, her mother Dolores Sanchez and her uncle Robert Sanchez, *Muwekma* elders

be done. Second, archaeological excavation of pre- and post-contact native civilization in the Bay Area can proceed without regard for the cultural sensitivities and research priorities of Ohlone descendants since, again, none exist. Last, the authority of Kroeberian and pseudo-Kroeberian pronouncements of extinction suggests that isolated individuals may possess enough Ohlone ancestry to act as consultants for CRM firms, but firmly discounts revitalized tribal governments among the Ohlone people (Leventhal et al. 1992). Since, as Kroeber's statement in 1955 (about clarifying what anthropologists mean when they say something is extinct) attests, modern descendants do not possess the knowledge about language and other cultural traits that pedigrees them as "proper" Indians in the eyes of some anthropological authorities. A number of academic based anthropologists, CRM archaeologists, university museum curators, and historians have, until very recently, alleged that contemporary tribal organizations have little or no legitimacy, especially as it relates to each tribe's ancestral and present-day heritage (e.g., PL 101-601, Native American Graves Protection and Repatriation Act).

Elsewhere, we have detailed the precise sequence of events, starting in the mid-1970s, during which Ohlones throughout the Bay Area responded to the specific kind of disempowerment posed by some CRM archaeologists (see Field, Leventhal, Sanchez and Cambra 1992a). At first, acting as individuals and often in a spontaneous manner, the *Muwekma* Ohlone families began taking direct action to protect ancestral sites which feature elaborate mortuary complexes replete with aesthetically sophisticated material culture. In the case of the East and South Bay *Muwekma* Ohlone Tribe in particular, the ever-increasing threat to their ancestral dead created the impetus that obliged them to reach beyond their family-based survival strategies, and motivated them to initiate new inter-family community organizations. The *Muwekma* Tribe established its own archaeological consulting firm, Ohlone Families Consulting Services (OFCS), in order to transform the archaeological management of their ancestral sites by taking control of its past. Recognized by the Department of the Interior under the Buy Indian Act as a Native American owned firm, OFCS has carried out excavations and written interpretive reports of a professional caliber in collaborative relationships with federal, state, county and city agencies. By taking control of their history, they have established control over their tribal identity and their collective future.

Nevertheless, much of the archaeological community in the Bay Area has been slow to break with the anthropological ideas of Kroeber and Heizer. Ohlone demands for both repatriation of already excavated remains and control over new excavations have led many local CRM archaeologists to align with political action groups organized by anthropologists and other "concerned" scientists who are attempting to blockade repatriation. One such group, called ACPAC (American Committee for Preservation of Archaeological Collections) is presently supported by Constance Cameron (Museum of Anthropology, California State University) and Clement W. Meighan (Emeritus Professor of Anthropology, UCLA) and a number of others. This group publishes a politically charged informational newsletter that has made the Ohlones something of a *bête noire*. In 1993, E.J. Neiburger's article "Profiting From Reburial" declaimed:

> Public money for reburials is the latest growth industry for numerous activists: $135,000 of taxpayers' money was used to pay off land-owners, lawyers, archaeologists and activists in an effort to bury 146 poorly understood skeletons in Saline, Kansas. Religious and historic traditions, accurate identifications and the desires of the next-of-kin have little influence on many activists who demand reburial of all remains under a variety of self-styled "traditional" religions. Thus, Stanford University has released 550 Ohlone skeletons to individuals who had identified with this tribe (the last recognized member of which died in the early 1800s) (Originally published in Nature 1990, 344:297; republished in ACPAC Newsletter, March 1993:3).

OFCS has thus gone to battle with a professional community among which many resist rethinking the legacy of Kroeber's extinction sentence and insist upon retaining exclusive control over archaeology in the Bay Area.

CONCLUSION

By working collectively to obtain control of archaeological excavation of ancestral sites, which embodies their claim to their own past, the East and South Bay *Muwekma* Ohlone Tribe rejected extinction. The professional collaborative relationships they established in their archaeological work have built a foundation for public acceptance of both their continued existence and their important role in the contemporary Bay Area.

The establishment of OFCS aided in the process of self-empowerment and formal regrouping of the East and South Bay Ohlone families as the *Muwekma* Ohlone Tribe. Through their excavation work and the writing of interpretive reports that, like this chapter, challenge the conceptual framework that has supported the erasure of Ohlone identity, the *Muwekma* have documented their historical and cultural continuity. This documentation is also the precondition for federal acknowledgment of their tribal status, for which they filed in 1989.   Federal acknowledgment, a crucial emblem of political empowerment for Native Americans, will enable the *Muwekma* Ohlone to re-establish their land base, initiate economic development, and create the basis for a new and revitalized Native American community.

The leadership of both the *Amah-Mutsun* Band and the Esselen Nation has worked closely with the *Muwekma* to coordinate the tasks of historical revision and reconstruction that lays the basis for empowering all these descendants of "extinct" peoples. This process thus entails a reversal of each step of the historical disenfranchisement of the native peoples of the Bay Area. Coming "back from extinction" has put these peoples on the road toward a new cultural, political and economic revitalization.

REFERENCES CITED

Bancroft, Hubert H.
1874   The Native Races of the Pacific States of North America, Vol. 1, Wild Tribes. New York: D. Appleton and Company.

Basin Research Associates
1984   Excavations at Ca-SC1-6EAST and Ca-SCl-268, A Limited Data Recovery Operation, Santa Clara County, California. Report on file at the Northwest Information Center, Sonoma State University.

1985   Cultural Resources Monitoring Report of Orchard Properties, Inc. Projects 515 and 1001, including Sites Ca-SCl-418, -553, -559 and -569H, San Jose, California. On File at the Northwest Information Center, Sonoma State University.

1990   Analysis of Native American Skeletal Remains Recovered During Emergency Disinternment at Ca-Ala-514/H, The Hidden Valley Ranch Site, City of Fremont, Alameda County, California. On File at the Northwest Information Center, Sonoma State University.

Bean, Lowell J.
1976   Social Organization in Native California. *In* Native Californians: A Theoretical Retrospective. Pp. 99-123. Lowell J. Bean and Thomas C. Blackburn, eds. Menlo Park: Ballena Press.

1978   Social Organization. *In* Handbook of North American Indians, Vol. 8 (California). Pp. 673-682. Robert F. Heizer, ed., William C. Sturtevant, gen. ed. Washington, D.C.: Smithsonian Institution.

1992   Indians of California: Diverse and Complex Peoples. *In* California History: Indians of California. Vol. LXXI (3) Fall. California Historical Society, San Francisco.

Bean, Lowell J. and Thomas King, eds.
1974   ?Antap: California Indian Political and Economic Organization. Ballena Press Anthropological Papers 2, Lowell J. Bean, ed. Ramona: Ballena Press.

Bean, Lowell J. and Harry Lawton
1976   Some Explanations for the Rise of Cultural Complexity in Native California with Comments on Proto-Agriculture and Agriculture. In Native Californians: A Theoretical Retrospective. Pp. 19-48. Lowell J. Bean and Thomas C. Blackburn, eds. Menlo Park: Ballena Press.

Bean, Lowell J. and Thomas Blackburn, eds.
1976   Native Californians: A Theoretical Retrospective. Menlo Park: Ballena Press.

Bean, Walter and James Rawls
1988   California: An Interpretive History. McGraw-Hill Book Company.

Beeler, Madison S.
1961   Northern Costanoan. International Journal of American Linguistics 27:191-197.

Blackburn, Thomas C.
1976   Ceremonial Integration and Social Interaction in Aboriginal California. In Native Californians: A Theoretical Retrospective. Pp. 225-243. Lowell J. Bean and Thomas C. Blackburn, eds. Menlo Park: Ballena Press.

Blackburn, Thomas and Kat Anderson, eds.
1993   Before the Wildnerness: Environmental Management by Native Californians. Ballena Press Anthropological Papers No. 40, Thomas C. Blackburn, ed. Menlo Park: Ballena Press.

Brady, Victoria, Sarah Crome and Lyn Reese
1984   Resist! Survival Tactics of Indian Women. In California History Volume LXIII (2) Spring. California Historical Society, San Francisco.

Brown, Alan K.
1975   Pomponio's World.   The San Francisco Westerners
               Argonaut Number 6.

Buckley, Thomas
1989   Suffering in the Cultural Construction of Others: Robert
               Spott and A.L. Kroeber.   *In* The American Indian
               Quarterly, Journal of American Indian Studies. Special
               Issue: The California Indians, Volume XIII (4) Fall.

Cartier, Robert R., ed.
1990   Archaeological Excavations at Ca-SCl-6W, the Lick Mill
               Boulevard Site. 3 Volumes. Report on File at City of
               Santa Clara.

Castillo, Edward D.
1978   The Impact of Euro-American Exploration and
               Settlement. *In* Handbook of North American Indians,
               Vol. 8 (California). Pp. 99-127. Robert F. Heizer, ed.,
               William C. Sturtevant, gen. ed.   Washington, D.C.:
               Smithsonian Institution.

1989   An Indian Account of the Decline and Collapse of
               Mexico's Hegemony Over the Missionized Indians of
               California. *In* The American Indian Quarterly, Journal
               of American Indian Studies.   Special Issue: The
               California Indians, Volume XIII (4) Fall.

Chagnon, Napoleon
1970   Ecological and Adaptive Aspects of California Shell
               Money.   University of California, Los Angeles,
               Archaeological Survey Annual Report, 1969-1970:1-25.
               Los Angeles.

Chartkoff, Joseph L. and Kerry K. Chartkoff
1984   The Archaeology of California.   Stanford: Stanford
               University Press.

Cook, Sherburne F.
1976a   The Conflict Between the California Indian and White
               Civilization. Berkeley: University of California Press.

1976b   The Population of the California Indians, 1769-1970.
               Berkeley: University of California Press.

1978   Historical Demography.   *In* Handbook of North
               American Indians, Volume 8 (California).   Pp. 91-98.
               Robert Heizer, ed., William C. Sturtevant, gen. ed.
               Washington, D.C.: Smithsonian Institution.

Crapo, Richley H.
1987   Cultural Anthropology: Understanding Ourselves and
               Others. Connecticut: Dushkin Publishing.

Cronon, William
1983   Changes in the Land: Indians, Colonists, and the Ecology
               of New England. New York: Hill and Wang.

Cutter, Donald C.
1990   California in 1792: A Spanish Naval Visit. Norman:
               University of Oklahoma Press.

Davis, James T.
1961   Trade Routes and Economic Exchange Among the
               Indians of California.   University of California
               Archaeological Survey Reports 54:1-71. Berkeley.

Dixon, Roland B., and Alfred L. Kroeber
1913   New Linguistic Families in California.   American
               Anthropologist 15(4):647-655.

1919   Linguistic Families of California.   University of
               California Publications in American Archaeology and
               Ethnology 16(3):47-118. Berkeley.

Dobyns, Henry F.
1966   Estimating Aboriginal American Population: An
               Appraisal of Techniques with a New Hampshire
               Estimate.   Current Anthropology Volume 7:395-416,
               440-444.

Dorrington, L. A.
1927   Letter written to the Commissioner of Indian Affairs,
               June 23. Roseburg File, the 1907-1939 Bureau of Indian

Affairs Classified Files. Washington, D.C.: National Archives.

DuBois, Cora
1939   The 1870 Ghost Dance. University of California Anthropological Records 3(1):1-157. Berkeley.

Fages, Pedro
1937   A Historical, Political, and Natural Description of California by Pedro Fages, Soldier of Spain (1775), Herbert I. Priestly, trans. Berkeley: University of California Press. (Reprinted by Ballena Press, Ramona, California, 1972).

Field, Les, Alan Leventhal, Dolores Sanchez, and Rosemary Cambra
1992a   A Contemporary Ohlone Tribal Revitalization Movement: A Perspective from the Muwekma Costanoan/Ohlone Indians of the San Francisco Bay Area. *In* California History: Indians of California Vol. LXXI (3) Fall. California Historical Society, San Francisco.

1992b   A Contemporary Ohlone Tribal Revitalization Movement: A Perspective from the Muwekma Costanoan/Ohlone Indians of the San Francisco Bay. San Jose: Muwekma Ohlone Indian Tribal Press.

Field, Les, Alan Leventhal and Joseph Mondragon
1994   Bridges Between Two Worlds: The Life and World of Ascencion Solorsano de Cervantes a Amah-Mutsun Doctor. Manuscript by Loyola Fontaine. Amah-Mutsun Tribal Press.

Fowler, Melvin L.
1971   The Origin of Plant Cultivation in the Central Mississippi Valley: A Hypothesis. *In* Prehistoric Agriculture. Stuart Struever, ed. American Museum Source Books in Anthropology. New York: The Natural History Press.

Fried, Morton
1967   The Evolution of Political Society. New York: Random House.

Garaventa, Donna M., Robert M. Harmon, Sondra A. Jarvis, Michael R.
Fong
1991   Cultural Resources Survey and National Register
                Evaluation for Guadalupe River Project, City of San
                Jose, Santa Clara County, California. On File at the
                Army Corps of Engineers, Sacramento District,
                Sacramento, California.

Gifford, Edward W.
1914   Handwritten Linguistic Notes on San Lorenzo Costanoan
                (6 pages). Ethnographic Document 194 on file at the
                University of California Archives, Bancroft Library,
                Berkeley.

1926   Miwok Cults. University of California Publications in
                American Archaeology and Ethnology 18(3):391-408.
                Berkeley.

1927   Southern Maidu Religious Ceremonies.   American
                Anthropologist 29(3):214-257.

Goldschmidt, Walter
1951   Nomlaki Ethnography.   University of California
                Publications in American Archaeology and Ethnology
                42(4):303-443. Berkeley.

Gordon, Robert
1992   The Bushmen Myth: The Making of a Namibian
                Underclass. Boulder, Colorado: Westview Press.

Harrington, John P.
1921-1939   Costanoan Field Notes: Chochenyo Linguistics. On
                microfilm at San Jose State University Library. New
                York: Kraus International Publications.

Hauke, C. F.
1916   Letter to J. Terrell, Special Commissioner, Bureau of
                Indian Affairs, August 19. Roseburg File, the 1907-1939
                Bureau of Indian Affairs Classified Files. Washington,
                D.C.: National Archives.

Heizer, Robert F.
1974a   The Destruction of California Indians: A Collection of
            Documents from the Period 1847 to 1865 in Which are
            Described Some of the Things that Happened to Some of
            the Indians of California. Santa Barbara, California:
            Peregrine Smith.

1974b   The Costanoan Indians. Local History Studies Volume
            18. California History Center, DeAnza College,
            Cupertino, California.

1978a   Handbook of North American Indians, Vol. 8
            (California). Robert F. Heizer, volume editor, William
            C. Sturtevant, gen. ed. Washington, D.C.: Smithsonian
            Institution.

1978b   Trade and Trails. *In* Handbook of North American
            Indians, Vol. 8 (California). Pp. 690-693. Robert
            Heizer, ed., William C. Sturtevant, gen. ed. Washington,
            D. C.: Smithsonian Institution.

1978c   Treaties. *In* Handbook of North American Indians, Vol.
            8 (California). Pp. 701-704. Robert Heizer, ed.,
            William C. Sturtevant, gen. ed. Washington, D. C.:
            Smithsonian Institution.

1979   Federal Concern about Conditions of California Indians,
            1853-1913: Eight Documents. Ballena Press
            Publications in Archaeology, Ethnology and History
            Number 13. Menlo Park, CA: Ballena Press.

Hester, Thomas Roy
1978   Esselen. *In* Handbook of North American Indians,
            Volume 8 (California). Pp. 496-499. Robert Heizer, ed.,
            William C. Sturtevant, gen. ed. Washington, D.C.:
            Smithsonian Institution.

Hittell, John S.
1879   The Resources of California Comprising the Society,
            Climate, Salubrity, Scenery, Commerce and Industry of
            the State. San Francisco: A. L. Bancroft and Company.
            7th Edition.

Holterman, Jack
1970   The Revolt of Estanislao. The Indian Historian 3(1):43-
            54.

Hoopes, Chad L.
1975   Domesticate   or   Exterminate.   Redwood   Coast
            Publications.

Hunter, David E. K.
1985   Subsistence Strategies and the Organization of Social
            Life. *In* Anthropology: Contemporary Perspectives.
            David E. K. Hunter and Phillip Whitten, eds. 4th Edition.
            Boston: Little, Brown and Company.

Hurtado, Albert L.
1988   Indian Survival on the California Frontier. New Haven,
            Connecticut: Yale University Press.

Jackson, Robert H.
1992   Patterns of Demographic Change in the Alta California
            Missions: The Case of Santa Ines. *In* California
            History: Indians of California Volume LXXI (3) Fall.
            California Historical Society, San Francisco.

Kehoe, Alice B.
1992   North American Indians: A Comprehensive Account.
            2nd Edition. Prentice Hall.

Kelly, Isabel T.
1932   Ethnographic Field Notes on the Coast Miwok Indians.
            Manuscript on file at the Bancroft Library. University of
            California, Berkeley.

1978   Coast Miwok. *In* Handbook of North American Indians,
            Vol. 8 (California). Pp. 414-425. Robert Heizer, ed.,
            William C. Sturtevant, gen. ed.   Washington, D. C.:
            Smithsonian Institution.

1991   Interviews with Tom Smith and Maria Copa: Isabel
            Kelly's Ethnographic Notes on the Coast Miwok Indians
            of Marin and Southern Sonoma Counties, California. M.
            E. Trumbull Collier and S. B. Thalman, eds. San Rafael,
            California: Miwok Archaeological Preserve of Marin.

Kelsey, C. E.

1913   Map and accompanying letter to Commissioner of Indian Affairs, October 4. Roseburg File, the 1907-1939 Bureau of Indian Affairs Classified Files. Washington, D.C.: National Archives.

King, Chester D.

1974   Northern Santa Clara Ethnography. *In* Environmental Impact Report, San Felipe Water Distribution System, Archaeological Resources by T. King and G. Berg. Appendix I. Report prepared for Santa Clara Valley Water District.

1977   Matalan Ethnohistory. *In* Final Report of Archaeological Test Excavations for Construction of Freeway 04-SCI-101 Post Miles 17.2/29.4 by S. A. Dietz. Chapter IV. Report prepared by Archaeological Consulting and Research Services for Cal-Trans, District 04, San Francisco.

1978a   The Historic Indian Settlements of San Jose. *In* Archaeological Investigations at Ca-SCL-128: The Holiday Inn Site. J. C. Winter, ed. Chapter XI. Report prepared for the Redevelopment Agency, City of San Jose.

1978b   Almaden Valley Ethnogeography. *In* The Archaeological Mitigation of 4-SCI-132 Alamitos Creek, San Jose, Ca. Robert Cartier, ed. Report on file, City of San Jose.

King, Thomas F.

1970   The Dead at Tiburon. Northwest California Archaeological Society, Occasional Papers 2.

1974   The Evolution of Status Ascription Around San Francisco Bay. *In* ?Antap: California Indian Political and Economic Organization. Lowell J. Bean and Thomas F. King, eds. Pp. 35-54. Ballena Press Anthropological Papers 2, Lowell J. Bean, ed. Ramona: Ballena Press.

Kroeber, Alfred L.
1904   The Languages of the Coast of California South of San
                Francisco. University of California Publications in
                American Archaeology and Ethnology 2(2):29-80.
                Berkeley.

1910   The Chumash and Costanoan Languages. University of
                California Publications in American Archaeology and
                Ethnology 9:237-271. Berkeley.

1925   Handbook of the Indians of California. Bureau of
                American Ethnology Bulletin 78. Washington, D. C.

1948   Anthropology: Race, Language, Culture, Psychology,
                Prehistory. 2nd Edition. New York: Harcourt, Brace
                and Company.

1955   Nature of the Land-holding Group. Ethnohistory
                2(4):303-314.

1962   The Nature of the Land-holding Groups in Aboriginal
                California. Pp. 19-58 in Two Papers on the Aboriginal
                Ethnography of California. D. H. Hymes and R. F.
                Heizer, eds. University of California Archaeological
                Survey Reports 56. Berkeley.

Kroeber, Alfred L. and Robert F. Heizer
1970   Continuity of Indian Population in California from
                1770/1848 to 1955. University of California
                Archaeological Research Facility Contribution 9:1-22.
                Berkeley.

Lantis, David W., Rodney Steiner, and Arthur E. Karinen
1963   California: Land of Contrast. Belmont, CA: Wadsworth
                Publishing Company.

Lanyon, Milton and Laurence Bulmore
1967   Cinnabar Hills: The Quicksilver Days of New Almaden.
                Los Gatos, California: Village Printers.

Latham, R. G.
1856   On the Languages of Northern, Western and Central
                America. Trans. of the Philological Society, pp. 82-84.

Leventhal, Alan M.
1993   A Reinterpretation of Some Bay Area Shellmound Sites:
            A View From the Mortuary Complex From Ca-Ala-329,
            the Ryan Mound. Master's thesis, Department of Social
            Sciences, San Jose State University.

Leventhal, Alan, R. Cambra, A. Miranda, J. Mondragon, A. Slagle and
I. Zweirlein
1992   Anthropology—A Continued Process of Colonialism or
            California Indians Are Still Only Objects of Study.
            Paper presented at the Ohlone Indian Symposium,
            Southwestern Anthropological Association 63rd Annual
            Meeting. Berkeley, California.

Levy, Richard
1978   Costanoan. *In* Handbook of North American Indians,
            Volume 8 (California). Pp. 485-495. Robert Heizer, ed.,
            William C. Sturtevant, gen. ed.   Washington, D.C.:
            Smithsonian Institution.

Lewis, Henry T.
1973   Patterns of Indian Burning in California: Ecology and
            Ethnohistory. Ballena Press Anthropological Papers 1:1-
            101. Lowell J. Bean ed. Ramona, California: Ballena
            Press.   Reprinted 1993 *In* Before the Wildnerness:
            Environmental Management by Native Californians. Pp.
            55-116. Thomas C. Blackburn and Kat Anderson, eds.
            Ballena Press Anthropological Papers No. 40, Thomas C.
            Blackburn, ed. Menlo Park: Ballena Press.

1993   In Retrospect. *In* Before the Wilderness: Environmental
            Management by Native Californians. Pp. 389-400.
            Thomas C. Blackburn and Kat Anderson, eds. Ballena
            Press Anthropological Papers No. 40, Thomas C.
            Blackburn, ed. Menlo Park: Ballena Press.

Luby, Edward
1991   Social Organization and Symbolism at the Patterson
            Mound Site: Ala-328, Alameda County, California.
            California Anthropologist 18(2).

Margolin, Malcolm
    1978   The Ohlone Way: Indian Life in the San Francisco-
                    Monterey Bay Area. Berkeley: Heyday Books.

Mason, J. Alden
    1916   The Mutsun Dialect of Costanoan Based on the
                    Vocabulary of de la Cuesta. University of California
                    Publications in American Archaeology and Ethnology
                    11(7):399-472. Berkeley.

Merriam, C. Hart
    1967   Ethnographic Notes on California Indian Tribes, III:
                    Central California Indian Tribes. Robert F. Heizer, ed.
                    University of California Archaeological Survey Reports
                    68(3). Berkeley.

Milliken, Randall T.
    1978   Ethnohistory of the Lower Napa Valley. *In* Final Report
                    of Archaeological Investigations at the River Glen Site
                    (Ca-Nap-261). Prepared by Archaeological Consulting
                    and Research Services, Mill Valley, California.

    1981   Ethnohistory of the Rumsen. *In* Report of
                    Archaeological Excavations at Nineteen Archaeological
                    Sites for the Stage 1 Pacific Grove-Monterey
                    Consolidation Project of the Regional Sewerage System.
                    Stephen Dietz and Thomas Jackson, eds.

    1982   An Ethnographic Study of the Clayton Area, Contra
                    Costa County, California. *In* Part 2 of Cultural Resource
                    Evaluation of Keller Ranch, Clayton, California. Miley
                    Holman, Principal. Limited publication by Holman
                    Associates, San Francisco.

    1983   The Spatial Organization of Human Population on
                    Central California's San Francisco Peninsula at the
                    Spanish Arrival. Master's thesis, Interdisciplinary
                    Studies: Cultural Resource Management, Sonoma State
                    University.

    1988   Ethnographic Context. Chapter 4 in Archaeological
                    Investigations at Elkhorn Slough: Ca-Mnt-229, A Middle
                    Period Site on the Central California Coast. Stephen

Dietz and William Hildebrandt, principals. Papers in Northern California Anthropology, Number 3.

1990   Ethnogeography and Ethnohistory of the Big Sur District, California State Park System During the 1770-1810 Time Period. Report submitted to Department of Parks and Recreation, Sacramento.

1991   An Ethnohistory of the Indian People of the San Francisco Bay Area from 1770 to 1810. Ph.D. dissertation, Department of Anthropology, University of California, Berkeley.

1993   Historic Overview of the San Felipe Sink Area (Part 1) and Native Peoples (Part 2). Chapters in Archaeological Test Excavataions at Fourteen Sites Along Highways 101 and 152, Santa Clara and San Benito Counties, California, Volume 2: History Ethnohistory, and Historic Archaeology. Far Western Anthropological Research Group, Report submitted to Caltrans District 4. Oakland.

Monroy, Douglas
1990   Thrown Among Strangers: The Making of Mexican Culture in Frontier California. University of California Press.

Moratto, Michael J.
1984   California Archaeology. New York: Academic Press.

Munoz, Jeanne
1983   Ethnographic Background. *In* Archaeological Research of the Southern Santa Clara Valley Project: Located in the Route 101 Corridor, Santa Clara County, California. William R. Hildebrandt, Principal. Report Prepared for Caltrans.

Neiburger, E. J.
1990   Profiting From Reburial. Nature, 344:297. Republished *in* American Committee for Preservation of Archaeo-logical Collections Newsletter, March 1993:3.

Norick, Frank
1989   Interview Excerpted from Angle of Repose article by
              Steve Hiemhoff in Express: The East Bay's Free Weekly
              Newspaper. July 21, Vol. 11, No. 41.

Pastron, Allen G. and Michael R. Walsh
1988   Archaeological Excavations at Ca-SFr-112, the Stevenson
              Street Shellmound, San Francisco, California. Archives
              of California Prehistory 21. Salinas: Coyote Press.

Peoples, James and Garrick Bailey
1994   Humanity: An Introduction to Cultural Anthropology.
              3rd Edition. New York: West Publishing.

Pitt, Leonard
1968   The Decline of the Californios. University of California
              Press.

Powell, John Wesley
1877   Linguistics. *In* Tribes of California. Stephen Powers.
              Pp. 439-613.   Contributions to North American
              Ethnology 3. Washington: U.S. Geographical and
              Geological Survey of the Rocky Mountain Region.

Powers, Stephen
1877   Tribes of California. Contributions to North American
              Ethnology 3. Washington: U.S. Geographical and
              Geological Survey of the Rocky Mountain Region.

Rappaport, Joanne
1990   The Politics of Memory: Native Historical Interpretations
              in the Colombian Andes. Cambridge: Cambridge
              University Press.

Rawls, James J.
1986   Indians of California: The Changing Image. University
              of Oklahoma Press.

Salomon, Frank
1981   Weavers of Odavalo. *In* Peoples and Cultures of Native
              South America. Daniel Gross, ed., Pp. 463-492. New
              York: Natural History Press.

Salzman, Philip C.
1967   Political Organization Among Nomadic Peoples. *In*
            Proceedings of the American Philosophical Society
            Volume 3:115-131.

Service, Elman R.
1962   Primitive Social Organization: An Evolutionary
            Perspective. New York: Random House.

1975   Origins of the State and Civilization: The Process of
            Cultural Evolution. New York: Norton.

Shipek, Florence C.
1989   Mission Indians and Indians of California Land Claims.
            In The American Indian Quarterly, Journal of American
            Indian Studies. Special Issue: The California Indians,
            Volume XIII, Number 4, Fall.

Smith, Carol
1990   Guatemalan Indians and the State: 1540-1988. Austin:
            University of Texas Press.

Stewart, Omer C.
1978   Litigation and its Effects. *In* Handbook of North
            American Indians, Volume 8 (California). Pp. 705-712.
            Robert Heizer, ed., William C. Sturtevant, gen. ed.
            Washington, D.C.: Smithsonian Institution.

Struever, Stuart, ed.
1971   Prehistoric Agriculture. American Museum Source
            Books in Anthropology. New York: The Natural History
            Press.

Terrell, J., Special Commissioner, Indian Service
1916   Letter to Commissioner of Indian Affairs, October 16.
            Roseburg File, the 1907-1939 Bureau of Indian Affairs
            Classified Files. Washington, D.C.: National Archives.

Underhill, Ruth
1953   Red Man's America: A History of Indians in the United
            States. University of Chicago Press.

Vayda, Andrew P.
  1967   Pomo Trade Feasts. *In* Tribal and Peasant Economies:
                Readings in Economic Anthropology.   Pp. 494-500.
                George Dalton, ed. Published for the American Museum
                of Natural History. Garden City, New York: Natural
                History Press.

Wiberg, Randy S.
  1984   The Santa Rita Village Mortuary Complex: Evidence and
                Implications of a Meganos Intrusion. Master's thesis,
                Department of Anthropology, San Francisco State
                University.

Winter, Joseph C., ed.
  1978a   Archaeological Investigations at Ca-SCL-128: The
                Holiday Inn Site.   Report prepared for the
                Redevelopment Agency of the City of San Jose.

  1978b   Tamien: 6000 Years in an American City. Report to the
                City of San Jose Redevelopment Agency. San Jose.

Yates, Lorenzo G.
  1875   The Relics of the Mound Builders of California.
                Alameda County Independent, June 19.

NOSO-N
"IN BREATH SO IT IS IN SPIRIT"
THE STORY OF INDIAN CANYON

Ann Marie Sayers[1]

I was born and raised here in Indian Canyon as was my brother Christopher Sayers. Indian Canyon is a very peaceful place. Dreams have come true and have been fulfilled here, I believe, because of the Canyon and its natural elements. The waterfall is a sacred area. We still carry on our traditions and ceremonies. As I did when I was a child at age three or four, my daughter Kanyon Sayers-Roods goes to the waterfall quite frequently, sometimes with guests and sometimes alone, and offers prayers and blessings using sage and other traditional herbs.

My people are of the *Mutsun* language group of Costanoan people. In the late 1700s Spanish missionaries recorded the first inter-actions with the *Mutsuns* at Mission San Juan Bautista. In the early 1800s, Rev. Fr. Felipe Arroyo de la Cuesta recorded more extensive information on the *Mutsuns*. In an Index he compiled 2,284 phrases of the *Mutsun* language as spoken at Mission San Juan Bautista, together with his Spanish translations. For this I am particularly grateful because we are now reviving our language. In 1814, de la Cuesta responded to the *interrogatorio* issued by the Spanish Government requesting information on the customs and beliefs of the native people (Arroyo de la Cuesta 1821). I found some of his statements to contain some factual information, but they show the priest's profound lack of understanding and sensitivity towards the cultures at the mission. I should like to quote a few sentences from the answers to the *interrogatorio*:

---

[1]Transcribed and edited with the help of Ismana Crater.

These people had scarcely any idea of the soul, nor of its immortality; nevertheless, they would say that when an Indian died, his spirit would be in sacred places which the sorcerers had and still have for the purpose of asking pardon of the devil. From this arose the fear they had when they passed such an oratory, which consisted of but a pole painted red, white and black, and some bows and arrows or other things lying at the foot of the pole. This pole was called Chochon, where they would also place some pinole or parched corn, beads, and a pouch of tobacco. Others would say that the spirits of the dead went to the west; but they could not tell what they did there. For this reason, they never name the dead. Indeed, it is the greatest grief and injury even to name the dead before them; and the pagans still observe the foolish custom. Of hell, bosom of Abraham, limbo, purgatory, resurrections, final and universal judgement they never had any knowledge, nor did they speak of the Author of nature, nor of heaven; yet they say in one of their stories that there exists a people above, and that the stars are the refuse of those inhabitants. Now our neophytes have the knowledge that there is One Creator, God of heaven and earth and of all things. They know about hell, purgatory, heaven, and all the fundamental truths of our holy Faith and Christian Religion.

This is an active Mission where people, who have wandered astray in the mountains, have been collected and are together; who had no idea of letters or characters, and whose history amounts to ridiculous fables, which are passed from generation to generation, and who relate them only for the purpose of passing the time, laughing or to entertain the boys.

The response to the *interrogatorio* mentions that some Indians "return[ed] to the mountains as fugitives." When I was a child, my mother told me that Indian Canyon has always served as a safe haven for some of those who did not like the restrictions of the mission. Today Indian Canyon still serves as a place of healing and renewal.

The eminent anthropologist John P. Harrington produced the primary ethnographic studies of the *Mutsun* People of San Juan Bautista. These studies, based on field work carried out between 1920 and 1935, are critical in providing evidence that the *Mutsun* language and cultural identity were distinct from those of the numerous other indigenous peoples living at the mission. *Mutsun* is one of the eight languages spoken within the area today known as "Costanoan Indian" territory, a term introduced by the Spaniards to lump together all the coastal people in the San Francisco/Monterey Bay Area. It was spoken by a number of distinct tribes that lived within a geographical area bounded on the east side by the Mount Diablo mountain range, on the north by what is now San Jose, on the west by Monterey Bay, and on the south by King City. They traded, socialized and married with neighboring tribes as far afield as the Miwok, Salinan, Yokut, Esselen, and Chumash. And perhaps even further.

My people occupied Indian Canyon, formerly known as Indian Gulch, 15 miles southwest of the city of Hollister. Artifacts found in the Canyon suggest that it was inhabited well before European contact. The Canyon is surrounded by hills and mountains and has several waterfalls and small streams running through it. At the mouth are open lands that were originally swamps, making it a safe hideout for those who knew how to cross them.

Our culture was shaped by the environment in which we lived. The Canyon is filled with oak, pine, sycamore, bay and manzanita. Our economy was based on gathering acorns, berries and many other plants, supplemented by game such as deer, wild turkey, rabbit, elk, quail, and

Figure 12.1. Occupants of Indian Canyon late nineteenth century

others. The social organization that maintained the Indian families in the Canyon, and governed the relationships between the Canyon *Mutsun* band and neighboring groups was informal, but it was adhered to over long periods of time. Those of us who are left in Indian Canyon derive our heritage from our ancestors, who were originally from Chualar, Carmel, San Luis Obispo, Soledad, Santa Cruz, and the San Juan Bautista area.

The documented history of the *Mutsun* Indians of Indian Canyon began in 1897 when my great-grandfather, Sebastian Garcia, (B.I.A. Roll Number 6502) submitted his petition for an Indian Allotment under the Indian Allotment Act of 1887. The heading on the form that my great-grandfather filled out for his allotment boldly proclaims NON COMPETENT INDIAN. Sebastian Garcia, his wife Maria Robles Garcia, and their twelve children, along with several other Indian families, had been residing in Indian Canyon most of their lives.

My mother Elena Sanchez was designated Tribal Leader of the small band in Indian Canyon by her grandfather Sebastian Garcia just before his death in the 1930s. At the time a problem arose with access to the Canyon. A local rancher/farmer who owned the property that provided the only unencumbered access to Indian Canyon tried to prevent Elena and the others of her tribe from entering and exiting through his property. Luckily, another local farmer, Howard Harris (now 84 years old), intervened and convinced the landowner that the right of egress and ingress had always been a *Mutsun* Indian right. The Indians had always come and gone from the Canyon through his property. Why stop them now? Adjudication prevailed and Elena and her people could freely live and move in and out of the Canyon.

My mother was a strong and wise woman. She successfully petitioned the United States government to issue her the "Fee Deed" to the property in 1945. Throughout my mother's lifetime she maintained traditional ties with the *Mutsun* families living in the Canyon and with native people in the outlying area.

Every weekend she held a gathering at which she provided food for all. People brought gifts of fruit, vegetables or other things and left sometimes with more than they came with. During these traditional gatherings, she would often speak about her family's mission days and struggles and tell stories relating to the spiritual values and codes of conduct of our people. She instilled in us a respect for the land. From her, I learned that the proper way to pick oregano was to thank the plant for providing itself. I felt that all the natural elements, and its substance (i.e. air, wind, water, rocks, trees, plants, animals, etc.) were part of a living whole in which we also participated. She spent her life nurturing

Figure 12.2. Joe Wellina and Maria Garcia

her family. She is spoken of to this day with respect and admiration, and is referred to as "the Indian lady from Indian Canyon." She passed to the next world in 1974.

Although my brother Christopher and I were raised in the Canyon and exposed to our tribal heritage by our mother, we also grew up in the "white world," being educated in our modern school system and finding our way in modern society. Having been attracted to adventure and places with paved roads and electricity, I moved to southern California when I was 20 years old. Always selling, be it commodities, stocks and bonds, or New Guinea art work, I found the greatest sense of place when I came home to visit mother. As a child, I had always known I would one day build my permanent home on my great grandfather's homesite at the head of the Canyon. The homesite had collected the positive energies of generations of my ancestors that had lived there, and I could feel their powerful presence. It was one of these visits to mother that I realized the time had come to start planning to build. While I was chasing around the globe after money to build my cabin on Sebastian's homesite, my brother, Chris, was in the Canyon caring for mother and our affairs. However, we have both served as tribal leaders of the *Mutsuns* here in Indian Canyon, and in 1981 we began the process of formalizing the *Mutsun* tribe. I am presently Tribal Chairperson, and since 1980 have interacted and negotiated with city, county, state and federal authorities on behalf of our tribe. In 1988, the enormous effort put out by myself, my family, friends and supporters resulted in our reclaiming my family's ancestral lands in Indian Canyon. It is this story that I would like to relate.

In 1980, I realized that the area at the head of the Canyon, which included my great grandfather's homesite, was not included in the property my mother had inherited from him. Sebastian and Maria had simply continued tradition by building on their family's homesite. This area comprised the central portion of Indian Canyon, and now fell under the jurisdiction of the Bureau of Land Management. This is due to the fact that the southern boundary of Sebastian's allotment as described on the fee deed is 200 feet north of his actual homesite. I decided to petition for the property, and purchase it if possible. It had no value for anyone else; it was landlocked and no one could get to it. My ancestors have lived on this land for many generations. In Folsom, California I met with a Bureau of Land Management (BLM) representative. He brought it to my attention that all petitions for public auction under their jurisdiction had been returned. Alan Thompson, Bureau of Land Management Director, said that at the time (1980), people who had petitioned for land at public auction had their petitions returned because the BLM was not participating in the public auction or exchange programs. My response was to ask if there was any vehicle that I might utilize to purchase the property, so that I could build on my great grandfather's homesite.

I brought to his attention the Indian Allotment Act of 1887:

> Under section 4 of the General Allotment Act of February 8, 1887 (24 Stat. 389; 25 U.S.C.A. 334) an Indian not residing on a reservation or for whose tribe no reservation was provided may apply for an allotment on the public domain.

This act was responsible for breaking up communal landholdings on some reservations, allotting parcels of 40 to 160 acres to individual Indians. Further, it provided that allotments might include an area not to exceed 160 acres of nonirrigable grazing land. On some reservations the remaining available lands on the various reservations were put up for sale to non-Indians. This proved disastrous on many levels to the tribes involved. Basically, it was a law drawn up by the people who were in power at the time. There were many people coming west and the Indians were in the way. It was thought that if the native peoples were turned into farmers and allocated a particular amount of land, the balance of their lands could be sold or homesteaded by settlers heading west. Nation-wide, ninety-one million acres of Indian lands were taken away as a result of this act. It was completely disastrous for the native people who were not farmers, and did not have the same concepts of land "ownership."

The Allotment Act had a tremendous effect, somewhat similar to that of the Mission System here in California, which for the most part affected coastal people. People who had highly sophisticated and complex societies found themselves dislocated from their own culture and tradition.

So, here we are now, trying desperately to revitalize our language and our culture, bits and pieces that we come across with visions that are coming back in dreams. . . . And, in contrast here in California the provision of the Indian Allotment Act that said that non-reservation Indians might apply for an allotment benefitted many California Indians who did not have reservation lands. Hundreds of allotments from public domain lands were granted. Many of the grantees and/or their descendants still own their trust allotments today.

Once I brought this information to his attention, the Bureau of Land Management representative did look up the Indian Allotment Act. He brought up the fact that it was a very old, archaic law somewhat like a Native American Homestead Act, and that it would be almost impossible to meet the requirements. My response was, "If the land can meet the requirements, they will be met."

One of the most important things the Department of the Interior considers in making a decision about allotments under this law is its policy that an Indian allotment should contain land that is good enough to support an Indian family. In most recent cases, the soil has been found too poor or without enough water to support an Indian family, and virtually all of the applications have been turned down. After much research, having the property surveyed, and further discussions with the Bureau of Land Management, I finally met the requirements. These included showing that I could generate revenue via grazing without irrigation and live on the property for two years in a house that met the county planning commission codes (a stipulation that the BLM added to the requirements; it proved to be illegal, and once again a classic example of government agency/Indian interaction—it's rather common). Under the Indian Allotment Act of 1887, after the requirements are met, the land goes into trust for 25 years. The land is considered "Indian Country."

While the land is in trust, you do not pay property taxes, you are not governed by the state, county, or city regulations. Additionally, anything which requires your signature has to be approved in writing by the Bureau of Indian Affairs, and you cannot sell or encumber the property. Originally, I was required to generate enough revenue to support an individual Indian, but halfway through the process, the Bureau of Land Management brought it to my attention that, in fact, I was required to generate enough to support a famiiy of four, or $12,000.

By 1983 I had a prepared proposal that met all the requirements. Indian Canyon is hilly, rocky, brushy and very beautiful. It would also support five cows for three months, an economic unit that was not acceptable to the Department of the Interior because it was not enough to generate the money required. It took three years of considerable activity in the gathering and arduous investigation of various information to meet the archaic requirements of this Indian Allotment Act in order to regain the property my ancestors had lived on for generations. With the help of the University of California, Davis; University of California, San Diego; University of Oregon, Portland; the United States Department of Agriculture Soil Conservation Service; the Bureau of Land Management; the Bureau of Indian Affairs; the United Indian Development Association; Howard Harris, specialist in riparian rights; and adjacent landowners, I met all the requirements of the Allotment Act. What I proposed (I should say, "we proposed," because so many made contributions), was raising West African pygmy goats. They graze, and they do not need irrigated grazing lands. The nature of the Canyon land was such that it could support pygmy goats. They are very hardy and were domesticated on the western coast of Africa where they have lived for hundreds of years. Over a long period of time, primarily because of neglect and lack of food, they diminished in size. They are bred for show in the United States. Pygmy goats proved to be the answer to my needs at the Canyon; to show that I could generate revenue without requiring irrigation.

When I did meet the land requirements of the Bureau of Land Management, I said "Fantastic!" Now I had to build a cabin on the property. I had two years to do it. Then I discovered that all the conventional financial institutions could not or would not loan me the money I required because I could not put the property up as collateral (the land being in trust). Anything concerning the property that requires my signature must go through the approval process at the Bureau of Indian Affairs.

I wrote to President Reagan, and he had Bureau of Indian Affairs official Sid Mills respond to my letter. Mills in his response pointed out a revolving loan account with the Bureau of Indian Affairs in Sacramento, and gave me a name and number to contact. As a result of

Figure 12.3. Pygmy goats with horse

my contacting the Bureau of Indian Affairs in Sacramento, I received a packet of information from Weldon Smith, the loan officer at the time. I had by this time completed a 5-year feasibility study on raising pygmy goats for pets and for show, with the help of the United Indian Development Association. I called Weldon Smith concerning available funds from the revolving loan account. He informed me that the funds had been reallocated, and said, ". . . but it really doesn't matter anyway, because you are not eligible for a loan from this account. It is only for federally-recognized tribes." "What! This is a fine time to tell me. . . what is a federally recognized tribe?" I said. He sent me another packet! The Costanoan/Ohlone Indians, which comprise between forty to forty-five individual groups or tribes with their own languages, their own mythological stories, their own origins and their own lifeways are not federally recognized because they were brought into the Mission System, and were considered fully assimilated by the time California became part of the United States.

In 1852 there were eighteen treaties negotiated with California Indian groups throughout the state. These treaties would have cancelled the aboriginal land claims of the groups that signed them, setting aside approximately 8.5 million acres for reservations. They were never ratified by Congress, primarily due to the objections raised about "giving" potentially useful lands to the Indians. The eighteen treaties just "disappeared," and were relocated in 1905, I believe, in a bottom drawer by an office clerk who came across them unexpectedly. They had actually been sealed and kept out of public view for fifty years by a government that had only the economic interests of the dominant non-Indian population in mind, beginning with the California Gold Rush, which directly impacted the original Senate vote to deny ratification of the eighteen treaties.

After the discovery of these treaties in 1905, it began to be realized that technically the Indians still owned California.

This was quite incredible at a time when 75% of the native population in Northern California was homeless. On October 13, 1909 in San Francisco at the Commonwealth Club, Mr. C.E. Kelsey best described why:

> It should be understood that from the American occupation of California to the Dawes Act (Indian Allotment Act) in 1887, no Indian could acquire title to land from the public domain. Only citizens can homestead land, and the Indian was not a citizen. The Indian was not an alien. He had no foreign allegiance to renounce. He, therefore, could not be naturalized, become a citizen and take up land.
>
> The Indian was therefore precluded from acquiring title to even his own home for a period of some forty years after the American occupation. By this time everything but the most remote and worthless land had been appropriated. The price of land has risen to such a high figure that not an Indian in a thousand can hope to buy a home. It was upon these facts, first, that the national government had taken the Indian lands without payment; and, second, that the laws had barred Indians from acquiring lands until all land was gone, that the California Indian Association based its great campaign to ask Congress for an appropriation to buy lands for the landless and homeless Indians of California.

Seventeen years later the efforts of such organizations as the California Indian Association, the Mission Indian Federation, and others resulted in the passage of state and federal legislation that permitted the Indians of California to sue the federal government for not paying them for the land taken from them. How much? Well, what was the value of land in the state of California in 1852? The United States government came to the conclusion that it was worth 41¢ an acre.

All of the living descendants of the Indians were entitled to that money. The need to identify these descendants resulted in the 1928 California Indian Census. The census forms were sent to all the Indian people of California who could prove that they had ancestors in the State of California in 1852 when the eighteen treaties were drawn up.

The usual insensitivity and lack of real concern for justice and fairness for tribal peoples were evident, in that questionnaires were sent without provision for illiteracy. The problem was that many Indians did not read, write, or understand the true significance of this document for themselves or their descendants. Indians had to make great efforts to find people to assist them with the document, and those who could verify that the Indians were giving accurate information. A great many Indians were not contacted; many others were denied. California Indians who were living out of state, in Nevada or Arizona, for example, were denied a final roll number because they were a "Non-resident of California on May 18, 1928." This was the reason most frequently given for a claim rejection.

Fortunately or unfortunately, my great-grandfather, Sebastian Garcia, Maria his wife, and several of their children did fill out the Census questionnaire. Because we were approved, we received a Bureau of Indian Affairs identification number. We became recipients of the California Land Claims Settlement and as such, in 1950 we each received a check for $150.00. Now this was the final settlement of a case decided in 1944, when the courts awarded $17 million for reservation land that had been promised 92 years before. Then there were "offsets" of $12 million that the government kept for earlier outlays, or goods and services. In 1972 we received $668.00 for the remaining 91 million acres of California that excluded the proposed reservations, already paid for; the Spanish and Mexican land grants and other allotments.

At present, many individual California Indian groups are still not federally acknowledged, even though their members may be registered with the Bureau of Indian Affairs. It is very difficult to become a tribe in accordance with the requirements dictated by the Federal Acknowledgement Branch of the Bureau of Indian Affairs in Washington D. C. I had originally assumed that we would be able to meet the requirements. We have a land base; and we still carry on our ceremonies. As I began the process of petitioning for federal recognition, I realized that there are many active groups here in the Costanoan/Ohlone territory, and not one of us is federally recognized as a tribe. Throughout the state of California, there are currently thirty-six groups or bands that are petitioning for federal recognition. The personal experiences of being rejected by one's own people because of federal regulations are many. One of our people (a Costanoan/Ohlone lady) was in urgent need of help, and went to the Indian Health Service in San Jose, very close to where she was raised. She was turned down; "You're not a member of a federally recognized tribe. We're sorry but we cannot help you . . . ."

While I was being introduced to this new problem, I had a cabin to build. Generating the money for it was an immediate need. I did talk to a number of representatives of federally recognized tribes both here in California and out of state. The feedback was the same everywhere. Government cuts were drastic. There was certainly no money for one Indian who was trying to reclaim ancestral land. So it was then that Howard Harris, a neighbor and friend, came into the picture and donated money to put in a road. It was one of the most exciting days, seeing the road actually in place! Howard was seventy-five at the time. He was driving the bull-dozer. His wife, Bess, was seventy-eight. She was picking up rocks along the way, with me following behind. I counted four hundred and sixty-eight rocks that I picked up in a short period of time. And I was wondering, "What am I doing?" The thought lasted only a moment when I looked up at Bess Harris, and there she was smiling and humming as she continued to pick up rocks that kept multiplying. I finally sold off some of my inheritance, using the proceeds to benefit everyone. We were able to erect the cabin and purchase the pygmy goats. During the interim, the two-year period in which I had to complete the work came to an end. I was granted a one year extension and then another. I was so happy! Enough money was

Figure 12.4. Log cabin. Same home site as great grandfather Sebastian Garcia

generated to pay 50% down on a log cabin, and the rest when it was delivered. I had the blueprints drawn up. The corral was going up, and I was going to bring my goats up here (they were still boarded out). I saw the dream about to become a reality.

But at this juncture another major obstacle was thrown in my path. The Bureau of Land Management brought it to my attention that the National Wildlife Federation had a lawsuit against them. It seemed that the National Wildlife Federation had an injunction on all Bureau of Land Management lands, including Indian Canyon. I was told, "We (the Bureau of Land Management) regret to inform you that you have three options. Drop your application; continue but be aware that we cannot guarantee that we can issue a trust patent; or have Congress change the ruling." Naturally, I was devastated, but I began attending different Indian gatherings, Pow Wows, and native arts and crafts shows to get people to sign their support for my exclusion from this lawsuit. We got in excess of three thousand signatures.

At this point California Indian Legal Services (CILS) came into the picture. Their Attorney Steve Hirsch was in full agreement with me, and as outraged, when he said, "They are putting requirements on you that are totally illegal. This is ridiculous--a trust patent should have been issued when you met the stated requirements."

We were determined to continue with our plans. Howard Harris, my friend, came up with a 1934 Presidential proclamation that stated that if land was occupied before 1934, that property would not be subject to classification by the federal government. CILS attorney Steve Hirsch also took that view, and gathered testimonies from local people who knew that my parents and great-grandparents had lived in Indian Canyon since the Mission Period. We put our case before the Board of Appeals in Washington, D.C., and they concurred. Thus, through people-power, the Trust Patent was finally issued.

My story would not be complete without acknowledging the help of one of the most important people in it. While I was in Southern California in 1987, generating revenues to complete the improvements in the Canyon, I met a commercial artist from New York, Richard Roods. Richard had been commissioned to produce a work of art depicting Fr. Junipero Serra for the city of Ventura. The fact that this priest was being honored in this way devastated me because of the atrocities perpetrated on my people in the name of Christianity and the Mission System by men like these! I shared the Native point of view with Richard in such a way that he donated a year of his life to helping me reclaim my ancestral land. I have never seen a man work so hard. I fell in love with him, and little did he know that one year would turn into two, and now seven, during which time we brought a beautiful daughter, Kanyon Sayers-Roods, into this special place. Meanwhile, the cabin went up with the help of many who shared my dream and love of the Canyon. It was incredible. The structure went up in two-and-a-half days. The Trust Patent was forthcoming in August, 1988.

We still live here, we still carry out our ceremonies. I believe that I had to go through eight years of effort to reclaim my ancestral lands in order to fully understand, through experience, why California Indians are in this predicament.

We are all in need of traditional lands upon which to carry out our traditions and live our culture. In view of this, we have opened up my mother's property as a Living Indian Heritage Area. We have our own ceremonies—the Honoring of the Land Ceremony, the Talking Feather, Moon, and many others. We are also making the area available for the use by native people who do not have traditional land for ceremony.

Figure 12.5. Arbor area. Site of many ceremonies

REFLECTIONS ON THE PRESENT

I want to emphasize that Indian country exists within the Costanoan/Ohlone territory, Indian Canyon. Native peoples live here and conduct ceremonies. Currently, this land is being developed into an educational, cultural and spiritual environment, one that includes what is now registered with the Native America Heritage Commission as a

Figure 12.6. Traditional sweat lodge

"Living Indian Heritage Area." The Canyon is home to a newly-built traditional *Tupentak* (central California Indian sweat lodge), and an outdoor dance arbor. We are currently in the planning stages for the construction of a *Tupen-Tah-Ruk* (Round House or Assembly House) to be completed in 1995. The sweat lodge is available for purification ceremonies and spiritual well-being and is utilized by various tribal groups in our area. The dance arbor serves as a place for *Tcite-s-mak* (dancers), gatherings, and educational programs. The Round House will provide an environment conducive to holding tribal meetings, guest speakers, dances and ceremonial activities such as the *Tchokin* (Sacred Staff), or *Ritca Sipas* (Talking Feather Circle). All of these spiritual, cultural and educational activities revolve around the concept *Noso-N* which translates in *Mutsun* as "Breath, so it is in Spirit." *Noso-N* is central to the well-being of *Ahmah* (the People), as well as the natural and spiritual world we live in. On January 30, 1993 we had a "Completion of the Tupentak Ceremony." We invited many of those who came to visit my mother when she was alive—so it was a happy and significant reunion in many ways. These are people who want to feel their native roots again, who want to become involved in their ancient ways and traditions.

State and federal agencies are starting to acknowledge our existence. For example, they request input from the native peoples of a given area on the archaeological sensitivity of that area if a project (such as a dam or new road, etc.) is being planned. The South of the Delta Project west of the San Joaquin Valley includes at least five locations which are highly sensitive archaeologically. Some are sizeable religious sites, and the possibility that a Visitor's Center may be built is being discussed. Just the fact that we are being included in this project with a view to our interests and needs is extremely important and necessary.

We have been working with our local County Planning Commission to get an ordinance for the preservation of Native American sites for San Benito County. We accomplished this task in 1992. This provides another example, on the county level, of government agencies working with the Native American population on projects which benefit both the native and non-native people of an area. We appreciate the support given, for example, by John Fritz of the University of California at Santa Cruz, and Charles Smith of Cabrillo College, Santa Cruz. In their "Archaeological Overview of Pinnacles National Monument," they reflect clearly this new and positive trend in their recommendations regarding the involvement of local Native Americans in the management of cultural resources:

> Many Native Americans wish to be involved in the control and management of cultural resources created and used by their ancestors. Some groups have articulated this wish as part of a general program for Native American welfare, for example, the Native American Movement, or as the chief focus of their organizations. . . These groups have been instrumental in the formation of the California State Indian Heritage Commission. This Commission is developing broad responsibility for the management of Native California cultural resources owned or controlled by the State.

The Repatriation Bill signed by President Bush on November 16, 1990, came in part out of Costanoan Indian concern about their territory. This new law addresses the rights of Native Americans to their cultural and sacred objects and to the burial remains of their ancestors which lie (sometimes in dire neglect) in museums and archival storerooms. It also addresses ownership and protection of these same sacred objects when they are found on Indian lands. Many local indigenous people, including myself, were instrumental, together with Stanford University and the Native American Heritage Commission in beginning the process towards repatriation. Now, instead of our sacred burial objects, including the bones of our ancestors, being dumped in a dusty corner wrapped in old newspapers, they are being returned to their people for proper reburial. Many artifacts are being returned to the "most likely descendants."

Another current issue to be addressed by all native peoples in this country is that of our freedom to practice our respective religious ways. Many of us face limitations and restrictions and have to fight for our rights to the ceremonial elements necessary to the full expression of our religious rituals.

In our case, water is an essential ceremonial element at Indian Canyon, as it is in Native American religion in general. However, our water is being diverted upstream by a neighboring corporation, and we are currently unable to practice our ceremonies in full. The owner of this corporation, whose actions have dried up our stream and waterfall, claims that the use of the waterfall for religious purposes is not recognized under the law of California as a reasonable beneficial use. The American Indian Freedom of Religion Act, which has not stood up in court since its implementation in 1978, gives us no legal redress.

Figure 12.7. Indigenous conference area with waterfall in background

Indian Canyon is the only "Indian Country" within the Costanoan/Ohlone territory, a region with one of the largest Native American populations in the United States. The Canyon is open to all peoples of Native American heritage who are in need of traditional lands for their ceremonies. More than a thousand people come to Indian

Canyon annually from many nations across the United States. We participate in both tribal and intertribal ceremonies that may involve gatherings of up to two hundred people at a time. Smaller gatherings may spend several days in the Canyon.

The waterfall at Indian Canyon is its primary sacred area. Water is essential for both ceremonial and practical purposes. The waterfall, flowing in its natural water course, is a sacred and essential part of all ceremonies here in the Canyon. Spiritual leaders from different tribes take water from it and use it in their ceremonies elsewhere. Sweat lodge purification ceremonies, a major aspect of Native American religious practice, cannot be held without water. It is used to create steam inside the sweat lodge and to quench thirst brought on by the loss of body water. Both large gatherings and small extended gatherings need water for drinking, sanitation and cooking. But the waterfall has been dry every summer for five consecutive years since the water was first diverted upstream.

We need to emphasize to the people of this government that a strong and legally enforceable Native American Free Exercise of Religion Act of 1993 (NAFERA), S. 1021, would ensure that the religious freedom of the Native American could be protected in a court of law. This would not only be ethically in line with United States policy, it would carry many other benefits. The freedom to practice one's religion restores dignity to individuals, increasing the mental, spiritual and physical health of the community. This would result in less government spending on community programs and thus, will benefit society in general. One of the principle needs in amending the American Indian Freedom of Religion Act is the setting down of clearly written, indisputable statements guaranteeing to Native Americans full use of the ceremonial elements essential to the practice of our religion. In our case, water is the ceremonial element being denied to us.

The sound of water, the movement of water, our placement of everything revolves around our water in Indian Canyon. It is extremely important. We were successful in our Petition to have water included in the amendments to the NAFERA, and this is very good. I believe this will be very important in future years. We will still be able to participate in our ceremonies fully. And the Native American Free Exercise of Religion Act of 1993 will ensure that.

That there is recognition of California Indians and their unique situation is a tremendous step forward. I believe particularly that the experience of having to negotiate and to establish effective working relationships with state and federal government agencies will continue to enhance the recognition that indigenous "intellectual property rights" provide an appropriate basis for land uses. Traditional land is dependent upon the knowledge and skills of the indigenous people, the practice of this care can only blossom if the Californian communities realize the benefits from our heritage and wisdom regarding the land. As an example, as I write, the on-going government interference with the land stewardship issue of the Chemehuevi Tribe[2] is an illustration of the inappropriate relationship between government attitude toward the native resources and the indigenous relationship to those same resources. Whether deliberate or not, this kind of manipulation of intellectual, spiritual and material "property rights" is continuing today throughout California and especially among the non-federally recognized tribes. We had highly sophisticated and complex ideas and attitudes during our pre-contact history. We still do have them, and they are starting to emerge in a way that is very good. Slowly we are being given recognition and dignity for who we are as the indigenous people of this land.

This country is built on the lives and deaths of Indians who are environmentally aware; whose societies operated within traditional systems of authority and law, and who lived culturally rich and deeply spiritual lives centuries before the Spaniards arrived. Until this is recognized and there is truth in history, the life of the natural world, which is the real foundation of the well being of this country, will continue to be lost.

I would like to end this story with a *Mutsun* word, *Noso-n*. It means "breath, so it is in spirit." There is no English word that comes close to the description of life for all living things, "*Noso-n*".

---

[2] The Chemehuevi Tribe was federally recognized in 1970 and they were displaced to nonarable lands when the Parker Dam was constructed (1936-1940).

REFERENCES CITED

Arroyo de la Cuesta, Felipe
   1821   Idiomos Californias. Manuscript in Bancroft Library, University of California, Berkeley.

Kelsey, C.E.
   1909   Speech given at the Commonwealth Club, San Francisco, October 13. Commonwealth Club Archives.

INDEX

CONTRIBUTORS

Henry "Hank" Alvarez, *Muwekma* Ohlone Elder and Tribal Council Member, active in both tribal and community affairs, with wife Stella is influential in the community organization PACT (People Acting in Community Together).

Gary Breschini, Ph.D., is a SOPA certified archaeologist and physical anthropologist who has spent over 20 years researching the prehistory of the Central California coast.

Alan K. Brown (Ph.D., Stanford University) is a medievalist and Associate Professor of English at The Ohio State University. He is completing an in-depth historical introduction to the Crespí journals.

Rosemary Cambra, chairwoman, *Muwekma* Ohlone Tribe, and member, Federal Advisory Council on California Indian Policy's task force for unrecognized tribes, has also been active in cultural resource management and repatriation issues.

Edward D. Castillo is a Cahuilla-Luiseño Indian and a Professor of Native American Studies at Sonoma State University. He is an authority on the ethnohistory of California Indians.

Jeff Fentress (M.A., Anthropology, California State University, Hayward), a Ph.D. candidate and Teaching Assistant in the Anthropology Department, University of Oregon, also works as an archaeologist in both California and Oregon.

Les Field (Ph.D., Duke University, 1987), Assistant Professor of Anthropology at the University of New Mexico, and staff ethnohistorian for the *Muwekma* Ohlone Tribe, has co-authored numerous articles with the tribe.

Trudy Haversat, M.A., is a SOPA certified consulting archaeologist and physical anthropologist with an extensive background in cultural resource management and Central Coast prehistory.

Mark G. Hylkema has worked on numerous California archaeological projects, with a particular focus on the Central Coast. He currently works as an archaeologist for the California Department of Transportation (Caltrans).

Robert H. Jackson (Ph.D., University of California, Berkeley) is a specialist in Borderlands history. His research interests include the social, demographic, and economic history of the northern frontier of New Spain/Mexico.

Chester King, Ph.D. is an archaeologist/ethnohistorian. He has conducted ethnohistoric research concerning Ohlone, Chumash, Tataviam and Tongva settlements to aid in understanding the distribution of archaeological sites.

Alan Leventhal, College of Social Sciences at San Jose State University, has worked as an archaeologist and ethnohistorian for the *Muwekma* Ohlone Tribe, the *Amah-Mutsun* Ohlone, and the Esselen Nation.

Randall Milliken (Ph.D., University of California, Berkeley, 1991), a student of J.A. Bennyhoff's ethnohistoric approach, began building a computerized list of mission baptismal entries, now numbering 26,955, in 1978.

Beverly O. Ortiz, a Ph.D. candidate in social/cultural anthropology at the University of California, Berkeley, is an ethnographic consultant, park naturalist, and columnist for *News for Native California*.

Breck Parkman (M.A., Anthropology, California State University, Hayward) is a State Archaeologist with the California Park Service, and a Research Associate at the University of California, Berkeley.

Alex O. Ramirez (*Rumsen* Ohlone), author of *Tjatjakiy-matchan (Coyote) A Legend from the Carmel Valley* (1992) and Indian Education instructor, has served on several American Indian program boards in Santa Clara County.

Ann Marie Sayers, chair of Indian Canyon Mutsun Band of Costanoan People, is also the chairperson of Costanoan Indian Research, Inc., and founder of the Indian Canyon Native American Library.

Linda Yamane (*Rumsien* Ohlone) is a freelance writer, illustrator and cultural interpreter living in the Monterey area. She has been active in retrieving Rumsien basketry, language, folklore and songs.